DARK BOTANY

The Herbarium Tales

Edited by

Prudence Gibson
Sigi Jöttkandt
Marie Sierra
Anna Westbrook

OPEN HUMANITIES PRESS

London 2024

OPEN HUMANITIES PRESS

Open Humanities Press is an international, scholar-led, open access publishing collective whose mission is to make leading works of contemporary critical thought freely available worldwide.

More at http://openhumanitiespress.org

The editors acknowledge the traditional custodianship of lands by First Nations peoples and present this body of texts in gesture toward the connected threads of humanity around the world. The earthbound nature of new leaves and probing roots joins plants and people from diverse communities and cultures across the globe. It pays attention to, and honours, quiet resistance and peaceful refusal. This book suggests plant-like reciprocity, joining the past to the future.

TABLE OF CONTENTS

Introduction

There exists a night-blooming cactus, the 'Queen of the Night,' that flowers only for a single night in the year. It starts out fairly innocuously—just a small bulge on the side of the cactus's flat fleshy stem—but in a quick few days the flower bud morphs into a fist-sized tulip-shaped bulb, whitish but with pink twining tendrils like a net or a corset that will soon be unlaced. When the Queen does make her resplendent appearance, these threads will fan out behind her as a train or lattice, providing the immense, almost insupportable white flower with her unique proto-textual frame. The 'Queen of the Night' is a dark botanical entity—rarely seen unless watched for closely, a figure for another "spell of creation," to recall the words of a kindred night-dweller, the artist Louise Bourgeois.

The essays collected in this volume explore the spell of this 'dark botany,' a concept we have gently prised from the inspiring leaves of Timothy Morton's *Dark Ecology* and watched flower in this SeedBook. For Morton, "dark ecology" takes you to an umbral zone where thought and things thread together in the co-existent logic of a Möbius strip. Dark ecology, a form of eco-gnosis, impels one to enter into the inherent strangeness of worlds and words, tracing a pathway that will also loop back upon us to reveal how strange we are to ourselves. In Morton's "dark ecology", the very notion of space itself, understood as a constant site of presence and presencing, and of time as the medium through which life unfolds, collapse beneath the weight of unseen dark matter whose gravity affects and thwarts the fantasy of Euclidean space, "the convenient fiction of White imperialist humans" (Morton 10).

A 'dark botany' performs a comparable estrangement of the Herbarium as the traditional repository of Enlightenment knowledge and Imperial desire. Each chapter in this volume is entangled with the darkly botanical, not only telling truths about the Herbarium's dark histories and darker contemporary currents, but also training a microscope's lens on the complexity of texture, movement, memory, compound structure, chemical emissions and rapid evolution of plants and languages. What one discovers is that herbaria are not static: they are as vital and energetic and enigmatic as the plants in their collections, and as diverse.

In this collection of Herbarium Tales, 'dark botany' emerges as a reflexive mode of counter-narrative form and function. It is a means of owning up to the violence, erasure and oppression of plants by humans. It is a process of acknowledging the ill-effects of colonial pursuits. It is also a project of re-collecting and re-configuring our relation to the plant world's "dark shimmering" (Morton 6). Dark botany elicits what Betty Russ evokes as a "vegetal vocal signifier" that would de-erase the voices from botanical history's official pages. It is also an invitation to "walk beside" Indigenous peoples to learn more about Country and its rich cultures.

Opening Part I with her titular essay summoning the concept of 'dark botany', Prudence Gibson hovers over an uneasy connection between certain plants and Australia's legacy of imperial expansionist colonial history. Gibson warns that "sometimes the secrets of the herbarium—sheets of plant specimens with collection data on them—offer up stories we'd prefer not to know." Among these are the stories of the 18th century Antiguan painter Lydia Byam and the 19th century botanist, Amalie Dietrich, whose herbarium collection offers a pre-colonial vision of Australian flora.

As Anna-Sophie Springer reminds us, dark botany exposes the archiving impulse as simultaneously an inscription and an erasure, each 'leaf' in the Herbarium a palimpsestic trace of "the surveys, evaluations, and land-use changes that have engendered irreversible biospheric and socioecological modifications". Dark botany also invites one to see how the plant "gives the lie", as Elaine Miller puts it, to the desire to see ourselves reflected in nature. The "eyeless, brainless plant", she contends, is uncanny. If we look at it too long, far from seeing 'ourselves', it returns as a figure for "the absolute other", "unplumbed" by human intelligence but also somehow strangely too close for critical and theoretical understanding. Yet it still demands the work of thought. To say, with Derrida, the word "animal" is already not to understand. But to say the word "plant" seems to open onto an even more abyssal non-knowledge and non-identity.

Tapping into a more ancient mode of relation to plants than we are accustomed to when encountering the vegetal world—where they normally present to us their heliotropic, sun-loving 'faces' as the world's predominant food sources, materials for habitation, and their eco-services roles as the lungs of planet Earth, giving oxygen and absorbing carbon—'dark botany' is also, as other contributors here recognise, a profoundly intimate affair. It rekindles practices that have been lost through the changes in agriculture during the late 19th century, changes in the movement of plants around the globe for profit and power, in medicine away from local care to big pharma, in food and plant production that necessitates monoculture, and even changes in gardening away from utility and as a construct of aesthetic imagination. To write about plants as kin and as egalitarian knowledge holders thus also transforms our relation to them in unexpected ways.

With his concept of a "speculative phytopoetics", Giovanni Aloi invites us to (re-)encounter this relation in terms of a "subtle and elusive form of interspecies communication" between humans and plants, which is arrived at by inhabiting plant rather than capitalist 'time'. Matthew Beach traces the history of house-plants back to the mysteries of ferns, once thought to hold magical properties, including the gift of invisibility. Might this history offer ways of rethinking the house-plant beyond its nominal framing of "home" to open onto forms of care that respond to the plant's "postcolonial" and "queer identities" that have been driven underground, forging rooty connections with other species?

This dual nature of plants, as dwellers of both aerial and chthonic worlds, invites a cosmic turn in thinking, Vanessa Lemm argues. The plant's sense of co-existence and inter-relationality between living beings and living matter upends habitual distinctions of inside and outside, asking us to become "cosmic mediators", rooted in our "home" on Earth, and as co-habitants of an inter-planetary star system. We can bring back the insights from this tarrying among the spheres, Lemm proposes, and regard the Earth itself as a micro-planetary system by paying attention to "the many worlds that are found here on earth, in a multi-species and symbiotic sense of co-existence and inter-relationality between living beings and living matter."

A collision of beings and matter is how Heather Rogers and Nick Lawrence ask us to reconceive the Herbarium, that is, as a sensuous "site of convergence" of multiple materialities in a constant process of deterritorialization and reter-ritorialization. Herbaria specimens come alive as assemblages of vibrant chemical, elemental, biotic matter intra-acting with the humans who gathered, saved, examined and re-stor(i)ed them in the archive. A considerable part of archival desire is bound up with naming. Bart Vandeput pressurizes names in a 'pata-botanical' experiment. Inspired by the seeming paradox of Latvian microbiologist Anete Boroduska's discovery that "the Berry is an Apple", Vandeput takes us

on a revelatory journey arriving at an almost unpronounceable, scarcely readable new name for a plant that 'chokes' back every nominal expression it spawns.
Yet if we simply 'listen' to plants, and the stories around them they inspire,
Anna Perdibon suggests in her recounting of Edelweiss fairy tales, we engage
in "a searching revaluation of philosophy, politics and art" (Morton 159), one
that attunes us to thinking and feeling at other scales, simultaneously Alpine
and micro-scopic. Both become condensed in the eternal form of the noble
mountain star.

A living herbarium is the focus of Juliann Vitullo and Arina Melkozernova's
essay, which escorts us further along the Alpine paths to the Italian town of
Colobraro, renowned for "sorcery and bad luck". But this village's 'dark' history,
shrouded with magical practices involving plants, has borne unusual and unexpected fruit, a "Museum of magic" that overturns the seeming inevitability of
extinction narratives. Such an enterprise fits within a larger darkly botanical
project of phyto-séancing that Nick Koenig and Anna Lawrence engage in, in
their exploration of the collections of the Kentucky botanist, Mary E. Wharton,
and the New Zealand gardener Mary Frederica Marshall, both tuning in, in
spectral ways, to query how one can respond ethically to the twin impulses of
the archive as both inscription and erasure.

This thread of inscription is taken up by both Sigi Jöttkandt and Edward
Colless who, in their respective essays, focus on a not-quite imaginable literary heritage that haunts the philosophical as a Derridean supplement. Jöttkandt
uncovers in D. H. Lawrence a counter-rhetorical tradition that thrives in the
sun-baked Tuscan hills. She notes how the incarnation of words as flowers, literary language's most beloved and undying trope for naturalising the system of
representation, yields in Lawrence to a de-naturing repetition, without origin
or end. Colless pursues "the most mysterious book in the world". The Voynich
manuscript is a fifteenth-century illuminated codex that resembles a herbalism guide written in a still-as-yet undeciphered script in an utterly unknown
language with illustrations of plants that remain completely unidentified. The
competing theories about it seem to suggest it is either in a lost language or is a
hoax. For Colless neither theory quite accounts for the unsettling alienness of
the document, prompting him towards new concepts: exobotany or xenobotany.

Together, the essays in Part I are alert to the challenges of the attempt to
access the agency and secret wisdom of the vegetal world. Cognisant of the risk
of flattening plant aesthetics, of stifling plant agency, of slipping back into colonial mastery, of adding to data without contributing to reparations or changed

perceptions of plants, the contributors nevertheless tell alternate stories of plants, original stories of plants and humans and find the courage to reveal negative stories that might reflect poorly on humans, and on ourselves. This, too, is a dark botanical undertaking, one that comprises story-telling, creative endeavours, poetic devices, philosophical investigations and the ancient wisdom of over 65 000 years of Aboriginal and Torres Strait Islander traditional plant knowledge.

Research-based art practice is a slippery discipline that resists and refuses to conform to either theory or art. Instead it hovers over art disciplines as a meta-praxis, where alternate pasts and futures burst into the present. Housed in Part II are specimens of the new forms of creative evolution emerging from the more 'theoretical' explorations in Part I. In this part, an international community of plant+art writers and artists answered our call to respond to the vicissitudes of the Herbarium and its colonial history of collection, presentation and re-presentation. The fruits of that search ripen in the form of independent and polyphonic voices.

Anna Madeleine Raupach writes about her work, *Vivid Frequencies*, an Artificial Intelligence artwork created as a responsive reaction to plants and trees at Mt Annan, NSW, one of the three Royal Botanic Gardens properties. Unpacking the audio visual code of plant databases, Raupach's digital analysis and layered imaging shows us the multiplicities of vegetal time. As part of the same Tellus Project, Erica Seccombe shares her community-facing experience of endemic plants growing at Bundanon. In a collaboration with Walbunja Elder Aunty Deidre Martin, Seccombe dismantles conventional colonial approaches to the botanical world, through intimate consultation and 'biocultural exchange.'

Rebecca Mayo's Plant Sensibilia Machine is a hand-cranked dying press that sat on the banks of the Shoalhaven River. The steam, scents, sounds and voices of humans' manual printing labour, alongside plants, revives plant knowledge that once was an intimate part of inter-species lives. Such plant knowledge is also plant wisdom: Christina Stadlbauer introduces her artwork, "The Phytonic Oracle", foretelling other futures through planty divinations that keep a beat to planty time.

In Aunty Deidre Martin's and Lisa Gorton's poem, "Acacia Longifolia", we encounter a calendric principle based on the signifiers of the natural world. With Jacob Morris, we meet Arawarra and Cararura—warriors, protectors, heroes of Country who remind us that one of the guiding principles of herbaria collections is curatorial care. The connection between plant care and art is an aesthetic of mutuality. Maya Martin Westheimer acquaints us with her curatorial work focussed on Neilsen Park in Sydney. Artists responded to a specific intertidal stretch of Sydney Harbour, where rock platforms meet coastal scrub and Sydney algae. Her waves of reflective analysis mimic those tidal patterns. Verena Kuni, too, reflects on various artists who have either responded to herbarium collections or whose work functions like an herbarium. The idea of augmented herbarealities exposes two different modes of preservation, herbaria and photography, to each other across five artworks, in the process constructing new affinities between image-making, plant preservation and the ethics and politics of world building.

The creative contemplation of the herbarium germinated slowly in the earth. Verdant tendrils emerged, arching inevitably toward light and water. Diverse in form, with unexpected knots and twists; the artist, the poets, and the writers all probe relationships, rebel against taxonomy, and unbalance the weight of the "I" to throw the soft animal of the body against vegetal benign indifference. Betty Russ explores the concept of "invasive species" and the jagged currency of colonisation via her spectacular practice of kinetic sculpture, sound, and installation. Tamryn Bennett and Ryan Gordan expand and contract from the galactic to the spore, touching knowledges, mourning their attempted erasure, opening to the infinite. Georgina Reid takes on with tenderness the role of the gardener, nudging against what brutality lurks within the bucolic. Anna Westbrook delves into the wound, the regrowth, and the scar. Form unfettered; these contributors are playful, tentative, liminal, and rhizomatic in imagination.

If there is a tone that weaves across all the contributions, both creative and scholarly, that tone is a sincere desire to think more laterally about plants. It's an attempt to understand what plant-human relations have been in ancient cultures, how the imperial pursuit of scientific knowledge affected human relations with plants during colonial epochs, and how urgent the need to reconnect with plants. *Dark Botany* engages the material and sensorial wonder of plants—their energy, their mysterious allure, their capacities and skills, their independent might. We invite you to attend their opening.

Acknowledgements

The editors would like to thank the contributors, the Australian Research Council, and our Linkage project collaborators Sophie O'Brien from Bundanon Trust, Brett Summerell from Sydney Botanical Gardens Herbarium, and Gary

Hall from Open Humanities Press. Our particular thanks to Joanna Zylinska, Kimberley Skelton, Baron Chau and David Ottina.

Works Cited

Morton, Timothy. *Dark Ecology: For a Logic of Future Coexistence.* Columbia University Press, 2018.

PART I

...unseen buds, infinite, hidden well...

—Walt Whitman, *Leaves of Grass*

1 Dark Botany

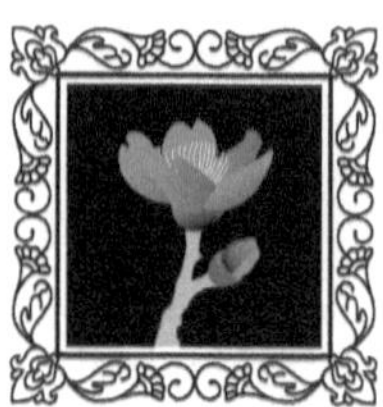

Prudence Gibson

Introduction

Conventional botanical discourses sometimes forget to acknowledge women botanists. They sometimes fail to note Aboriginal and Torres Strait Islander contributions to white Australian botanical history. They sometimes erase First Nations knowledge entirely.

Such discourses also tend to avoid challenging or disputing colonial naming systems, which rarely include Indigenous names. They do not admit to malevolent witchcraft or actively stand against plant theft, or against agricultural monocultures and illegal use of psychedelic plants (Gibson). These botanical discourses often forget the vast and dark history of colonial imperial discovery—those epic and sprawling nationalistic voyages to distant lands to collect, colonise, and enslave plants and peoples (Baber; Barndt). If we do not pay attention to the failures of conventional botanical discourse, humanity risks repeating the same mistakes (Ogburn). This is why we need Dark Botany, to reconnect humans with the plant world, both dark and light.

Dark Botany is a sapling discipline, a field of research within critical plant studies. Critical plant studies re-examine human relationships with plants, in response to new plant science data concerning sentience, communication, memory, and learning (Calvo; Gagliano; Souza; Trewavas). My contribution to this field has been in the feminist context of visual art and herbarium collections. It became clear that the work I was contributing is best described as "dark botany," which is also a methodology of counter-narratives ("The Dirt Witches' Counter-narrative" 2023).

As a methodology, dark botany approaches and actively respects the independent agency of plants. A counter-narrative approach that tells stories outside the conventions of traditional botanical discourse, it focuses on narratives that are not mainstream and may not have been intended for public knowledge. Counter-narratives are needed to redress the preconceived notion that plants are inert and passive, and only make sense within a taxonomic system of naming and classifying.

Dark botany is a methodology of counter-narratives that acknowledges the systematic instrumentalisation of plants in botany, in philosophical thinking, and in its effects on aesthetics (Aloi). This methodology is one that notes monoculture and extinction threats, food security, and biodiversity problems. It tells true stories of colonial plant oppressions and historical extraction for profit, known as "green imperialism" (Groves). Even "robotany," a term I coined in *The Plant Contract* in 2018 to describe the use of technology to improve plant life and mimic it, has its place in the dark botany of hyper-efficient agricultural systems, because of the industrial chemicals that speed up flowering times for increased profit.

A darker botanical approach demands personal decolonisation. This refers to a better self-awareness of white, educated privilege and a consequential practice of consultation for Indigenous best practice. It is a means of critical enquiry and curiosity applied to plant-human relations. The process is one of searching for the stories beneath colonial botanical propaganda. An example of this propaganda is the argument that the collection and ownership of all plants is for the betterment of all people. Such propaganda forgets that botanical and agricultural knowledge during colonial epochs of expansion did not improve the lives of all people equally. This situation endures today.

Darker stories extend to the damage done to enslaved peoples and their enslaved plant kin, such as plantations where cotton and sugar were grown and harvested for profit (Brixius). As Donna Haraway and Anna Tsing have said, "the capacity to love and care for place is radically incompatible with the plantations" because plantations were places of interruption and disorder for both humans and their ecologies ... even the fungi went feral (2019). Darker stories also extend to the burning of leaves, bark, and seeds to make apotropaic charms to ward off evil spirits (Stewart) or to the adding of plant poison to the tips of spears (Lombard).

And dark botany does still more. As a disciplinary focus, it cools the heat of climate change rage, so that we can attend to survivalist tactics. It is a better way to slow the pace of plant overuse. A better way to urge restoration of endangered plant ecologies, and to advocate for an aesthetics of plant care. A better way to strengthen our decolonising muscles and stoke the embers of rebirth, within *this* earth's life (Marder).

Philosophically, dark botany responds to Timothy Morton's "dark ecology" enquiries. Dark ecology is an evocation of ecological awareness. For Morton, "dark" implies "pretty depressing" and "uncanny." Dark, as in abject sweetness.

Morton suggests that darkness, weirdness, and loops, which can, in turn, be weird and uncanny, are desirable (Morton 22). They reflect the desire to face horror—in Morton's case the horror of climate change—so that it becomes a driver of human spiritedness. In Morton's loop, or Möbius strip, the loop is twisted so that you can only see one side. While Morton is referring to climate change during the Anthropocene, that image reminds me of how I have been hoodwinked by an Australian school and university education in the 1980s that chose not to tell me who Aboriginal and Torres Strait peoples really were or are. And that I may be implicated in that wrongdoing.

My conception of dark botany is a response to Morton's "monster in the dark mirror" (Morton 134). I have to stay within the darkness of Australian colonial plant stories, whether I like it or not. I have to face the monster, the monster that might be me. This is what Morton calls "radical self knowledge." I need to remember the botanists and botanical guides who were erased from the herbarium archives. I need to recall the stealthy theft of Indigenous knowledge and land by Australian colonial settlers (Head et al). There is a constant necessity to remind audiences of the colonial British mindset in Australia, which allowed such things as blackbirding (enforced labour and/or enslavement of Pacific Islander peoples) in nineteenth- and twentieth-century Queensland for sugar cane profits.

These concepts may be uncomfortable and difficult. Many have been hidden for a long time. Dark stories are often trapped inside herbaria archives and embedded in colonial correspondences. Such histories reached their zenith in colonial epochs via slave plantations, plant and mineral extraction, and the frenzied and rapacious appetite to develop natural history collections during colonial eras (Shiva; Deloughrey). Bringing them out into the light is a counter-narrative process because the darkness of botanical histories can show those of us in the plant humanities the truth of the past and the light of the future.

Currently, there are equally compelling dark botany issues to face in Australia. One such counter-narrative is the annihilation of psychedelic plants growing in the bush. There is a species of acacia in the Australian state of New South Wales that is on the brink of extinction. It just barely grows on a coastal mountain, but its family of acacias has been wiped out by people who know it is high in Dimethyltryptamine (DMT). If prepared and imbibed, DMT causes a psychedelic experience. Those in the know find these acacias growing in national parks and along highways, and steal the bark, the roots, and the leaves, effectively killing the trees (DCCEEW).

Another counter-narrative is to truly accept the troubling activity of gardening, which must suffer the critique of ongoing colonialism (Mondragon). Even for those of us who love gardening, it is nevertheless a biopolitical entanglement. Gardening is a type of cultivation that is implicit in the negative effects of human activity on the earth since industrialisation. This activity creates sites of contestation (Sandilands and Gersdorf 1).

Yet another counter-narrative is the story of an Australian woman who is an experienced wild mushroom forager and who was recently arraigned for the death of three people and attempting the murder of two more by feeding them poisonous mushrooms harvested from the bush (Singh). Hallucinatory experiences aside, such stories reveal a different, darker side of plants: the weaponising of plants for malevolent means. This could also be interpreted as the plants' refusal to remain benign.

Therefore, like Morton's dark ecology, dark botany is a multiplicity of radicality, even of epiphanic joy, in the face of dark knowledge. Three dark botany counter-narratives reveal how it works:

Part 1: Silk Cotton Tree

In 1797, Lydia Byam illustrated a book entitled *A Collection of Exotics from the Island of Antigua*. Lydia's family were planters. That is, her family owned some of the biggest and most productive sugar plantations on the Caribbean island of Antigua. Slave plantations profited from enslaved and free workers, who were a mixture of salaried and convict staff. Slaves were branded and sometimes chained. The Byam family owned Cedar Mills, a grand and established property, for over two hundred years. The mills were where the sugar off-cuts were brought to make rum. Work began at the first of the Byams' plantations in 1688. By 1829, there were 266 slaves, and the estate was about five hundred acres.

The first illustration in Lydia's book is of *Bombax gossypium*, or the silk cotton tree. Two specimens are included in the illustration. One cutting has flower buds and small blossoms: this is the silk cotton tree. The other has leaves and small seeds and is *apocynum erectum*, or wild ipecacuan. For some reason, Lydia pairs her plants in this book. Under the silk cotton tree, she has written: "It bears a Flower without Smell, with long Filaments of great Fineness." Under the wild ipecacuan, there is the more compelling note that "A strong vegetable Poison and Medicine" (Byam 3).

Lydia was born (or rather baptised, which presumably was not too long after her birth) in 1772 on the island of Antigua. There is very little information about her, except for this book and a second publication *Fruits of the West Indies*, dated 1800. All that is known is that she was lost at sea, presumably after 1800, when she was twenty-eight. I have noted that in the travel memoir of Maria Riddell, a Scottish woman who was the same age as Lydia, it is clear that Maria visited Antigua in 1800 and also the family home of the Byams. There is a high likelihood that the two women, both interested in botany, met. But there is no evidence.

What is interesting about Lydia's book is that while the silk cotton tree seems relatively tame compared to the poisonous or medicinal wild ipecacuan, the silk cotton tree has its own story to tell. It is poisonous in large doses, but smaller doses were considered beneficial for the treatment of diarrhoea, dysentery, and male sexual disorders (Jain).

These kinds of alternative medicines would have been apparent to Lydia Byam not from conventional British medicine tomes, but through local knowledge. In her 1844 book entitled *Antigua and the Antiguans*, Mrs Lanaghan refers to the "exceedingly harsh laws passed respecting the slaves, and the shocking executions of those concerned in the insurrection in 1736" (vii). The first three people whom Mrs Lanaghan acknowledges in her book, which she describes as an "impartial view of slavery," are members of the Byam family. An important Antiguan plantation family, the Byams were planters.

Lydia Byam would have found out the uses and properties of the local Antiguan plants through means other than advice from her family. However, no enslaved persons, who would have been stolen or purchased during African stopovers from Europe to the West Indies, are acknowledged. Judith Carney has observed:

> The decades following 1492 launched an era of European overseas expansion, which led to an unprecedented intercontinental exchange of plant and animal species. The movement of African plant and food animals across the Atlantic Ocean in the initial period of plantation development depended on the transatlantic slave trade for their dispersal. Plants and animals arrived on slave ships together with African captives for whom the species were traditional dietary staples, medicinals, and food animals (168).

In Lydia's book, there is no referenced source material for her plant information regarding poisons and cures. Readers are left to guess how she came upon

Prudence Gibson

this information. It is hard not to speculate that local, enslaved women gave her the local botanical knowledge about the plants she chose to include.

While Lydia does not reveal nor acknowledge her sources, she conveys a sycophantic tone in her introduction—a tone that is self-deprecating and almost unctuous. This appears to be common across the writings of eighteenth-century female writers. Repeatedly, we find an almost snivelling feminine meekness, a modesty intended to cause as little trouble as possible. The deferential and submissive tone in Lydia Byam's preface is addressed to a woman, the Viscountess of Galway. While the addressee is a woman, there seems to be an implication that men will be "checking it." Lydia writes: "It is not from motives of vanity that I prefix your ladyship's name, but from the highest opinion of your judgement and taste; and, if I am so happy to meet your approbation, I shall then think I have some merit" (3). To make matters worse, Lydia Byam is too meek (or strategic) to use her own name for the book, preferring the self-effacing "By a Lady" (Byam).

I feel puzzled by Lydia's modesty and lack of appropriate acknowledgement. However, I understand the times, the politics, and the injustices that women must have endured. Those injustices would have been mild compared to the lives of enslaved women, who were routinely raped, beaten, poisoned, and falsely accused of poisoning. Lydia was caught up in this era of bioprospecting. As Londa Schiebinger says of bioprospecting, "The most pressing motivation for investigating tropical medicines, however, was to keep European troops and planters alive in the colonies. Colonial botany was crucial to Europe's successful control of tropical areas, where voyagers from temperate zones became sick and died in alarming numbers" (2005b, 321). Most likely, the illnesses included male infertility and erectile dysfunction.

Schiebinger has also written at length about the use of plant abortifacients in the Caribbean (2005a). This use of plants to cause miscarriages increased after the 1830s emancipation of enslaved people on Antigua. Rather than liberating women during this period, men were given waged jobs, leaving women and children abandoned and compromised more than ever, as the systems of enslavement shifted into a different dark and racist beast (Dawes).

While sugar was the main product of Antigua while Lydia was alive, and rum came in second, there was also an appetite for natural history knowledge. Was Lydia merely providing that new knowledge for a European audience, or was she complicit in the barbaric treatment of enslaved people on the island of

Antigua? As Georgia Fox says, the dynamics of sugar plantations on Antigua created a "legacy of bitter memories" (1).

The silk cotton tree had no smell, according to Lydia Byam, but it could treat male sexual disorders. If only it treated other male disorders of the time.

Part 2: Dieffenbachia

The cures and the curers. The history of plants as medicine, salve, and cure has an ongoing association of moral goodness. Plants can play the part of moral beings because they can "help" humans survive. Putting aside the exceptionalism of these ideas of plants as cures *for humans*, there is also an aesthetic effect of plants as cures. Think of images of medicine bottles, of dispensaries filled with row upon row of tiny little tinctures and glass bottles of burned, seeped, and ground plant matter.

The multiplicity of the chemist, the pharmacy, and the dispensary are visually attractive, not unlike the art shop, the candy store, or the car outlet, depending on your fancies. Not to mention the more recent corner marijuana shop on any block in New York or Los Angeles with hundreds of bongs, dried flowers, and cannabis oils. So much stuff. Along with the multifaceted aesthetic of plant cures, there is the mythology and narrative of the local medicine person: the priestess, the shaman, and the alchemist. These are the people entrusted with the highest order of plant knowledge. They are appealing figures in history, and that appeal continues today.

In Pablo Gomez's book *The Experimental Caribbean*, he writes about the "Caribbean priests, slaves, natural philosophers, historians, Mohanes [Peruvian shaman], balbalawos [West African priest], babanga [African shaman], botanists, alchemists and cooks" who were all healing practitioners in the West Indies during the colonial epoch (122). He refers to a Spanish barber surgeon who travelled to the Caribbean in 1575 and who had scorpion ointment, cinchona bark, laudanum, centipedes, and Florentine lilies in a wooden travel cabinet, ready to salve and save as part of a social pharmacopeia.

One of the plants that act as both cure and poison is dieffenbachia, or dumb cane. It gets its name from the fact that the leaves are toxic and were notoriously used as punishment on plantations in the Caribbean during the late eighteenth and early nineteenth centuries. The toxins from the plant's leaves make the human tongue swell when it is eaten. It was used by plantation owners in the West Indies to silence their enslaved labour, hence "dumb cane." It also caused muteness, pain, and difficulty in breathing.

   Prudence Gibson

According to Arditti and Rodriguez, dieffenbachia stems render victims speechless for days, and even in non-fatal cases, dieffenbachia causes corrosive burns, accelerated heart rate, muscle twitching, and respiratory failure. Like the silk cotton tree, Arditti and Rodriguez confirm, dieffenbachia was used as a cure for dropsy and sexual impotence. Inhabitants of the Caribbean chewed it to bring about male sterility that lasted for twenty-four to forty-eight hours. For women, the sterility lasted thirty to fifty days (295). Arditti and Rodriguez also note that dieffenbachia was used in the upper Amazon by Indigenous peoples to make poisonous arrows (296).

Plant medicine was brought to Antigua and other Caribbean islands, but it was also developed there. According to Sasha Turner Bryson, there were constant accusations of poisonings during the years of plantation slavery. White planters feared obeah, local Indigenous medicine, and the violence of black enslaved peoples (Sheridan). But the use of poisons was also attributed to enslaved peoples, and obeah was subsequently vilified as fraudulent witchcraft (Bryson).

Plants during this period were used for malevolent reasons, but not by obeah practitioners. The use of dieffenbachia was different from the subtle balance between cure and poison or underdose and overdose. There were instances of purposeful and malicious violence. Dieffenbachia can now be bought all over the place, such as at your local hardware store or garden nursery in Australia. My local Flowerpower, for instance, sells dieffenbachia tropical tiki, dieffenbachia compacta, dieffenbachia memoria corsi, dieffenbachia camille, dieffenbachia marina, and so on—to give you an idea of how many varieties are available, just down the road.

The temporary sterility of those who chew the dieffenbachia stem or leaves introduces another interesting question around plants: sterility and abortifacients. The use of dieffenbachia as enforced sterility was also accompanied by a parallel knowledge that it could terminate pregnancy. This supports the scholarship of Londa Schiebinger in her work on abortifacient use in the colonial Caribbean.

In Germany during World War II, there was a perverse and sickening interest in dieffenbachia. It emerged during the Nuremberg tribunals that research had been undertaken regarding how dieffenbachia, when injected, could cause ongoing sterility in women (Arditti and Rodriguez 296). The Nazi SS officer Heinrich Himmler heard of Dr Madaus's research into these properties of the dieffenbachia. Himmler conducted experiments in concentration camps and also considered developing plant propagation in large amounts. However, Himmler was unable to cultivate or import enough of the dieffenbachia from South America for his purposes, and the project stalled.

There are two dieffenbachia specimens in the Sydney Herbarium collection. Both were collected in 1970 from New Caledonia, both had to be treated for fungal damage, and both have French labels from The French Museum in Paris. The plants look a little waterlogged, as though they never dried out properly. They seem to have been acquired from Paris, rather than being collected directly.

These specimens are a reminder of the movement of specimens between herbarium institutions for knowledge sharing, for security, and for research. There is an uneasy connection between certain plants and Australia's legacy of imperial, expansionist, and colonial history. Sometimes the secrets of the herbarium—sheets of plant specimens with collection data on them—offer up stories we would prefer not to know. The secrets are too dark. But that is the perverse adventure of opening drawers and unwrapping specimen sheets. There is a kind of adrenalin rush whenever you go hunting through an archive, which has something to do with the possibility of discovery.

I recently pulled out the specimens for dieffenbachia one more time. Now that I knew how malevolently they had been used by humans, I searched the water stains on their leaves and the stubby roots that look a bit like sugar cane for answers.

But those specimens gave nothing away. They were just plants pressed onto a page. Perhaps they are innocent victims of human instrumentalism. Perhaps they are conscious (on some molecular level) of the destruction they are capable of. Dieffenbachia sit in our living rooms and on our balconies. Pets and kids brush past them, unaware of the secret harm they hold. We tend to think of plants only in the context of goodness. That is one of the many mistakes that humans may have made in their relations with nature.

Part 3: Dark Collecting

Amalie Dietrich (1821-91) was a self-taught naturalist and chemist. She lived in what would become East Germany in the 1850s-60s. Amalie's mother taught her about the wild plants and their medicinal uses when she was growing up in Saxony. Her husband Wilhelm was a pharmacist who collected plants for pharmaceutical products and relied on his wife to assist him. When Wilhelm began an affair with their nanny, Amalie chose to leave their daughter Charitas

and Wilhelm in Germany to follow her collecting passion and did not return to
Germany for nearly a decade.

In 1863, Amalie Dietrich was commissioned, after many attempts over several years, by the wealthy shipping merchant Johann Cesar VI Godeffroy to
assist him in his grand, imperial vision to establish a major natural history collection. She embarked on a voyage from Hamburg to Australia to collect specimens for the newly established Museum Godeffroy (Gibson).

Amalie faced harsh conditions in Australia. As a female collector travelling
alone during the late colonial period, she probably found it difficult. Mostly
in remote regional Queensland, she collected plants, rocks, and animals. Her
enviable and rigorous collections were widely respected and had an enormous
impact on zoological and botanical knowledge for many subsequent decades.

She was able, despite the imposing physical and cultural challenges she faced
in Australia, to constantly ship back specimens to Hamburg for the Godeffroy
Museum. The collection was later moved to the National Museum of Hamburg,
the ethno-collection to Leipzig, and the plants to the Hamburg Herbarium. In
World War II, the collections were moved again and were then only rediscovered in the 1980s.

The National Herbarium of New South Wales in Sydney holds 368 duplicates
of Amalie's collection. Its director Hannah McPherson says, "specimens become
the truth." Specimens do become the truth, because they can reveal some dark
stories about our important natural history and plant collections. And about
our collectors.

Amalie's collections "constitute the first records of many Australian species
and provide a unique record of the Australian flora prior to land-clearing for
expanding agriculture and urbanisation. Dietrich's immense contribution to
natural history was recognised by her peers and successors, and many species
are named in her honour," says Hannah McPherson, who also noted that a large
portion of her collections has still not been catalogued (Gibson 2023, 162).

In a photograph of Amalie Dietrich, she has clear, round eyes and thin lips
pressed together in a calm expression. Not at all unattractive, despite the severe
hair style of the day—a middle part with the hair pulled back in a curve halfway
down the ear and tied into a nape bun. The Amalie I saw looks like she was
capable of anything, and, in effect, she was. A strenuous sea voyage, even in
the 1860s, and a brutal life on the bushranger backroads of Queensland would
not have been easy for anyone, let alone a woman on her own. Over those nine
years, she amassed what was then the most significant spider collection in the

world, along with marsupials, beetles, butterflies, coral, sea slugs, and 20,000 plant specimens.

In October 1866, a catalogue entitled "Plants of New Holland collected by Mrs. Amalie Dietrich at the Brisbane river, Col., Queensland by order of Mr Joh. Ces. Godeffroy & Son in Hamburg" was issued. It contained a list of almost 350 plant species available for purchase in sets. Amalie also collected ethnological specimens such as canoes, cubs, and spears and amassed 266 species of birds.

While in Rockhampton, she obtained one of her most important specimens: a brown snake that was new to science at the time and would later be commonly known as the taipan snake. Her collections remain as evidence of a unique period in the expansion of the natural sciences and global exploration by German botanists—a rich period that also included Ferdinand von Mueller and Ludwig Leichhardt. Aside from their cultural and historical value, the specimens collected by Amalie Dietrich also remain highly relevant and important to the scientific community.

However, there was a dark side to the story of Amalie Dietrich that must be told. She retrieved eight Indigenous Australian skeletons, five male and three female, from the Bowen area, plus a skull from Rockhampton.

Conclusion

Clearly, there is darkness in the history of botanical discourses and botanical practice. Plants have been used and abused, reduced and flattened—and weaponised. Dark botany seeks to redress the darkest stories by facing them, by acknowledging and even apologising for them. What becomes clear is that violence and erasure are not limited to the past.

Rather than hoping for a utopian, decolonial botanical future, dark botany is situated in the present with all of its atemporal variations. It is a method and a conceptual means of making sense of cruelty and inequity, but it also allows for some rocking good tales. If colonialism is and was the problem, story-telling—visually, conceptually and textually—is the answer. I make amulets and ash-bottles to give to my children to ward off bad spirits and rotten luck. This shows me that plant culture, in all its forms, is ongoing.

Works Cited

Aloi, Giovanni. *Lucien Freud Herbarium.* Prestel Verlag 2019.

Antonelli, Alexandre. "Director of Science at Kew: It's Time to Decolonise the Collection." *The Conversation,* 19 Jun. 2020, https://theconversation.com/director-of-science-at-kew-its-time-to-decolonise-botanical-collections-141070. Accessed 5 Dec. 2023.

Arditti, Joseph, and Rodriguez, Eloy. "Dieffenbachia: Uses, Abuses and Toxic Constituents." *Journal of Ethnopharmacology,* vol. 5, 1982, pp. 293-302.

Baber, Zaheer. "The Plants of Empire: Botanical Gardens, Colonial Power and Botanical Knowledge." *Journal of Contemporary Asia,* vol. 46, no. 4, 2016, pp. 1-21.

Barndt, Deborah. *Tangled Routes: Women, Work, and Globalization on the Tomato Trail.* Rowman and Littlefield 2007.

Bousfield, Dan. "Settler Colonialism in Vegetal Worlds: Exploring Progress and Resilience at the Margins of the Anthropocene." *Settler Colonial Studies,* vol. 10, no. 1, 2020, pp. 15-33.

Brixius, Dorit. "From Ethnobotany to Emancipation: Slaves, Plant Knowledge, and Gardens on Eighteenth-Century Isle de France." *History of Science,* vol. 58, no. 1, 2020, pp. 51-75.

Bryson, Sasha Turner. "The Art of Power: Poison and Obeah Accusations and the Struggle for Dominance and Survival in Jamaica's Slave Society." *Caribbean Studies,* vol. 41, no. 2, 2013, pp. 61-90.

Byam, Lydia. *A Collection of Exotics from the Island of Antigua.* 1797.

Calvo, Paco, Monica Gagliano, G. M. Souza and A. Trewavas. "Plants Are Intelligent, and Here Is How." *Annals of Botany,* vol. 125, 2020, pp. 11-28.

Carney, Judith Ann. "African Traditional Plant Knowledge in the Circum-Caribbean Region." *Journal of Ethnobiology,* vol. 23, no. 2, 2003, pp. 167-85.

Dawes, William. "The Papers of William Dawes, Missionary 1816-78." *Empire Online,* https://www.amdigital.co.uk. Accessed 2 Dec. 2023.

DeLoughrey, Elizabeth. "Globalizing the Routes of Breadfruit and Other Bounties." *Journal of Colonialism and Colonial History,* vol. 8, no. 3, 2008, pp. 1-40.

DCCEEW Department of Climate Change, Energy, Environment and Water. "Acacia courtii," https://www.dcceew.gov.au/environment/biodiversity/threatened/nominations/comment/acacia-courtii Accessed 6 Feb. 2024.

Fox, Georgia L. "Transformations, Economics, and Bitter Outcomes." *Economic Anthropology,* vol. 3, 2016, pp. 228-239.

Gibson, Prudence. *The Plant Contract*. Brill 2018.

---. *The Plant Thieves*. New South Publishing, 2023.

---. "The Dirt Witches' counter-narrative: a response to Murray Bail's 'Eucalyptus.'" *Ecozon Journal September*, 2023.

Godeffroy, Johann Cesar VI. "Plants of New Holland Collected by Mrs. Amalie Dietrich at the Brisbane River, Col., Queensland by Order of Mr Joh. Ces. Godeffroy & Son in Hamburg." Catalogue, Godeffroy, 1866.

Gomez, Pablo F. *The Experimental Caribbean*. University of North Carolina Press, 2017.

Grove, Richard, *Green Imperialism: Colonial Expansion, Tropical Island Edens and the Origins of Environmentalism, 1600–1860*. Cambridge University Press, 1995.

Haraway, Donna, and Tsing, Anna. "Reflections on the Plantationocene." Podcast, https://edgeeffects.net/haraway-tsing-plantationocene/ Accessed: 1 Feb. 2024.

Head, Lesley, et al. "Vegetal Politics: Belonging, Practices and Places." *Social & Cultural Geography*, vol. 15, no. 8, 2014, pp. 861-870, https://doi.org/10.1080/1464936 5.2014.973900.

Jain, Vartika. "Myths, Traditions and Fate of Multipurpose Bombax Ceiba – An Appraisal." *Indian Journal of Traditional Knowledge*, vol. 8, no. 4, 2009, pp. 87-94.

Kenny, Michael. "A Darker Shade of Green." *Social History of Medicine*, vol. 15, no. 3, 2002, pp. 481-504.

Lanaghan, Mrs. *Antigua and the Antiguans*. Self published, 1844.

Lombard, Marlize. "The Tip Cross-sectional Areas of Poisoned Bone Arrowheads in Southern Africa." *Journal of Archaeological Science: Reports*, vol. 33, 2020, p.102477.

Marder, Michael. *The Philosopher's Plant*. Columbia University Press, 2013

Mondragon, Brittany. "Uprooted Doorway Gardens." *History in the Making*, vol. 15, 2022, pp. 161-204.

Morton, Timothy. "This Interview Has Also Been Published as Part of Living Earth – Field Notes from Dark Ecology Project 2014-2016." http://www.sonicacts.com/shop. Accessed 5 Jan. 2024.

Ogborn, Miles. "Talking Plants: Botany and Speech in Eighteenth-Century Jamaica." *History of Science*, vol. 51, 2013, pp. 251-282.

Sandilands, Catriona. "Floral Sensations: Plant Biopolitics." *The Oxford Handbook of Environmental Political Theory*, edited by Teena Gabrielson et al., Oxford University Press, 2016, pp. 226-237.

---. and Gersdorf, Katrin, eds. "Gardening (Against) the Anthropocene." *Ecozon*, vol. 14, no. 1, 2023.

Schiebinger, Londa. "Agnotology and Exotic Abortifacients: The Cultural Production of Ignorance in the Eighteenth Century Atlantic World." *Proceedings of the American Philosophical Society*, vol. 149, no. 3, 2005a, pp. 316-43.

---. *Plants and Empire: Colonial Bioprospecting in the Atlantic World.* Harvard University Press, 2005b.

Sheridan, Richard. "Slave Medicine in Jamaica: Thomas Thistlewood's 'Receipts for a Physick,' 1750–1786." *Jamaican Historical Review*, vol. 17, 1991, p. 118.

Shiva, Vandana. *Biopiracy: The Plunder of Nature and Knowledge.* North Atlantic Books, 2016.

Singh, Namita. "Survivor of Suspected Mushroom Poisoning Was Experienced Forager of Wild Fungi." *The Independent*, 16 Aug. 2023, https://www.independent. co.uk/news/world/australasia/beef-wellington-mushroom-poisoning-australia-b2393987.html.

Stewart, Amy. *Wicked Plants.* Algonquin, 2009.

2   Palimpsests of Imperial Desire

Anna-Sophie Springer

During colonial times, mountains were displaced, rivers rerouted,
forests destroyed, and plants, animals, and humans moved around.
Postcolonial ideology of development followed the same logic:
nothing would stop human desire to shape its environment and
remake it in its own image.

—Françoise Vergès, "Like a Riot" (33)

Plants can tell us their and our story;
we need to learn to listen.

—Robin Wall Kimmerer, *Braiding Sweetgrass* (10)

There is no other biome that symbolises a healthy and fecund ecology more
than the tropical rainforest. Drawing from my collaborative, exhibition-led
research and co-curatorial initiative *Reassembling the Natural* (2013–23, henceforth RN), this essay challenges the conventional image of the tropical primary
forest as it was constructed in a Eurocentric cultural and geographic imagination. The reflections here on RN's work in botanical collections and science
museum exhibitions in Germany and Indonesia problematise how conventional
natural history continues to champion a sense of scientific and universal objectivity with regards to "tropical nature," but tends to eclipse the transactional
role played by colonial natural science for Western economic growth and imperialism in the formation of this exotic "tropical nature." In contrast to conventional natural history, I offer a materially grounded perspective that critically
asserts tropical specimens as under-studied evidence of a more mundane mindset of investment and accumulation, as well as of the connected assumptions,
desires, and violent transformations. Botanical specimens here are reminders of
the surveys, evaluations, and land-use changes that have engendered irreversible biospheric and socioecological modifications. The preservation of these

specimens also invites questions about the global infrastructures of collecting and taxonomic classification required to maintain a planetary approach to natural history—with its under-acknowledged links to extractive capitalism, racialisation, and epistemicide (de Sousa Santos).

My discussion is based on a selection of museum objects, plant specimens, and botanical arrangements at the Bogor and Cibinong Botanical Gardens in Java as well as the Herbarium Hamburgense (HBG) in Hamburg. In what follows, I unpack how a repurposing of these collections that stretches beyond their uses specific to botany can invoke more complex understandings of the geopolitical, scientific, and commercial economies that contributed to the establishment of herbaria, *xylothèques*, and botanical gardens—which in turn shaped the emergence of asymmetrical hierarchies and systems of representation. In this context, herbarium sheets become dense palimpsests of layered meanings and reinscription. Even though these sheets are now an outmoded scientific sample technique in the field of botany itself, they can be used to situate and *denaturalise* the stories and assumptions that comprise the usual image of tropical nature.

As a whole, the essay touches upon what I have termed the "ecocidal gaze"—a worldview that is deeply anti-ecological, stridently hierarchical, and rigorously utilitarian. Through a discussion of concrete examples from RN's collaborative investigations, I show that specific botanical specimens and related visual artefacts can prompt reflections about the significant roles of "dismemberment" and "extractability" in imperial botany, colonial plant collecting, and the birth of scientific forestry. As the botanical specimens and objects discussed below allow us to foreground the interconnections between the appropriation of plants, land, and labour, analysis of them also contributes to a productive conversation about the imperial plantation system and the current ecological threat posed by intensive monocultures. It is important to note that the so-called (colonial) "useful plants" are typically excluded from the museum imaginary of the rainforest—even though mono-crop plantations and agroforestry have mostly supplanted immense sylvan areas in the tropics and elsewhere. Overall, the argument of this chapter is that old botanical collections constitute palimpsestic evidence for the accumulative processes of extraction and investment that continue to structure the political, economic, and social classifications of lives today. I thus assert that specimens embody their own material-conceptual argument for why it is crucial to rethink the status and public potential of botanical collections in the present, interwoven crises of climate, biodiversity, pollution, and social justice.

Colonial Negatives

In 2014, a research travel grant from the Goethe Institute made possible my initial visit Indonesia to begin the preparations for *Reassembling the Natural*'s first major exhibition, *125.660 Spesimen Sejarah Alam* (125,660 Specimens of Natural History). Planned to open one year later at the art gallery of Komunitas Salihara, a progressive arts and culture organisation in Jakarta, this collaborative experiment explored contemporary perspectives on Alfred Russel Wallace's nineteenth-century collecting expedition that gathered 125,660 natural historical specimens from Southeast Asia for museums in Europe. Over a period of six weeks, my Co-Principal Investigator, the philosopher Etienne Turpin, and I contacted, met, and interviewed several Indonesian expert natural scientists and collection curators at the Lembaga Ilmu Pengetahuan Indonesia (the Indonesian Institute of Science, LIPI) in Java about the cultural and environmental impact and legacy of colonial collecting. In the process of these meetings, we established crucial partnerships between RN and LIPI's Museum Zoologi Bogor (the state zoological museum, MZB), Pusat Penelitian Biologi (LIPI's Biology Research Center), Kebun Raya Bogor (Bogor Botanic Garden), and Herbarium Bogoriense (the Bogor Botanic Garden's collection of plant specimens), which is located in Cibodas, near Bogor. Several months later, we returned to MZB-LIPI with a group of young Indonesian artist-researchers who had been assembled via an open call to participate in the project; this call was disseminated on our behalf by Salihara. The travel to build up RN's multi-year research and its crucial partnerships took time. Therefore, when, as co-curator of RN, I speak of "exhibition-led research," I think of the various lines of investigation and transformative experiences we encountered, albeit without ever fully predicting their potential trajectories and outcomes. In other words, the people, interactions, and conversations at archives and collections such as LIPI significantly guided and formed where we would go next, whom we would meet, and with whom we would discuss our ideas. Often, these personal encounters would alter how we reflected on the materials, sites, communities, and information we came across. Most of the components featured in RN's projects are connected to such moments of serendipity and intercultural and transdisciplinary connection.

In February 2015, after several previous working visits with the collection curators of MZB-LIPI, I received an email from Mohammed Irham, an

Anna-Sophie Springer

ornithologist and the keeper of bird specimens. He asked if we would like to return again soon and suggested we come to look at the hundreds, maybe thousands, of colonial photographs that the Pusat Penelitian Biologi in Cibinong was storing, in addition to the zoological specimens accumulated across more than a century. When our group arrived, we were led to a storage room with miscellaneous items, including numerous boxes filled with 13- x 13-centimetre glass negatives and a folio-sized ledger containing a handwritten catalogue consisting of numbered entries in Dutch and Bahasa Indonesia. Though evidently stored with care, everything was in rather poor condition; many plates were cracked, and the edges of the lists were severely torn and creased. As the negative pictures on the glass plates were hard to discern with bare eyes when held up against the light, we soon crowded around the ornithologist's computer screen and pored over black-and-white images someone had digitised and inverted back in 2008: low-resolution files, smaller than 50 kilobytes, these days hardly larger than their own preview thumbnails. We clicked through pixelated, lead-grey scenes recognisable as the colonial botanical garden called Lands Plantentuin te Buitenzorg (Kebun Raya Bogor's predecessor), surrounding tree plantations and mountain landscapes, the white villas and laboratories of the European elites, as well as some interior views of agricultural factories, botanical greenhouses with palm trees, and open-air gatherings of Javanese workers.

Historically, botanical gardens have been among the most important tools for colonial expansion and accumulation (Brockway). The botanic garden at Buitenzorg in West Java was no exception. Established in 1817 with the appointment of German chemist, naturalist, and Dutch colonial official and royal gardener Caspar Reinwardt (1773–1854) as its founding director, the garden was a symbol of Dutch power in the East Indies and beyond. Its establishment was unthinkable without the funding and support of the Dutch king and colonial government (Weber, 2014 301). Even its location was selected to be adjacent to the estate and menagerie of the governor-general's palace—today, Indonesia's summer presidential palace in Bogor (Weber, 2012 129). Translated into English as "Outdoor Care," one of Buitenzorg's objectives was to provide a prominent location for facilities dedicated to the collection, survey, and cultivation of trees and other plants from all over the Dutch East Indies. For instance, at Kebun Raya, on my first research visit, I happened to traverse a grove of the large tree-ferns Wallace had been so fascinated with in Sarawak (Wallace, n. d. 259). However, besides any decorative specimens, the foreign plant collectors, gardeners, and administrators were mostly interested in, of course, the edible and medicinal plants known in Sundanese, Javanese, Malay, and Chinese local cultures, as well as the famed Moluccan spices, exotic fruits, and native hardwoods for shipbuilding and other commercial purposes. Furthermore, the Buitenzorg Botanic Garden was also used to conduct acclimatisation and agricultural experiments with non-native species from other continents and botanic gardens. It thus functioned as an open-air laboratory to test scaling and economic potential, especially of indigo, sugarcane, and coffee and then later of cinchona, rubber, and oil palm.

The strategic role of the Buitenzorg Botanic Garden becomes particularly clear when we realise that it was founded after the corporate governance of the Vereenigde Oost-Indische Compagnie (VOC) had officially dissolved in 1800, and one year after the Dutch colonial administration had returned in 1816 to replace the British interregnum represented by Thomas Raffles (who eventually founded Singapore in 1819). Economic and environmental historian Peter Boomgaard has provided detailed analyses of the decades-long struggles of the Dutch to introduce into Java systems of forestry management, cash-crop cultivation, and the accompanying authorities and surveys (Boomgaard). With their government support, the facilities of Buitenzorg Lands Plantentuin (also known as Hortus Bogoriense) served as central hubs for the accumulation of useful knowledge and the development and application of economic botany. Here, we must note that prior to the nineteenth century, it had been the Dutch East India Company (VOC) which had employed naturalists and collectors to maximise an economic understanding of tropical vegetation. When the VOC's trading posts were nationalised, however, the Dutch East Indies colony was established, and the Dutch government sought to subjugate Aceh north of Sumatra and the Moluccas near Papua New Guinea at the eastern edge of the Malay Archipelago. Simultaneously, the botanical sciences were increasingly professionalised and funded to strengthen a new society under colonial rule. The different phases of this gradual colonisation throughout the nineteenth and into the twentieth century are reflected in the changing role and profile of Buitenzorg Botanic Garden (Adam). In the first decades, naturalists aimed to expand their knowledge of native flora. With the economic liberalisation of the 1840s to 1860s, the new challenge became to administer nature more effectively so that European private investors could settle profitably, comfortably, and healthily; this period was marked by the beginnings of quinine production and palm oil monocultures. Eventually, botany was institutionalised, and the focus turned to international networks of professional scientists and laboratory practice. The historian Andrew Goss has summarised the economic and political impact of these intertwined historical trends in his study of colonial science in Indonesia under the Dutch:

> anthropologists and doctors to cartographers and geophysicists … were tentacles of colonial power, creating knowledge about the people and places of the archipelago, as well as suggesting ways in which to control them. Colonial officials turned to scientists when confronted with new problems created by recent territorial acquisitions, economic demands, or social unrest. Naturalists, from the colonial state's point of view, were useful as expert managers of tropical nature in all its complexity (5).

With regard to Buitenzorg Botanic Garden, the wishful aspect of such a centralised vision is evident in Wallace's disappointed comments in *The Malay Archipelago*, where he mentions the slow and difficult practice of acclimatising and domesticating even native plants—while, somewhat paradoxically, claiming to have seen the same species in significantly better condition in the engineered greenhouses of faraway Kew (85). Both the landscaped garden and the tropical greenhouse are idealised forms of exotic nature created in the eye of the totalising "master." Other than the unruly "junglewoods," (Wallace) the planted arrangements in these man-made gardens give an image of the tropics much more in line with Eurocentric assumptions about order and taxonomy (Prest). Robert Pogue Harrison, Richard Grove, and others have illuminated the roles of rational design and geometric perfection across such botanical gardens (Harrison; Grove). Like many botanic gardens in the tropics, Buitenzorg also functioned as an exclusive retreat for the colonial elites. Its purposefully carefree views are memorialised in hotel postcards, paintings, and photographs celebrating colonial progress and civilization (Protschky 51-60). Against this background, it is little surprising then that even Wallace would conclude his account of Buitenzorg by admiring the "avenues of stately palms" (Wallace 85).

In our own meeting in Bogor, while looking at the digital photo files, we learned from Mohammed Irham that the biologists at MZB-LIPI had no use for this historical photography and were not sure which type of negatives these glass plates were, or how to restore or preserve them. He imagined we would be interested in engaging with the material for our project. The first daguerreotypes made in Java were made in the mid-1840s (Newton 13). But I have since identified the negatives in the LIPI collection as silver gelatin, dry plate negatives. This type of negative was in use from 1880 to the late 1920s and was the most modern type of glass negative until the invention of celluloid film (Reilly). In *Images of the Tropics*, Susie Protschky opens with the reminder that pictures of

> Indies landscapes formed colonial notions of the Indies' past and future and expressed the impulses driving colonial conquest. ... Palm trees, volcanic mountain ranges, verdant valleys and shimmering rice fields gave texture and colour to Dutch imaginings of a distant colonial possession. ... Where painters tended to focus exclusively on images of stasis, ... photographers regularly depicted the transformations that colonial rule had wrought upon Indies landscapes. Such images of the Indies were cornerstones of the triumphant, positivist discourses that supported colonial exploitation and expansion (16).

The LIPI photographs—judging from the cars, industrial machinery, European fashion, and a calendar on a wall—were made in the 1920s, some perhaps a little earlier, some possibly later. Many motifs appear repeatedly, in merely slight variation. Dry silver gelatin plates were commercially produced and were more convenient to handle than their wet predecessors. Some of the frames thus could be outtakes. Perhaps the negatives disclosed to us at LIPI were indeed leftovers, intentionally allowed to remain and not incorporated into the large holdings of Dutch institutions such as the Koninklijk Instituut voor de Tropen (KIT) or the Koninklijk Instituut voor Taal-, Land- en Volkenkunde (KITLV) (*Southeast Asian & Caribbean Images*). A sequence of pictures shows rubber, coffee, corn, and cinchona plantations, as well as saplings and more mature individual plants. Often, a person (usually young native men) is included in these frames to provide a point of comparison for height; sometimes, these people hold up a tall ruler to allow for more precise measurements. A few of the pictures also document agricultural labour in action, with groups of native women among the coffee trees or men on motorised ploughs tilling the soil.

One of the pictures stands out as a single image of its kind in this repository. It has a portrait format and shows a rectilinear forest parcel that has been clear-cut and a drainage canal. On the canal's left side as well as on the horizon beyond the logged area, the trees are still intact, while on the canal's right side, it is possible to make out a boy standing in front of the expanse of arboreal debris left over from the felling of the trees. Here and there across the scene, columns of smoke rise up. Even despite such an evocative document of colonial

Anna-Sophie Springer

clear-cutting for plantation development, none of LIPI's pictures appears to depict recognisably problematic events, such as soil erosion, flooding, or corporal punishment; these events can be found in the other, larger European collections.[1] Rather, what is evident in these glass plate negatives is the aim to celebrate the industriousness, efficiency, and neatness of this undertaking in exotic botany. The negatives are indeed typical of a certain type of Dutch colonial photography. However, it is important that we encountered these images in the repository of a post-colonial science centre in Java rather than in Dutch, British, or German archives, which are the collections of former imperial powers. These images prompt the following question: if they were used in the past to assert sovereignty over landscapes, people, and ecosystems while promoting hegemonic conduct and new consumption habits, how can they be repurposed and recontextualised today?[2]

Indeed, a century later, the desperate state of the ledger's pages, the fractured, oxidised, and crazed negatives, as well as their low-resolution, pixelated digital inversions, seem above all to mark the *failure* of colonial-scientific positivism and the long-term—both local and planetary—burdens of its legacies. LIPI's photographs are not just significant pictorially, as visual documentation of colonial (agri)culture, imagination, and scientific ambition to "improve" tropical nature. It is also necessary to consider these forgotten silver gelatin negatives that captured the activities of Buitenzorg Botanic Garden in the hinterland of Batavia as part of a residual, physical detritus indicative of the material and multiscalar feedback loops of empire. This consideration invokes the resources that were necessary to produce, distribute, and manipulate botanical and photographic technologies and affects the role of inherited institutional infrastructures, as both built and epistemological form (Azoulay; Campt). Primarily, then, the botanical, glass-plate images seem to *per-form*, through their physical-visual defectiveness, what Ann Laura Stoler in *Along the Archival Grain* has described as the "epistemic uncertainty" that constantly unsettled and undermined the colonial dream of perfect, cultivated order (42). In addition, the digitised inversions of these images facilitates their circulation, reproduction, and multiplication, all of which enhance their epistemic mobility by making them potential agents in processes of decolonisation (Supartono and Moschovi).

Seeing the Forest like a State

For the rational and utilitarian treatment of the plants captured in the images, one of the most forceful analyses is offered by James C. Scott in his seminal

Seeing Like a State. Serving as an opening parable for his book on the control mechanisms of the modern state, his short chapter on German forestry science has been indispensable for my ecopolitical reading of the planetary significance of the glass-plate negatives from Buitenzorg. In his account of the simplification and profit-oriented optimisation of old-growth forests, Scott traces how the forest as habitat was "replaced by the forest as an economic resource to be managed efficiently and profitably" when individuals in the eighteenth-century German-speaking states began to equate usefulness with quantifiable mass and monetary profit (13). According to Scott, this process is a prime example of the normalisation of a highly "selective reality" whose reduction and abstraction enables even higher degrees of quantification through manipulation and control. In its most radical form, scientific forestry subjected dense ecosystems with their multitude of intersecting ways of life—human activities included—to the reductive logic of "powerful institutions with sharply defined interests" and "standardising techniques for calculating the sustainable yield of commercial timber" (15). Everything that is not immediately relevant to this narrow, capitalistic scheme is not only deemed useless but actively disavowed and excised. Through scientific forestry, the crisscrossing of ecological relations across scales was replaced (or "replanted") with an economy of the straight row—the nature of investment. This straight row marked the invention of rectilinear monoculture, about which Scott says that it

> could be synoptically surveyed by the chief forester; it could be more easily supervised and harvested according to centralised, long-range plans; it provided a steady, uniform commodity, thereby eliminating one major source of revenue fluctuation; and it created a legible natural terrain that facilitated manipulation and experimentation (18).

Referencing a seminal text by Henry Lowood (Lowood), an expert in the history of German forestry science, Scott teases out the paradoxes of the forest mathematics scheme: the more perfect, or "normal," such a transformed forest becomes, the fewer variables it contains; the more the forest resembles a rational construct, the more easily its orderly form can be anticipated and replicated. Through such radical simplification into a single raw material and commodity, the "forest" itself, in its very ontology, is *expendable* because abstraction is now reality—at least in an ideal sense.

For Scott, his descriptions of German forestry are metaphors for other contexts, especially the administrative management and fiscal governance of states

Anna-Sophie Springer

and cities with organically grown, diverse demographics and heterogeneous quarters that developed across centuries and where political autonomy stands in contrast and resistance to top-down rule and urban planning. Yet, while the skills and knowledge of German foresters such as Heinrich Cotta, Dietrich Brandis, and Franz Wilhelm Junghuhn were in high demand throughout the tropical colonies—and foreign colonial administrations in the nineteenth century employed them all over the world—this ground-breaking investment in nature also fundamentally shaped how authorities instrumentalised the methods of seeing the forest like a state in Nusantara. In fact, as government-sponsored colonial science in the Dutch East Indies maintained its characteristically condescending attitude towards local people and their natural knowledge, the favoured views among scientific government officials were those that connected taxonomy with economic possibility. As Goss, the author of *Floracrats*, aptly states: "Its framework for understanding nature was imported from outside" (31). In other words, when German scientific forestry tried to impose its principles of uniformity to entire old-growth landscapes in Southeast Asia, the imposition of these principles was not simply the application of a European framework for understanding nature; it was also, particularly, a framework whose methodology was remarkably anti-ecological.

Theatrum Botanicum's White Curtain

In the months leading up to our exhibition at Komunitas Salihara, big efforts were made at MZB-LIPI to rescan and invert some of the glass negatives in higher resolution. The collection curators and their director had agreed to loan a selection of zoological specimens that would evoke Wallace's original collection for public display in *125,660 Specimens of Natural History*, and they expressed the wish that we incorporate their discovery of the glass-plate negatives, too. With the gallery built as a huge oval room, our exhibition was an experimental blending of workshop-led artistic commissions and scientific specimens; RN developed a structure of modular tables that would hold everything conceptually together in the space. These tables themselves were modelled after the 21st century laboratory and storage furniture we had observed during our visits to MZB-LIPI, and they created an expansive, archipelagic landscape in the gallery. The exhibition did not need to be traversed according to a preconceived—let alone linear—narrative or argument. Rather, the setup evoked various trajectories and ways of looking, which, in turn, brought changing relationships into view.[3] With twenty-five artworks and dozens of newly exhibited mammal, bird, and insect specimens arranged on the viewing tables, the curved wall of the gallery space remained a visible constant in the background; we made the decision not to erect any vertical partitions.

It was along this curved wall that we placed seven large, plywood panels on which short texts in Bahasa Indonesian summarised the concerns of the main sections of Wallace's *The Malay Archipelago.* Offering the only text in the exhibition, other than a selection of quotes from Wallace and our exhibition catalogue, these panels stood in evenly spaced gaps between the large-format, colour prints by photographer Fred Langford Edwards, which showed Wallace's original specimens now in British museum collections.[4] Referencing Wallace's *Malay Archipelago* book and his Malay specimens as two types of primary records of colonial collecting, the gallery wall thus formed an equatorial-conceptual horizon and clear investigative frame. The artworks, collaborative research materials, and zoological specimens loaned from MZB-LIPI, on the other hand, were installed in the centre of the gallery. The artworks explored a variety of themes, such as practices of collecting, processes of commodification and consumption, realities of land-use transformation and urban ecologies, agricultural exploitation, and species extinction, in addition to the contradictions at play in the longing for authentic experience through travel and the will to knowledge.

RN's proposal for *125,660 Specimens of Natural History* was highly unusual both to the artistic and the scientific communities in Jakarta—as well as to us as foreign, visiting curators and project initiators. Everyone eagerly explored the possibilities to shape this exhibition-driven, collaborative experiment. As our small RN team was coordinating and preparing the installation at Salihara, MZB-LIPI finally shared a hard drive with us of all the digitised glass plates. There was talk of bringing actual glass negatives themselves so that we could lay them out on one of the illuminated table vitrines we had built; however, in the end, we decided to reproduce a few details in the printed exhibition panels and to dedicate a double page of the accompanying catalogue to a selection of additional images.[5] The most noteworthy of these images, however, became the lead image for the panel at the entryway of our exhibition. The unforgettable scene in the photograph captures everything that is anti-ecological about colonial botany. It is like an emblem of the ecocidal gaze.

This scene differs from other images in the LIPI repository because it is more performative than documentary—at least in the sense that the composed moment was evidently staged specifically for the photograph—even though its purpose was nothing less than to produce a botanical *document,* a

Anna-Sophie Springer

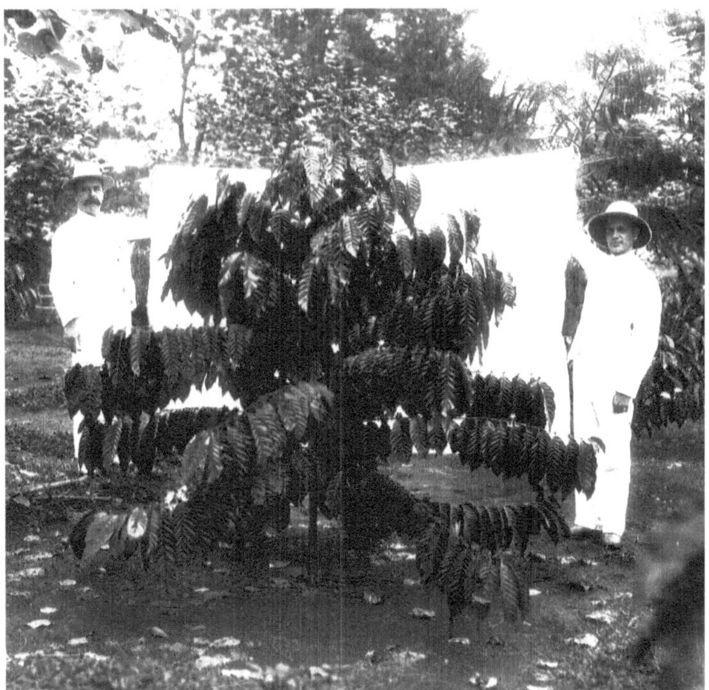

Figure 1. Dutch botanists photographing a coffee plant in front of a white sheet in Java, circa 1920s; digitised image (inverted) glass plate negative.

photographic specimen. The image is also rare because its black-and-white contrasts are very high, even too much in comparison with the leaden or silvery grey of many other images. Moreover, the photograph is clearly divided into a foreground, a background, and indeterminate surroundings. The protagonist in the foreground is a bushy coffee tree. Its single stem grows out of a dark patch of earth from which the underbrush has been removed; there are just some leaves from the coffee tree itself. The tree is identifiable as a *coffea* from its tiny white blossoms and the oval shape of its leaves, which hang down low from the branches, are tightly bunched, and are visible as black-and-white patterns that highlight their typical glossy and grooved surfaces. Most likely, the tree is an earlier arabica variant—an ancestor of the coffee plants still lining the fertile Prianger Mountains of West Java today—and a descendant of the even older plants that the VOC had monopolised in *Insulinde*[6] through forced cultivation since the early 1700s (Breman). For a long time, these plants provided coffee with its nickname of "Java." The tree could also be a specimen of the once popular "Liberia" coffee variety, which Buitenzorg's agricultural entrepreneurs had begun to request from Joseph D. Hooker at Kew Gardens in the 1870s and which introduced a series of fungal coffee leaf rot diseases that substantially damaged Java's mono-cropping industry (Burck).

Yet, despite these historical facts, the plant in this photograph is identifiable to us as coffee by the characteristics of its leaves because of the sleight of logic performed just behind the bushy tree. Two European men immediately behind the tree frame it; their task is to hold up a rectangular white sheet: economic botany's revelatory curtain. This screen in the hands of the two white-suited men with pith helmets assumes the role of the botanist's knife that cuts the branches bearing leaves, flowers, and fruits to make herbarium samples. It performs the narrowing of vision that objectifies *Coffea* by separating it from its environment and thereby rendering it extricable from its wider ecology. *Coffea* here is the Normalbaum [standardized tree] that Scott writes about when he asserts that scientific forestry's "view of its forests was abstract and partial" (13). Indeed, what is performed in this photograph is the transformation of a plant into a study object and commodity that, as an image of nature, can be appropriated and circulated for knowledge and consumption.

It is the gaze of these scientists, straight into the lens of the camera and burnt into a forgotten glass negative, that organises the relationships between the colonised land and the colonial herbarium into the accumulated positive of the coffee-drinking metropoles. Because of their gaze, noticing the third plane of the image is particularly important; it turns all the other, surrounding vegetation deemed uninteresting in this theatrical moment of botanical fixation into nameless noise and disorderly chaos. What is recorded with this image is a moment of the ecocidal gaze in action—a gaze that dismembers species into resources without habitats and promises of potential exploitation. Colonial botanic records, like this stunning photograph, but also like every herbarium sheet, are thus also analogous to receipts for currencies entered into a database for future investments and forlorn failures. They are tallies of the severing of ecosystems into so-called "useful plants" and the worthless "refuse" left over after deforestation.

Encountering the glass-plate negatives at MZB-LIPI in the process of our exhibition-driven research profoundly affected how we conceived of the urgency and responsibility that comes with curatorial practice in the context of the socioecological violence inherent in archival, botanical, and zoological specimens. While only a few reproductions of the photographs featured in *125,660 Specimens of Natural History*, our unexpected introduction to this

uncatalogued, damaged colonial repository in a postcolonial institution nevertheless deeply shaped how, as curators and project initiators, we continued to
think and work towards all later projects.[7] Rather than underscoring how environmental deterioration emerged from "recognised standards of archiving and
records management" (Buckley), the damaged negatives ask us to imagine and
care for a different kind of positive—that is, to engage in forms of decolonial
praxis with the aim of disassembling the ecocidal gaze and beginning to assemble a different understanding of our multispecies nature in a world of bonds
threatened by extinction.

Reassembling Herbarium Hamburgense

In conjunction with this process of generating a new positive, it is equally
necessary to read, situate, and reinscribe actual botanic specimens into their
roles as evidence of coloniality, erasure, and extraction. This aim was the focus
of my work with Matthias Schultz, the head of the Herbarium Hamburgense
(HBG) when, in 2017, we developed a wall installation of historical herbarium
sheets that was included in all three phases of *Disappearing Legacies: The World
as Forest*, RN's three-part exhibition project in Germany that followed the
Jakarta exhibition.

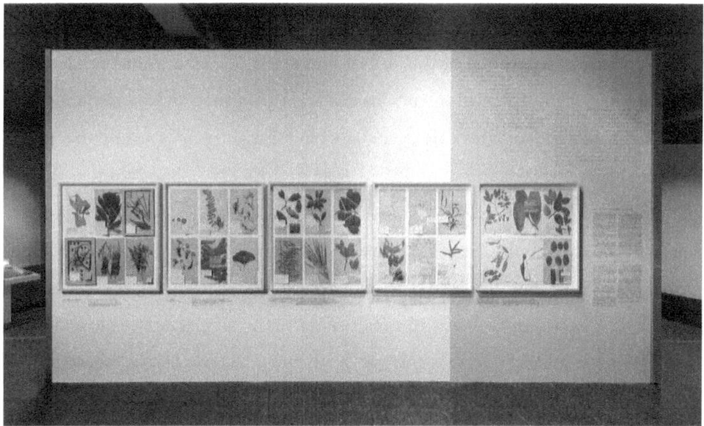

Figure 2. Exhibition view of Reassembling the Herbarium, installation by RN in
collaboration with Matthias Schultz with herbarium specimens from the Herbarium
Hamburgense, University of Hamburg, in *Disappearing Legacies: The World as Forest*.
Photo: Michael Pfisterer for RN at the CeNak Zoological Museum, Hamburg, 2017.

In this essay's final section, I revisit *Disappearing Legacies: The World as Forest* and conceptualise the botanical herbarium sheet as a palimpsest of (post)colonial meanings, correction, and reinscription. The project demonstrates that paying close attention to the purpose, circulation, and components of herbarium sheets reveals some of the structural parallels and intersections between tropical colonisation, climate change, and plantationocene extinction. I show that botanical specimens—unlike objects in ethnographic collections, which it might make more sense to repatriate—can be repurposed for decolonial work in exhibitions by redefining colonial science collections as mirrors of political, social, and economic dynamics that have shaped the environments of the world we live in today. The installation is also an interesting example of a successful interdisciplinary collaboration between RN and an expert collection curator who normally focused on other topics in his daily work. As an intervention should, our herbarium installation managed to intersect with and shed a different light on otherwise firmly assumed botanic principles and everyday conventions.

The HBG is a scientific research collection in the University of Hamburg's biology department. A port city and global metropolis since the Middle Ages, Hamburg itself has a rich history of intercontinental trade, import, export, finance, and industrial manufacture. Having suffered no damage during World War II (when large parts of the Berlin herbarium collection were destroyed), the city's herbarium is one of the largest herbaria in Germany and the world—storing more than 1.8 million specimens. Kept on paper and in alcohol, these specimens include mosses, algae, lichen, and fungi from around the globe. But, as the herbarium was founded in 1883 and its early years coincided with the period of German colonialism, the collection is particularly rich in specimens from the tropical regions, especially Amazonia and Borneo, as well as former German colonies in Africa and the South Pacific.[8] In the context of RN's research, it is important to recall that botanical specimens preserved by Wallace, such as the palm samples at Kew and the fern herbarium sheets at Cambridge, are unusual; in contrast, he collected tens of thousands of zoological specimens. Yet, Wallace's detailed observations and descriptions of tropical fauna, his biogeography, and his Victorian morals and activities as a scientific collector offer useful insight into the accumulation of "natural" knowledge of the tropics. As Susanna Hecht and Alexander Cockburn state in their seminal book on the transformation of tropical forest ecologies, *The Fate of the Forest*: "In contrast to the robust bandeirantes who were spurred by gold and imperial

Anna-Sophie Springer

favour, the nineteenth century naturalists—Humboldt, Darwin, Bates, Wallace, Martius and Spix—expressed a more genteel version of what is now called, in the jargon of development economists, natural resource assessment" (10). In my investigation with the HBG's head curator, I was interested in exploring how we could make the interconnections between natural history, economic application, and colonial exploration explicit in RN's developing exhibition—and thereby also reveal how the transnational matrix of coloniality underpinned the herbarium itself.

At HBG, the pressed samples are stored in the typical black archival boxes. Close to thirty thousand of these boxes fill rows and rows of floor-to-ceiling shelves across several floors of the repository. Specimens stored in the wet collection are kept in plastic crates on shelves in specific rooms elsewhere in the building. Remote researchers can access the datasets of thousands of these specimens via an online catalogue that is still being updated constantly.[9] Or, one can ask to meet Matthias Schultz and look at the specimens in the university's Biocenter Klein Flottbek. In addition to being head curator, Schultz is an expert lichenologist. When I first began to visit him at his office, he had recently participated in a scientific expedition to Kenai Fjords National Park, Alaska in order to create an inventory of the local ecology of lichens; his desks were covered with small containers holding tiny lichen samples in folded paper envelopes. Besides studying and preparing these samples for inclusion in the HBG's collection, he explained to me, he regularly devoted much time to administration and correspondence with scientists from around the world who requested reference information or specimen loans for their research. When I noticed a box on top of a cupboard in the corner of his office with the name Dietrich Brandis written on it, Schultz told me that records of famous collectors were kept separately. That is, the herbarium is not only organised by genus and species, but also sometimes according to the names of collectors. Imagining such an individualised approach to history of science was actually the mindset with which Etienne and I initially went to the London Natural History Museum in 2013, in order to start *Reassembling the Natural*. We asked the entomologist George Beccaloni to show us the "Wallace collection," only to learn that such a category was not coherent with the principles of objectivity that zoological collections and museums traditionally followed (Springer and Turpin 71). Instead, scientific specimens are absorbed into the collections "systematically" and "taxonomically," while the individual perspectives of the collectors, the native guides, the agents who sell the specimens, the scientists who receive them, those who prepare them, and so on are moved as far away from the science frame as possible. This process is to allow us to behold and encounter nature—or its ideal (type) specimens of flora and fauna, at least—as separately from subjectivity and human (in other words, cultural, historical, and political) impact as possible. Talking with Schultz, however, I was reminded of the two colonial botanists visible in LIPI's glass photo from Buitenzorg: if the catalogue of Herbarium Hamburgense already offered a direct path to the dried plant collections via the names of collectors, what if we used our research in the herbarium to interweave our forthcoming exhibition that would unpack the museum image of the tropics with local—that is, with Hamburg-focused—stories of tropical collecting?

Let us remember that although the point of the white textile sheet on the LIPI photograph was to depict the coffee tree as an isolated, extricated specimen, the presence of the two men in their white suits reveals the scene's extraordinary tension between that which is meant to be noticed and that which is meant to be disregarded. The paradox of mastery and suppression necessary to *unsee* a lived world of interrelations in favour of modes of erasure, dismemberment, hierarchy, and exploitability is what I call the ecocidal gaze. Like the botanists' curtain, herbarium sheets provide blank backgrounds on which plants are positioned so that botany can document and reorder them. However, in reality, the sheets of archival paper are also marked with information concerning the place, the year, the collector, and the botanical assumptions about the species sampled. These data also often include revisions, such as different plant names, added later by someone else. Drawing attention to such para-texts highlights the processes of erasure and reinscription, visibility and invisibility essential for the production of scientific specimens and the image of nature they create together. From this perspective, the herbarium sheet is like a palimpsest whose layers, structures, and references can change the way we view plants in the museum and beyond, thereby also transforming our understanding of the profound impact and continuities of ecological imperialism and environmental destruction in the twenty-first century. In Germany, where the legacies of colonialism are still rarely included in school curricula, such a move in the public forum of a conventional natural history museum has a striking potential.

As Schultz and I opened the black boxes in the collection depot, we began to investigate how these records of the history of botany could tell a story of imperial desire. Wallace's *Palm Trees of the Amazon and Their Uses* (1853) offered a concrete starting point for our selection because it merges naturalist and economic perspectives. Published the year before Wallace's departure for southeast Asia,

                                                            Anna-Sophie Springer

the 218-page book discusses his travels in the "neotropical" region of Brazil and combines morphological drawings with taxonomic and biogeographical observations and descriptions of Indigenous peoples' uses of local trees and forest products. Despite Wallace's ethnobotanical concern for Indigenous cultures, including his interest in the native names of the palms, the scope of the book cannot be separated from the Western quest to increase the palette of useful colonial plants. Wallace evidently sought to evaluate and classify species according to their potential industrial benefits. Yet, as a collector focusing on the more lucrative zoological specimens, he was certainly exemplary for the many collectors who, in the early to mid-nineteenth century, could not make a living from selling their herbaria. Later, research into biodiversity in the colonies promised not only new knowledge, but also new raw materials, in addition to consumer and trade goods. Prussian forestry and agricultural science provided novel approaches and techniques for extending state control over forested areas while at the same time restricting use by local residents.

In Hamburg, the Botanical Museum (the HBG's predecessor) was an important adviser for the trading companies based in the city, such as C. Woermann and Jantzen & Thormählen. The plants and plant raw materials imported by ships, notably the oil palm *Elaeis guineensis* Jacq. or substances like rubber, were analysed and classified by scientists according to a primarily colonial understanding of nature and economics. With this in mind, Schultz and I arranged our final selection of thirty herbarium sheets for *The World as Forest* to recalibrate the display of tropical plant specimens as an interconnected tableau of the herbarium's evolving economic purpose in light of the world's geopolitical transformations.

All of the sheets were grouped in thematic sextets and hung on the wall in five large, museum frames specifically made for our exhibition. The first set of six sheets included sample parts of the same palm species Wallace had encountered at the Amazon and Rio Negro. The second sextet featured fern species from Amazonia, and there were six additional fern samples from the Malay Archipelago in the third set. Another sextet included examples of the native and nowadays critically endangered dipterocarp hardwood tree and pitcher plant species from Borneo, and the central set contained the most important "useful colonial plants." Though departing from references to Wallace's palm book, all plant samples on the sheets had been collected and brought to the Herbarium, or to the earlier Botanical Museum, by various explorers. The diverse biographies of these explorers—ranging from the very first German naturalists going to Amazonia in the 1820s to late-twentieth-century academics and employees of the University of Hamburg—let us demonstrate connections that situated the HBG within the history of colonial science in the tropics.

Four of the six palm samples we showed, for instance, were of species "discovered" and named for Western botany by Carl Friedrich Philipp von Martius (1794-1868), who was most famous for publishing the encyclopedia entitled *Historia naturalis palmarum* (1823-50). Von Martius's "discovery" has been considered the first modern classification of Brazilian palm species and was an inspiration for Wallace, who himself "discovered" and named another palm species of von Martius's *Leopoldinia* genus, as we showed in the exhibition. The specimen labelled "L. major Wallace" in the exhibition, however, was retrieved in 1988 by Klaus Kubitzki (b. 1933), HGB's emeritus director, in the flooded blackwater igapó forests near Manaus. Just as it helps to realise that the genus name *"Leopoldinia"* has rendered palm trees memorials to colonisation (it honoured an archduchess of Austria who became the first empress of Brazil) because it is a reminder that the naming of places, people, and species is an inherently political act often connected with power, control, and erasure, the overall selection of herbarium sheets, and all the traces available on and through them, foregrounded a densely interwoven web of cultural, social, and economic markers intersecting across scientific practice (Haraway).

The fern species from Borneo matched some of the forty-one Wallace specimens held at the University of Cambridge, but they had instead been collected by German botanists working for the Dutch colonial government, such as Caspar Reinwardt, the previously mentioned founder of the Buitenzorg Botanic Garden, as well as Justus Haßkarl (1811-94), whom the Dutch ministry of colonies had sent to the Andean highlands on a mission to smuggle living specimens of cinchona trees, the source for quinine, the drug that cured malaria, to Buitenzorg in the 1850s (Goss 33-58; Junghuhn). The oldest specimen of Amazonian fern and the oldest specimen of Bornean fern were also among the HBG's oldest herbarium sheets; they dated back exactly two hundred years, to 1817. The fern collected in Java by Haßkarl, on the other hand, was from 1844, the year when Buitenzorg's colonial herbarium was founded. In contrast, the hardwood and pitcher plant samples from Borneo only dated back to 1959-64 and were gathered by Eberhard Brüning, a professor of global forestry at the University of Hamburg, when he still worked as a surveyor for the—then British-controlled—Sarawak Forest Department near Kuching (the area where Wallace stayed for the longest time during his trips to collect specimens). Since the Malay timber boom of the 1970s, the old-growth forests from which these samples originated, have mostly and swiftly disappeared (Brüning; Ross).

Currently, the region is dominated by oil palm plantations, which cover Sarawak and other vast regions in southeast Asia. This land-use change was evoked in the middle sextet of our exhibition; we devoted this set to different moments of colonial agroforestry booms, showing cinchona leaves collected both as native specimens in Bolivia and as crops in the Dutch colonial plantations near Bogor in Java, *hevea* from near the Rio Negro, and an oil palm frond from a plantation in Cameroon, when the country had been a German colony. As the seeds of cinchona, rubber, and oil palm were smuggled, nursed, and acclimatised across the tropical belt for their healing bark, rubbery sap, and honey-coloured, versatile oils, they became linked to different social groups and involuntary actors in capitalist reproduction and monoculture, as well as forms of vernacular and unintended proliferation. For instance, from the 1880s until the 1940s, Indonesia was the world's leading exporter of quinine—the drug that promised to make the tropics "safe" for colonists and soldiers. But before the cinchona trees (whose medical properties were first known to the Quechua peoples in the Andes) had successfully taken root in plantations across the hillsides of West Java, F. W. Junghuhn, Wallace's contemporary, had experimented—and failed—with planting them for nearly a decade. It was during his experiments with the cinchona trees that Junghuhn began to speculate and write about the correlations between large-scale deforestation, monoculture reforestation, rainfall, and local climate change (Springer and Turpin). In our exhibition, this multilayered history was evoked by a cinchona specimen explicitly marked as "cultivated" and "medicinal" and labelled with the logo of "Museum Botanicum Horti Bogoriensis" as well as the local Malay name, *Pohon kina.*

The oil palm frond from 1910 was also marked as "cultivated," but it originated in the German-owned plantations of west Africa, which had been colonised. Encountering this sample was interesting because it was only this single oil palm sheet that we could find in the collection. The sheet was even more remarkable, however, for its handwritten labels that identified the collector as "comm. Woermann," one of Hamburg's old, traditional trading and shipping family businesses.[10] Palm oil was one of this company's most profitable trading goods; in fact, Carl Woermann, the company's founder, had initially begun a career in colonial trade by exchanging liquor and weapons for palm oil. By 1883, the year when Hamburg's Botanical Museum was established, Carl's son and heir Adolph had become an important protagonist in the preparation of a formal

German colonial empire and participated in the Congo Conference under Bismarck of 1884-85. Moreover, as the official administrator of Cameroon as a German "protectorate" for the palm-oil trade from 1884 onwards, the Woermann company significantly expanded its maritime infrastructure and shipping lines between Europe and Africa. In 1904, the Woermann-Linie ships not only transported soldiers, horses, and military supplies from Germany to Namibia, making enormous financial profits from the ensuing colonial genocide against the Herero and Nama (Woermann-Linie); in the words of historian Kim Todzi, "the Woermann-Linie and its directors were enablers of the genocide" (Todzi, 407; my translation). This violent corporate-colonial-military entanglement was also suggested in our exhibition by the herbarium specimen.

In the same archival box as the Woermann oil palm sample, beneath an old newspaper page, we found another pressed and mounted sample; this second sample had been collected near Monrovia (Liberia) in the 1950s by a Swiss botanist working at the University of Hamburg. Because the box was shelved in the *Arecaceae* (palm tree) family area, it was surprising that the sample was of a fern species, *Nephrolepis biserrata*, which is quite familiar as a potted plant. However, as the label states, this sample was taken from an epiphyte growing on the trunk of an oil palm. Thus, rather than being taxonomically, and therefore spatially, separated across aisles of the alphabetised herbarium, heterogeneous species commonly seen together "in the field" were united in this unusual box. We mounted the two sheets side by side in the exhibition. *Nephrolepis biserrata* indeed tends to grow in landscapes that have been altered by humans and is among the few plant species that one can still find in abundance in the rows of oil palm trees lining monocrop plantations. In her feminist polemic on the Anthropocene, "Earth Stalked by Man," Anna Tsing writes: "In the uneven proliferation of plantation ecologies, the patchy Anthropocene becomes apparent. And here I arrive back at Man, capital M, who makes resources for progress through plantations" (4). Building on the reality that botany, like any other knowledge system, develops out of the relaying, familiarity, comparison, and revision (or even removal) of information, experiences, and accounts of various individuals, we decided to overlay the herbarium specimens in our exhibition with a layer of scattered commentary written on the glass. One such comment remarked that in English as well as in German, *Nephrolepis biserrata* has the vernacular name of "Macho fern"—a reference to its capacity to spread in radically simplified landscapes.[11] When the thirty sheets in our exhibition were returned to their black archival boxes, Matthias Schultz made sure each of them

Anna-Sophie Springer

acquired a new note in their digital datasheets: "selected for exhibition Die Welt als Wald," thus creating a minuscule trace that RN had made a lasting mark on the collection.

By focusing our herbarium wall displays on the collectors, we emphasised the professional, commercial, and geopolitical interconnections underpinning tropical collecting and so highlighted questions about crucial issues that often remain unacknowledged in permanent natural history exhibitions; these issues included: the specimens' origins and provenance, as well as the circumstances of their acquisition. However, selecting and annotating the sheets we showed must not merely be seen as some kind of resolute confrontation with a contentious past peeled away like the layers of a palimpsest. Standing in for millions of dismembered multispecies, lived worlds and collected species, the thirty mounted botanical specimens together invoked an evidentiary "tableau mort" of the impact of the transnational and multi-centred fabric of social, material, and financial processes that have increasingly homogenised planetary ecologies. In its multiplicity of components, relationships, and local perspectives, our exhibition also challenged the idea of a universal, abstract global system. It is in this sense that the herbarium wall summoned a kind of ethical attentiveness that encourages us to think differently in and about the ecological present.

Notes

1 See, for instance, an image in the Dutch East Indies photographic archives at the Nationaal Museum van Wereldculturen. This image is entitled "Administering Corporal Punishment, Binjai (Sumatra)," [1880–1895, TM-60007721] and can be seen at: commons.wikimedia.org/wiki/File:Collectie_NMvWereldculturen,_TM-60007721,_Foto,_%27Voltrekking_van_een_lijfstraf%27,_fotograaf_onbekend,_1880-1895.jpg.

2 See also the section narrating the encounter of a crumbling imperial map by Franz Wilhelm Junghuhn in Perpustakaan Nasional, Indonesia's State Library in Jakarta, in Springer and Turpin, 11-22.

3 On the liminality of the archipelago as a figure of thought, see Glissant.

4 The long-term photographic research of Fred Langford Edwards consists of locating and photographing original Wallace specimens in collections around the world; the medium-format images can be enlarged far beyond the dimensions of the documented objects. Edwards was first introduced to RN in 2013 by George Beccaloni, director of the AR Wallace Correspondence Project. A series of Edwards's photographs is also reproduced in Springer and Turpin, eds., 136-51.

5   The 2015 catalogue in Bahasa Indonesia can be accessed online: drive.google.com/
     file/d/1pqptgMYUE2nf4zYxQyLUefRgz6ZswwWk/view.

6   Insulinde is an antiquated, colonial term for Malay Archipelago which was used in
     the nineteenth and early 20th century by the Dutch and the Germans.

7   For an investigation of the emotional response-ability of curators vis-à-vis colonial
     photography, see Modest, 21-41.

8   Type specimens—including "holotypes," "isotypes," and other subcategories—are
     biological samples that first indicated a species new to science and that were physi-
     cally used when the species was named by a botanic "author" for the first time. The
     number of such sheets increases the value and importance of a botanical collection;
     they are usually visually marked by a special red tag and often kept separately.

9   https://portal.wissenschaftliche-sammlungen.de/DigitalCollection/179652 As part
     of the Global Plants Initiative funded by the A.W. Mellon Foundation, digital high-
     resolution scans of thousands of the herbarium sheets can also be accessed. See
     Biozentrum Klein Flottbek und Botanischer Garten der Universität Hamburg.

10   Today, the Woermann company exists forth as C. Woermann GmbH & Co. KG,
     offering agricultural, transport, construction machinery, and logistical exper-
     tise to clients primarily in Ghana, Nigeria, and Angola. See: c-woermann.de/
     englisch_de/homepage

11   The existence of plants is unthinkable without the soils in which they grow. Yet
     we have only once encountered a sort of dismembered, disaggregated soil (in the
     anthropological teaching collection of the University of Toronto Mississauga).
     Of course, it would be hard to collect "soil," since it is made up of microbial living
     organisms that would perish.

Works Cited

Azoulay, Ariella Aïsha. *Potential History: Unlearning Imperialism.* Verso, 2019.

Biozentrum Klein Flottbek und Botanischer Garten der Universität Hamburg. Global Plants,
     JSTOR, plants.jstor.org/partner/HBG. Accessed 18 August 2021.

Boomgaard, Peter. "Forest Management and Exploitation in Colonial Java, 1677–1897."
     Forest & Conservation History, vol. 36, no.1, 1992, pp. 4-14.

Breman, Jan. *Mobilizing Labour for the Global Coffee Market: Profits from an Unfree Work
     Regime in Colonial Java.* Amsterdam University Press, 2015.

Brockway, Lucile H. *Science and Botanical Expansion: The Role of the British Royal Botanic
     Gardens.* Yale University Press, 2002.

Brüning, Eberhard F. "On the Seasonality of Droughts in the Lowlands of Sarawak
     (Borneo)." *Erdkunde,* vol. 23, no. 2, 1969, pp. 127-33.

                                         Anna-Sophie Springer

Buckley, Liam. "Objects of Love and Decay: Colonial Photographs in a Postcolonial Archive." *Cultural Anthropology*, vol. 20, no. 2, May 2005, pp. 249-70.

Burck, William. "Koffiebladziekte en de Middelen om haar te Bestrijden." *Mededelingen Uit 's Lands Plantentuin, Mededelingen Uit 's Lands Plantentuin*, vol. 4. Lands-Drukkerij, 1887.

Campt, Tina. *Listening to Images*. Duke University Press, 2017.

De Sousa Santos Boaventura. *Epistemologies of the South: Justice against Epistemicide*. Paradigm Publishers, 2014.

Goss, Andrew. *The Floracrats: State-Sponsored Science and the Failure of the Enlightenment in Indonesia*. Wisconsin University Press, 2011.

Glissant, Edouard. *Traité du tout-monde*. Gallimard, 1997.

Grove, Richard. *Green Imperialism: Colonial Expansion, Tropical Island Edens and the Origins of Environmentalism 1600–1800*. Cambridge University Press, 1997.

Haraway, Donna. "Situated Knowledges: The Science Question in Feminism and the Privilege of Partial Perspective." *Feminist Studies*, vol. 14, no. 3, Autumn 1988, pp. 575-99.

Harrison, Robert Pogue. *Forests: The Shadow of Civilization*. University of Chicago Press, 1992.

Hecht, Susanna, and Alexander Cockburn. *The Fate of the Forest*. University of Chicago Press, 2010.

Junghuhn, Franz Wilhelm. "Der Zustand der angepflanzten Chinabäume auf Java." *Bonplandia: Zeitschrift für die gesammte Botanik*, vol. 188, 1858, pp. 70-107.

Kimmerer, Robin Wall. *Braiding Sweetgrass: Indigenous Wisdom, Scientific Knowledge and the Teachings of Plants*. Penguin, 2020.

Lowood, Henry E. "The Calculating Forester: Quantification, Cameral Science, and the Emergence of Scientific Forestry Management in Germany." *The Quantifying Spirit in the Eighteenth Century*, edited by Tore Frängsmyr, J. L. Heilbron, and Robin E. Ride, University of California Press, 1990, pp. 315-42.

Luthfie, Adam. *Cultivating Power: Buitenzorg Botanic Garden and Empire-Building in the Netherlands East Indies, 1745-1917*. 2020. Northwestern University, PhD Thesis.

Modest, Wayne. "Museums and the Emotional Afterlife of Colonial Photography." *Certain Images: Museums and the Work of Photographs*, edited by Sigrid Lin and Elizabeth Edwards, Routledge, 2014, pp. 21-41.

Newton, Gael. "Silver Streams: Photography Arrives in Southeast Asia 1840-1880s," in *Garden of the East: Photography in Indonesia 1850s-1940s*, edited by Gael Newton, National Gallery of Australia, 2014, pp. 12-31.

Prest, John. *The Garden of Eden: The Botanic Garden and the Recreation of Paradise.* Yale University Press, 1981.

Protschky, Susie. *Images of the Tropics: Environment and Visual Culture in Colonial Indonesia.* Brill, 2011.

Reilly, James M., *Care and Identification of 19th-Century Photograph Prints.* Eastman Kodak Co., 1986.

Ross, Michael L. "Sarawak, Malaysia: An Almost Uncontrollable Instinct." *Timber Booms and Institutional Breakdown in Southeast Asia.* Cambridge University Press, 2009, pp. 127-56.

Scott, James C., *Seeing Like a State: How Certain Schemes To Improve the Human Condition Have Failed.* Yale University Press, 2008.

Southeast Asian & Caribbean Images (KITVL). Leiden University Libraries, 2016, digitalcollections.universiteitleiden.nl/imagecollection-kitlv. Accessed 23 November 2021.

Springer, Anna-Sophie and Etienne Turpin. "The Science of Letters." *Reverse Hallucinations in the Archipelago*, edited by Springer and Turpin, K. Verlag and Haus der Kulturen der Welt, 2017, pp. 11-22.

Springer, Anna-Sophie and Etienne Turpin, eds. *Reverse Hallucinations in the Archipelago.* K. Verlag and Haus der Kulturen der Welt, 2017.

---. et al. "Worlds after Wallace." *Reverse Hallucinations in the Archipelago*, edited by Springer and Turpin, K. Verlag and Haus der Kulturen der Welt, 2017, pp. 68-83.

Stoler, Ann Laura. *Against the Archival Grain: Epistemic Anxieties and Colonial Common Sense.* Princeton University Press, 2009.

Supartono, Alexander, and Alexandra Moschovi, "Contesting Colonial (Hi)Stories: (Post)Colonial Imaginings of Southeast Asia." *Southeast Asian Studies*, vol. 51, no. 3, Nov. 2020, pp. 343-71.

Todzi, Kim. *Unternehmen Weltaneignung: Der Woermann-Konzern und der deutsche Kolonialismus 1837–1916.* Wallstein Verlag, 2023.

Tsing, Anna. "Earth Stalked by Man." *Cambridge Journal of Anthropology*, vol. 34, no.1, 2016, pp. 2-16.

Vergès, Françoise. "Like a Riot: The Politics of Forgetfulness, Relearning the South, and the Island of Dr. Moreau." *South as a State of Mind*, vol. 6, Fall/Winter, 2015, 26-41.

Wallace, Alfred Russel. *The Malay Archipelago: The Land of the Orang-Utan and Bird of Paradise* [1869], Singapore: Periplus, n. d.

---. *Palm Trees of the Amazon and Their Uses.* John van Voorst, 1853.

Anna-Sophie Springer

Weber, Andreas. *Hybrid Ambitions: Science, Governance, and Empire in the Career of Caspar G. C. Reinwardt (1773–1854)*. Leiden University Press, 2012.

---. "Bitter Fruits of Accumulation: The Case of Caspar Georg Carl Reinwardt (1773–1854)." *History of Science*, vols. 52/3, 2014, pp. 297-318.

Woermann C. c-woermann.de/englisch_de/homepage. Accessed 18 January 2022.

Woermann-Linie, ed. *Die Woermann-Linie während des Aufstandes in Deutsch-Südwest-Afrika*. Hamburg, 1906.

3 What Is Orientation in Plant Thinking?

Elaine Miller

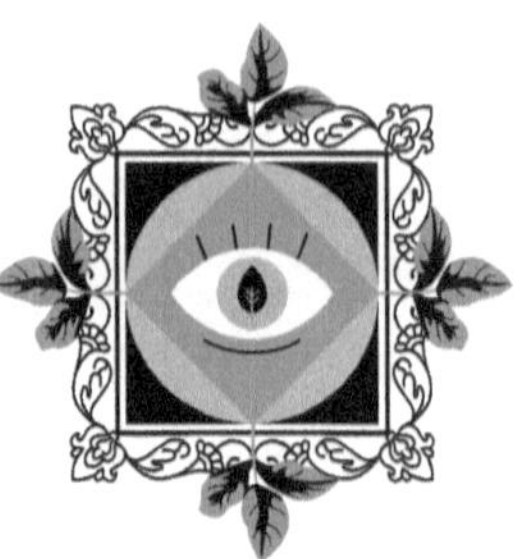

However exalted the application of our concepts, and however far
up from sensibility we may abstract them, still they will always
be appended to image representations, whose proper function is
to make these concepts, which are not otherwise derived from
experience, serviceable for experiential use.

—Immanuel Kant, "What Does It Mean To Orient Oneself in
Thinking?" (Kant 1970, 237)

Philosophy exists in order to redeem what you see in the look of
an animal. If you feel that an idea is supposed to serve a practical
purpose, it slithers into the dialectic. … The mark of authenticity
of a thought is that it negates the immediate presence of one's
own interests.

—Theodor Adorno, radio conversation with Max Horkheimer,
1956 (Adorno 2011, 71)

The plant gives the lie to our desire to see ourselves in the eye of nature. In
"What is Orientation in Thinking?" Immanuel Kant considers the phenomenon
of proprioception, by means of which, through orienting ourselves in our bodies (that is, by knowing where various parts of our body are in relation to each
other without having to look at them), we are also able to orient ourselves in the
sensible (and ultimately supersensible) world. Kant draws our attention to the
origins of the concept of orientation—the focus on the east as the direction of
the rising sun (239). If I see the sun in the east, I can find west, south, and north
as well. For such an orientation, however, Kant says, I must be able to perceive
differences not only on the horizon, but also within my own body. Such a proprioception is not conceptual; although we might alternatively be able to chart,

say, the position of constellations in the sky or the arrangement of furniture in a familiar room by measuring and mapping them, "orientation," as Kant discusses it here, is based on a *feeling* of our subjective (bodily) outline, our parts in spatial relation to each other. Presumably, most animals share this (not necessarily conscious) capacity for proprioception, and even plants have been shown to exhibit proprioception in the form of complex, rotational growth patterns and differentiation between up and down. We would nonetheless be hard pressed to understand the "blind" spiral rotation of a plant as orientation in the way that Kant makes an analogy between left-right spatial and rational proprioception, and it is not my intention to argue that plants are like animals.

A *New York Times* article recently reported scientific findings that suggest that in order to locate an object in space, human brains must become attuned both to sound waves and to the shape of their own ears (Greenwood). Moreover, human ears (and presumably all animal ears) adapt over time to sound patterns and so reveal that the very morphology of our bodies, then, is not static, but conforms to stimuli around us, just as a plant grows toward the light. At the same time, the particular shape of the ears that we are born with also modifies the ways in which we hear sound. Thus, proprioception is not just about self-generated movement in space; it is also about the ways in which our bodies respond to and are shaped by the environment. Perhaps the connection between humans and other living beings lies in our fundamental capacity for self-location in relation to space rather than the possession by all living beings of a subjectivity or personhood.

In *Plants are Persons*, the botanist and philosopher Matthew Hall outlines the parallels between animals and plants. Animals have a sense of sight; a plant, too, has an eyeless sense of sight. Animals have a sense of smell; so, without a nose, does a plant. Animals have a sense of touch; plants too. We can hear; the plant, too, responds to sounds. Plants, research has shown, have a form of proprioception, and a plant can even remember. Plants, the argument goes, like animals, are sentient and even aware (if not conscious) beings, and, consequently, they have moral standing. Michael Marder's "What Is Plant Thinking?" goes further, urging humans to practice the non-cognitive, non-ideational, and non-imagistic mode of thinking that is unique to plants, both in our thinking about plants and in our relations to the plant world; that is, he urges us to become more like plant persons (Marder 134-43).

However, what if trying to think like a plant is something we can do only by forgetting the idea of plants as persons? In the late eighteenth century,

Johann Wolfgang von Goethe, Kant's contemporary, wrote in the introduction to his scientific work "On Morphology": "What would we say of an architect who entered a palace by the side door and then tried to relate everything in his description and drawings to the minor aspect he encountered first? Yet in the sciences this happens every day" (Goethe 1988, 42). The "minor aspect" we encounter first, in this case, is our own condition as humans—as definitively individuated, embodied living beings. In reality, as Goethe writes in *On Morphology*: "No living thing is unitary in nature: every such thing is a plurality. Even the organism that appears to us as individual exists as a collection of independent living entities" (Goethe 1988, 64). Nietzsche, in early notes for his dissertation on Kant's *Critique of Judgment*, insists that our misconception that all organisms, and by extension, all concepts, are distinctly individuated comes from "an unrefined (*grobe*) perspective, perhaps first taken from the body of the human being" (388). Personhood, presumably, implies some form of individuation.

Goethe was in part reacting to the anthropomorphisation of plants found in Linnaeus's work. In Aphorism 146 of *Sexes of Plants* (1760), Carl Linnaeus describes plant sexuality almost exclusively in the coy terms of eighteenth-century heterosexual marriage, identifying the calyx as the "bedchamber" and the corollas as the "curtains" that shield from view the anthers (the "testes"), the stigma (the "vulva"), and the style (the "vagina") (qtd. in Ritterbusch 110; Schiebinger 25; Müller-Wille). Goethe, by contrast, articulated a depersonalising theory of morphology as a basis for discovering "the underlying unity in the vast diversity of plants and animals" according to a formative drive (*Trieb*) that would explain nature's organisational power (in contrast to *Kraft*, or mechanical force) (Goethe 2009, xvi). In *The Vegetative Soul*, I argued that, following Goethe, plant metamorphosis became a figure for human subjectivity in its intertwining with the natural world in nineteenth-century German Romantic and Idealist philosophy and literature. I read this figuration as pushing back against a more familiar, modern, "animal" figure of subjectivity interpreted as autonomous, individuated, and oppositional. By "figure," I mean the human tendency to append imagery to our concepts—the tendency that Kant describes in his "Orientation" essay—as well as the ways in which the particular morphology of individual body parts, such as ears, shape our reception of the world around us. At that time, I contrasted "animal" subjectivity, which thinks organisms and concepts in terms of their strictly individuated contours and analytically distinguishes one contour from the other, with "plant" subjectivity, which understands subjectivity, intersubjectivity, and other concepts, including the human relationship to nature, fluidly and relationally. Goethe recognised that all of nature, including humans, shares a vegetative drive that shatters our capacity to imagine nature. Humans are plantlike, but plants are not like people. Kant's philosophy, too, preserves a lacuna between substance and subject, between what we can know and how the natural world is.

Goethe suggests that the use of the word *Gestalt* (form) in the German studies of natural history of his time is misleading, since "with this expression they exclude what is changeable and assume that an interrelated whole is identified, defined, and fixed in character" (Goethe 1988, 63). Goethe substituted the word *Bildung* (formation) for *Gestalt* in order to convey the perpetual motion of all metamorphic change. He argued that scientists' manner of approaching nature cannot be judged simply quantitatively—by the amount of information that they gather or the number of phenomena their theory may explain—but must also be questioned qualitatively, in terms of the way nature is configured by it.

We can find the precursor of this argument in Kant's *Critique of Judgment*. Kant introduced reflective judgment in the third "Critique" as a way of addressing the lacuna between his two critiques of theoretical reason and of practical reason, both of which rely on determinative judgment. Determinative judgment is the power to subsume a particular under a (pre-established, or *a priori*) universal. This type of judgment proceeds from a concept, rule, or principle given by the understanding to the faculty of judgment in theoretical judgments, or by reason in practical judgments. In reflective judgment, by contrast, the point of departure is not an *a priori* concept or universal, but rather a sensuous particular, and judgment's task is to search for a universal to which that particular can refer, even though, importantly, the universal will be indeterminate. The two spheres of human experience that Kant believed particularly required reflective judgment are aesthetics and the quest for systematicity in organising discrete laws of nature into a purposive whole (what we might call a unified scientific theory).

In the case of both reflective judgments of beauty and of teleology in nature, the *a priori* principle of judgment at play is subjective formal purposiveness, by which Kant means a principle that is transcendental, that is, assumed a priori as the condition of making a reflective judgment in the first place (in contrast to an external, teleological principle). It is important to insist on this point because Kant's theory of reflective judgment, while it is linked closely with concrete experience, nonetheless is not primarily empirical. Reflective judgment is also notably distinct from induction, where the repetition of particulars with a given similarity can lead to a generalisation ("all swans are white"); in reflection, Kant is adamant that only a *singular* is given.

Kant firmly draws a line between our judgment, which is based on a singular presentation, of nature as beautiful or purposive, and nature itself, whatever it is in itself. We are not justified in asserting as grounds for knowledge the argument that the world is in any objective sense peculiarly suited to humans' presence in it or even to our perception of it, even if the way in which our cognition works at its best subjectively and necessarily gives rise to the idea that nature is suited to humans' presence and perception. Kant thus draws a line that cannot be crossed between a mediated knowledge of appearances and what he indicates negatively as *noumena*, which are only accessible to an intuitive intellect fundamentally different from our own.

So when thinking about our orientation toward nature, it is important not to focus on the determination of theoretical judgment or moral judgment, where there is a tendency toward what Karen Houle calls "onto-stabilization." By looking instead toward reflective judgment, we may engage in "thinking otherwise," as Houle urges us to do; we can resist dominant modes and habits of imagining, while nonetheless tracking the enduring sway of these concepts in order to destabilise their domineering power. "To think otherwise," she writes, is to "strenuously resist the premise of the animal," the constitutive "onto-stabilization" that is central to Western philosophy's past. We can thus open up a new conceptual space distinct from our dominant ways of thinking about communication and intersubjectivity (Houle 40).

Jeffrey Nealon and Lynn Huffer have noted Foucault's argument in *The Order of Things* that attention to the bodily contours of an organism as a figure for human thinking shifted historically from the plant to the animal in the move from what he calls the "classical" age to our modern world (Nealon, 7; Huffer 135). Despite Foucault's convincing argument that classical natural history gave precedence to classification and "vegetable values," while biology and the concept of "life," privileged the animal, with its invisible, internal organic structure, in the nineteenth century, I would argue that Goethe's concept of plant *Bildung* already has the connotations of a hidden, ideal force that binds together the various stages of the development of all life forms, and that plant metamorphosis is thus divided from the animal only in terms of its open display of the lack of individuation in living beings.

Elaine Miller

Kant's philosophy has been characterised as positing an unbridgeable divide between the subject and the realm of nature, and this interpretation is correct at the level of epistemology. According to Kant, intuitively enough, I cannot unsee or unfeel my body and the structure of my human cognition. Even if I can use my imagination to try to think otherwise, I can never know, for example, whether what I project onto plant intelligence really captures the experience of a plant. At the level of what is real, Kant is not a subjective idealist, however. Knowledge of appearances, as shaped by the *a priori* forms of intuition and the categories of the understanding, is possible, necessary, and consistent across humans. What we cannot know for certain is how all of these discrete phenomena and discrete laws of nature fit together in a systematic whole. Projecting a unity onto nature is the work of reflective judgment, which has to presuppose that such a harmony is possible in order even to undertake the process of trying to understand nature. Kant asserts that we cannot know nature as a whole; what goes beyond the contours of the particular intelligence that we have been assigned by nature will always be a matter of reflective judgment, urged on by the regulative principles of reason. Our human strength and our limitation is the ability to imagine the true structure of nature yet not to be able to definitively verify what we know without slipping into dogmatism.

For Kant, the use of images to orient oneself in purely mental space is analogous to the subjective use of bodily proprioception to orient oneself in physical space. Kant writes that it is a natural, even unavoidable, human tendency to append images to the pure, abstract concepts of the understanding (concepts that, in his view, are not derived from experience), in order to make them "serviceable" for experiential use. Since we feel ourselves bodily as stable and enduring in a particular identity over time, we attribute a similar stability to other organic beings if their bodily structure seems similar to our own, and also to important concepts, even though no such perceptual quality belongs to them. Such a tendency to append images to concepts is both an individual's limitation and his or her only opportunity for orientation in the world. Nietzsche repeats Kant's claim that the human being most effectively and aesthetically unifies its conception of itself and of nature as a whole through reflective judgment patterned after the form of the organism, yet he criticises the human tendency to limit that unification to the crude outlines of the human body. We can imagine ourselves as individuated entities capable of spontaneous, intentional movement, or we can imagine ourselves as indefinite, relational networks with no specific telos or centre. Either way, however, we are imagining, and a certain number of "fictions" follow from the path we choose.

By "fiction," I do not mean something that is untrue, necessarily, but rather an idea constitutive of human thought that results from particular human limitations and motivations; "fictioning" (*dichten*, a word Kant uses) means positing, poetising, creating, animating, and perhaps reifying as "natural" that which is originally a human construct. The fiction that I will consider follows from the undeniable truth that humans dominate and manipulate nature for their own ends. It says something along these lines: in order to liberate nature and free ourselves, we must let it (nature) be what it truly is in itself. In *Dialectic of Enlightenment*, Adorno and Horkheimer point out that this conception of nature as the "healing antithesis of society" is paradoxically nothing more than a presentation of society's own control mechanism. Therefore, it is not liberatory but conservative, "absorbed into that incurable society and sold off" (119).

In his discussion of the beauty of nature in *Aesthetic Theory*, Adorno writes that *phusei*, or nature, is that realm which is "not merely for the subject ... what, in Kantian terms, would be the thing itself" (63). What is at stake in the difference between thinking of nature as a healing anthithesis to society and understanding it as the thing in itself is the permanent unknowability and indeterminability of the thing in itself, according to Kant. For Adorno, the phrase "beauty of nature" indicates this fundamental quality of the objective realm in its nonidentity with our subjective grasp of it. Karl Kraus, to whom Adorno refers in his discussion of natural beauty in *Aesthetic Theory*, was a journalist who sought, through a particular mode of writing, to vindicate "what capitalism has oppressed: animal, landscape, woman" (Adorno 63)—a project to which Adorno links his reorientation of aesthetic theory toward natural beauty. Kraus's method of quoting without comment greatly interested Walter Benjamin, who saw in this practice of summoning a word by its name, wrenching it from its context, and precisely thereby calling it back to its origin a means of doing justice to a concept that other forms of linguistic practice could not (Benjamin 453-54). Both Adorno and Benjamin refer to a "language of nature" distinct from human language, one in which the object rather than the subject might "speak." While for Benjamin it is nature itself that speaks, Adorno grants the potential for speech to the beauty of nature (Adorno 73).

Specifically, with the concept of nature, in particular of natural beauty, Adorno pushed back against a perceived danger, namely, that specifying nature as the antithesis of society and a respite from instrumental reason immediately and paradoxically co-opts it into the sphere of what it means to oppose—the leisure industry, the aesthetic appreciation of nature, or the care of nature as a care of the self—just as vegetable energy was co-opted into animal consumption. Natural beauty "points to the primacy of the object" rather than the subject, even "in subjective experience" (Adorno 71). Adorno thus argues that the beauty of nature, like Kant's thing in itself, is a cipher for what he calls the nonidentical, a noumenal realm inaccessible to subjectivity, which, though forever unknowable, precisely in its inaccessibility to thought holds the promise for things to be otherwise than the way our concepts represent them (including, especially, those concepts that dominate nature for our own purposes). Natural beauty, Adorno writes, is the trace of the nonidentical in things under the spell of universal identity created by the modernist illusion that our concepts fully capture and subtend reality.

Importantly, the thing in itself, by definition, lies beyond the scope of human knowledge. There can be no human project, no matter how beneficent, that will unearth the truth of nature. The promise of natural beauty is not a glimpse of a mysterious utopia that will come to be someday. For Adorno, the only human production that might possibly give us insight into the beauty of nature is nonrepresentational art. This is because art's role, in Adorno's theory, is to acknowledge and make visible nature's invisible suffering, suffering that directly results from human domination. Art that represents nature mimics nature's forms without admitting its own status as techne, and, in so doing, both occludes and replaces nature, transforming natural beauty into human artifice. In fact, as Camilla Flodin puts it, "To express the suffering of nature, an artwork cannot pretend to be an organic unity... authentic artworks are artworks that do not pretend to be authentic and harmonious, but in fact admit their inauthenticity" (3). For this reason, Adorno was interested in the phenomenon of dissonance in musical works, calling dissonance a memorial to the suffering caused by the domination of nature, a memorial that at the same time might give "a voice to nature" (Adorno 66). Art that pretends to transparently represent nature and that does not acknowledge its own artificiality co-opts nature into subjective artistic intention, making it into the correlate of human desire. I worry that plant ethics does or might do the same thing.

To my mind, the way in which we can distinguish the contemporary attentiveness to vegetal being from that of Kant, Goethe, and the early German Romantics lies in the way in which each of them considers plant metamorphosis in relation to human thinking. I think we must openly acknowledge our necessarily anthropocentric/limited perspective, while at the same time respecting the plant as an absolute other.

During a 1956 radio conversation with his friend and intellectual interlocutor Max Horkheimer, Adorno claimed that the purpose of philosophy is "to redeem what lies in the look of an animal" (Adorno 2011, 71). The gaze of the animal would be a gaze beyond the human's capacity to represent nature, beyond the spell of the identical, which posits that our concepts capture the truth of objectivity. For Adorno, even in philosophically reflecting on nature, we almost do it an injustice. He writes, "Any claim that this is how nature speaks cannot be judged with assurance, for [nature's] language does not make judgments." At the same time, "neither is nature's language merely the deceptive consolation that longing reflects back to itself" (Adorno 1997, 73).

Looking into the eyes of an animal, or admiring it from afar, we attribute a parallel nature to it, even if we fear it, because of the similarity of its features to ours. Nevertheless, what the animal sees is opaque to us. When Adorno says that philosophy exists in order to redeem what we see in the eyes of the animal, to do justice to what is not in our own interest, I wonder if there is still some significance to the fact that it is the animal's eyes to which he appeals. The eyeless, brainless plant is the real figure for the absolute other, representing both itself and animal nature as unplumbed by human intelligence. A plant is in fact uncanny to us if we consider it for too long, not in the sense of that which is strange or other but in the sense of what is closest, most familiar, yet repressed, as Freud insists (Freud 1981, 245). It is not that plants are persons, but rather that persons are plant-like, and this is not something that we can understand.

Plants seem so completely other to humans. Plants have a double life, above ground and below, and for at least half of plant life, we have no reference point. As botanist Hope Jahren writes in the popular memoir *Lab Girl*, "Plants are not like us. They are different in critical and fundamental ways … they are beings we can never truly understand. Only when we begin to grasp this deep otherness can we be sure we are no longer projecting ourselves onto plants" (Jahren 2017, 279). Jahren goes on to catalogue the ways in which humans have reduced plants to three things: food, medicine, and wood. Plants are not mirrors in which to reflect ourselves back.

It is essential to acknowledge, in a Kantian way, the ineluctably anthropocentric orientation of our concept of nature. This entails acknowledging our insurmountable limitations, the impossibility of knowing whether our concepts are adequate to what they indicate. Nonetheless, following Kant's account not of determinative, theoretical judgment, as in discrete judgments about specific natural phenomena, but of the capacity of reflective judgment to posit the ways in which all the individual laws of nature work together in a system, it is also imperative for us to engage in "thinking otherwise." Only by acknowledging the ineluctably anthropocentric orientation of our human concepts of nature and plant life can we also acknowledge our limitations. By recognising the non-identical—the gap between subjective categories and the objects they point to—we may properly respect the otherness that we may only gesture toward with phrases such as "the eyes of the animal" and "the fragility, multiplicity, and relationality of the plant."

Works Cited

Adorno, Theodor. *Aesthetic Theory*, translated by Robert Hullot-Kentor, University of Minnesota Press, 1997.

Adorno, Theodor, and Max Horkheimer. *Dialectic of Enlightenment*, translated by Edmund Jephcoft, Stanford University Press, 2002.

---. *Towards a New Manifesto*, translated by Rodney Livingstone, Verso, 2011.

Benjamin, Walter. *Selected Writings*, edited by Michael W. Jennings et al., vol. 2, part 2. Harvard University Press, 2005.

Chamowitz, Daniel. *What a Plant Knows: A Field Guide to the Senses.* Farrar, Straus and Giroux, 2016.

Flodin, Camilla. "The Wor(l)d of the Animal: Adorno on Art's Expression of Suffering." *Journal of Aesthetics & Culture*, vol. 3, no. 1, 2011, pp. 1-12.

Freud, Sigmund. "The 'Uncanny.'" In *The Standard Edition of the Complete Psychological Works of Sigmund Freud*, edited by James Strachey, vol. 17, Hogarth, 1981, pp. 217-256.

Goethe, Johann Wolfang von. *Scientific Studies*, edited and translated by Douglas Miller, Suhrkamp Publishers, 1988.

---. *The Metamorphosis of Plants*, edited by Gordon L. Miller, MIT Press, 2009.

Greenwood, Veronique. "How the Shape of Your Ears Affects How You Hear." *The New York Times*, 6 Mar. 2018, https://www.nytimes.com/2018/03/06/science/ears-shape-hearing.html.

Hall, Matthew. *Plants as Persons: A Philosophical Botany.* SUNY Press, 2011.

Houle, Karen. "Animal, Vegetable, Mineral: Ethics as Extension or Becoming?" *Symposium*, vol. 19, no. 2, Fall 2015, pp. 37-56.

Huffer, Lynne. "Foucault's Fossils: Life Itself and the Return to Nature in Feminist Philosophy." *Foucault Studies*, vol. 20, 2015, pp. 122-41.

Jahren, Hope. *Lab Girl*. Knopf Doubleday, 2017.

Kant, Immanuel. "What is Orientation in Thinking?," translated by H. B. Nisbet, *Political Writings*, edited by H. S. Reiss, Cambridge University Press, 1970, pp. 237-249.

Linden, Ari. "Quoting the Language of Nature in Karl Kraus's Satires." *Journal of Austrian Studies*, vol. 46, no.1, 2013, pp. 1-21.

Marder, Michael. "What is Plant Thinking?" *Klesis – Revue Philosophique*, vol. 25, 2013, pp. 124-143.

Müller-Wille, Steffan. "Linnaeus and the Love Lives of Plants." *Reproduction: Antiquity to the Present Day*, edited by N. Hopwood, R. Flemming, and L. Kassell, Cambridge University Press, 2018, pp. 305-18.

Nealon, Jeffrey. *Plant Theory: Biopower and Vegetable Life*. Stanford University Press, 2015.

Nietzsche, Friedrich. *Werke: Historische-Kritische Gesamtausgabe*, vol. 1, no. 3, edited by Hans Joachim Mette and Karl Schlechta, C. H. Beck'sche Verlag, 1935.

Ritterbusch, Philip. *Overtures to Biology: The Speculation of Eighteenth Century Naturalists*. Yale University Press, 1964.

Schiebinger, Londa L. "The Private Lives of Plants." *Nature's Body: Gender in the Making of Modern Science*, Rutgers University Press, 1993, pp. 11-39.

4 Speculative Phytopoetics: Towards Vegetal Kinship

Giovanni Aloi

A cactus in a terracotta pot sits near a life-size photographic reproduction of itself, which is, in turn, positioned close to a dictionary definition of the word "plant":

> **Plant:** 1. A young tree, shrub, or herb, ready to put into other soil for growth to maturity; a slip, cutting, or set. 2. Any living thing that cannot move voluntarily, has no sense organs, and generally makes its own food by photosynthesis; vegetable organism, as distinguished from an animal organism; any tree, shrub, herb, etc. 3. A soft-stemmed organism of this kind, as distinguished from a tree or shrub.

Potted plant, photograph, and definition are the essential parts of Joseph Kosuth's 1965 *One and Three Plants*—one of the many iterations of the iconic work entitled *One and Three Chairs*. Oozing conceptual prowess, this pioneering artwork aptly shows how, for a long time, we have thought of plants in art as nothing more than objects.

Returning to Duchamp's early twentieth-century notion of the ready-made, Kosuth prioritised this concept over manual skills evidencing the world-forming power of language. He was strongly influenced by French structuralist philosophy—a movement that, since the 1960s, has functioned as the interpretative key for a conspicuous amount of art. *One and Three Chairs* is a philosophical conundrum focused on the essence of being and the world-forming agency of language. But it perhaps inadvertently also demonstrates how language can far too easily flatten the diversity of the natural world.

One and Three Hammers, One and Three Tables, One and Three Clocks, One and Three Shoes, One and Three Shovels: each of Kosuth's iterations of the original work bolstered the artist's message. However, *One and Three Plants* is special because instead of reaffirming Kosuth's linguistic certitude, it short-circuits the theoretical framework that anchors it. Plants are not man-made objects; they are not inert. They are living beings. As such, more than a hammer or a chair, they always further entangle the ties that bind language to reality. Unlike the shovel, the shoe, and the chair, the plant grows. And despite the claims made by the dictionary definition on the wall, a plant can move voluntarily, and it is sentient. Perhaps involuntarily, *One and Three Plants* perfectly works as a metaphor for the innate plant-blindness that has afflicted Western philosophy over centuries.

Following Kosuth's prescription, *One and Three Plants* can be staged by curators with any plant species of their choosing. So far, cacti have been preferred over others because of their sculptural presence and minimal need for water and light. They are some of the easiest plants to keep alive for months in an art gallery. Cacti are slow-response plants. They can endure hardship for extended periods of time. They will survive—hopefully until the end of the exhibition. In truth, curators tend to see cacti as design objects, admiring their texture, verticality, and linearity. Some museums have opted for other resilient species like rubber plants (*Ficus elastica*) or majesty palms (*Ravenea rivularis*). The interchangeability of plant species in this artwork is another symptom of the relentless objectification that tends to obscure plant life in the late modernist paradigm. While this objectification might have been acceptable for the 1960s, posthumanist perspectives make it hard not to see its limitations.

Over the past ten years, philosophers Michael Marder and Matthew Hall have uncovered the vegetal myopia of Western philosophy (Marder, 2013, 2015, 2016; Marder and Irigaray; Hall). The research of evolutionary ecologist Monica Gagliano and plant neurobiologists Paco Calvo and Stefano Mancuso has uncovered plants as complex and sentient beings able to problem-solve, learn, and remember (Gagliano, 2018; Calvo; Mancuso). Potawatomi Nation scholar Robyn Wall Kimmerer has combined Western scientific research and Indigenous knowledge to bypass the cultural limitations that have denuded our modern world of its mythological magic (Kimmerer, 2015). Biologist Merlin Sheldrake has evidenced the importance of mycorrhizal entwinement between fungi and tress—the previously overlooked and yet quintessential connectivity upon which much of the health of our planet relies (Sheldrake).

And all along, artists have engaged with plants in de-objectifying and exciting ways. Bio artists Špela Petrič, Suzanne Anker, and Eduardo Kac have explored at length biological continuities between plants and humans; Indigenous artists Abel Rodriguez and Maria Theresa Alves have harnessed the political power of plants to give voices to silenced or erased histories; Uriel Orlow, Kapwani

Kiwanga, and Nathalie Bikoro have engaged with plants as powerful agents of decolonisation; while Zachari Logan and Precious Okoyomon have worked with weeds as emblems of resilience for LGBTQIA+ communities and racial minorities. The work of these artists has deliberately bypassed the linguistic strictures of Western philosophy through both careful consideration of the radical alterity of plants and a direct engagement with them. Art historians like myself and Prudence Gibson have devised new contextual frameworks through which past and present representations of plants in art can be renegotiated through the lens of critical plant studies (Aloi, 2011, 2018a, 2018b, 2019, 2023a, 2023b; Gibson, 2015, 2018a, 2018b, 2023). These examples of pioneering engagement are all committed to combating plant-blindness, our inability to perceive vegetal life as postulated by botanists Wandersee and Schussler in 1999 (Wandersee and Schussler).

How can we learn from artistic approaches to unlearn ideas and attitudes that define our relationships with the vegetal world in meaningful and lasting ways? The concept of the Anthropocene invites us to focus on sublime vegetal domains like tropical forests and plantations but reconsidering the importance of our domestic vegetal companions might be the first step towards a genuine engagement with the more vast and distant realities in which plants play essential ecosystemic roles. Failing to develop empathy with plants close to us will inevitably diminish the importance of plants far away—those that live in seriously endangered environments. As a result, these distant plants will seem akin to anonymous and replaceable specimens filed in an inaccessible herbarium. How can houseplants serve as empathic bridges to the larger and often elusive dimension of the biosphere?

I suggest looking no further than the potted plant in the room where you are sitting right now. This challenge, as simple as it might seem, involves a radical shift in mindset. It entails re-educating ourselves to make space for what I call "speculative phytopoetics": an immanent model of vegetal/human, empathy-based engagement derived from the relational modalities of contemporary art that can enable us to reclaim plants from the cultural objectification of capitalism.

Speculative Phytopoetics

Many of us are more inclined to give attention to an artwork than focus with some intensity on a plant. Think about the intent and focus with which we approach a work of art in a gallery space. Our behavioural mode shifts upon entering the white cube. In his seminal book *Inside the White Cube*, Brian O'Doherty traces a compelling genealogy of the gallery space from the ancestral time of myth to the transcendentalism of medieval cathedrals to contemplative spatialization of otherworldly purity and timelessness (O'Doherty). Much has been said about the negative aspects of this utopian space that erases the past in order to gain control of the narratives of the future. The white cube is intrinsically biophobic. Bio artists know this very well. It is afraid of contamination and is, in essence, exclusivist. It decontextualises the object from the world, endlessly reiterating the separation between nature and culture as an ineluctable fact.

Nowhere in the history of art do these paradigms shine more brightly through the whiteness of the gallery walls than in the creative milieu we call minimalism. Stemming from abstraction in the late 1950s, minimalism proposed a radical departure from the transcendentalism of modern art. In a sense, minimalist art exemplified the essence of the gallery space by owning, like no previous movement, the proclaimed disconnectedness of the gallery space from the rest of the world. The experience of the minimalist art object was intentionally decontextualised to stage a closed encounter with form and matter; the object was enigmatic, constantly withdrawing, unavailable, a questioning entity. In *Art and Objecthood*, originally published in 1967, Michael Fried acknowledged that minimalist artists like Donald Judd and Robert Morris challenged the ways in which the viewer developed a relationship to the art object (Fried). While classical art engaged in purely affirmative storytelling and mythmaking, modern art aimed to transport viewers elsewhere, challenging their understanding of their own physicality and cultural certitude. But the objecthood of minimalism has crafted an engagement modality that we still carry with us today whenever we enter the gallery space, regardless of the art we encounter. We feel that we owe a debt to the art—that we have to engage in a speculative-aesthetic contemplative state of heightened attention. We seem to be under the impression that the more we concentrate and look harder and harder, the more we can gain access to recondite mysteries of the art object. We certainly approach art this way, bringing an open mind to our experience. We give an artwork a chance to say something, even if it seems like the chance that the object might have something to say is slim. Today, we approach art with extreme patience and caution, eager to engage in a speculative-aesthetic manner. We talk about "spending time with the art" as a badge of honour—the confirmation that we are prepared to invest substantial amounts of time and energy to allow the art to do something to us. But when it comes to plants, most of us are not prepared to put in the effort required by an encounter with an otherness that exceeds any minimalist object ever created and that, given the opportunity, might reward us in ways that an art object never could.

Like encounters with cryptic art objects, speculative phytopoetics requires closeness, constancy, patience, and determination.[1] Speculative phytopoetics is a coded language we co-produce with plants through our daily living with them. It is among the most subtle and elusive form of interspecies communication, yet to experience it, we do not even need to leave the house—we just have to slow down, observe time and time again, and develop an intimate attunement with vegetal being. Speculative phytopoetics is a set of non-verbal, non-written codes we develop with individual plants in our home. Think of it as a secret language between you and the plant, but not as a dialogue either between two humans or between a human and an object. Speculative phytopoetics is a subcategory of biosemiotics, the field concerned with prelinguistic, meaning-making production and interpretation of codes in living systems.[2] It is specific to one individual plant and is subject to change if the plant is relocated to a different space in your home. Speculative phytopoetic codes are often non-transferable to other plants of the same species. They are site-specific. They constitute the perceptible framework of the plant identity—an identity dispersed across branches and leaves and extended throughout the geography of the domestic space that plants share with us. Phytopoetics are speculative because they entail a leap into the darkness of being that separates human from non-human. However, this leap relies on the knowledge that such darkness is not a negative space—as in the conception of the Enlightenment—but co-produced by and productive of a kind of freedom.

I use here the term "speculative" in the context of Quentin Meillassoux's 2006 *Après la finitude*, that revived enthusiasm (and hope) in Western philosophy at the beginning of the new millennium (Meillassoux). This term implies the renewed investment in the materiality of objects that, in the field of Speculative Realism, has been more concretely addressed by the philosophical movements of Object-Oriented Ontology and New Materialism. "Speculative" acknowledges the intrinsic impossibility of gaining complete access to the otherness of the non-human. However, it sees this limited accessibility not as a diminishing factor or limitation but as a productive opportunity to attempt to creatively bridge human and non-human worlds. Speculative phytopoetics is one of these bridges.

Sharing time and space with an individual plant is the essential prerequisite. But speculative phytopoetics has nothing to do with the infamous plant-communication experiments of the 1960s, in which researchers speculated that plants could hear us or read our minds. Cleve Backster's experiments with plant perception were published in the *International Journal of Parapsychology* (1968), and then popularised by a New York Times bestseller entitled *The Secret Life of Plants* and written by Peter Tompkins and Christopher Bird. *The Secret Life of Plants* has given any domestic human-plant communication a bad name (Tompkins and Bird 1973). Speculative phytopoetics, however, is not related to New Age ideas that plants enjoy listening to classical music.

Is there a houseplant in your home that has been with you for many years? One that has moved with you from one apartment to the other? Might this be the one that survived your holidays abroad as well as the forgetfulness that takes hold whenever work gets too busy, or the kid is sick? If you have shared your life with this kind of resilient vegetal companion, chances are that you might have already, perhaps unknowingly, engaged in some kind of speculative phytopoetics.

Can you sense when one of your plant companions is unhappy because of the way their leaves are angled, or when a plant looks slightly discoloured or appears dull? Can you tell at a glance when a plant needs water? And can you read the signs of a plant's ill health before it is too late? These signs are part of the biosemiotic vocabulary we instinctually develop with our vegetal companions. It is a kind of secret sign language. Given the opportunity, the same relationship could be developed with plants in the garden or trees in the wild. But the privacy of the domestic environment, the individualisation of the plant, and its isolation from the elements make it easier to detect otherwise imperceptible changes in vegetal bodies. To a point, and perhaps paradoxically, the objecthood of minimalist art can provide us with an aesthetic-contemplative modality upon which we can rearrange and attune our attention economies towards the biosemiotics of vegetal being.

Capitalist Miseducation

Capitalism deliberately frustrates our biosemiotic communication with plants. It sells us a plant in the hope that we will kill it and buy another one every few months, or ideally more frequently. Production, consumption, and waste are the three key stages of most capitalist transactions. During the 1970s-80s, with the rise of economic stability across the global north, manufacturers

Giovanni Aloi

of mass-produced goods began to incorporate strategically planned depreciation into their products. This is why the lives of domestic appliances have considerably shortened over the past twenty years. Productivity is the oxygen of capitalist ecologies, and capitalist multinationals know how to bring more oxygen to their business. Plants, like other commodities, are subject to the same principles. The oldest plant in your home, then, is a monument of resistance to capitalism. It is a vegetal statement of defiance. A living rejection of the way capitalism defines our relationship with nature as disposable, superficial, and ephemeral.

In our capitalist world, very basic, often inaccurate plant care information is crammed on tiny labels stuck in the soil that fills plastic, tiny pots. Perhaps not surprisingly, the aesthetics of care it deploys speak a language of mechanisation. Part shade, full sun. Keep moist. Water every three weeks. Maintenance, not kinship, is the framework. Capitalism tells us very little about the plant we buy at the moment of purchase because it does not know much about the plant, beyond the point of production. An alarm clock manual has ten times the information that normally comes with a plant. Speculative phytopoetics subverts this consumerist framework by replacing maintenance with a specific and individualised interaction between human and non-human that is grounded in empathy. It frees potted plants from the shackles of consumerism and returns them to the realm of the living.

Capitalism thrives on our insecurity. For everything we buy, there is an expert on hand. There is always, too, another opportunity to spend more money. So many magazines, tools, gadgets, and books to buy. Deep down, the message is clear: we are inadequate. Capitalism miseducates us to make us dependent on plant-diagnosis resources. There is more than one Facebook group called "What's wrong with my plant?" Over a dozen books share different iterations of that title. These can be useful sources of information, and all plant lovers need some kind of basic reference. A plant that thrives in full shade will die if it is placed in full sun. It is important to know such information from the start. Capitalism is kind enough to at least tell us that. After all, it is true, plants that belong to the same species are likely to have similar requirements. But then, why can we miserably fail even when instructions are followed to the letter? Why is keeping a plant happy not as straightforward as these books and labels claim?

We have been miseducated about plant time. With plants, everything tends to take longer; vegetal beings are intertwined with time much more intimately than we are. They live on different timescales. In order to find common ground upon which to craft speculative phytopoetics with them, we need to slow down and understand their response phases and rhythms. This does not require spiritual meditation, but rather keen observation, good visual memory, and plenty of care. We need to look and look again, with patience and determination. We need to build a mental archive of the biosemiotics signals that the plant sends under certain circumstances and learn how to decode them. This takes time and dedication.

Speculative phytopoetics has a lot to do with art in its poetic dimension; it is linked to the expressive essence lying at the core of all art making—the key feature that separates the factual from the interpretative. Poetry is about simultaneously blurring, sharpening, contracting, expanding, and twisting language. It asks the reader to surrender to a different flow, to trace, and to follow. It is about inventing new semantic structures, as well as collaboratively dismantling, fragmenting, discarding, and reconfiguring old ones, to find out what can be said from the fragments that can be rearranged afterwards. Poetry is a shared intimacy of momentary and yet eternal presence. It can be revelatory, shattering, or exhilarating. Poetry nurtures respect for its subjects and objects by moulding, casting, and outlining, always allowing for a certain kind of darkness to rest undisturbed at the margins of the light cast by scientific and religious knowledge.

The modalities of observation invited by paintings, photographs, sculptures can change us in many ways, but one of the most powerful demands most art makes of us is to slow down to truly see beyond the veneers of appearances, beyond the pre-inscribed truths institutions have imparted upon us. One of the most valuable lessons imparted by the minimalist object in the gallery space is its demands on the viewer; the focus and concentration it requires is a call to overcome cultural blindness and to embrace the alterity of the other. In speculative phytopoetics, poetics is conceived as the elusive essence that breathes life into contemporary art. It draws on the principle that Umberto Eco uses to connect the poetics of the open work to the interpretative, improvised creation involved in some instrumental music: the performer's freedom to interpret, and therefore simultaneously decode, existing text, as well as to produce new text (Eco). According to art historian Peter Osborne, poetics in contemporary art, works in opposition to word theory, especially its rules and systematic approaches (Osborne). Speculative phytopoetics also relates to Édouard Glissant's argument in favour of opacity in the sphere of the relational:

Giovanni Aloi

"an alterity that is unquantifiable, a diversity that exceeds categories of identifiable difference" (Krauss and Thajib 11). Thus, speculative phytopoetics unfurls in twilight.

The space of indeterminacy that is allowed to unfold is a field of poetic opportunities: relationships held together and made accessible, line after line, brushstroke after brushstroke, and gesture after gesture. These opportunities are always open-ended, never fully exhaustible, inescapably opaque. Poetics fills the blanks of life with a flicker. It stretches language to the point at which it crumbles into abstract images. It emerges where meaning dangerously teeters along the edge that separates materiality and mythology.

Often, contemporary artists present viewers with highly idiosyncratic and cryptic work that requires a suspension of judgment and an abandonment to the "ways of the other." The viewer is expected to patiently negotiate time and space with the art object, to carefully consider the demands made by the encounter with the object, and to expect very little answer back. Much contemporary art raises questions without providing answers; it is not affirmative. In many ways, human-plant relations unfold on similar trajectories. The modalities of observation that contemporary art invites can become a training ground for attention and focus, expectation and negotiation—skills essential to productive human-plant relations.

The Truth About Your Potted Plant

The bodies, identities, and characters of houseplants are defined by their pots, the quality of the soil they grow in, the humidity in your bathroom or kitchen, and the quality of the air. Plants are intimately enmeshed with their surroundings and with the elements from which they draw nutrients. The structure of a plant is a poetic manifestation emerging from all these factors and the care you provide. How can online plant care instructions engage with this wealth of unwritten specific knowledge you and you alone have? Speculative phytopoetics maps the territory of complicity between plant, domestic space, and human.

Plants often come from nurseries where they are deliberately pumped up to biological breakdown levels. The nurseries where plants are produced by the millions know one thing: most species of domesticated plants produce more leaves and flowers under stable and regular conditions. In nurseries, plant lives are ruled by timers. Regular watering, consistent lighting for exactly the same amount of time every day, slightly warmer days and cooler nights, reliable humidity levels, and good airflow allow plants to grow bigger than they ever could in a natural environment.

Plants are keen planners. Although they might not "think" in a centralised way, every part of their vegetal bodies knowingly responds to their surroundings. They constantly sense and evaluate the environment around them, while calculating their next move. How many blooms can be carried at once is defined by the "knowledge" the plant develops about how much water and light, as well as how many nutrients, it can safely rely upon day after day. Overreaching can mean death.

But there is more. The plant you have just bought from the gardening centre or saved from the supermarket stand is on drugs—literally. It has been regularly sprayed with a growth retardant called chlormequat chloride. Formulated in the late 1950s by Dr N. E. Tolbert, a chemistry professor at Michigan State University, chlormequat drastically inhibits stem elongation and promotes bushiness (Runkle). The greenness of leaves on chrysanthemums, poinsettias, and other species is also accentuated by this chemical. Your new plant thus often looks sassy, compact, and full of life because its natural growth processes have been seriously tampered with. Capitalism has taught us to associate these aesthetic qualities with good health and prosperity. It has miseducated us to recognise these aesthetic values as "natural," even though they are forced and wholly artificial. This mindset greatly interferes with the development of speculative phytopoetics. When plants enter our homes, adjusting to our less than ideal habitat is inevitably traumatic, and coming off the drugs is a drag: they are like addicts gone cold turkey.

After a period of detoxication (usually a month, sometimes a bit longer), you can truly begin to get to know your plant and engage in speculative phytopoetics. Depending on the species of plant, speculative phytopoetics can become quite rich and complex. And when you think you and your plant have a connection, the plant suddenly comes up with a new signal that you cannot decipher. Capitalism has taught us to read such moments as failures: the inexplicable yellow leaves, the aborted bloom, and the unusually elongated stems.

Of course, one must learn about parasites and fungal diseases too. The curling of leaves, the discolouring, various marks—these are all codes we need to identify the pest and diagnose a cure. But these are not failures. They are essential parts of living with plants. Capitalism has fooled us to believe that if we cannot keep our plants constantly happy so that they look the same all the time, then we are failing. In its quest to objectify plants, capitalism has repressed and ignored vegetal life cycles.

Orchids are regularly and knowingly mis-sold as plants that only flower once. Often, labels ignore the fact that if cared for in a certain way, the plant will rebloom next year. Capitalism will not allow us to wait a year for that bloom. There is an orchid in bloom all year round in a shop near you.

Amaryllis, a winter favourite, shares a similar fate. Labels rarely, if ever, instruct one about how to re-nourish the bulb after flowering, how to let it recharge in summer, and how to stop watering in early autumn so that it will go dormant and flower again.

Poinsettias (*Euphorbia pulcherrima*) are among the most abused species in the context of domestic vegetal commoditisation. Pumped with fertilisers, put through a laborious process of photoperiodic training entailing fourteen hours of complete darkness per day, and drenched with chlormequat to make them compact, poinsettias can be literally programmed to bloom a few weeks before Christmas. The intensely coloured bracts then stay fresh-looking for up to two months. Millions of poinsettias are sold around the world in December, but only a minuscule fraction will survive for a second Christmas. Away from the greenhouse-regulated environment and off the vegetal-steroid dripper, the leaves begin to yellow and fall. The label never tells us it is possible to care for the plant and make it rebloom. Why would capitalism share that piece of information? It would save you some money, prevent the waste of so much heat, water, electricity, gas, pesticides, and plastic, all of which go into the making of each poinsettia every year. Speculative phytopoetics helps prevent all of that waste.

Re-Educating Ourselves

At the core of speculative phytopoetics lie two Japanese Zen philosophies: Wabi-sabi and Kintsugi (Kore; Yutaka). Wabi-sabi nurtures all that is authentic by acknowledging three simple realities: nothing lasts, nothing is finished, and nothing is perfect. A philosophy of acceptance, Wabi-sabi teaches us to appreciate the straggliness and often non-symmetrical structure of our houseplants because their look is the result of cohabitation with us in our homes. In the shape of their branches is written our shared history; their identity is enmeshed with ours and the space we share.

Kintsugi invites us not to be ashamed of what is damaged or broken and to celebrate the scar as a sign that life has occurred. In gardening centres, supermarkets, and big-box chain stores, imperfect and unblemished plants are thrown out. Capitalism has devalued plant life so much that it would rather let live plants perish than pay a worker to water them. Plants are ultimately cheaper to produce than the worker's wage. The markup on house plants is enormous. The sale of one plant covers the economic loss caused by the many that will die on the shelf.

How can art help us sidestep capitalist strategies of objectification and commodification? It can teach us to develop some of the key skills necessary to craft speculative phytopoetics with our vegetal companions. For far too long, the presence of plants in a gallery space has been intended as a humorous counterpoint to the serious rationality of the white cube. Most often, plants have been brought into the exhibiting space to metaphorically offset the timelessness of artworks and our obsession with purity and preservation. At other times, they have been posed as tokens of nature—as that which can only truly exist outside the culturally defined perimeter of the gallery. But since the beginning of the new millennium, plants in art have come to mean so much more. The slowing down, the mindfulness, and the presence we experience upon encountering a work of art in a gallery space, or a plant presented as a work of art, lie at the heart of speculative phytopoetics, especially its emphasis on the potential for a fuller world in which we make efforts to meet the non-human halfway instead of repressing it from a distance, objectifying it, or erasing it. Through the engagement modalities of art deployed in these new kinds of plant encounters, there is the possibility for a heightened sense of perceptive awareness to emerge and to make space for what capitalism has told us we should really have no time for. At stake is the opportunity to make space for a fuller and more sustainable world enriched by a sense of respectful affinity and attunement with the radical otherness of other earthlings built on the intimacy of care; all this can start with your potted philodendron.

Notes

1   This term is not to be confused with the term "phytopoetics," which was coined by John Charles Ryan in 2017. To Ryan, "[t]he notion of 'plant poetics' (or 'phytopoetics') embraces the ancient grounding of poetry in *poiesis*—in the creative act of making, becoming, bringing-forth or emerging. ... With language as the transformative medium, we might thus become more conscious of the shared florescence of plants, places, people and all else that exists" (Ryan, online: https://plumwoodmountain.com/poem/editorial-plant-poetics/). Nor should my use of this term be confused with the use it by Joela Jacobs, according to whom "phytopoetics entails both a poetic engagement with plants in literature and moments in which plants

          Giovanni Aloi

take on literary or cultural agency themselves (see Moe's [2014] emphasis on agency in zoopoetics, and Marder, 2018). In this understanding, phytopoetics encompasses instances in which plants participate in the production of texts as 'material-semiotic nodes or knots' (Haraway, 2008, p. 4) that are neither just metaphor, nor just plant (see Driscoll & Hoffmann, 2018, p. 4 and pp. 6-7)" (Jacobs 1). The term "speculative phytopoetics" that I use here emerges especially out of: Bachelard; Eco; Bishop; and the conception of Speculative Realism in philosophy (Bryant et al.; MacKay et al.).

2   See, for instance, Wheeler; Hoffmeyer and Favareau.

Works Cited

Aloi, Giovanni, ed. "Why Look at Plants?," "Beyond Morphology." *Antennae: The Journal of Nature in Visual Culture*, vols. 17 & 18, 2011.

---. *Botanical Speculations.* Cambridge Scholars, 2018a.

---. *Why Look at Plants?: The Botanical Emergence in Contemporary Art.* Brill, 2018b.

---. *Lucian Freud: Herbarium.* Prestel, 2019.

---, ed. *Estado Vegetal,* University of Minnesota Press, 2023.

---, and Michael Marder, eds. *Vegetal Entwinements in Philosophy and Art: A Reader.* MIT Press, 2023.

Bachelard, Gaston. *The Poetics of Space.* Penguin Books, 1958.

Backster, Cleve. "Evidence of a Primary Perception in Plant Life." *International Journal of Parapsychology*, vol. 10, 1968, pp. 329-48.

Bishop, Claire. *Artificial Hells: Participatory Art and the Politics of Spectatorship.* Verso, 2011.

Bryant, Levi R., et al. *The Speculative Turn: Continental Materialism and Realism.* re.press, 2011.

Calvo, Paco. *Planta Sapiens.* National Geographic Books, 2023.

Cunningham, David, and Peter Osborne. "Poetics of Contemporary Art." 28 Mar. 2019. Kingston University, London, UK. Conference paper.

Driscoll, Kári, and Eva Hoffmann. *What Is Zoopoetics?: Texts, Bodies, Entanglement.* Palgrave Macmillan, 2018.

Eco, Umberto. *The Open Work.* Harvard University Press, 1989.

Fried, Michael. *Art and Objecthood: Essays and Reviews.* University of Chicago Press, 2011.

Gagliano, Monica. "Green Symphonies: A Call for Studies on Acoustic Communication in Plants." *Behavioral Ecology*, vol. 24, no. 4, 2012, pp. 789-96.

---. *Thus Spoke the Plant: A Remarkable Journey of Groundbreaking Scientific Discoveries and Personal Encounters with Plants.* North Atlantic Books, 2018.

---, et al. "Towards Understanding Plant Bioacoustics." *Trends in Plant Science*, vol. 17, no. 6, 2012, pp. 323-25.

---, et al. "Tuned In: Plant Roots Use Sound to Locate Water." *Oecologia*, vol. 184, 2017, pp. 151-60.

Gibson, Prudence. *Janet Laurence: The Pharmacy of Plants.* University of New South Wales Press, 2015.

---. *The Plant Contract.* Brill, 2018a.

---. *The Plant Thieves.* NewSouth, 2023.

---, and Baylee Brits. *Covert Plants: Vegetal Consciousness and Agency in an Anthropocentric World.* Brainstorm Books, 2018b.

Glissant, Édouard. *Poetics of Relation*, translated by Betsy Wing, University of Michigan Press, 1997.

Hall, Matthew. *Plants as Persons.* State University of New York Press, 2011.

Haraway, Donna Jeanne. *When Species Meet.* University of Minnesota Press, 2008.

Hoffmeyer, Joseph, and Donald Favareau. *Biosemiotics: An Examination into the Signs of Life and the Life of Signs.* University of Scranton Press, 2009.

Jacobs, Joela. "Phytopoetics." *Catalyst: Feminism, Theory, Technoscience*, vol. 5, no. 2, 2019, pp. 1-18.

Kimmerer, Robin Wall. *Gathering Moss: A Natural and Cultural History of Mosses.* Oregon State University Press, 2003.

---. *Braiding Sweetgrass: Indigenous Wisdom, Scientific Knowledge and the Teachings of Plants.* Milkweed Editions, 2015.

Koren, Leonard. *Wabi-Sabi for Artists, Designers, Poets & Philosophers.* Imperfect Publishing, 2008.

Krauss, Annette and Thajib, Ferdiansyah. "In The Vortex of Institutional Lives." *ARTMargins* 2022; 11 (1-2): 10–28, doi: https://doi.org/10.1162/artm_a_00313

Mackay, Robin, et al. *Speculative Aesthetics.* MIT Press, 2019.

Mancuso, Stefano, and Viola, Alessandra. *Brilliant Green: The Surprising History and Science of Plant Intelligence.* Island Press, 2015.

Marder, Michael. *Plant-Thinking: A Philosophy of Vegetal Life.* Columbia University Press, 2013.

---. *The Philosopher's Plant.* Columbia University Press, 2015.

---. *Grafts: Writings on Plants*. University of Minnesota Press/Univocal, 2016.

Marder, Michael, and Luce Irigaray. *Through Vegetal Being*. Columbia University Press, 2016a.

Meillassoux, Quentin. *After Finitude: An Essay on the Necessity of Contingency*, translated by Ray Brassier, Continuum, 2006.

O'Doherty, Brian. *Inside the White Cube: The Ideology of the Gallery Space*. University of California Press, 1986.

Osborne, Peter. *Anywhere or Not at All: Philosophy of Contemporary Art*. Verso, 2013.

Runkle, Eric. "Using Chlormequat Chloride with Success." *Greenhouse Product News*, 2014, https://gpnmag.com/article/using-chlormequat-chloride-success/

Ryan, Charles. "Editorial: Plant Poetics." *Plumwood Mountain*, vol.7, no. 2, https://plumwoodmountain.com/editorial-plant-poetics/

Sheldrake, Merlin. *Entangled Life: How Fungi Make Our Worlds, Change Our Minds & Shape Our Futures*. Random House, 2021.

Tompkins, Peter, and Christopher Bird. *The Secret Life of Plants: A Fascinating Account of the Physical, Emotional, and Spiritual Relations between Plants and Man*. Harper and Row, 1973.

Wandersee, James H., and Elisabeth E. Schussler. "Preventing Plant Blindness." *The American Biology Teacher*, vol. 61, no. 2, 1999, pp. 82-86.

Wheeler, Wendy. *The Whole Creature: Complexity, Biosemiotics and the Evolution of Culture*. Lawrence & Wishart, 2006.

Yazawa, Yutaka. *The Little Book of Japanese Living*. White Lion Publishing, 2020.

5   Herbaria, Creative Practice, and the Postcolonial Houseplant

Matthew Beach

Introduction

This chapter connects academic and creative critiques of the herbarium as an imperial knowledge project with a recently increased interest in houseplants, arguing for the need to view European houseplant cultures as always post-colonial. In recent years, calls to (re)examine the imperial legacies of plant science have intensified. For example, the Director of Science at the Royal Botanic Gardens, Kew, United Kingdom argued for the need to tackle the structural racism surrounding its historic collections and their contemporary use (Antonelli). A wider science and humanities partnership between Kew and Royal Holloway, University of London explored how collections could be decolonised, in part through interviews with current staff (Driver and Cornish). In creative practice, the Decolonising Botany working group brings together artists from Europe, east Asia, and southeast Asia to prioritise decolonial "undoings and solidarity" (Burns). These collaborative endeavours are illustrative of the productive space between plant science and the humanities and social sciences, which often include elements of creative practice.

While the herbarium as a structure that produces botanical knowledge is often hinted at for considering decolonisation (Delves; Subramanian), there is space for further scholarly and/or creative work that addresses the aesthetics of the herbarium and its legacy within contemporary houseplant cultures. Creative practice is key here because it allows for the production of new objects that subvert existing practices and present alternative ones. Many of these projects include an affective, caring dimension to working with botanical material, whether by drawing attention to development injustices, seeking to understand anthropogenic disaster effects on plants, or physically cultivating and tending to plant material. These affective aspects point to a wider interest in care practices as integral to decolonisation (Parreñas; Motta).

In this chapter, I first outline scholarly work that has interrogated herbaria aesthetics and situate these critiques within two creative projects invoking the herbarium as a methodology useful for highlighting Indigeneity and locality. The artists' focus on ferns opens up a broader discussion of colonial knowledge production concerning ferns and their transition from dried herbaria to indoor cultivated plants—a transition that has in part led to the creation of wider European houseplant markets via Wardian cases. These early types of glass terrariums were employed to display plants as well as transport them between imperial centres and colonies. Charting this colonial history allows me to link imperialism to both scholarship on contemporary houseplants and creative projects invoking herbaria methodologies (creative herbaria) as a decolonising method. I present a meditation on one of my own creative engagements with the herbarium as a critical view of houseplant care practices and relations in the aftermath of imperialism. Practices and relations of houseplant care are impor-tant objects of discussion because of the herbarium's persistence in knowledge production (Heberling and Isaac; Dion and Aloi), the evocation of its aesthetic in various mass-produced elements of home decor (Ikea; Khadou), and the resurgence and continued interest in houseplants (Bond; Tolentino; Hughes; Kirk-Ballard). Neither a survey of herbarium implementation or subversion in creative practice, nor a critical, postcolonial examination of contemporary houseplant practice has been conducted within the plant humanities. Thus, my contribution strives to merge these two research strands in order to argue for looking backwards as humans imagine and create new, affective human-plant futures within interior domestic settings.

Herbaria, Imperialism, and Creative Practice Critique

A herbarium is comprised of a collection of dried and pressed plants (some-times including flowers, seeds, and/or berries). Each plant is typically indi-vidually mounted on light-coloured cotton paper and arranged according to a classification system tailored to a specific area of enquiry, for example: taxonomic/floristic study, documentation for medicinal and economic pur-poses, and verifiable and repeatable botanical research (Forman and Bridson; Flannery; Heberling and Isaac). Many European herbaria follow the practice of the fifteenth-century Italian botanist Luca Ghini (Sprague and Nelmes), and his approach became the favoured imperialist method of documenting large-scale plant distribution (Massey).

In 2017, Emma Lansdowne extensively interrogated the herbarium as an imperial practice. She argued that herbaria convert plants into aesthetic objects by removing them from their wider environments and ecologies; they become uprooted, displaced, and lifeless as singular entities divorced from indigeneity. Thus, placed within their historical setting, herbaria signify the construction of a particular kind of bias and value system in botanical knowledge creation because of their aesthetic nature, as well as their authors. This is a system that privileges whiteness, maleness, and historic wealth in a broader framework of natural-cultural extraction; it is a "way of possession through knowledge" (Lansdowne). Lansdowne traces this aspect of the colonising project, which exists between science and aesthetics, by theorising about human desire and sensorial pleasure. Her framework is linked to abstract and material expressions, including taxonomical systems, gardens, and herbaria, as well as world-making practices of drawing borders to create social, economic, and political divisions. The herbarium becomes a material expression of this cartographic practice: an aesthetic knowledge object that perhaps says less about the "natural" world than it does about possession, power, and subjectivity, in addition to the positionality and desire of the collector-extractor.

Creative practice and art making in the work of artists Melissa Oresky and Anselm Kiefer offer one process by which to confront these imperial, botanical legacies; both artists challenge normative understandings of herbaria practices. The artists' engagement with ferns is particularly useful for setting up further discussion of the way in which herbaria collections have been transformed into houseplant cultivation. Oresky's *Finder* (n. d.) subverts the herbarium by layering sixteenth-century botanical engravings from *Herball* (1597) and *Fern Finder: A Guide to Native Ferns of Central and Northeastern United States and Eastern Canada* (2001). Together with the historian Keith Pluymers, Oresky approaches this subversive layering as a process of creative composting (Pluymers and Oresky). Here, creative composting enables new forms of historical storytelling through layering, accretion, and decay and offers a way to answer the call by Robin Wall Kimmerer, a member of the Citizen Potawatomi Nation and an environmental biologist, to challenge scientific ways of seeing. Oresky highlights Kimmerer's distinction between practising science and being trained in a "scientific" world-view; the latter has a compromised colonial legacy. Composting offers a way to intimately know plants in the creative herbarium. Oresky claims that we can learn to see the local, embodied, and experiential as new ways of finding. In this way, her work attends to decolonising attempts in the context of challenging histories of fern cataloguing.

Similarly, Kiefer subverts historical herbarium practice in his 2007 project *The Secret of the Ferns.* The work takes its title from a poem of the same name

Matthew Beach

by Paul Celan, a Romanian Jew and Holocaust survivor whose work consists of imagery of greenery, shadows, and ferns placed within themes of mystery and dread (Batsaki). Kiefer's herbarium has mixed media; it contains dried plants alongside other elements such as fabric, glass, plastic, clay, and metal. *The Secret of the Ferns* reminds viewers of more intimate human relations with ferns by deploying wall text and physical inscriptions in the works. An example is the use of the phrases "La nuit de Saint Jean," "Johannis Nacht," "Saint Jean," and "Nacht Saint Jean" to allude to historical rituals associated with the summer solstice. One ritual, in fact, involved adorning households with fern foliage for protection from poor weather and ill-meaning supernatural phenomena (Batsaki). These rituals were eventually discontinued by the Christian church because of the assumption that they were tied to magic and/or witchcraft (Corne). What I want to emphasise in my survey of these two creative herbaria projects is their focus on humans having intimate caring relations with specific plants, that is, various species of ferns.

Ferns have long histories of use value in European societies; initially, they were associated with quests for knowledge and with folklore. Because of their reproduction by spores rather than seeds, they often had connotations of magic and mystique. Until the sixteenth century, ferns were employed for summer solstice rituals, in which humans would spread cloth or metal plates to capture seeds that could then bestow invisibility upon the holder of the plate (Corne). Ferns also had economic roles since they were used in the production of dyes, fats, fibres, flavourings, medical remedies (e.g. a cure for intestinal worms), and fragrance (Moore; May). Underscoring the ways in which imperial economies dominated relations between humans and ferns offers the opportunity to open up a broader discussion of ferns in histories of European empire, colonial expansion, and domestic cultivation. I turn next to the process by which ferns became mass-produced, foliar fascinations, as well as aesthetic objects of desire.

Placing Human-Fern Relations within Imperial European Houseplant Cultivation

Moving from magic, folk relations, and knowledge production concerning fern species towards positivism and imperial science led to an increased emphasis on studying living flora as well as those in herbaria. This shift was closely tied to the rise of economic botany, which was one of the primary considerations in early colonial expeditions and bio-prospecting (De Vos; Schiebinger). It became desirable to find a way to transport plants and provide care for them both in colonial settings and imperial centres, and new technologies allowed more people to cultivate plants indoors across Europe. The transition from assembling herbaria to mass-producing some of the first domestic plants demonstrates how herbaria practices directly led to the initial conceptualisation of the houseplant. This means that discussion of domestic plant cultivation arising out of herbaria cannot occur without a postcolonial conceptualisation. What follows is a charting of the transition from herbaria to houseplant in order to ground a subsequent, postcolonial analysis of contemporary houseplant scholarship, as well as an argument for how we think about the postcolonial houseplant through herbaria and creative practices.

The most influential invention associated with the rise of mass interior plant cultivation was Nathaniel Bagshaw Ward's Wardian case. One of Ward's primary reasons for constructing his cases was to be able to cultivate living ferns outside his extensive herbarium collection within London; at that time, it was not possible to grow ferns in open air due to the significant air pollution, or smog (Ward).[1] Wardian cases were eventually mass produced, which made indoor plant cultivation accessible to those outside the highest economic strata (Eckel). Thomas Moore's writings of 1859 on ferns and their relatives was aimed at popular readership and in fact dedicated to Ward (Moore). Sophie Ruppel argues that this influx of plant cultivation publications targeted at a wider readership was associated with the broader rise of the middle class and changes in domestic culture across Europe (Ruppel; Allen; Whittingham). While Ruppel focuses on the Bouché family in Germany, she notes a similar phenomenon appeared in other European countries (Easterby-Smith; Easterby-Smith and Hill). She examines the articles and magazines published by the Bouchés within the German genre of *Stubengärtner* (room gardener); this genre coincided with what was termed "botanophilia," or enthusiasm for botanising (collecting, drying, and categorising plants). Botanophilia collapsed the distinction between trained botanists and professional as well as amateur gardeners, which in turn began to shift the location of the interior plant from studies and libraries to other rooms in the home.

Thus, interior fern cultivation is one example of the ways in which plants originally extracted for economic means entered the sphere of the ornamental. This shift from economic to decorative can also be seen in descriptions of urban ornamental plant markets. For instance, *The Leisure Hour*, a popular Victorian general-interest periodical, published an article describing the origins of a young girl's pet fern that was given to her as a gift (Gordon). The subheading "Foliage Plants" includes a walk through a flower market that showcases the

Matthew Beach

best practices for ornamental plant purchases in London, specifically plants that are mass-produced and require smaller pot sizes to save shelf space. The tour of the flower market also addresses plant care with the mention of needing to immediately repot one's new companion and advice about the necessity of fertiliser. The collapse between botanists and amateur gardeners is hinted at, as the manufacturers in the story prefer to employ those without a background in conventional outdoor domestic gardening. They want to specifically teach pot gardening in order to emphasise the importance of good watering and seed sprouting practice. In the case of ferns, after spores were sprinkled on the surface of soil-filled pots, they were left to germinate and grow into thousands of small plants reminiscent of sheets of moss, before being gently picked apart and moved into several iterations of larger pots, ultimately being sold at the greengrocer.

An emphasis on plant care waned as mass domestic material culture increased. There was particularly a marked difference in the latter half of the nineteenth century, when popular literature shifted away from a view of plants as living creatures and companions and towards a conception of them as decor and an aesthetic concern (Ruppel 727). According to Ruppel, this shift likely occurred in part because of the advent of "plant furniture," such as larger cases and shelves, which made plants mobile around the home with their wheels. I want to especially highlight this shift since I argue that it is happening again in the current resurgence of houseplant culture that is emerging with tailor-made plant care accessories, including greenhouse cabinets, grow lights, and 3D-printed plant supports. Humans are at a crossroads; we are repeating some of the same domestic culture tropes in our current social, political, and economic era as we attempt to produce new futures, and we need to consider these histories if we are to make progress in the work of decolonising houseplants. I have sought here to explore the ways in which European houseplant culture rose out of an imperial context. Next, I want to theorise contemporary scholarship on houseplants with this postcolonial lens before examining creative herbaria as a decolonising practice.

Shifting Contemporary Houseplant Relations towards Decolonising Discourse and Practice

While some critical studies of plants have considered the experiences of those living under colonial agricultural regimes, these analyses do not focus on houseplants (Jackson; Brooking and Pawson; Torget). Similarly, scholarship on houseplants does not trace imperial lineages. While some research focuses on extraction and illicit trading of plants intended for interior domestic care in the context of the loss of biodiversity and wider environmental destruction (Chen; Margulies), most social scientists relegate houseplants to the topic of effects on human mental health (Bringslimark et al.; Davidoff; Wallsten). Other scholars have acknowledged that while understanding the relationship between mental health and plants is important, there is potential to consider houseplants in other contexts. Two examples include the increased interest in houseplants amidst the Covid-19 pandemic as a move towards more than human solidarities (Carabelli); and links between pandemic crises, human response, considerations of human-plant relations, and their (re)configurations in the context of war and displacement (Tsymbalyuk). Central to Carabelli's and Tsymbalyuk's arguments is an emphasis on a multispecies, relational care ethics (Puig de la Bellacassa). Care in the practice of keeping indoor plants has also been researched as a way in which humans can benefit from improved air quality, enhanced mental health, and home beautification (Phillips and Schulz 378).

What is important to note here is that care of houseplants has not been conceptualised outside the home. These plants' native habitats are rarely mentioned, and the issue of how humans might care for these plants from a distance is likewise not addressed (Silk). The question remains: what kinds of research would instruct us about how to care for the postcolonial houseplant? There is scope to extend this scholarship into wider, decolonial contexts that exist between critical plant studies and vegetal geographies, including amending hegemonic plant thought, emphasis on species nativism cloaking anti-immigrant sentiments, and colonial and state presence in forests (Lawrence 638). One scholar has also gone as far as to state "House plants in art are the next phase in the critical plant studies revolution!" (Aloi). Here, I argue that there needs to be further decolonising work on some of the colonial legacies of specific species and genera of houseplants.

We need not only more "conventional" scholarly work, but also creative pursuits that operate in different public spheres. In addition to contemporary art galleries, another useful space might be the Royal Horticultural Society's (RHS) annual Chelsea Flower Show in London. In 2022, the RHS hosted Tayshan Hayden-Smith's nonprofit platform Grow2Know, which was aimed at decolonising horticulture. The garden evoked histories of racism, poverty, and violence in the Notting Hill suburb of London during the 1960s and 1970s, as well as today (Quinn). The RHS is well poised to continue doing this work for houseplants because of their recent addition of houseplant studios (Jayes; Royal Horticultural Society). To stress a more normative contemporary art outlet, however, I now describe my own recent project's attempts at decolonising houseplant practice with the creative herbaria.

Houseplants and Creative Herbaria in the *Propagations* Series

The *Propagations* series debuted in my 2021 exhibition *The Herbarium's Shadow* at San Mei Gallery, London. Comprised of twenty-four framed cyanotypes embedded in support paper with chine-collé and depicting young plantlet propagations (Fig. 1), each print displays a representation of the still-living foliage recently removed from stem cuttings of a *Philodendron pedatum vine*.[2] The title refers to the process of cloning a particular plant by cutting a section of stem that includes a leaf, aerial roots, and a growth point. Once the plant section is removed and allowed to callus, it can be placed in damp growing media or water. The aerial roots will then develop into a new root system, and the growth points will activate to start a new plant.

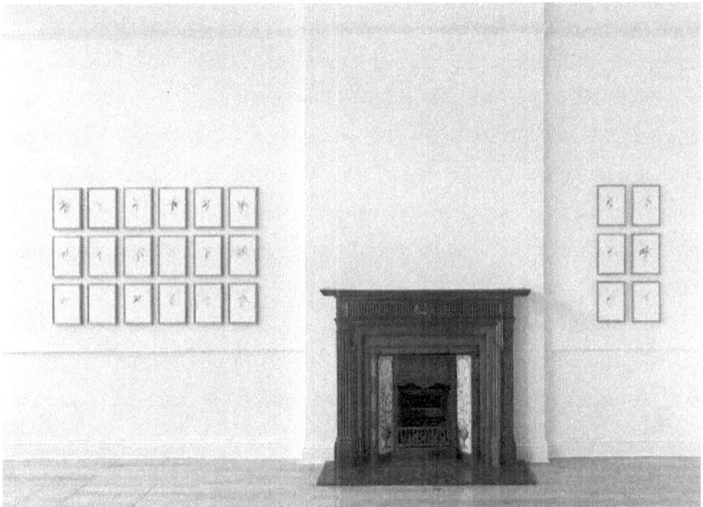

Figure 1. *Propagations.* 2020. Propagations installation view. (Image courtesy of Theo Christelis).

I chose *Philodendron pedatum* (rather than a fern species) as the subject of my creative herbarium for several reasons. My own entrance into forming relationships with houseplants was for their purported mental health benefits. *Philodendron pedatum* was one of my first houseplants, and I found it rewarding and easy to grow. Philodendra are largely an epiphytic species, beginning life on the forest floor and slowly crawling towards the bases of trees for support, before climbing up into the canopies of trees. Upon reaching flowering maturity, Philodendra produce inflorescences (blooms) that, when open, emit strong odors to attract pollinator beetles of the *Cyclocephala* or *Erioscelis* genera. These beetles then provide food in the form of a resin-like substance and a space for reproduction (Gibernau et al.). Other relations between Philodendra and insects include some ant species who harvest seeds and place them within nest structures in tree canopies (Jolivet), and some bee species who use the resin-like substance produced during blooming to construct nests (Murphy and Breed). An example of human relations with *Philodendron pedatum* is the use of the foliage by some Indigenous communities in Brazil. Prepared with oil, the leaves have been deployed as a dressing for gout pains (Plowman).

In addition to such multispecies relations, which have been excluded from contemporary houseplant discourses, *Philodendra* also are useful for discussing economic value creation. Over the last few years, a new phenomenon dubbed "Aroid Mania" (Tinyplants) has been used to describe the desire for plants from the *Aracaea* family, which includes *Philodendra*. This impulse to possess and collect harkens back to the colonial Tulipomania (Dash), Pteridomania (fern fever)(Allen;Whittingham), and Orchidelirium (Larner). *Philodendron* was one of the genera profiled in the 2019 article "How Much Would You Pay for a Houseplant?," which listed plants selling for thousands of dollars in the United States (Chapman). *Philodendron pedatum* falls into the wider category of houseplants known as "rare plants" (McGurk), albeit perhaps one of the more "uncommon" and less coveted varieties. The economic value placed on various species of *Philodendron* reinforces the idea of the plant as a singular aesthetic object and excludes consideration of the destruction of native ecologies, imperial cultivation histories, and the economic, social, and political geographies of contemporary large-scale cultivation.

Thus, *Philodendron pedatum* highlights two strands of possible analysis: it allows the plant to be placed in existing critiques of the herbarium as a scientific practice of exclusion, and it provides entry points into speaking about how houseplant practice, which is predicated on knowledge production, excludes other topics. It is worth noting briefly that the herbarium as an object producing colonial botanical knowledge did not and does not exist in isolation. The knowledge available about *Philodendron pedatum* comes from herbaria, in-situ observations, captive cultivation, and a range of other sources. However, the placement of a plant in a herbarium frames it as a singular object isolated from its relations with other beings and materials (Lansdowne). Something similar may be said about the various artworks discussed here. They, too, do not exist in isolation but rather in a variety of broader contexts: for instance, exhibitions, public events, workshops, writings, and conversations. I want to now discuss how my implementation of a houseplant herbarium works to continue the project of subverting this framing in the context of care.[3]

Care as Decolonisation in the Creative Herbarium of *Propagations*

"The living archive" concept was coined to describe an expansion of the botanical archive beyond Enlightenment thinking's nature/culture binary; it is an archive that is multi-sited, co-produced between art and science, that embraces non-dominant knowledge practices, and that is relational and informed by feeling and affect embedded in shared communities concerned with "community arts practice, activism, pedagogy, and radical gardening" (Bristow et al.). *Propagations* situates itself within this concept, extending the creative herbarium by establishing an archive that continues to expand through living plants' growth facilitated via the care act of propagating.

Propagating the entirety of a matured vine is an act of deconstruction. Such an act subverts colonial knowledge-making practices grounded in conceiving of "nature" as a divided whole. Presenting the entirety of the vine in a herbarium display alongside growing vines highlights the futility of documenting an ever-changing world. As a practice, deconstructing by propagating might be proposed as care if a plant has been attacked by insects, has been grown in less than favorable conditions, and/or has roots that are beginning to degrade. Propagating a healthy plant, however, might be seen more as an act of assault, containment, and mastery. When I separated out the *Philodendron pedatum* for my project, it had reached the ceiling of the room it was inhabiting. The room faced south, had temperatures fluctuating between 18 and 26 degrees Celsius, and had 45-70% humidity, which are appropriate conditions for this plant to grow successfully an interior domestic setting. Except for saving space, there was no practical need to cut the plant. However, one way of envisioning propagating as caring is to consider one practice of the plant, namely, sexual reproduction. Propagation is asexual reproduction, in essence creating clones of a plant; thus, growing cuttings could be considered care because one is collaborating with the plant to provide greater chances for it to practise sexual reproduction. This is an element of my own houseplant hobby beyond creative practice; I

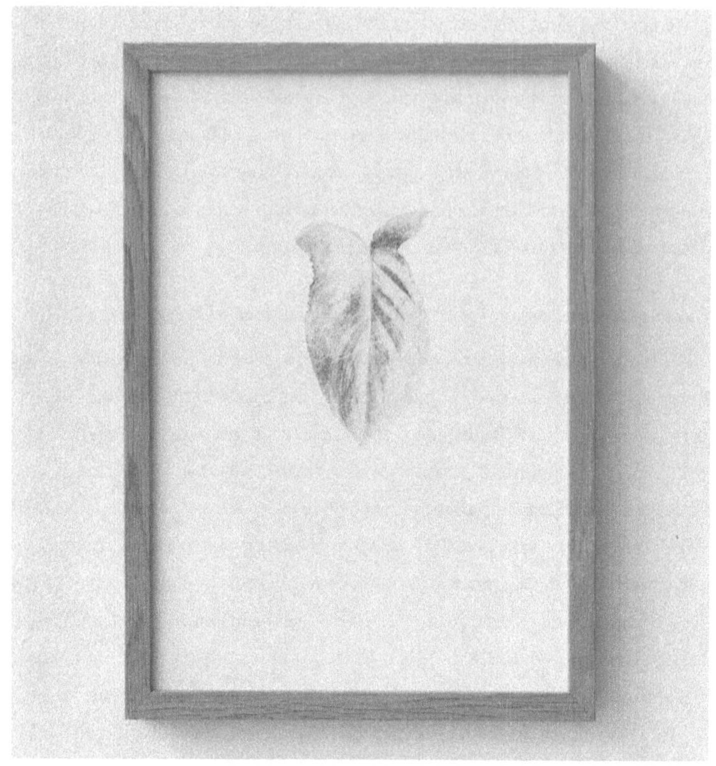

Figure 2. *Propagations*. 2020. Propagations (#20). (Image courtesy of Theo Christelis).

attempt to mature several vines in the same pot for a greater number of annual blooms. Additionally, while the plants' native pollinators are thousands of miles away, there is anecdotal evidence of insects in non-native geographies pollinating *Philodendron* in botanical garden greenhouses (Summer Rayne Oakes).

Once the plant was cut, I left the thirty individual stem pieces to callus over, in order to discourage any rot that may occur once they were placed in damp growing media (in this case, sphagnum moss). The plants were situated in an indoor, tabletop greenhouse with seedling mats for heat, small fans for air circulation, and a grow light. The plants were also treated with preventative insecticide, which is an act of care for the cuttings but less so for any pests looking for a meal (Ginn, 2013, 2016; Pitt). About a month after the plants were placed in the greenhouse, I severed the leaves from the stem cutting to photograph them for my herbarium. This was not an act of care, as it slowed down the ability of the cutting to grow into a new plant. In the words of contemporary plant hobbyists, I turned them into "wet sticks." There is less guilt associated with this

Matthew Beach

action because the leaves would have eventually fallen off when the plant used its energy to create new growth, but it remains an uncaring act. Throughout this process, I maintained a practice of negotiating scales of care, short-term uncaring actions in service of a wider approach to construct the notion of the postcolonial houseplant in an art exhibition setting.

While the wet sticks were growing roots, my attention was devoted to producing each new plant's corresponding cyanotype within the herbarium (Fig. 2). The tissue paper employed for the process was Bib Tengujo 12 gsm, a 100% manilla hemp fibre, sourced from Shepherds in London. This paper was chosen because of its uses in conservation for securing plant material to herbarium sheets. Because the tissue paper is plant-based, the cyanotype emulsion will adhere to it. All leaves were photographed and reproduced true-to-scale as new photographic negatives. When exposed to the cyanotype-coated tissue paper, the resulting image is a positive. In this way, *Propagations* becomes a lively herbarium, too, through its emphasis on documenting living plant material, rather than dried and pressed foliage.

It is a herbarium that looks outward onto future relations between *Philodendron*, humans, and other species. Composed of a deconstructed *Philodendron pedatum* vine, the herbarium is an object that is not botanically useful because the foliage captured consists of abstractions created via photographs. The documented leaves retain visual expressions of three-dimensionality. The tissue paper becomes the pressed foliage, meaning there is no scope for DNA analysis; but even if there were, all the genetic information captured within *Propagations* is identical. Instead, my herbarium points to the mass production of houseplants. The use of the photograph is tied to the practice of propagating: the cut of the stem is akin to the exposure, as the axillary bud is latent with new growth and the cyanotype print latent with areas of light and shadow. The exposure, too, relates to care, with the greenhouse lit by a 36-watt SANSI grow light bulb. This same bulb produced the cyanotypes: its emulsion is sensitive to ultraviolet light.

Photography has been linked to the herbarium through the practice of indexing in nature printing. In this process, the object depicted is also the printing block, inked and sandwiched with paper to create an impression. Developing in parallel with herbarium practice, nature printing has become a valuable tool during winter when living plants are not available. Herbaria, nature printing, and early photography each facilitate a frozen moment, stopping the life cycle of the plant (Artaker). *Propagations* subverts these practices. Rather than stopping the plant's life cycle, the act of propagating encourages it to continue. As a method of indexing, the cameraless photographs present in the series capture less of a physical relationship to the *Philodendron* plantlets. Placed in the wider exhibition context, the photographs present a lively archive that undermines knowledge-making practices in botany, conservation, and domesticity. Through working to contextualise (Demos) the native environments and interspecies connections embedded in *Philodendron*'s lively materiality, as well as those histories that are left out of houseplant care and cultivation narratives, *Propagations*'s creative herbaria continues the decolonising practice of subverting herbarium collections.

Conclusion: The Case for the Postcolonial Houseplant

In an era when houseplants are resurging in popularity and botanists seek to take advantage of this renewed interest to combat plant blindness (Wandersee and Schussler; Burke et al.), how we orient ourselves towards these shared futures matters. Forming relationships with houseplants offers an opportunity to move beyond the botanising practices of nineteenth-century Europe and reconceive of plants as living entities who have also experienced extractive violence through imperialism and colonialism. With the current emphasis on the usefulness of houseplants for mental health benefits and on their roles as aesthetic objects that can sometimes also be valuable investments (University of Cambridge), there is a need to emphasise the postcolonial identities concealed within our leafy companions. Moreover, these identities must also encompass aspects of queerness (Seymour), acknowledging bodies that are both terranean, reaching towards the light, and subterranean, making rooty connections in the darkness below (Castro; Simard).

Rather than viewing houseplants as stationary decor, we must build upon the 1970s interest in interior domestic plant communication, plant sentience, and plant intelligence (Castro). We must understand that to be in the presence of a houseplant means to stand in solidarity with them against the biopolitical capitalist regime that seeks to standardise and commodify vegetal life. Understanding the presence of houseplants means contemplating their existence beyond brief encounters, working to bridge sensorial gaps that create distance in our relating to plants (Aloi). To do so requires lingering in the presence of our houseplants, paying attention to their changing morphology and to their growth habits as they move towards the light; we must consider the climbing green plant as a relational being rather than a potentially invasive other (Sanders).

Across this text I have moved through a series of botanical drifts (Zinnenburg Carroll), foregrounding plants as protagonists in critiques of colonial herbaria, surveys of creative herbaria practice, histories of and contemporary thought concerning houseplant cultivation, and my own creative attempts, in order to construct what I am terming the notion of the postcolonial houseplant. The postcolonial houseplant disrupts our normative relations within the interior domestic sphere. Creative herbaria offer one method with which to confront this disruption, but there are also other possibilities and opportunities for further scrutiny—for instance, through mapping imperial ornamental plant commodity flows, looking at cultivar breeding programs, interrogating the politics embedded in "common" naming, drawing attention to local knowledges around specific plants, examining the development of various plant societies, or elucidating various houseplants' relations to their native ecologies. Wherever these strands of decolonising discourse drift, we must continue to creatively subvert the extractive colonial legacy embedded in our companion flora.

Notes

1   Ferns were not only extracted and transported to imperial centres, but also exported to settler colonies (Giles).

2   Chine-collé is a process in which a thin piece of dampened paper is coated with an adhesive, placed onto a thicker backing paper, and run through a printing press. To produce an herbarium, often plant matter is attached to a support paper using a piece of collagen-based, glue-soaked, Japanese, vegetal-fibre-based tissue paper. This collagen-based glue will adhere to tissue paper but not "unprocessed" plant matter, and thus becomes a useful method within herbarium production.

3   While I am working to enliven the herbarium based on earlier scholarship that link pressed plants to death, there are other ways of considering herbarium liveliness—for instance, through archive geographies (Ogborn).

Works Cited

Allen, David E. *The Victorian Craze: A History of Pteridomania*. Hutchinson 1969.

Aloi, Giovanni. "Presence, Bareness, and Being-With." *Why Look at Plants?: The Botanical Emergence in Contemporary Art*, edited by G. Aloi. Brill, 2019, pp. 183-190.

@AloiArtTalk (Giovanni Aloi). "House plants in art are the next phase in the critical plant studies revolution." *Twitter*, 20 Jun 2021, 8:42pm, https://twitter.com/AloiArtTalk/status/1406457456025288705.

Antonelli, Alexandre. "Director of Science at Kew: It's Time to Decolonise Botanical Collections." *The Conversation*, 19 Jun. 2020, https://theconversation.com/director-of-science-at-kew-its-time-to-decolonise-botanical-collections-141070.

Artaker, Anna. "The Birth of Photography from the Spirit of the Herbarium." *Unlikely*, vol. 4, 2017.

Batsaki, Yota. "The Apocalyptic Herbarium: Mourning and Transformation in Anselm Kiefer's Secret of the Ferns." *Environmental Humanities*, vol. 13, no. 2, 2021, pp. 391-413.

Bond, Casey. "Why Millennials Are Suddenly So Obsessed With Houseplants." *The Huffington Post*, 6 May 2019, https://www.huffingtonpost.co.uk/entry/millennials-obsessed-houseplants-instagram_l_5d7a976de4b01c1970c433b9

Giles, Juliet. "The History of Terrariums: The Wardian Case." *Gardens Illustrated*, 28 Aug. 2019, https://www.gardensillustrated.com/plants/the-history-of-terrariums-the-wardian-case/.

Bringslimark, Tina, et al. "Psychological Benefits of Indoor Plants in Workplaces: Putting Experimental Results into Context." *Hortscience*, vol. 42, no. 3, 2007, pp. 581-87.

Bristow, Tom, et al. "Editorial." *Unlikely*, vol. 4, 2017, https://unlikely.net.au/issue-04/editorial-225.

Brooking, Tom, and Pawson, Eric. *Seeds of Empire: The Environmental Transformation of New Zealand*. Bloomsbury Publishing, 2011.

Burke, Rory, et al. "Botanical Boom: A New Opportunity To Promote the Public Appreciation of Botany." *Plants People Planet*, vol. 4, no. 1, 2022, pp. 326-34.

Burns, Laura. *Decolonizing Botany*, 2022, http://www.lauraburns.co.uk/decolonising-botany. Accessed 10 Jan. 2023.

Carabelli, Giulia. "Plants, Vegetables, Lawn: Radical Solidarities in Pandemic Times." *Lateral*, vol. 10, no. 2, 2021, https://csalateral.org/forum/corona-affects-effects/plants-vegetables-lawn-radical-solidarities-pandemic-times-carabelli/

Chapman, Gray. "How Much Would You Pay for a Houseplant?" *The New York Times*, 11 Nov. 2019, https://www.nytimes.com/2019/11/11/style/tropical-plants-rare.html.

Castro, Teresa. "The Mediated Plant." *E-flux*, vol. 102, 2019, https://www.e-flux.com/journal/102/283819/the-mediated-plant/

---. "The 1970s Plant Craze." *Antennae*, vol. 52, 2020, pp. 173-89.

    Matthew Beach

Chen, Jim. "Across the Apocalypse on Horseback: Biodiversity Loss and the Law." *Biodiversity and the Law: Intellectual Property, Biotechnology and Traditional Knowledge*, edited by C.R. McManic, Earthscan, 2007, pp. 42-57.

Corne, F. E. "Ferns: Facts and Fancies about Them: II." *American Fern Journal*, vol. 14, no. 3, 1924, pp. 77-82.

Dash, Mike. *Tulipomania: The Story of the World's Most Coveted Flower and the Extraordinary Passions It Aroused.* Crown Publishers, 1999.

Davidoff, Alexandra. *Relationship between Psychological Stress and Houseplants.* 2021. Belmont University, BA Thesis.

Delves, Jay. *Decolonize Herbaria and Specimen Data; Quantifying the Contribution of Local Herbaria to Biodiversity Patterns.* 2021. University of Edinburgh, MA Thesis.

Demos, T. J. *Decolonizing Nature: Contemporary Art and the Politics of Ecology.* Sternberg Press, 2016.

De Vos, Paula S. "The Science of Spices: Empiricism and Economic Botany in the Early Spanish Empire." *Journal of World History*, vol. 17, no. 4, 2006, pp. 399-427.

Dion, Mark, and Giovanni Aloi. "Herbarium Perrine: Interview with Mark Dion." *Why Look at Plants?: The Botanical Emergence in Contemporary Art*, edited by G. Aloi, Brill, 2019, pp. 250-54.

Driver, Felix, and Caroline Cornish. *Plant Humanities: A Scoping Report on RHUL-Kew Collaboration.* Royal Holloway, University of London and Royal Botanic Gardens, Kew, 2020.

Easterby-Smith, Sarah. *Cultivating Commerce: Cultures of Botany in Britain and France, 1760–1815.* Cambridge University Press, 2018.

Easterby-Smith, Sarah, and John Hill. "Exotic Botany and the Competitive World of Eighteenth-Century Horticulture." *Fame & Fortune: Sir John Hill and London Life in the 1750s*, edited by C. Brant and G. Rousseau, Palgrave Macmillan, 2018, pp. 291-313.

Eckel, Molly K. "'A Little World within a World': The Wardian Case of Tropical Ferns in the Victorian Home." *Immediations*, vol. 4, no. 2, 2017, https://courtauld.ac.uk/research/research-resources/publications/immeditations-postgraduate-journal/immediations-online/2017-2/molly-k-eckel-a-little-world-within-a-world-the-wardian-case-of-tropical-ferns-in-the-victorian-home/.

Evans, Meredith. "Becoming Sensor in the Planthroposcene: An Interview with Natasha Myers: Visual and New Media Review," *Fieldsights*, 2020, https://culanth.org/fieldsights/becoming-sensor-an-interview-with-natasha-myers

Flannery, Maura C. "The Herbarium as Muse: Plant Specimens as Inspiration." *Biology International*, vol. 53, 2013, pp. 23-34.

---. *In the Herbarium: The Hidden World of Collecting and Preserving Plants*. Yale University Press, 2023.

Forman, Leonard, and Diane Bridson, eds. *The Herbarium Handbook*. Kew Royal Botanical Gardens, 1992.

Gerard, John. *Herball*. John Norton, 1597.

Gibernau, Mark, et al. "Beetle Pollination of Philodendron Solimoesense (Araceae) in French Guiana." *International Journal of Plant Science*, vol. 160, no. 6, 1999, pp. 1135-43.

Ginn, Franklin. "Sticky Lives: Slugs, Detachment and More-Than-Human Ethics in the Garden." *Transactions of the Institute of British Geographers*, vol. 39, no. 4, 2013, 532-44.

---. *Domestic Wild: Memory, Nature and Gardening in Suburbia*. Routledge, 2016.

Gordon, W. J. *Flowers of the Market: The Leisure Hour: An Illustrated Magazine for Home Reading*, vol. 43, 1894, pp. 86-91.

Hallowell, Anne C., and Barbara. G. Hallowell. *Fern Finder: A Guide to Native Ferns of Central and Northeastern United States and Eastern Canada*. Nature Study Guild Publishers, 2001.

Hughes, Alice. "Average Briton Spends Hundreds of Pounds on Houseplants Each Year, Poll Finds." *The Independent*, 16 Jul. 2021, https://www.independent.co.uk/life-style/uk-adults-houseplants-poll-gen-z-b1885308.html.

Ikea. "Indoor Plant Ideas for Your Living Room," 2022, https://www.ikea.com/gb/en/ideas/indoor-plant-ideas-for-your-living-room-pub32022f0.1 Accessed 4 Jul. 2022.

Jackson, Joe. *The Thief at the End of the World: Rubber, Power, and the Seeds of Empire*. Penguin Books, 2008.

Jayes, Phoebe. "Houseplant Studios at Chelsea Flower Show." *The English Garden*, 21 Sept. 2021, https://www.theenglishgarden.co.uk/news-and-events/chelsea-flower-show/houseplant-studios-chelsea-flower-show/.

Jolivet, Pierre. *Interrelationship Between Insects and Plants*. CRC Press, 1998.

Koestlé-Cate, Jonathan. "The Currency of Belief: Jonathan Koestlé-Cate Profiles the Artist John Newling." *Art and Christianity*, vol. 74, 2013, pp. 1-5.

Khadou, Céline. "Shopping: je veux du vert!." *FrenchFancy*, 2015, https://frenchyfancy.com/shopping-deco-objet-couleur-vert/. Accessed 15 Jul. 2022.

Kirk-Ballard, Heather. "Houseplants Are Making a Big Comeback." *Magnolia Reporter*, 14 Jul. 2022, http://www.magnoliareporter.com/living_and_learning/education/article_a873b1d2-0269-11ed-9fea-177d456063c2.html.

Lansdowne, Emma. "Curatorial Subjectivity: The Universal Aesthetics of Herbaria." *Unlikely*, vol. 4, 2017.

Larner, Stacey. *Orchidelirium: When Love Turns to Obsession*. State Library of Queensland, 2021, https://www.slq.qld.gov.au/blog/orchidelirium-when-love-turns-obsession. Accessed 19 Jul. 2022.

Lawrence, Anna. "Listening to Plants: Conversations between Critical Plant Studies and Vegetal Geography." *Progress in Human Geography*, vol. 46, no. 2, 2021, pp. 629-51.

Massey, Jimmy R. "The Herbarium." *Vascular Plant Systematics*, edited by A. E. Radford, Seiler Harper & Row, 1974, pp. 751-74.

Margulies, Jared D. "Korean 'Housewives' and 'Hipsters' Are Not Driving a New Illicit Plant Trade: Complicating Consumer Motivations behind an Emergent Wildlife Trade in Dudleya Farinosa." *Frontiers in Ecology and Evolution*, vol. 8, 2020, pp. 1-8.

Mason, Heberling J., and Bonnie L. Isaac. "Herbarium Specimens as Exaptations: New Uses for Old Collections." *American Journal of Botany*, vol. 104, no. 7, 2017, pp. 963-65.

May, Lenore W. "The Economic Uses and Associated Folklore of Ferns and Fern Allies." *The Botanical Review*, vol. 44, 1978, pp. 491-528.

McGurk, Stuart. "Pots of Gold: The World's Most Expensive House Plants." *The Guardian*, 17 Apr. 2022, https://www.theguardian.com/lifeandstyle/2022/apr/17/gold-leaves-meet-the-30000-pound-houseplants-sparking-a-new-green-crimewave.

Moore, Thomas. *A Popular History of the British Ferns and the Allied Plants, Comprising the Club-Mosses, Pepperworts, and Horsetails*. Routledge, Warne, and Routledge, 1859.

Motta, Sara C. "Decolonizing (Critical) Social Theory: Enfleshing Post-Covid Futurities." *Thesis Eleven*, vol. 170, no. 1, 2022, pp. 58-77.

Murphy, Christina M., and Michael D. Breed. "Nectar and Resin Robbing in Stingless Bees." *American Entomologist*, vol. 54, no. 1, 2008, pp. 36-44.

Oakes, Summer Rayne. "3,700 AROIDS in One Greenhouse!: Anthurium, Philodendron & More: Part 1 – Ep. 261." *Plant One on Me*, 10 Feb. 2022, https://www.youtube.com/watch?v=ua9WyM6V4ag. Accessed 19 Jul. 2022.

Oresky, Melissa. *Books & Prints*, https://melissaoresky.com/Books-Prints. Accessed 22 Jul. 2022).

The National Archives. *Currency Converter: 1270–2017*, 2018, https://www.nationalarchives.gov.uk/currency-converter/. Accessed 18 Jul. 2022.

Tinyplants. "Is Aroid Mania the New Orchid Mania?" *Tinyplants*, 2020, https://tinyplants.biz/blogs/tinyplants/is-aroid-mania-the-new-orchid-mania. Accessed 19 Jul. 2022.

Ogborn, Miles. "Archive." *The Sage Handbook of Geographical Knowledge*, edited by J. Agnew and D. N. Livingstone, Sage, 2011, pp. 88-98.

Parreñas, Juno S. *Decolonizing Extinction: The Work of Care in Orangutan Rehabilitation.* Duke University Press, 2018.

Phillips, Catherine, and Eily Schulz. "Greening Home: Caring for Plants Indoors." *Australian Geographer,* vol. 52, no. 4, 2021, pp. 373-89.

Pitt, Hannah. "Questioning Care Cultivated through Connecting with More-Than-Human Communities." *Social and Cultural Geography,* vol. 19, no. 2, 2018, pp. 253-74.

Plowman, Timothy. "Folk Uses of New World Aroids." *Economic Botany,* vol. 23, no. 2, 1969, pp. 97-122.

Pluymers, Keith, and Melissa Oresky. "Composting in the Herbarium." *Antennae,* vol. 52, 2020, pp. 156-71.

Puig de la Bellacasa, Maria. *Matters of Care: Speculative Ethics in More Than Human Worlds.* University of Minnesota Press, 2017.

Quinn, Ben. "Mangrove Nine Garden Brings Activism to Chelsea Flower Show." *The Guardian,* 24 May 2022, https://www.theguardian.com/lifeandstyle/2022/may/24/mangrove-nine-garden-activism-chelsea-flower-show-notting-hill

Royal Horticultural Society. "Houseplant Studios Return to RHS Chelsea," 2022, https://www.rhs.org.uk/shows-events/rhs-chelsea-flower-show/news/2022/houseplant-studios-return. Accessed 18 Jul. 2022.

Ruppel, Sophie. "Houseplants and the Invention of Indoor Gardening." *Routledge History of the Domestic Sphere in Europe,* edited by J. Eibach and M. Lazinger, Routledge, 2020, pp. 1282-1320.

Sanders, Dawn L. "Seeing Green: The Climbing Other." *Why Look at Plants?: The Botanical Emergence in Contemporary Art,* edited by G. Aloi. Brill, 2019, pp. 195-97.

Schiebinger, Londa. *Plants and Empire: Colonial Bioprospecting in the Atlantic World.* Harvard University Press, 2007.

Seymour, Nicole. "Queer Ecologies and Queer Environmentalisms." *The Cambridge Companion to Queer Studies,* edited by S. B. Somerville, Cambridge University Press, 2020, pp. 108-24.

Silk, John. "Caring at a Distance." *Philosophy & Geography,* vol. 1, no. 2, 1998, pp. 165-82.

Simard, Suzanne. *Finding the Mother Tree: Discovering the Wisdom of the Forest.* Knopf, 2021.

Sprague, Thomas A., and Enid Nelmes. "The Herbal of Leonhart Fuchs." *Botanical Journal of the Linnean Society,* vol. 48, no. 325, 1931, pp. 545-642.

Subramaniam, Banu. "Methodologies for the Pressed: Cartographies for Adisciplinary Sciences." *Science, Technology and Society,* vol. 28, 2022, pp. 1-9.

Tolentino, Jia. "The Leafy Love Affair Between Millennials and Houseplants." *The New Yorker*, 18 Apr. 2019, https://www.newyorker.com/culture/culture-desk/the-leafy-love-affair-between-millennials-and-our-houseplants.

Tondeur, Anaïs. "Chernobyl Herbarium," 2011, https://anaistondeur.com/chernobyl-herbarium. Accessed 20 Jul. 2022.

Torget, Andrew J. *Seeds of Empire: Cotton, Slavery, and the Transformation of the Texas Borderlands, 1800–1850.* University of North Carolina Press, 2015.

Tsing, Anna L., et al. *Feral Atlas: The More-Than-Human Anthropocene.* Stanford University Press, 2021.

Tsymbalyuk, Darya. "Lockdown and Locked In: Houseplants and Covid-19." *Seeing the Woods*, 29 Jun. 2022, https://seeingthewoods.org/2020/06/29/lockdown-and-locked-in-houseplants-and-covid-19/. Accessed 3 Jul. 2022.

University of Cambridge. "Inaugural Entrepreneur-In-Residence Appointed." *King's College Cambridge*, 2022, http://www.kings.cam.ac.uk/news/2022/inaugural-entrepreneur-residence-appointed. Accessed 20 Jul. 2022.

Wandersee, James H., and Elisabeth E. Schussler. "Preventing Plant Blindness." *The American Biology Teacher*, vol. 61, no. 2, 1999, pp. 82-86.

Ward, Nathaniel B. *On the Growth of Plants in Closely Glazed Cases.* John Van Voorst, 1852.

Wallsten, Brittani. "Houseplants as Mental Health Supports for Dorm Occupants during the Lockdown Period at Portland State University." *Anthós*, vol. 11, no. 1, 2022, pp. 11-19.

Whittingham, Sarah. *Fern Fever: The Story of Pteridomania.* Frances Lincoln, 2012.

Zinnenburg Carroll, Khadija von. "The Useless and Confusing: Vegetable Philosophies and Performances in the Kew Economic Botany Collection." *Botanical Drift: Protagonists of the Invasive Herbarium*, edited by K. von Zinnenburg Carroll, Sternberg Press, 2017, pp. 5-18.

6 Rooted in Other Worlds

Vanessa Lemm

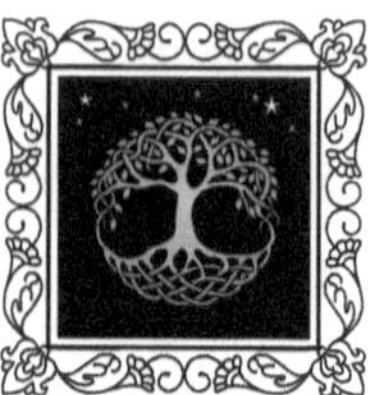

What can we learn from plants and the way they are rooted in Earth and planetary life about the nature of the human being and its place in the world? This contribution seeks to connect two recent developments in the humanities and social sciences—a "plant turn" and a "planetary turn"—and bring both to bear on the question of how we should inhabit this planet now that our own actions are making it uninhabitable for so many members of the community of life. I ask what plant life can teach us about how to bridge worlds and reconnect humans to Earth and planetary life by focusing on images of rootedness in other worlds in Plato and Dostoevsky.

The Planetary Turn

Until recently, many assumed that, for human purposes, the Earth was an inert background: always there, meaningless, the backdrop for our human drama. But we now know that this is not the case. Rather, this backdrop is a complex Earth-system that makes our lives possible and that our capitalist, industrial civilisation is in the process of destabilising.

In a recent book, the postcolonial historian Dipesh Chakrabarty, one of the world's leading experts on the history of climate change, distinguished between "global" and the "planetary" perspectives (Chakrabarty). Whereas the term "global," as in "globalization," refers to "a story of how we created this world, how we converted this planet into a spherical human domain" in which technology, empire, and capitalism run their course, for Chakrabarty the same term "global" in the expression "global warming" refers to an entirely different history, a planetary history. This history highlights a much older dimension of existence that does not include the human species. It is a history of life on Earth in which the Earth-system is the main actor and needs to respond creatively to changed external circumstances—for instance, when the very slight change in the Earth's inclination towards the sun led, through a complex process, to a change in the atmosphere as new oxygen levels eliminated previous life forms based on nitrogen and led to life forms that thrive on oxygen and to our current atmospheric composition.

The planetary perspective is relevant for plant studies insofar as plants, that is, organisms capable of photosynthesis, were the key players in this transformation of the atmosphere. This transformation has been termed the Great Oxygenation Event or Oxygen Catastrophe and led to the spread of aerobic forms of life and the extinction of non-aerobic forms. Thus, plant life not only is one of the oldest forms of life (over 350 million years old) in comparison to *homo sapiens* (approximately 300,000 years old), but also shows, as plant biologist Monica Gagliano put it, that "plants are perhaps the most fundamental form of life, providing sustenance, and thus enabling the existence of all animals, including humans" (Gagliano et al. vii). Plants represent about 99% of the Earth's biomass, and it is thanks to them that the Earth produces an atmosphere that makes life possible for the vast majority of species.

From an anthropocentric perspective, human life and the circumstances in which we find ourselves are both subject to human design: we have the capacity to design these circumstances as an enveloping medium that closes us off from the meaninglessness of sheer existence, while at the same time protecting and comforting us, like a warm house in the middle of a cold winter (e.g. Sloterdijk). In contrast, the point of contemporary plant studies is precisely to break through our artificial environments and to connect us to unknown earthly and aerial worlds, such as the plant's unique position in the world, that hold together earth and sky. Plants live two kinds of lives. An earthly life, with their roots deeply immersed in the soil, underground, chthonic, nocturnal. And an aerial life, turned towards our star, immersed in its sunlight, visible and interacting with other species. This is why the Italian philosopher Emmanuele Coccia argues that plant life "is the most intense, radical, and paradigmatic form of being in the world" and that, therefore, we need to interrogate plants if we want to understand the meaning of human existence and its dependence on environmental constraints that are not simply at its disposal and that cannot be custom designed or re-engineered (Coccia 5).

Perhaps it is because we are so dependent on plants for our planetary existence that they bear the brunt of our drive to find security within artificial worlds of our own making. It is not only the clearing of land to make space for urban dwelling, for animal husbandry, and for mining. It is not only that the industrialisation of agriculture requires massive use of pesticides that poison our daily lives without our being aware of it. Plants also bear the brunt of most genetic manipulation and engineering. The patents of 90% of genetically modified crops grown in the United States are owned by a handful of powerful seed and pesticide manufacturers (Nealon). Precisely because human life is so plant-like, there is something particularly uncanny about the genetic modifications of plants in so far as these modifications suggest the ease with which we are in the process of transitioning to a so-called "trans-human" future in which genetically enhanced human life will itself be patented, and possibly owned by the equivalents of Bayer, the former Monsanto (Robin; Holmes).

Plants as Cosmic Mediators

In order to resist an anthropocentric ecology that sunders an irrational Earth from our meaningful world, plant philosopher Michael Marder speaks of "the environmental sagacity" of plants that stand in relation to their environment both as radically context-dependent and open systems thanks to "a series of internal communicative networks (e.g. biochemical and hormonal channels, or synaptic cell-cell communication) and external communication pathways that connect it to its environment" (Marder 1370; Lemm). Plants are inseparable from their environment, and, vice versa, their environment is inseparable from them to the point that one can no longer distinguish between an inside and an outside. Completely immersed in their environment, the lives of plants are fully enmeshed with the life of others. Plants are radically non-identitary, always exposed and open to the other and always also growing in communities with others (e.g. Lemm).

This insight into the lives of plants has important ethical implications because our Western political and legal traditions teach that our security ultimately depends on distinguishing ourselves from what surrounds us by erecting borders between those who are our friends and those who are our enemies, borders between what is mine and what is thine (Lindahl). Conversely, what we may learn from the life of plants is what it means to be human on a planet that must be necessarily shared with other forms of life and what it takes to coexist with and co-depend on other forms of life.

New ways of communicating with non-human forms of life are required for us to reconnect with the Earth and the cosmos, including plants. This would mean cultivating new forms of respect and care for human and non-human life. We need to reject the Aristotelian hierarchy of the souls and learn from plants how to communicate with our environment. This insight has led scholars in plant biology to ask the question of whether a plant language exists. According to Gagliano, plants invite us to "a speaking without words, a listening without hearing, that humankind must learn to cultivate for the sake of the future we wish to share with each other and with other beings" (Gagliano et al. xx).

What appears remarkable about plants is their "double nature," that is, their capacity to gather and hold together both the earth and the starry heavens, in the form of sunlight, and thus to participate in fashioning the atmosphere for life on this planet. These characteristics of plant life have led Coccia to speak of plants as "cosmic mediators" (Coccia 81). From an Earth-system science perspective, plant life can also teach us that we need to be mindful not only of the atmospheric conditions of life on Earth, but also of the astral dimensions of life, which nowadays are studied by astrobiology. The findings of astrobiologists are bringing about a renaissance of an ancient belief, namely, that life on Earth may have come from the stars and that we ourselves are made up of the same stuff as stars (Cumont; Hokari).

So, if plant life suggests the need to be in communication with non-human worlds, then we must be open to the possibility of what Nietzsche calls a "star friendship" (Nietzsche, *Gay Science*, aphorism 279, 523-4). In the Western philosophical tradition, the idea that the secret of human nature is hidden in the stars finds probably its most prominent source in Plato, who himself absorbed and reworked the science and the myths received from older African and Asian cultures. In *Timaeus*, Plato defines the human being as a celestial plant whose roots are in heaven, in the stars. Plato imagines the human being as rooted upwards in the divine cosmos.

> We should think of the most authoritative part of our soul as a guardian spirit given to each of us by God and living in the summit of the body; this spirit can properly be said to lift us from the earth towards our home in heaven, as if we were a heavenly (and not earthbound) plant. For where the soul first grew into being, from there our divine part attaches us by the head to heavens, like a plant by its roots, and keeps our body upright (Plato, *Timaeus* 88).

The notion that our rootedness in other worlds distinguishes us and underpins our capacity for intellectual transcendence was not uncommon among the ancient Greeks. For the ancient Greeks, philosophy was, above all, cosmology because they thought that it is in the perfect, circular movement of the starry vault, the supra-terrestrial dimension of the cosmos, that we find orientation and moral guidance. Therefore, philosophers with a Platonic orientation were typically depicted as gazing upwards into the heavens in contrast to Aristotelians, whose philosophical perspective was oriented downwards, towards the exploration of material forms of life, such as plants and animals. The upward gaze is of course a pitfall that the Greeks were well aware of. According to Plato's anecdote of the Greek sage and astronomer Thales, he left his house to look at the stars and fell into a ditch, causing his slave to burst out in laughter (Plato, *Theaetetus* 174a; Blumenberg 14-21, 46-53). The message here is clear: no matter how deep and far we think, we should keep our feet well planted on the earth because we are not only celestial beings, but also earthlings.

Now, there is also another version of Thales's story. In this version, Thales intentionally went into the earth and dug a well in order to observe more clearly the night skies. He did so because he wanted to understand and predict the weather; he was developing the science of meteorology; with this knowledge, he speculated on the grain market and became very wealthy. The study of the cosmos has always had a speculative side to it, speculative in a philosophical and mathematical sense, but also speculative in an economic sense. Today this speculative drive behind the exploration of space seems to animate individuals like Elon Musk who are on a "transhumanist" mission to abandon the Earth and transform *homo sapiens* into a "multi-planet species and true spacefaring civilization," viewing planets and stars from the perspective of their inexhaustibly extractivist potential (Sheetz). But who owns the heavens? Nowadays, there is a race to space to be outsourced to astropreneurs, with space becoming the final frontier that is for sale to the wealthy few (Gorman).

The problem with looking at the stars from Plato's perspective, according to French ecological thinker Bruno Latour, is that we project onto space a mathematical geometry that gives us the illusion that we can formulate and so anticipate the trajectories of everything under and beyond the sun (Latour). The danger of such celestial visions is that they make us lose sight of the contingencies of our earthly atmosphere, of the unpredictable and far messier and more fragile systems of feedback cycles and loops that characterise the Earth. But do we have to choose between earth and heavens? What can the dual nature of plants tell us about how to be doubly rooted, above and below?

Rooted in Two Worlds

I would like to close with a literary image drawn from Fyodor Dostoesvky's masterpiece, *The Brothers Karamazov*. This image is paradigmatic of a different sense of rootedness, a rootedness in other worlds that draws us back to the Earth and our responsibility for it. The image is from "Conversations and Exhortations of Father Zossima" and is about Alyosha, one of the three Karamazov brothers, who decides to become a monk and adopts Father Zossima's teaching that the root of all love emerges from our living bond with other worlds: "We have been given a precious mystic sense of our living bond with the other world, with the higher heavenly world, and the roots of our thoughts and feelings are not here but in other worlds" (245). For Zossima, our displacement on Earth is due to our rootedness in other worlds. On this point, Zossima stands in the Platonic tradition of orientating ourselves towards the cosmos, but for Zossima, our position is not due to reason as abstract from lived experience but due to a "living bond with other worlds":

> On earth, indeed, we are, as it were, astray … Much on earth is hidden from us, but to make up for that we have been given a precious mystic sense of our living bond with the other world, with the higher heavenly world, and the roots of our thoughts and feelings are not here but in other worlds. That is why the philosophers say that we cannot apprehend the reality of things on earth (245).

Unlike Plato, Zossima acknowledges the limits of human knowledge. Whereas Plato seeks to overcome these limits through the human being's capacity for transcendence, Zossima believes that only our living bond with other worlds can make life on Earth worth living. Plato's humanism is centred on the human being's rational capacity to know other worlds that transcend the world of lived experience. Instead, Zossima's spiritual existentialism is based on the idea that to realise our human nature means to connect with these other worlds. We need to be like plants, orientated towards both Earthly and planetary life, immanent and transcendent. And also like plants, we need to turn ourselves inside out, expose, offer, and give ourselves to the other. Adopting the model of the life of the plant requires an externalisation based on the acceptance that our role in this world depends on something other than human for our lives to be meaningful and worth living. This otherness is expressed through the image of the divine seed, which withholds the secret of our existence. For Zossima, our happiness on Earth depends on our capacity to receive this gift (seed) and realise that it is through our connection and relationship with others that our lives take on meaning:

God took seeds from different worlds and sowed them on this earth,
and His garden grew up and everything came up that could come up,
but what grows lives and is alive only through the feeling of its contact with other mysterious worlds. If that feeling grows weak or is
destroyed in you, the heavenly growth will die away in you. Then
you will be indifferent to life and even grow to hate it. That's what I
think (245).

In contrast to Plato, who understands our divine origin in other worlds
as symbolic for our capacity for knowledge, as a centre of gravity pulling us
upwards and away from the Earth, Zossima inverts Plato's celestial plant and
reconnects us with life on earth: "Love the animals, love the plants, love everything. If you love everything, you will perceive the divine mystery in things.
Once you perceive it, you will begin to comprehend it better every day. And you
will come at last to love the whole world with an all-embracing love" (244).

For Zossima, not reason and knowledge, but love and compassion are the
nature of the human being. However, rather than belonging to us, this nature
is a gift we received from other worlds, a gift that comes with a calling, the
responsibility of care for the Earth. According to Zossima, our role in the world
is all about responding to our relationship with others. Like a plant, we are
called to be cosmic mediators, building bridges between worlds and acknowledging our dependency on other forms of life, human and non-human. Love
and care for the Earth allows us to see that everything is in everything and
that everything belongs to everything. As such, our rootedness in other worlds
does not make us strangers to the Earth, as in Plato. Instead, it predestines us
to be open to alterity, to multiple worlds and perspectives. The responsibility
of love and care for the Earth obliges us to question the mindless extrapolation
from the Earth.

Where does Zossima's teaching about human nature and our place in the
world leave us? Today, in the face of climate change and environmental catastro-
phes, love and responsibility of and for the Earth is perhaps needed more than
ever. Especially, to challenge those who are on the "transhumanist" mission of
abandoning this earth. Instead, what we need is attention to the many worlds
that are found here on earth, in a multi-species and symbiotic sense of coexistence and inter-relationality between living beings and living matter. This
is needed far more than setting out to "colonise" other planets. Interestingly,
Zossima's teaching resonates with Gayatri Spivak's postcolonial approach to

Vanessa Lemm

planetary thinking (Spivak). Echoing French poststructuralist philosophers, she avers: "To be human is to be intended toward the other." And like Zossima, she conceives the openness to the other through the figure of the gift, which we refer to by the name of "mother," "nature," "god," "earth," and so forth. Spivak invites us to imagine ourselves, like Zossima, as "planetary subjects rather than global agents, planetary creatures rather than global entities" and insists that to overcome the current predicament "[w]e must persistently educate ourselves into this peculiar mindset" (1223).

Works Cited

Blumenberg, Hans. *The Laughter of the Thracian Woman: A Protohistory of Theory*, translated by Spencer Hawkins, Bloomsbury Publishing, 2015.

Chakrabarty, Dipesh. *The Climate of History in a Planetary Age*. University of Chicago Press, 2021.

Coccia, Emanuele. *The Life of Plants: A Metaphysics of Mixture*. Polity, 2018.

Cumont, Franz. *Astrology and Religion among the Greeks and Romans*. Dover Publications, 1960.

Deleuze, Gilles, et al. *A Thousand Plateaus: Capitalism and Schizophrenia*. University of Minnesota Press, 1987.

Dostojevsky, Fyodor. *The Brothers Karamazov*. Global Grey Books, 2019.

Gagliano, Monica, et al., eds. *The Language of Plants: Science, Philosophy, Literature*. University of Minnesota Press, 2017.

Gorman, Alice, C. *Dr Space Junk vs the Universe: Archaeology and the Future*. NewSouth Books, 2019.

Hokari, Minoru. *Gurindji Journey: A Japanese Historian in the Outback*. University of New South Wales Press, 2011.

Holmes, Matthew. "Perspectives on Biotechnology: Public and Corporate Narratives in the GM Archives." *Plants People Planet*, vol. 4, 2022, pp. 476-84.

Latour, Bruno. *Facing Gaia: Eight Lectures on the New Climate Regime*. Polity Press, 2017.

Lemm, Vanessa. *Homo Natura: Nietzsche, Philosophical Anthropology and Biopolitics*. Edinburgh University Press, 2020.

---. "Posthumanism and Plant Studies." In *Palgrave Handbook of Critical Posthumanism*, edited by S. Herbrechter et al., Palgrave, 2022, pp. 1-18.

Lindahl, Hans. *Authority and the Globalisation of Inclusion and Exclusion.* Cambridge University Press, 2018.

Marder, Michael. *Plant-Thinking: A Philosophy of Vegetal Life.* Columbia University Press, 2013.

Nealon, Jeffrey, T. *Plant Theory: Biopower and Vegetable Life.* Stanford University Press, 2016.

Nietzsche, Friedrich. *Die Fröhliche Wissenschaft, in Kritische Gesammtausgabe.* De Grutyer, 1988.

Plato, *The Timaeus.* Gutenberg ebooks.

Robin, Marie-Monique. *The World* according *to Monsanto: Pollution, Corruption, and the Control of the World's Food Supply,* translated by George Holoch, New Press, 2010.

Sheetz, Michael. "Elon Musk Wants SpaceX To Reach Mars So Humanity Is Not a 'Single-Planet Species." *CNBC,* 23 Apr. 2021, https://www.cnbc.com/2021/04/23/elon-musk-aiming-for-mars-so-humanity-is-not-a-single-planet-species.html.

Sloterdijk, Peter. *Globes: Spheres II: Macrospherology.* MIT Press, 2014.

Spivak, Gayatri. "Planetarity." *The Dictionary of Untranslateables,* edited by Barbara Cassin, translated by Steven Rendeall et al., Princeton University Press, 2014, p. 1223.

Vanessa Lemm

7   **Against the Static Herbarium: Hidden Materialities of Spit, Fish Glue, and Mercury**

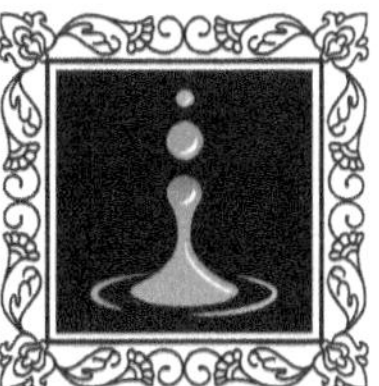

Heather Rogers and Nick Koenig

Opening the Cabinet Doors

Visiting a herbarium is truly a somatic experience: the unique scents as the cabinets open, the feel of the herbarium voucher paper as one carefully moves it out of the folders, the movement of dirt and botanical matter that gathered over time in the margins, surprise at the softness of the cotton within an orchid labella decades after it was delicately placed there. Examining a botanical voucher up close can reveal much more than the information captured on the voucher label. Herbaria are often perceived to be quiet, static repositories of botanical histories. Instead, if you look closely, herbaria reveal themselves to be sites of materialities converging, affecting, and (e)merging with one another across time.

However, before we enter the herbarium as a site of engagement, we first wish to foreground our own positionalities and places of writing, as these both are deeply woven into our own scholarship; we will do so through a brief presentation of our self-locations (Matsaw and Spang Gion; Liboiron; Haraway). We both hold within our pursuits of being scholars-activists (Ramasubramanian and Sousa) the importance of our queer identities and dedication to the more-than-human worlds—especially plants. Nick is a queer, genderfluid climate justice activist and tree-ring scientist who comes from a white settler background and is writing from the traditional homelands of the Nimíipuu, Palus, and Schitsu'umsh peoples. Heather is a queer, cisgender digital environmental humanist who comes from a white settler background and is writing from the traditional homelands of the Haudenosaunee and Anishinabeg nations. Pushing beyond a land acknowledgment (Stewart-Ambo and Yang), at the front of our thinking and understanding of herbaria is that the plants collected and housed in herbaria across the United States and Canada are from predominantly privileged, white cisgender-heterosexual-men who resided on stolen lands. Therefore, in our writing, we hope to explore the hidden materials within collections that have been marginalised by the dominant scientific arguments (Liboiron; Liboiron, Higgins, and Tolbert).

In addition to a new materialist approach to herbarium preservation, we apply the feminist epistemology of situated knowledge and make space to weave in our own situated experiences with herbaria collections. In doing so, we invite you, the reader, into our material, embodied experiences of plants. Applying a feminist epistemology to botanical history creates room for the situated knowledges of women and other historically marginalised communities. Coining the expression "situated knowledge," Donna Haraway's feminist epistemology advocates for elevating the position of the partial, subjective knower in knowledge creation. Situated knowledge thus opens up space for personal experiences and observations and, in doing so, argues for "a more adequate, richer, better account of a world, in order to live in it well and in critical, reflexive relation to our own as well as others' practices" (Braidotti 579). This approach unsettles the idea that only certain kinds of botanical knowledge creation are valued and, therefore, worthy of consideration. It instead advocates for a broader, more inclusive mosaic of human and vegetal stories. In turning to the histories of foregrounding embodiment, gaps in records and narratives about contributions to botanical knowledge creation and preservation can be filled by incorporating subjective, situated experiences. Moreover, a new materialist approach pushes back against the idea that the more-than-human around us is not worthy of notice or consideration. Bringing in a situated and material approach, our chapter focuses on preparation and preservation by centring our discussion on the material agents that can bind, extend, and even damage plant futures. Further bringing new materialism into the halls of the herbarium, we hope to extend our pursuit of an anticolonial framework for collecting, curating, and preserving plant life.

This chapter aims to experiment and play with these more-than-human stories through a new materialist reading of the herbarium as a site of convergence and emergence of multiple materialities. The effects of these material convergences can be found on each sheet and within each envelope, making their way onto or around the specimens years after they were first collected, and even affecting the human bodies who enter the herbarium. In turning our attention to not only the plants, but also the other elements of herbarium vouchers, such as glue, dust, spit, and mercury, we specifically draw on political scientist Jane Bennett's vibrant materialism, which calls for noticing the vibrant materialities around us that often get overlooked or are given less attention. As Bennett

Heather Rogers and Nick Koenig

posits in *Vibrant Matter*, "we are vital materiality and we are surrounded by it, though we do not always see it that way" (14).

Collections at First Glance

> *Heather: As I opened the herbarium cabinets at McGill University in search of an Ajuga pyramidalis collected a century earlier in the Swiss Alps, I was struck by that indescribable, earthy scent that all those who have entered a herbarium will be familiar with. The Lamiaceae cabinets were my favourites to sort through as I checked my way down a faded list of plants that I wanted to digitise. Despite many of the specimens dating well over a century, I was always greeted with the faint aroma of mint as I stood on the stepstool carefully searching the folder labels. When I found the voucher that I needed, I took a moment to peer down, letting my eyes move beyond the voucher label. Tiny air bubbles caught in the glue, small rust-coloured foxing dotted the paper, a slight ink smudge on the label, the tiniest flecks of dirt in the crease of the folder, someone's faded handwritten "Labiatae" in the bottom left corner. The more I looked, the more I forgot about recording information from the label that detailed where and when this plant was collected. Instead, I was fascinated by the material aspects that had made their way onto the sheet, merging with the flowers. The information on the label now seemed to be only part, and not the entirety, of this voucher's story.*

Although herbarium sheet labels vary in detail, they tend to highlight the human sets of relations involved in the collection and identification of the specimens, as well as the information included about the institutions where the voucher was housed. Often found at the bottom right corner of the voucher label are the scientific name and the common name of the plant, the date of collection, the name(s) of the person(s) who did the collecting, and the name(s) of the person(s) who made the identification. More detailed herbarium specimen labels might contain additional digitally printed, typewritten, or handwritten notes with first-hand accounts of the environment where the plant lived and the ecological assemblage that it was part of. Herbarium vouchers also speak to cultural understandings through the inclusion of common names in different languages, and to the plant's significance within local, Indigenous communities. Regardless of the size of the institution or the breadth of the collection, each herbarium is "a place, a landscape ... where the experience of people connecting with nature is revealed" (Humphreys 13). Stepping into a herbarium and opening up cabinets can reveal records of multispecies stories across time and place.

Literature: Grounding Our Conversations

New Materialism is an interdisciplinary field that foregrounds the vibrancy of matter in order to problematise and unsettle human-centred paradigms that deny matter agency and creativity. The term "new materialism" can be traced to Manual De Landa and Rosi Braidotti, who draw on the post-structuralist thinkers Gilles Deleuze and Felix Guattari in order to explore the idea of complex interconnectedness between bodies (Braidotti and Hlavajova 277). In focusing on the interconnectedness that links humans and more-than-humans, new materialists seek to unsettle the idea that agency is restricted to humans and instead point to the agency that exists with the more-than-human world. As Jeffrey Scott Marchand powerfully explains, an expanded understanding of agency "forces us to reconfigure and 'reterritorialise' the human within a volatile mix of agencies, beings, and forces, where the human is only one among a multiplicity of agents who are active in determining and enacting our (human or not) future possibilities" (Marchand 294). Humans are part of a vibrant web that can affect but, in turn, also be affected.

Challenging Cartesian dualistic paradigms of animate/inanimate, human/nature, subject/object, and human/nonhuman, New Materialism rejects the belief in the uniqueness of human agency that is opposed to matter's passivity. While some scholars critique this removal of dualisms as a flat ontology that completely erases differences between bodies, New Materialism instead offers a complex, interwoven framing of bodies. Moreover, by rejecting reductive and separate categories for humans and more-than-humans, New Materialism advocates for a relational ontology that acknowledges porous boundaries and complex interconnectedness. Such thinking underscores humans' connection to the material world through shared materiality and, in doing so, advocates for a system of justice, care, and inclusivity of the more-than-human world. In moving beyond binaries, New Materialism serves as a "research methodology for the non-dualistic study of the world within, beside and among ... the world that precedes, includes and exceeds us" (Van der Tuin 277).

New Materialists evoke the Deleuzoguattarian concept of assemblages to visualise the diverse and emergent convergences of matter. Within ecological studies, the term "assemblage" is used to describe meta-communities comprised of multiple species that often interact: the term also points to "variation

                                     Heather Rogers and Nick Koenig

in either species' behaviour, space or time that allows for the persistence of interlinked communities" (Stroud et al. 4761). Thinking through the literal and metaphorical meanings of the assemblage, as they are used across disciplines, can help to shift how humans see themselves in relation to the natural world (Stroud et al.). Moreover, in elevating the status of materiality, Bennett advocates for re-imagining humans' place in the order of things, not at the centre but in relation with more-than-human life. Entangled and linked, we argue for viewing herbaria through a new materialist lens in order to witness "a particularly rich and complex collection of materials" that can be found inside cabinets and on voucher sheets (Bennett 11).

In applying a New Materialist lens, we centre our discussion on the variety of intersections of human and more-than-human collaborations in herbaria. We choose to use the term "more-than-human" rather than "non-human" when describing beings within the natural world. As Carlos Roberto Bernardes de Souza Júnior explains, the term "more-than-human" encompasses the interconnectedness between, with, and beyond humans and thereby rejects the binary of nature and culture. Language is tricky, however, and, as Max Liboiron attests, both "non-human" and "more-than-human" inadvertently re-centre the human in discussions, when humans are not the focal point. One of the hopes of critical plant studies and New Materialist discourse is for new terminology that encapsulates interconnectedness and moves beyond humans as the centre (Souza Júnior; Liboiron). In focusing on herbarium collections, we extend this hope to include a new approach to analysing the practices of specimen collection, preparation, and preservation—especially to the methods and materials used in the preparation and mounting of specimens—so that we can move often unnoticed materialities to centre stage. A New Materialist attention to various materialities that constitute herbaria, we argue, helps us to fine-tune what we detect and turn our attention to how we can understand herbaria not simply as static, inactive rooms, but rather as sites of deeply vibrant botanical, chemical, and elemental materialities that continue to (inter)act with one another.

Digital and Material Futures of Herbaria

Before engaging with the physical materials of herbaria, we would be remiss if we did not consider the emerging materialities within herbaria during the twenty-first century—the digital technologies and renderings of specimens. The digital offers a multitude of ways to view, experience, and connect with the vegetal. According to Anna Lawrence, "speculative play with vegetal life invites different modes of attention" (Lawrence 640). Zooming in on an image of a preserved plant, one can see traces of cotton inside a flower, air bubbles in glue formed when a plant was mounted, discolouration on the paper in the shape of leaves once affixed to paper but lost at some point in time. Such zooming in can happen quite easily in a digital world, allowing us to discover the plant specimen from a new perspective and bringing previously un(der)noticed attributes into focus. There are affective elements to interacting with digital representations of materiality or "distant natures," that is, nature that is not experienced directly in person but transmitted using digital media and data (Jørgensen 109).

There are many significant, new insights that digitisation has granted to herbaria, conservation biologists, digital environmental humanists, environmental historians, and, more generally, anyone with computer and internet access. Quite literally, digitisation has opened the material cabinets—mercury-tainted and moth-ball-scented—to someone sitting across the world. However, this comes at the cost of removing the physical sensing of the plant and the material and political entanglements in which the specimen is situated. Unlike museum exhibits, herbaria present no barrier or divide between people and their collections. To hold an envelope containing preserved lichen and watch the broken pieces vibrate with each unfolding of the protective covering or to examine up close the wisps of a cotton ball that a botanist stuffed into an orchid's labellum decades before is to feel connected with a botanical memory. As John Charles Ryan explains, "memory is latent and affective—its dimensions contingent upon, and instigated by, the materiality of objects" (93). Ryan acknowledges a kind of botanical memory, which he defines as a "form of environmental or place-based memory focused on remembrances of plants; and encompassing individual and collective practices that instigate and sustain such recollections" (90). A New Materialist view thus reveals, to borrow an image from Ann Laura Stoler, the pulse of the herbarium—a vibrant, lively site of human-plant-material convergence in which all three elements continue to act upon one another even well after a plant has been collected and preserved (Stoler 232). In this way, it challenges the misconception of plants and herbaria as static. As Dani Stuchel reminds us, "though we may shape … material entities for human purposes, they are material things which change in ways proper to their materiality without regard for our desire to remember and prove" (14). Rather than viewing archives as sites of documents, Ann Laura Stoler coined the term "pulse of the archive" to capture the tensions and emotions within archival records of colonialism (228). A New Materialist approach to engaging with herbarium collections makes space for including the often missed or ignored elements and, consequently, allows us to take the "pulse" of the herbarium and come to understand its more-than-human stories in a deeper, richer way.

Herbaria as Sites of Vibrant Materiality

The botanical world, whether growing in the wild or preserved in herbaria, often goes unnoticed to devastating effect. The disenchanted misconception of plants as immobile, rooted beings, perpetually fixed in the ground where they sprouted up feeds into forgetting the presence of plants in our everyday life. This is an unfortunate reality so pervasive that it warrants its own term, that is, "plant awareness disparity" (Parsley 599), in which the "art of noticing" (Tsing 17) tends to start and stop at the charismatic megafauna (Tsing et al.). Also referred to as "plant blindness," a term introduced in 1999 by James H. Wandersee and Elisabeth E. Schussler, this concept is predominantly used to describe the tendency to overlook plants or relegate them to background figures. However, we choose to echo Kathryn M. Parsley's approach of using the term "plant awareness disparity" (PAD) as a non-ableist alternative (599). Rather than framing disability negatively, PAD speaks to the same issue of not noticing plants and instead advocates for raising individual awareness and appreciation of botanical lives.

A New Materialist perspective pushes back against such a misconception of plants as immobile and rooted, and indeed herbaria are ideal places for examining the convergence of different materialities since each voucher is an assemblage of chemical, elemental, and biotic matter. Herbarium preservation requires a keen understanding of the various materialities that make their way onto specimen sheets and storage cabinets. Curators and herbarium staff need a keen understanding of chemical interactions and integrated pest management (IPM), as well as knowledge of how plant chemicals and pheromones might react when introduced to agents meant to preserve and protect them. The process of collecting and preserving a specimen before mounting it is thus a delicate dance of timing, change, and both detected and undetected chemical reactions. As Iovino and Opperman explain, "all matter—even the one that we do not see, sense, or suspect—constantly interacts with other matter, whether in human or nonhuman forms" (7). Those familiar with herbarium preservation methods will have their own stories of material encounters involving glue, cotton, tape, dust, mould, and bugs. In viewing herbaria as sites of material convergences, we argue that herbarium specimens can be understood as lively material records that contain multiple stories of human-plant-matter entanglements. As Dani Stuchel explains, "what we regularly describe as conservation or preservation can be reinterpreted as the selective unfolding of material possibilities to create a desired assemblage of vibrant matter" (15).

Herbarium Roots

Herbaria find their origin in the work of Luca Ghini, a professor at the University of Bologna in the early 1500s (Thiers 14-15). Initially referred to as *hortus hiemalis* (winter garden) or *hortus siccus* (dry garden), the herbarium was created by gathering fresh plants and pressing them between sheets of paper to be flattened until they were ready to be mounted and described (Thiers 14). Each plant specimen, referred to as a "voucher," is "a pressed and dried sample of an individual containing aboveground structures (leaves, stems, flowers, and/ or fruits) and below ground structures when possible" (Culley 1). Diane Bridson and Leonard Forman recognise diverse types of herbaria that serve different audiences and functions (6). While some are meant for educational purposes and are housed in universities and colleges, others are analogous to museums and special collections, meant for both educational and public interest. Herbaria are increasingly considered valuable repositories of botanical history that can be analysed to understand both changes to ecosystems due to climate change and genetic aspects of genera and the occasional personal collections kept in private or public by passionate botanists. We use the word "value" here intentionally and critically, as the perceived "value" of herbaria is usually inscribed by powerful institutions and the dominant trends in science and is usually centred around how specimens are extracted for data and information rather than around the dazzling, entangled assemblages of storied histories that the herbaria offer. Additionally, scholars focused on the human side of herbarium collections can use the information included on voucher labels to research and credit collectors and identifiers from historically marginalised communities if relevant details appear on the specimen label. This disambiguation work could not be done without building networks of herbarium collections to create a web of links between botanists, collectors, and illustrators (Groom et al. 4).

Hidden Materials for Surveying & Exploring

Specimen Mounting—Spit

> *Nick: Mounting specimens is quite the queer and embodied experience. Sitting in the strictly temperature- and humidity-controlled room, I was wrapped in my jacket that usually sits on the Eastern Kentucky University herbarium wooden coat hook. The sun was shining brightly outside on the hot day as I was planted in the chilly indoors. I opened the file cabinet and grabbed a folder of newspaper-wrapped specimens. There they were, waiting to be affixed to the acid-free mounting paper. I gingerly opened the first specimen and saw running buffalo clover or Trifolium stoloniferum and knew what must be done—a salivary infusion. The "water"-activated, gummed cloth tape is the best way to mount more delicate plant materials like the clover's arm-like appendages—stolons—upon the paper. I cut out a long strip, placed it on the dorsal surface of my tongue, closed, and waited for the subtle taste of adhesive to titillate my tastebuds. Placing the slippery tape over the stolon onto the paper, I pressed and waited for it to air-dry. Finishing up, I grabbed the metal washers, laid them on the tape strips, and moved onto the next plant. Twenty-four hours later, the clover was filed away with its relatives in a storied world written on the label and embodied on the paper: spit and all.*

Other curators have since told me this practice is not necessary (Link-Perez, personal communication, 2021), and a small cup of water works just as well, but for the time being, I continue this practice for the sake of infusing and giving an offering of some sorts to the queer kinship in my curation practice (Hazard). The materiality involved in mounting specimens draws attention to the diversity of plant forms and bodies. Often when approaching a plant specimen for affixing it to the paper, curators give much consideration to the ways the specific species of plant will respond. Users of herbaria will frequently encounter, to borrow Dani Stuchel's phrasing, "frustrating and resistant materiality" (3), which can affect the longevity and appearance of specimens. For some species, it is necessary to apply a light wash of watered-down glue via a paintbrush to the specimen. Other plants might require a heavier dotting of glue followed by a strip of gummed cloth tape to secure the edges of leaves or other plant parts. The variety of mounting practices in itself—especially when we focus on the materiality of specimens—illustrates the embodied practice of the human-plant-glue entanglements situated within a single collection. Most curators who mount specimens are never mentioned in a specific collection, yet considering the gummed cloth tape materials evokes the mentioned and unmentioned histories of herbarium specimens. Not only are these tape materials entangled with one another, but the salivary offering is "rather saturated with other material, cultural, and cognitive elements" (Jue and Ruiz 9). The saliva embedded in the tape and plant traces an invisible history of humans tending to the futures of botanical collections; this history remains invisible—and maybe for the better?

Specimen Mounting—Glue

Along with human traces in specimen mounting, historical collections contain elemental and bodily remains of marine life. Known as ichthyocolla, or isinglass, fish paste made from the collagen-rich swim bladder of sturgeon fish was used to fix herbarium specimens to paper (Duffin). As Chris Duffin explains, an increasingly open trade between Russia and Europe made Russia the main exporter of beluga sturgeon for the production of Europe's isinglass in the seventeenth and eighteenth centuries. The application of isinglass as an adhesive for herbaria was recorded by Carl Linneaus, who detailed his use of ichthyocolla for his own plant collections. The merging of animal and plant matter continued to characterise herbarium specimen preservation. As William MacGillivray and William Withering detail in *A Systematic Arrangement of British Plants*:

> Let a number of narrow slips of different lengths be cut from a piece
> of the same paper, and let some prepared *isinglass* or dissolved gum
> tragacanth or gum arabic be in readiness, together with a camel-hair
> pencil. Take a dried plant, lay it upon a leaf of the fine cut paper, then
> fasten it down by means of a few slips of paper, to which *isinglass* or
> gum has been applied, across the stem and some of the branches ...
> In this manner all the dried plants destined to form part of the her-
> barium are treated (42; emphasis our own).

What might appear at first as just clear adhesive on historical specimens instead, when viewed through a New Materialist lens, can be described as a curious mix of animal, and sometimes human, elements collected and transported across space. These elements are, in turn, used to temporally preserve dynamic botanical histories. As Bennett explains, "vital materialists will thus try to linger in those moments during which they find themselves fascinated by

Heather Rogers and Nick Koenig

objects, taking them as clues to the material vitality that they share with them" (17). Lingering in these moments, we might ask: what more materials might be lurking in the files of vegetal matter? With a focus narrowed to the subtle levels of a voucher and by exploring the material convergences in herbaria that link together human and vegetal bodies, as well as chemical and abiotic matter, at the most minute levels, a New Materialist understanding of herbaria underscores that "we are entangled with their material agency and emerge together as storied beings" (Iovino and Oppermann 8). Plants, spit, glue, and everything in between.

Specimen Preservation—Mercury

Specimen preservation needs to take several factors into account that could alter or damage the specimen irreversibly. Insects are one such agent. Though small enough to be missed, the damage insects cause can have far-reaching effects. As Bridson and Forman explain, insect damage from aptly named herbarium beetles, booklice, and silverfish must be taken into consideration when preserving and maintaining herbarium collections (14-15). While specimens coming into the herbarium are placed in a freezer for "decontamination" before mounting, damage from potential insect damage must be factored in even after specimens are preserved and stored in the herbaria. Desiccant dust made from diatomaceous earth or silica can be spread around the cabinets to draw moisture out of the bodies of insects, thereby killing them before they can damage the specimens. Biocides derived from plants themselves, such as camphor, lavender oil-derived linalool, thymol, wild rosemary, and cedar oil, have also been used to prevent insect damage. Magdalena Grenda-Kurmanow notes that natural mixtures of clove and aloe as well as a concoction of wormwood and santonica were previously used for glue, although the latter was found to change the colour of the specimens after mounting (123).

Until the 1980s, collections in herbaria were often disinfected using a mix of mercuric chloride and ethanol (Havermans, Dekker, and Sportel). Positioned as a first line of defense against insect damage, mercuric chloride (also known historically as corrosive sublimate) was used to disinfect specimens when placing them in a herbarium collection. As J. P. Brown attested in an 1837 issue of *The Magazine of Natural History*, corrosive sublimate was declared to be more effective than camphor, another prevention method, because it not only shielded plants from insect damage, but also "preserv[ed] the colours and fresh appearance of the plants" (315). Walter Hough, who served as assistant curator for the ethology division from 1896 to 1910 and then later transitioned to the anthropology division in the United States National Museum, was technically curious in the cataloguing and preservation of museum collections (Judd 473). In 1887, Hough stated:

> The preservation of museum specimens is of no less importance than their acquisition. Periodically the attack of some new insect, or the infesting of some *new material*, is brought to the notice of curators, and hitherto many specimens have been destroyed which it would be now impossible to replace. In a great museum the abundance of the material will not permit its frequent examination, so that all specimens should be *thoroughly poisoned* before they get out of sight. There are many things which one would not think it necessary to poison, yet all should be, for nearly all organic structures have peculiar enemies in the insect world. As instances, woodwork, basketry, textiles, *botanical specimens, etc., should be poisoned* with corrosive sublimate, as it coagulates the albuminoid principles in vegetation and thereby prevents decay as well as the attacks of insects. (549; emphasis our own)

Hough later goes on to state:

> Before poisoning, all objects should be treated with benzine, by putting them in a close box or vessel, and pouring the benzine in, leaving them tightly closed therein for several days. This operation destroys any larvae or eggs (552-53).

While Hough was much concerned with botanical specimen preservation, his material considerations about specimen preservation are fascinating especially when considered in the context the modern health concerns. In the efforts to achieve long-term preservation of botanical specimens, there can be an inverse effect on human longevity through the introduction of toxic chemicals like mercury chloride. Moreover, John Havermans, René Dekker, and Ron Sportel have speculated that mercuric chloride's effect on herbarium specimens can be noticed up close as discoloration (7). Bridson and Forman echo this observation by explaining how mercuric chloride will often crystallise, giving the specimens a hairy appearance (20). Prior to the 1960s, plant collections were often soaked in mercury chloride to avoid the risk of introducing insects into the main herbarium cabinets (Webber, Ernest, and Vangapandu). The paper and the plants affixed to the paper were saturated with these toxic chemicals to

Heather Rogers and Nick Koenig

"protect" them from insects, while unintentionally posing a threat to humans (Jue and Ruiz).

The paradox of preservation within the materialities of herbaria was rendered tangible during Nick Koenig's time as the Assistant Curator of the Eastern Kentucky University Herbarium (EKY Collection), when there was discussion of adopting the University of Kentucky (UK) Herbarium. The merging of small- to medium-sized herbaria is becoming increasingly common within the United States due to decreasing funding for natural history collections. As of 2021, the future of many Kentucky herbaria remains uncertain because of the insufficient funding to housing these histories of botanical biodiversity. But the materiality of mercury can further complicate the futures of herbaria, for the presence of mercury has prevented the merging of the UK herbarium with many regional herbaria. Collections that have not used mercuric chloride are hesitant to adopt other collections that have deployed this chemical, as they would thus add these "poisons" to "unpoisoned" collections. Moreover, serious considerations and protocols must be taken by humans wishing to work with mercury-saturated vouchers, for the chemicals can sublimate even fifty years after preservation application (Webber, Ernest, and Vangapandu). Mercuric chloride thus complicates and collapses the material pasts, presents, and futures of plant collections, yet again pushing against the flat ontological paradigm written over herbaria.

Keeping the Cabinet Open

Across this chapter, we have explored how glue, spit, mercury, and a multitude of "planty," more-than-human, and non-human materials can be woven into New Materialist tales and create interactions among herbaria, environmental history, and personal narratives to push against the predominant notion of the static herbarium. Vouchers invite closer examination, not only of the plants themselves but of the materialities that allow us to study them across time and place. Traces of fish from global trade, human saliva from curators, and the chemicals once used to disinfect, in turn, pose invisible threats. A New Materialist examination of herbaria can spark curiosity, inviting us to look more closely and discover previously unnoticed and unwritten stories. As scholars with deep appreciation for herbaria, we wanted to include our own material experiences that left their marks on us. This exploration started out with the physical preparation of the plant and materials used in affixing the specimen to the paper with spit and fish glue. This is followed by a discussion of the elemental precarity of mercury's influence on the politics and preservation of plants. We hold ever present and at the forefront of our approach our own individual and shared self-locations, which are integral to the production of our writings with plants. These self-locations serve as invitations for fellow more-than-human activists, thinkers, and scholars to join us in pushing against plant awareness disparity. Lastly, we find these interventions and future collaborations with plants to be ever fruitful in amplifying the beautiful, storied worlds contained within herbarium cabinets. We invite you, reader, to think of your own material experiences in herbaria. By looking closer, what unwritten stories can you discover?

Works Cited

Anderson, M. Kat, and Michael J. Moratto. "Native American Land-Use Practices and Ecological Impacts." *Sierra Nevada Ecosystem Project: Final Report to Congress*, edited by University of California Davis: Centers for Water and Wildland Resources, vol. 2, 1996, pp. 187-206.

Bennett, Jane. *Vibrant Matter: A Political Ecology of Things*. Duke University Press, 2010.

Braidotti, Rosi. *Posthuman Knowledge*. vol. 2, Polity Press, 2019.

Braidotti, Rosi, and Maria Hlavajova, eds. *Posthuman Glossary*. Bloomsbury Publishing, 2018.

Brown, J. P. "On the Preservation of Botanical Specimens from the Attacks of Insects." *Magazine of Natural History*, Charlesworth Edition, vol. 1, 1837, pp. 311-15.

Culley, Theresa M. "Why Vouchers Matter in Botanical Research." *Applications in Plant Sciences*, vol. 1, no. 11, 2013, pp. 1-5.

Deleuze, Gilles, and Félix Guattari. *A Thousand Plateaus: Capitalism and Schizophrenia*. Bloomsbury Publishing, 1988.

Duffin, Christopher J. "Ichthyocolla: Medicinal 'Fish Glue.'" *Pharmaceutical Historian*, vol. 49, no. 4, 2019, pp. 116-22.

Forman, Leonard, and Diane Bridson, eds. *The Herbarium Handbook*. Royal Botanic Gardens, 1989.

Grenda-Kurmanow, Magdalena. "Review of Biocides Used as Prevention and Intervention Measures for Historic Artefacts, with Special Regard to Herbaria Collections." *Notes Konserwatorski*, vol. 21, 2019, pp. 121-61.

Groom, Quentin, et al. "The Disambiguation of People Names in Biological Collections." *Biodiversity Data Journal*, vol. 1, no. 10, 2022, pp. 1-37.

Heather Rogers and Nick Koenig

Haraway, Donna. "Situated Knowledges: The Science Question in Feminism and the Privilege of Partial Perspective." *Space, Gender, Knowledge: Feminist Readings*, edited by Linda McDowell and Joanne Sharp, Routledge, 2016, pp. 53-72.

Havermans, John, et al. "The Effect of Mercuric Chloride Treatment as Biocide for Herbaria on the Indoor Air Quality." *Heritage Science*, vol. 3, 2015, pp. 1-8.

Hazard, Cleo Wölfle. *Underflows: Queer Trans Ecologies and River Justice.* University of Washington Press, 2022.

Hough, Walter. "The Preservation of Museum Specimens from Insects and the Effects of Dampness." *Report of the United States National Museum for the Year Ending June 30, 1887 (Pt. 2 of the Annual Report of the Board of Regents of the Smithsonian Institution for the Year ending June 30, 1887)*, edited by The National Museum, 1897, pp. 549-558.

Humphreys, Helen. *Field Study: Meditations on a Year at the Herbarium.* ECW Press, 2021.

Iovino, Serenella, and Serpil Oppermann. "Introduction: Stories Come to Matter." *Material Ecocriticism*, edited by Iovino and Oppermann, Indiana University Press, 2014, pp. 1-17.

Jørgensen, Finn Arne. "The Armchair Traveler's Guide to Digital Environmental Humanities." *Environmental Humanities*, vol 4, no. 1, 2014, pp. 95-112.

Judd, Neil M. "Walter Hough: An Appreciation." *American Anthropologist*, vol. 38, no. 3, 1936, pp. 471-81.

Jue, Melody. "The Media of Seaweeds: Between Kelp Forest and Archive." *Saturation: An Elemental Politics*, edited by Melody Jue and Rafico Ruiz, Duke University Press, 2021, pp. 185-204.

Jue, Melody, and Rafico Ruiz. "Thinking with Saturation beyond Water: Thresholds, Phase Change, and the Precipitate." *Saturation: An Elemental Politics*, edited by Melody Jue and Rafico Ruiz, Duke University Press, 2021, pp. 1-26.

Kimmerer, Robin Wall, and Frank Kanawha Lake. "The Role of Indigenous Burning in Land Management." *Journal of Forestry*, vol. 99, no. 11, 2001, pp. 36-41.

Koenig, Nicholas, et al. "Phylogenetic Placement of Trifolium kentuckiense (Fabaceae), a New Member of the Native Eastern North American Clover Clade." *Castanea*, vol. 86, no. 2, 2022, pp. 283-95.

Lang, Patricia L. M., et al. "Using Herbaria to Study Global Environmental Change." *New Phytologist*, vol. 221, no. 1, 2019, pp. 110-22.

Lawrence, Anna M. "Listening to Plants: Conversations between Critical Plant Studies and Vegetal Geography." *Progress in Human Geography*, vol. 46, no. 2, 2022, pp. 629-51.

Liboiron, Max. *Pollution Is Colonialism.* Duke University Press, 2021.

Liboiron, Max, Marc Higgins, and Sara Tolbert. "In Conversation with Max Liboiron: Towards an Everyday, Anticolonial Feminist Science (Education) Practice." *Reimagining Science Education in the Anthropocene*, vol. 2, Springer International Publishing, 2023, pp. 343-361.

Marchand, Jeffrey Scott. "Non-Human Agency." *Posthuman Glossary*, edited by Rosi Braidotti and Maria Hlavajova, Bloomsbury Publishing, 2018, p. 294.

Marder, Michael. *Plant-Thinking: A Philosophy of Vegetal Life*. Columbia University Press, 2013.

Matsaw, Jessica, and Shanny Spang Gion. "Indigenous Mentoring Program Workshop Series." Apr. 2023.

Parsley, Kathryn M. "Plant Awareness Disparity: A Case for Renaming Plant Blindness." *Plants, People, Planet*, vol. 2, no. 6, 2020, pp. 598-601.

Ramasubramanian, Srividya, and Alexandra N. Sousa. "Communication Scholar-Activism: Conceptualising Key Dimensions and Practices Based on Interviews with Scholar-activists." *Journal of Applied Communication Research*, vol. 49, no. 5, 2021, pp. 477-96.

Ryan, John Charles. "Passive Flora?: Reconsidering Nature's Agency through Human-Plant Studies (HPS)." *Societies*, vol. 2, no. 3, 2012, pp. 101-21.

Ryan, John Charles. "The Substance of Memory: Plants, Objects, and Affect." *Journal of Literature and Art Studies*, vol. 6, no. 1, 2016, pp. 89-99.

Souza Júnior, Carlos Roberto Bernardes de. "More-Than-Human Cultural Geographies towards Co-Dwelling on Earth." *Mercator (Fortaleza)*, vol. 20, 2021, pp. 1-10.

Stewart-Ambo, Theresa, and K. Wayne Yang. "Beyond Land Acknowledgment in Settler Institutions." *Social Text*, vol. 39, no. 1, 2021, pp. 21-46.

Stoler, Ann Laura. "The Pulse of the Archive." *Ab Imperio*, vol. 3, 2007, pp. 225-64.

Stroud, James T., et al. "Is a Community Still a Community?: Reviewing Definitions of Key Terms in Community Ecology." *Ecology and Evolution*, vol. 5, no. 21, 2015, pp. 4757-65.

Stuchel, Dani. "Material Provocations in the Archives." *Journal of Critical Library and Information Studies*, vol. 3, no. 1, 2020, pp. 1-25.

TallBear, Kim. "Beyond the Life/Not-Life Binary: A Feminist-Indigenous Reading of Cryopreservation, Interspecies Thinking, and the New Materialisms." *Cryopolitics: Frozen Life in a Melting World*, edited by Joanna Radin and Emma Kowal, Duke University Press, 2017, pp. 179-202.

Thiers, Barbara M. *Herbarium: The Quest to Preserve and Classify the World's Plants*. Timber Press, 2020.

                                    Heather Rogers and Nick Koenig

Tsing, Anna Lowenhaupt. *The Mushroom at the End of the World: On the Possibility of Life in Capitalist Ruins.* Princeton University Press, 2015.

Tsing, Anna Lowenhaupt, et al., eds. *Arts of Living on a Damaged Planet: Ghosts and Monsters of the Anthropocene.* University of Minnesota Press, 2017.

Van der Tuin, Iris. "Neo/New Materialism." *Posthuman Glossary*, edited by Rosi Braidotti and Maria Hlavajova, Bloomsbury Publishing, 2018, p. 277.

Wandersee, James H., and Elisabeth E. Schussler. "Preventing Plant Blindness." *The American Biology Teacher*, vol. 61, no. 2, 1999, pp. 82-86.

Webber, W. Brent, et al. "Mercury Exposures in University Herbarium Collections." *Journal of Chemical Health & Safety*, vol. 18, no. 2, 2011, pp. 11-14.

Withering, William, and William MacGillivray. *A Systematic Arrangement of British Plants.* Scott, Webster, and Geary, 1841.

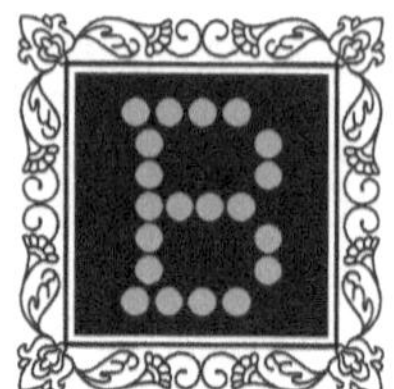

8 Baroa Belaobara: An Artist- and Plant-Based Work Tying Language and Creatures into Hybrid Beings

Bart Vandeput

Introduction

In 2009, I was first introduced to hundreds of plants in the wet clay soil just outside a town in the midwestern area of Latvia. These plants were presented to me as *Aronija*.[1] In 2015, a Latvian microbiologist stated at the arts centre near the plantation that *Aronija* is an apple and not a berry. During one of many wanderings on a rewilded berry-apple plantation also in this region, I suddenly hear and see the following dotted letter sequence: "Baroa belaobara." I interpret this experience as a signal of the name change that needs to be taken artiseriously: all human-given names for the plants, be they common or scientific, need to be replaced by "Baroa belaobara." Soon after, I perceive a mental graphic image. Instantaneously, I interpret it as the becoming-shape of the fruit of the plant.

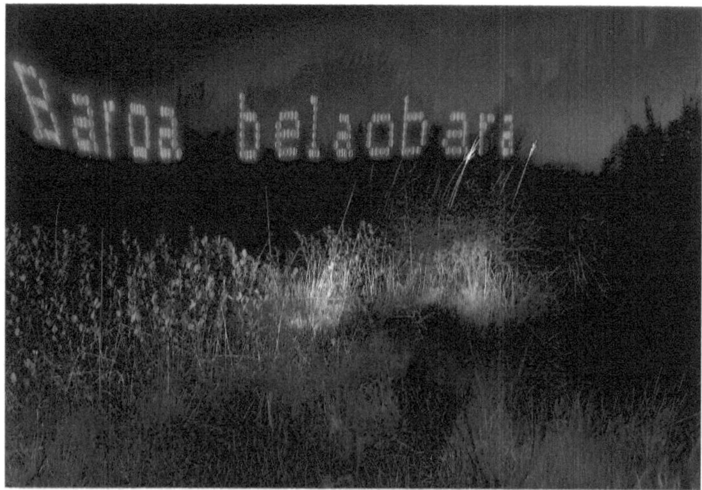

Figure 1. Reporting the new name Baroa belaobara to its plantation, using the Pixelstick device. (Image courtesy of Bartaku, CC-NC-SA 3.0).

Below I share the up-to-date findings of one strand of the artistic inquiries that are fused with this plant. These findings have to do with human and plant-human ways of referring to the plant through linguistic means, by naming.[2]

In the first section, I describe the visual and acoustic experience of "Baroa belaobara," which I interpret and commit to as a name change for the main plantation plant, *Aronija*. Next, I summarise the common and scientific naming of the plant. A restorative cutting of the rewilded plantation then creates the awareness that "Baroa belaobara" refers to *something* other than *Aronija*. In the subsequent discussion section, I aim to explore this evolving historical and situated naming narrative at the intersection of scientific, indigenous, and artistic naming approaches to a plant/ation. I conclude with a sense of yearning for an existing, ineffable[3] archive of naming.

Plant Renaming

Name Appearing

In what follows, I describe the mere happening of the renaming of the *Aronija* plant in the wet clay soil of midwestern Latvia. On a rewilded plantation, hundreds of 300-year old, wrinkly *Aronia m.* bushes are evolving. *Aronijas* are breathing and signalling with nearby blueberries, lichen, fungi, bird- and meadow-vetchlings, young birches, valerians, parsnips, and grasses. Spring, light-reflecting flowers are being pollinated by the pollinators and touched by the skins of deer, bat, bee, spider, tick, mosquito, and fox. Just beneath the Earth's crust, roots and microorganisms touch worms and moles while taking in water and minerals. Soon after, the leaves, stems, and fruits are emerging in the air, and human flesh is picking the purple-black, reflecting pomes and pushing them into their dark vacuoles. Soon after, when the tannins are softened by the cold air of short days, the feathered birds fly by to eat the leftover berry energy.

In the following decade, on various occasions, while wandering on the plantation land, more mere happenings occur: experiences that have a quality other than a fantasy, or inspiration. In an instant, unreflectively, I commit to them; I take these gifts that feel like an assignment artistically and seriously. I engage in art processes to make them tangible for the local community and for the plant/ation.

At times, the shared experiences and projects attract collaborating, more-than-*Aronija* entities, such as artists and researchers in residency at SERDE Art

Centre, which is a twenty-two-minute walk from the plantation. The art centre is the main driver behind artistic processes in this wide region.

In this essay, I limit myself to one mere happening that I have been describing as a nomenclature morphing (Vandeput 25). On 3 September 2014, I "see" in the cinema of my mind two groups of dotted graphic forms that the brain denotes as letters: Baroa belaobara. At an instant! While wandering amidst the *Aronija* bushes, the tension drastically drops. And in a split second and non-reflectively, I interpret these two separate sequences of concisely shaped, dotted letters as two nouns that, from this moment onward, should be read as the one and only name of *Aronija*. I perceive this name as the stable and single linguistic denominator for what before its appearing used to be locally named *Aronija*. Immediately, I commit to sharing this mere happening of "Baroa belaobara" with fellow humans using written and oral language and with the plant/ation using light and what I name "breath-wording," which emphasises the exchange of air and gasses between plant and nearby spoken word.

Before reflecting further upon this mere nomenclatural experience, I investigate the ways humans have been using language to refer to *Aronija*. But first I verify whether "Baroa belaobara" is already known to the human linguistic realm. Surprisingly, the undotted version of Baroa refers to a genus of oriental, noctuoid moths in the *Erebidae* family and in the *Arctiinae* subfamily. There are seven Baroa species that are living in the Philippines, Java, Thailand, China, and Nepal, far from the region of the Great Lakes in North America, where the "plant with the new name" is endemic, and from the Baltic region and Russia, where cultivated varieties have been spreading, as I will show below.

Latvian microbiologist Anete Boroduska's revelation to the visitors of a "Baroa belaboara" exhibition that "the Berry is an Apple" triggered my investigation into the relationship between language and the ways of classifying this plant in the human attempt to categorise and order the biological world (e.g. Rosch and Lloyd). How have humans been naming the plant, both the so-called "common names" given by the communities that relate to the plant—also referred to as a "bush"—and the botanical names given by science? This is a dynamic history, with much debate and many changes, especially in recent years due to DNA-based analysis that has created a lot of taxonomic re-shuffling.

Common Naming

Black chokeberry, wild gooseberry, choke pear, or dogberry are the common names in English that North American settlers have assigned to the plant.

Chokeberry is in use still today, with "choke" referring to the bodily sensation of choking and so the difficulties in swallowing due to the astringency of the tannin-rich sap of the fruits of the plant. The settlers knew from First Nation peoples in the region of the Great Lakes, such as the Potawatomi, that one could drink the sap as medicine for a cold.[4] The Forest Potawatomi refer to the plant as "niki'mînûn," "sakwako'mînûn," or "sakwako'mînawûnj" (Smith et. al. 75).

Aronia melanocarpa was transported to European botanical gardens in the eighteenth century, after which the species started new lives, growing new relations in new places due to the human appreciation of its aesthetic, ornamental, and medicinal qualities and value. Local common names appear in Russia, as "черноплодная рябина" (*Chernoplodnaya ryabina*; black-fruited mountain ash); in Poland as *Aronia czarna* (black *Aronia*); Sweden as *Svartaronia* (blackaronia); in Finland as *Marja-aronia* (*Aronia* berry); in France as *Aronia à fruits noirs, Aronie noire*, and *Gueule noire* (*Aronia* with black fruits, black *Aronia*, Blackmouth); in Germany as *Schwarze Apfelbeere* (black appleberry); and in the Low Countries as *Appelbes* (Dutch; appleberry).[5]

Science Naming

In scientific publications, the dominant name of the plant is *Aronia melanocarpa (Michx.) Ell.*, with *Aronia* as the genus, and *melanocarpa* as one of five species names, the others being *arbutifolia, prunifolia, mitschurinii*, and *melanocarpaS* (Brand et al. 290, 291). Originating from the Greek, *mela* means dark and carpa fruit. In scientific publications, this botanical name is very often accompanied by the common name of chokeberry (e.g. Suljević et al.). This might be explained by the ongoing volatility of the classification efforts of the Aronia genus and (sub)species. To make the taxonomical picture complete, according to the Flora of North America Editorial Committee (2014), the Aronia genus belongs to the family of Rosaceae, the order of Rosales, the class of *Dicotyledoneae*, which is classified under the phylum of *Anthophyta*. Ultimately, *Aronia* is part of the kingdom of *Plantae*.

At the turn of the nineteenth century, Russian and Eastern European breeders started significant *Aronia* breeding programmes exclusively to cultivate *Aronia* as an ornamental plant (Sennikov and Phipps 6). It was the horticulturist Ivan Vladimirovich Michurin (Mitschurin) who first attempted to grow black fruited *Aronia* as an edible plant during the 1890s (Skvortsov et al. 89). In his nursery in Kozlov (Michurinsk) in western Russia, he created a hybrid from

Sorbus aucuparia (rowanberry) and *Aronia melanocarpa*, or "Likernaya" (liquor rowan) (Sennikov and Phipps 36).

After his death, the new hybrid was named in his honour: *A. Mitschurinii*. Due to the medicinal properties of these new cultivars, plantations were established in the Soviet Union, including in Latvia during the 1970s.

Confusing

Returning to the plantation in Latvia in 2013, I wondered which scientific species name was to be replaced by "Baroa belaobara" as the all-encompassing expression for the plant entity introduced to me as *Aronija*? Would it be *Aronia melanocarpa* or *Aronia mitschurinii*, or a hybrid of both?

Due to the (agro-)political history of the Baltic region, the latter was more likely. However, holding plantation leaves and fruits in my hand, I felt that the fruits are too small to be *A. mitschurinii*. They seemed to be much more in line with the morphological descriptions in the literature of the plant in northeastern America that is called *A. melanocarpa* or "nîki'mînûn."

In the midst of this naming and classifying confusion, and with no local information available about the origins of the plantation plants, I turned to the technology for analysing plant DNA, with the help of a Finnish microbiologist. We hoped to ultimately determine the identity and classification of the plants in 2022. However, all our efforts yielded inconclusive results. In the same year, Brand and his group of scientists suggested the fifth species "*A. melanocarpaS.*" The "S" added to *melanocarpa* stands for "South" and indicates the location where specimens were collected: the southern part of the region of the Great Lakes. *A. melanocarpaS* is a species distinctly separate from all other taxonomic groups.

It is common for *A. mitschurinii* to be incorrectly identified as *A. melanocarpa* due to a lack of awareness of intergeneric hybridisation between Aronia and Sorbus. These erratic identifications are often caused by the "incomplete morphological information available when accessions were collected, but in other instances, the misidentification resulted from incomplete taxonomic descriptions in the literature and a poor historical understanding of speciation within the genus *Aronia*" (Brand et. al. 7). Using state-of-the-art gene analysis, Brand and his colleagues separated *A. mitschurinii* as a distinct branch from all other Aronia taxonomic entities.

However, if yet another name were added, it would reinforce the study's claim that the number of species in the genus *Aronia* has been enigmatic for decades, if not centuries (Brand et al. 7).

Earlier, I was insisting that "Baroa belaobara" be used as the ultimate way of naming the *Aronia* plant; it is a name that originated in the relating of *Aronija* and me.[6] Irreducible to the one or the other, I start to report the dotted letter sequence back to the plants, using breath (a o a e l a o a), pressure (B b), and vibration (r r). Simple breath-wordings in close encounters intensify the sensation of mutual dependency through the air, with every breath increasing the plant presence in myself—or myselves, rather. I developed further a way of speaking that could be sensed by fellow *homo sapiens*, but that was filtered by my interpretation of what the plants might be sensing in their biotope.[7]

Power C/u/t/

Having shown how multiple linguistic expressions have been used to represent the plant entity, I now ask the question: which one of them is to be replaced by "Baroa belaobara"? In 2016, just before the flowers began to blossom, I encountered a plantation that had been reduced to growing only Baroa belaobara plants. A human-machine cutting intervention restored the initial monoculture model, with most non-Baroa belaobara plants being cut. The remaining Baroa belaobaras were cut back to the minimum for optimised berry-apple growth. At an instant, the strong sense of bonding vanished, and I experienced a cathartic disconnection with plant and plantation land. I was confronting confusion and questions.

Discussion

And the king asked Jeanne d'Arc

why he could not hear the voices she had heard.

After all, he is the King.

Jeanne answered she had gone to the field to listen.

I interpreted the appearance of Baroa belaobara at the *Aronija* plantation as a signal to replace all humanly given names for the plant with the dotted letter sequence. It seemed a point of departure for botanical and taxonomical research and points to the ongoing difficulties to fix a name for the plant, even by using DNA analysis. However, a violent plantation cut disrupted the direct connection between Baroa belaobara and *Aronija*.

Taxonomy

Robin Wall Kimmerer points to the problematic, mostly scientific, aspect of naming something where the name becomes almost an end in itself for enquiry: "We're able to systematize it and put a Latin binomial on it, so it's ours. We know what we need to know" (Kimmerer, 2016). In an interview, she describes this problem for plants as "such a mechanical, wooden representation of what a plant really is. And we reduce them tremendously, ignoring all its relationships if we just think about them as physical elements of the ecosystem" (Kimmerer, 2016).

Perplexed by the emergence of Baroa belaobara, I initially related it to *Aronija*, the common Latvian name, and later to the scientific *Aronia m.*, only soon to be aware that the waters become somewhat murkier, as this "m.," which refers to the species name, could indicate the human-made *mitschurinii*, the "natural wild" *melanocarpa*, or even the recently "discovered" *A. melanocarpaS*. Consequently, *Aronia* retains its linguistic and taxonomic "wildness," with its identity continuously shifting within the taxonomical and botanical realm. This persistence showcases how the biological entity humanly named Aronia eludes attempts to be neatly classified. Meanwhile, I continue to learn directly from the plants, from local herbalists, from plant physicists and from microbiologists about *Aronia m.*'s ways of relational becoming and communicating. It helps me to articulate human plant/ation relationalities if I verbally report the name change back to the plants, in the form of an artistic gift.

Baroa belaobara emerged at a particular moment in the rewilded plantation, as many relationships between entities intertwined above and below the soil, mixing biochemicals, microorganisms, light, vibration, and rhythm. The cut made me doubt what the name "Baroa belaobara" was really referring to. Could "Baroa belaobara" mean the broader context of this plot of land as an ecosystem? Would it then lose its specific definition of one plant species, *Aronija?*[8]

Kimmerer suggests that "science and traditional knowledge may ask different questions and speak different languages, but they may converge when both truly listen to plants" (Kimmerer, 2020 165). And in the case of science, when done "with awe and humility in a powerful act of reciprocity with the more-than-human world, it can be a way of forming intimacy and respect with other entities that are rivalled only by the observations of traditional knowledge holders. It can be a path to kinship" (251). Natasha Myers argues further that plant

Bart Vandeput

scientists' sensoria "get 'vegetalised' over the long duration of their experimental inquiry" (42). Was I experiencing something of this kind?

Based on the artistic plantation practice surrounding Baroa belaobara, I suggest that this "vegetalising" can occur for artists and artistic ways of knowing. By "presencing" every year for various weeks across a decade at the plantation, through subtle conversations, explorations, and interventions, as well as through breathing processes of oxygen and carbon dioxide, I was in exchange with plants, bacteria, deer, fox, bird, lichen, and various other living entities. I then understood: Baroa belaobara originates from the land and its habitants.

While transformative learning may at times be marked by epiphanies—by crystallisations of knowing that suddenly coalesce when the time is ripe— place-based learning tends to be marked primarily by a slow, accretional process of change (Hathaway 319).

Name-Becoming through Plants

By practising the abovementioned breath-wording, the awareness of "becoming" increases through breathing and respiration. Plants breathe in what I breathe out and vice versa. So, as a porous entity, part of the respiration of plant molecules returns to me, making me susceptible to the breathing cycle in a shared process of becoming. Schrader, Nicolić, and Radulovic argue that the plant's performativity of mixing with the world is grounded in radical openness. It is an active, agential quest and experimentation for finding ways to respond that rely on capacities to be affected and entangled (Nicolić and Radulovic). Ultimately, this cyclical breath-wording points to a sense of mixed, in-between, hybrid, or queer identity, where, in the words of Emanuele Coccia, "everything is within everything" (71).

Name-Becoming through Land and Air

Ecologist and philosopher David Abram argues that through spoken wording and breathing "our animal senses awaken; we remember the primacy of the sensuous cosmos that reigns underneath all our theories." Additionally, "in indigenous lifeways, intuition is compelled by placing the spoken word centrally. For traditionally oral cultures, words are nothing other than shaped breath. Hence, the fluid air is the implicit intermediary in all communication, the very medium of meaning." And the breathing Earth articulates itself, he argues, "not in statistics but in seedpods and storms and spoken stories. The land's awareness slides easily in and out of our nostrils. We reclaim our membership in the Commonwealth of Breath" (Abram 313).

With the praxis of breathing, wording, and the cut, it dawned on me that Baroa belaobara must refer to more than just a plant. It originates from and is limited to a particular moment in time and space, situated in a mixed reality of plantation, land, and myself. In relational ontology, things are only existing if there is a relation. Indeed, it felt as if the plantation restoration had cut off all relations.

Baroa belaobara now increasingly resists further exploration and turns more into itself. It has morphed into a stable language entity, in line with the main intention of taxonomy and so explains the choice of a dead, stable language (Latin) in the naming system. Arguably, following Federico Campagna's line of thought on reality, Baroa belaobara thus shifts from the realm of "Technic," where its qualities, classification, and name can be continuously re-investigated, to the realm of "Magic," which, on the cosmological level, is "stable, eternal and ineffable" (Campagna 230). Baroa belaobara becomes part of a solid, measureless substratum that can endure the process of becoming "the alternative reality system and possible path towards the reconstruction of reality" (Campagna 230, 103).

Conclusion

The process of naming, or nomenclature, can be perplexing, as is exemplified here in the case of *Aronija* and the sudden appearance of Baroa belaobara, to which I responded with affect, responsibility, and commitment. I explored ways of sharing with the world and of reporting results back to the plantation.

Here and now, Baroa belaobara is what "it" is: a stable, enigmatic entity with various qualities, including visual, graphic, linguistic, ecological-respirational, and artistic aspects. I invite you, the reader, to practice the letter sequences aloud or in a whisper.

I like to speculate that Baroa belaobara is part of a growing, ineffable, living archive of preserved, non-sensical breath-wordings.

The naming of plants and our world can be equally bewildering. "Baroa belaobara" is depicted once more as a fixed entity with diverse attributes. Hopefully, these words will be revisited and pondered upon.

A herbarium is a collection of preserved plant specimens used for scientific research. "Baroa belaobara" could be considered as one entry in an expanding archive of preserved non-sensical wordings that come to life through presence, attunement, and affection in the realm where everything is in everything.

Notes

1   Aronija is the Latvian common name for Aronia m. (*melanocarpa(S)* or *mitschurinii*). I follow Kimmerer (2016, p. 385) in recognising the personhood of all beings as equally important, and, therefore, use capitals as well for the common name when it is a single Aronija plant, as opposed to referring to many aronija as a category.

2   For a detailed description of the research into the ethnobotanical and taxonomical history of *Aronia melanocarpa* and *Aronia mitschurinii*, see the chapter "Nomenclatureal Morphing" in my monograph *Baroa belaobara: Berryapple* from 2021.

3   For a consideration of this "ineffable, eternal and stable realm" as a reality of soothing magic, see Campagna (230).

4   In 1933, the ethnobotanist Huron H. Smith writes, "They steep the berry to make a tea to cure a cold. Among the whites, the berries are used for their astringent properties" (75).

5   Common plant names in Europe are based upon Wikipedia.

6   When using "me" and "myself," I mean in fact "myselves," a multispecies relational being that is becoming.

7   As an example, when sitting with a tiny Baroa belaobara next to a small path that is separating two parts of the Baltic Seashore, instead of writing that "many joggers pass by," I would say and write that "a blob passes by from where the sun rises towards where the sun sets, very shortly interrupting the rays—and thus food— reaching the plant".

8   See Terry Tafoya's *Principle of Uncertainty*, mentioned by Shawn Wilson in the context of relational accountability (8).

Works Cited

Abram, David. "The Commonwealth of Breath." *Material Ecocriticism*, edited by S. Lovino and Oppermann, Serpil, Indiana University Press, 2014, pp. 312-13.

Brand, Mark H., et al. "Ploidy, Genetic Diversity and Speciation of the Genus Aronia." *Scientia Horticulturae*, vol. 291, no. 110604, 2022, doi: 10.1016/j.scienta.2021.110604.

Campagna, Frederico. *Technic and Magic: The Reconstruction of Reality*. Bloomsbury Publishing, 2018.

Flora of North America Editorial Committee. *Magnoliophyta: Picramniaceae to Rosaceae Flora of North America North of Mexico IX*. Oxford University Press, 2014.

Hathaway, Mark D. *Cultivating Ecological Wisdom: Worldviews, Transformative Learning, and Engagement for Sustainability.* 2018. University of Toronto, MA Thesis.

Kimmerer, Robin Wall. "The Intelligence of Plants." *On Being,* The On Being Project, 25 Feb. 2016, https://onbeing.org/programs robin-wall-kimmerer-the-intelligence-of-plants-2022.

Kimmerer, Robin Wall. *Braiding Sweetgrass: Indigenous Wisdom, Scientific Knowledge and the Teachings of Plants.* Penguin Books, 2020.

Nikolić, Mirko, and Neda Radulovic. "Aesthetics of Inhuman Touch: Notes for 'Vegetalised' Performance." *RUUKKU - Studies in Artistic Research,* vol. 9, 2018, doi: 10.22501/ruu.372629.

Pessoa, Fernando. *The Book of Disquiet.* Serpent's Tail, 2018.

Sennikov, A. N., and J. B. Phipps. "Atlas Florae Europaeae Notes, 19-22: Nomenclatural Changes and Taxonomic Adjustments in Some Native and Introduced Species of Malinae (Rosaceae) in Europe." *Willdenowia,* vol. 43, no. 1, 2013, pp. 33-44, doi: 10.3372/wi.43.43104.

Skvortsov, A. K., et al., *"Cultivated Black-Fruited Aronia: Place, Time and Probable Mechanism of Formation"* [in Russian]. Bull. *MOIP, Otd. Biol.,* vol. 88, no. 3, 1983, pp. 88-96.

Suljević, Damir, et al. "Impact of Dietary Supplementation with Chokeberry (*Aronia melanocarpa, Michx.*) on Tetrachloride-Induced Liver Injury in Wistar Rats: Hematological and Biochemical Implication." *Cell Biochemistry and Function,* 2023, doi: 10.1002/cbf.3829.

Vandeput, Bartaku. *Baroa Belaobara: Berryapple.* 2021. PhD Thesis, Aalto University.

Wilson, Shawn. *Research Is Ceremony.* Fernwood Publishing, 2008.

Bart Vandeput

9   Weaving Myth, Extinction, Love and Magic: Some Edelweiss Stories

Anna Perdibon

Climate change is threatening the survival of sensitive Alpine species. With global warming dramatically changing habitats and Alpine plants being unable to move to higher, cooler places, mountain summits act like traps for fragile species. Indeed, if temperatures rise by a mere 2 degrees Celsius, it is estimated that trees and plants will move 300 to 400 metres higher. However, this movement is not possible for Alpine species, as has been documented by the World Wildlife Fund-supported GLORIA project, an initial attempt to systematically study vegetation changes in Europe's Alpine regions. As pointed out by Georg Grabherr, "a quarter of all flowering plants on the continent are only occurring in high Alpine zones. And yet unfragmented Alpine zones only make up 3 per cent of Europe's territory. Plants dwelling in these high regions are a particularly important part of Europe's biological diversity" (Paukovits).

A species that is particularly at risk of extinction in the Alps is the edelweiss (*Leontopodium alpinum*). This charismatic flower, often a symbol of the Alps, is a protected species: its scarcity and fragility has arisen not only because of climate change but also because of poaching and indiscriminate harvesting. These causes of plant extinction and habitat loss derive from the way(s) human relate with plants and the other non-human inhabitants of the land. Ultimately, ecological collapse can be viewed as caused by our detachment from and abstracted relations with the vegetal realms. By posing a conception of extinction as both collective death and individual death and by stressing the importance and loss of intergenerational inheritance, the field of extinction studies offers perspectives on plants deaths and show us the ways in which we are living and losing the world we belong to (Bird Rose et al. 1-19). As pointed out by Van Dooren about the loss of crows in Hawaii, local people realise that they have "lost the most intelligent and charismatic component of the forest" (Van Dooren 191).

Native to the Dolomites, the "Pale Mountains," the silvery, delicate, yet strong edelweiss flower is inescapably connected to its mountains. Conversely, the life of the mountains, with their melting glaciers and crumbling rocks, is entangled with the existence of their botanical inhabitants. The lives of mountains and plants are thus interconnected. The increasing rarity of the edelweiss, then, is not merely a loss of biodiversity; rather, it speaks to and embodies the death of the world we know, with its richness and depths of eco-cultural knowledge and relations. Not only are the flowers on the verge of extinction but also the old stories that tell us of a deep bond and knowledge of the Dolomites are languishing and being forgotten in our voracious world.

In these uncertain times of ecological collapse, we have much to learn from plant lives and stories. Exploring and perceiving the personalities of plants in their multifaceted soil, as well as in human encounters and the human imagination evident in stories and storytelling, can be(come) an antidote to the "collective dementia we are entangled in—a medicinal nectar that flows to allow a different ending to our story" (Gagliano 120). What follows is an attempt to restore and re-story the deep and never really lost connection of human people with plants and their local ecologies by recovering and translating old stories that still whisper under a thick or thin layer of soil, through the land, and in the mountains and forests.

In the rich, though neglected, repertoire of legends from the Ladin culture and language (a minority in the midst of the Italian Alps), the edelweiss emerges as an iconic and sacred botanical being. It is a co-protagonist of different stories that speak of a fragile and strong eco-cultural world, whose entangled histories involve the very existence of mountains, woods, plants, humans, and the other inhabitants of the woods. Tracing some of the almost forgotten stories of the edelweiss from the Dolomites, I attempt to weave together and highlight the connections between myth and reality, birth and death, sacredness and danger, strength and fragility, and care and greed through the language of story and poetry. In doing so, I explore and rely on the different ways in which plant narratives can nurture plant care in our compromised times of disease, fragmentation, detachment, and extinction. I wish to pause on how love and care are always matters of compromise and reciprocity, of understanding our respective natures, and of finding new, "third" ways to live together and to nurture a space where each of us can live and thrive to co-create the world we all live in and with.

Of Stars, Mountains, and Flowers

Many names, many stories: *Edelweiss* ("Noble White"), *Stella Alpina* ("Alpine Star") *Leontopodium alpinum* ("Lion's Foot of the Alps"), and *Fiore Eterno* ("Eternal Flower"). In these vernacular, scientific, and traditional names for the edelweiss, we can already sense the depths of its stories and relationships. Its names in different languages accompany us in tracing and rediscovering the complex and fascinating personality of this flower.

The Path of Light, Love and Magic: From Earth to Moon, from Moon to Earth

The name "edelweiss" derives from German and means "noble white." Its connections to nobility and whiteness are preserved in the legend of the Pale Mountains, the local name for the Dolomites. This legend is as follows:

> Once upon a time, there was a kingdom in the southern Alps where green pastures, shady forests, and steep mountains with black rocks thrived. Everyone was happy but the king's son, who was longing for the moon. On the nights when the full moon appeared, the prince was always gloomy and staring up at the moon.
>
> One day, the young prince got lost in the forest. When evening came, he slept in a meadow full of blooming red roses. He dreamed of a beautiful girl whom he had never seen before. His surroundings were entirely white, but he was holding red roses in his hand, and he handed them to the beautiful stranger. She was the daughter of Moon King.
>
> The prince finally woke up, and, hoping his dream would become real, he started growing the most beautiful red roses. One day, he suddenly met two old men. They revealed they were moon dwellers and were just about to return to the moon. They invited him to join them on their return trip. However, they warned the prince that no earthly creature could last long on the moon. "Everything is white there; everything shines in a silver glow. You will become blind very soon," one of the two men said. The other added, "A moon dweller cannot linger on the Earth, too, because of the dark colour of its mountains' rocks."

The prince did not hesitate, and followed the two men to the moon. There, he found a white landscape. While walking, he met a gardener. The man enquired, quite astonished, about the origin of the red flowers that the prince held in his hand. They were the red Alpine roses that he had picked at night. The gardener led the prince to the castle of the Moon King, an old man with a long silver beard. The king introduced the earthly prince to his daughter, the Moon Princess he had seen in his dream. She found great pleasure in the beautiful and rare flower, and the prince was invited to stay in the palace of the Moon King.

As in every good story, the prince and the princess fell in love. But, as in every real story, the relationship between the two began with some difficulties. One day, the prince woke up noticing that the intense brightness of the lunar landscape hurt his eyes, and he started to fear that he might go blind. All of a sudden, he decided to return to the Earth. Out of love, the princess followed him. She took with her a white and feathery flower, which started spreading throughout the Alps. It was called the edelweiss, or the noble flower and the flower from the moon.

On the Earth, the princess found a different environment, filled with dark and rich colors: black, red, green, brown, blue. The warm tones of the woods, soil, and pastures were beautiful to her, but too intense. And the darkness of the mountain caused her to feel sorrow. Soon, the princess became homesick, and sadness became intertwined with the love between the two. The suffering of the princess grew so strong that she fell severely ill. She had to return to the moon, and the prince decided to follow her, even though he remembered the warning of the two moon dwellers who brought him to the moon.

Once back on the moon, the princess recovered swiftly, but the prince was less and less able to see every day. He, then, had to leave his love and return to the earth. Longing for the moon and his beloved, he climbed the mountain peaks and stayed there all night long.

One day, walking in the forest, he met a strange little man with a long beard and crown. The man introduced himself as the king of the Salwàns, and narrated the sad fate of his people, who had been displaced after a foreign army had devastated their ancestral land. Moving from one kingdom to the next, the Salwàns were turned away everywhere. Some of them died; others had to disperse. The prince then told the Dwarf King the story of his princess. When the prince ended his story, the Dwarf King exclaimed: "Prince, rejoice, now we are both saved!" He suggested that the Salwàns could envelop the dark mountains from top to bottom with the white cloth of the lunar landscape, if the king of this Alpine kingdom allowed them to live here for good.

The prince immediately went to his father with the Dwarf King. His father was skeptical at first, but he changed his mind when the king of the Salwàns declared that his people would never lay claim to or descend to the valley bottoms, meadows, and fields. They would dwell in the woods and in the rocky wilderness. As soon as the Dwarf King and his people settled in their new home and the moon began to rise, they began their work.

Seven Salwàns appeared and started spinning the moonlight on each mountain peak. Then, they plucked apart their bundles of light and pulled the gleaming threads from the summit down the slopes below. They wrapped each mountain entirely in a net of light. Finally, they tightened all of their stitches until there were no dark spots. In just one night, they covered the kingdom's entire mountain range with the whiteness of the lunar landscape. The prince immediately traveled to the moon and asked the princess to come back to the Earth with him: he had woven a white world for them, where they could live together.

These words made the severely ill princess healthy again. After a while, she accompanied the prince back to the Earth. When she saw the landscape, pure joy filled her. The mountains were now a colorful Alpine garden, uniting the brightness of the moon with the rich colors of the earth. The princess never fell ill or felt homesick again.

The Pale Mountains still exist today, and they are called the Dolomites. The ancient kingdom has long since fallen apart, but the Salwàns still dwell in the rocky wilderness and forests.[1]

The legend of the Pale Mountains tells us of the origin of the Dolomites and its most iconic and "native" flower, the edelweiss. What we have here is a cosmogony in which the flower and the mountain are created so that their lives are inescapably intertwined. The story also conveys some precious lessons. In its play between light and darkness, whiteness and redness, love and pain, thriving life and disease, it reminds us of the dance of life itself. It underscores both the force of love and the need to belong to a place, to find a home where we can take root.

The story also demonstrates that only when we work and strive to locate a common ground, can a new, "third" way be created. This new way of living relies on an ongoing action of co-creation, of a multi-species collaboration with the non-human beings we live alongside. Moreover, we learn from this story that care and love are always possible when we listen and make space for our various natures to coexist, for our different and unique colours and shapes to just be. Finally, we are reminded that we all need a little magic in our lives.

We might dare to hint that the force of love between the prince and the princess is embodied in and represented by the edelweiss. The strength of the delicate yet tenacious flower is well reflected in the Latin name given to it by Linnaeus: *Leontopodium,* meaning "lion's foot." This name expresses the powerful love for life that allows the flowers to take root in a foreign place and to blossom.

Stella Alpina

Is it not curious that the flower native to the Alps has its origin in a faraway place like the moon? The foreign origin of the edelweiss is a traditional theme in the legends concerning the Dolomites. It is connected not only to the moon but also to the other inhabitants of the night sky, the stars. Indeed, the Italian name for the edelweiss is *Stella Alpina,* the "Alpine Star."

A legend that I listened to during a walk in the woods of the Dolomites recounts how a star, moved by compassion for a mountain enveloped in sadness and loneliness, decided to fall onto the mountain's sharp and cold rock and offer it company. After it fell, the star was transformed into a star-like, silvery flower, tenacious enough to take root in the barren and inhospitable rocky crevices. If my memory does not fail, the story runs like this:

A long time ago, a lonely mountain cried in silence.

Everyone looked at her, bewildered: the beeches, the firs, the oaks, the rhododendrons, and the periwinkles.

However, no plant could do anything to help the lonely mountain. Each plant was tied to the earth by its roots; not even a flower could blossom among its rocks.

Up in the sky, even the stars noticed the sadness of the mountain. One night, when the clouds had dispersed and the stars were playing among the branches of the tallest pines, one of them took pity on the crying mountain. The star came darting down from the sky and slipped between the rocks and crevices of the mountain, until she landed, tired, on the edge of a precipice.

It was cold on the mountain. The star began to wonder whether she had been out of her mind to leave the serene tranquillity of heaven. The mountain's frost would certainly kill her.

But, the mountain searched for a way to protect the star, grateful for that proof of heartfelt friendship. With its stone hands, the mountain wrapped the star in a soft, white fluff. Then, the mountain tied the star to itself with tenacious roots.

When dawn broke, the first edelweiss was born.

Only then did the mountain rejoice.

This second story shows how the life, happiness, and destiny of mountains and flowers are part of a shared narrative and so part of a single history. We learn too that generosity, sacrifice, and metamorphosis are part of one journey.

Touching the Flower: Sacredness and Fear, Life, and Death

Another name for the edelweiss is "eternal flower." These flowers have long been believed to be, and to be connected to, sacred beings that could gift not only immortality but also death, misfortune, and calamities if not appropriately approached. Indeed, the edelweiss should not be touched. In order to pick one, you need to get permission from the dwarfs of the mountain, who are the custodians of the edelweiss. The opportunity to pick an edelweiss is a wondrous gift that might become a life-transforming event.

The dangerous tension between greed and respect, death and life, love and selfishness is well portrayed in another legend from the Ladin valleys:

Once upon a time, at the foot of a mountain, there was a village run by a mayor. The man had a daughter, Berta, who was beautiful like the sun, but wicked like a witch.

Behind their house, a river flowed and moved the wheel of an old mill. The mill's owner was a young man named Hans, who, while working, watched the beautiful daughter, enraptured. "She is not for you; she is not for you!," his talking cat Peter kept warning him. But Hans did not heed such wise advice; he was consumed by a fruitless love, since Berta did not even deign to look at him.

One day, while hunting mice, the cat happened to pass under Berta's window, and he realised that she was secretly looking at the mill and its owner. When she noticed the cat, she even cuddled him, saying: "You are Hans's cat! Say hello from me." She was certain that the animal could not possibly communicate with its owner, but Peter could, and he told everything to Hans.

Hans, encouraged by these tidings, donned a magnificent robe and went to Berta. He would have expected anything except to be turned away impolitely. Berta exclaimed to him: "What do you want from me, poor miller? I refused much better proposals and cannot certainly go live in an old mill!" Hans was speechless, and Peter the cat baffled.

Dismissing both of them, Berta added contemptuously: "Let's see if you have courage! If you truly love me, you must bring me the water from the Dwarves' Spring, the Water of Life, which falls from the top of the rocks over there!" Hans shivered, as it was said that whoever tried to take even one drop of that water would be killed by the king of the dwarves, who was also was the king of the whole mountain. At his command, dangerous avalanches would fall, common stones would turn into sapphires and emeralds, and sources of water would suddenly emerge or disappear.

But love could be stronger than prudent reason. Hans set off up the mountain, while stones cascaded around him and new avalanches perpetually began. A big crow circled over his head and then landed

Anna Perdibon

at his feet, admonishing him: "Go back or you will die." Hans did not
want to surrender to fear, though; he climbed over the rocks until he
reached the miraculous spring.

It was not a spring, but a shining pond of white water. Hans tried to
immerse a jug in the water. Suddenly realising that the surface of the
pond was crystal, he took a stone and threw it on the surface, saying: "It is not for life, but for death that I take the water, for the love I
carry will be my death."

As he pronounced these words, something magical happened:
the pond disappeared, and, in its place, a thousand small edelweiss
appeared, white and velvety. Hans picked up a few of them, but the
dwarves blocked him, shouting: "You stole our treasure. You will
die!" They then lifted him and threw him over the precipice.

The following morning, Hans woke up at the foot of the cliff. Beside
him, Peter the cat was watching, incredulous. The flower that
his master still grasped in his hands had saved him: the flower of
life and death.

As for Berta, the legend concludes, Hans did not want to hear anything more about her. He married another woman, who was simpler,
gentler, and less greedy than Berta (Cattabiani 609-610).

This tale returns us to our exploitative and greedy Anthropocene present,
with its selfish and short-sighted lifestyles. The fragility of our ecosystems is
palpable to all of us who want to see and listen. The Pale Mountains are endangered on multiple levels and scales. But, as the delicate and strong Edelweiss
reminds us, the mountains and all that lives on them are also tenacious; life
and death are inescapably entangled. The third, cautionary legend of the edelweiss warns us of the dangerous slopes of extinction we currently occupy, of our
human greed, and of the importance of respecting nature. Plant stories and narratives that are embedded in the land are thus crucial and magically generative.

This final edelweiss story, together with the previous two legends narrated
here, calls for us to re-learn how to love and respect ourselves and the different
beings of our world. It asks us to remember that the mountains and their plants
and animals are sacred—that they should be allowed to live independently, in
their own ways. We should learn how to approach, relate to, and live with them,

but also to maintain a respectful distance. The three stories reveal how, rather than being opposites, delicacy and strength intertwine to offer a gentler and humbler path that we should fill with our own light, with the guidance of the stars and the flowers.

Finally, the edelweiss and its stories demonstrate that through care, love, sacrifice, and perseverance, life will emerge and thrive, even under the most difficult conditions. We should thus not waste our energy and time on those who are enveloped in greed. Instead, we should have the courage both to face death and to start anew, with simplicity and respect, if we want to become who we are meant to be. A world that does not exist yet is possible only if we walk the path of respect and of reciprocity, in collaboration with non-human beings. When everything seems impossible or lost, it is then that the imagination of human and non-human life and love performs its magic and turns death into life.

Notes

1   Freely inspired by Wolff 2016.

Works Cited

Bird Rose, Deborah, et al. "Introduction." *Extinction Studies: Stories of Time, Death, and Generations*, edited by Bird Rose et al., Columbia University Press, 2017, pp. 1-19.

Cattabiani, Alfredo. *Florario: miti, leggende e simboli di fiori e piante.* Mondadori, 1996.

Gagliano, Monica. *Thus Spoke the Plant: A Remarkable Journey of Groundbreaking Scientific Discoveries & Personal Encounters with Plants.* North Atlantic Books, 2018.

Kindle, Ulrike. *Le Dolomiti nella leggenda.* Editrice Frassinelli-Keitsch, 1993.

Paukovits, Andrea. "Edelweiss, the Queen of the Alps, in Danger!" *World Wildlife Fund*, 21 Aug. 2003, https://wwf.panda.org/wwf_news/?8421/Edelweiss-the-Queen-of-the-Alps-in-danger. Accessed 8 Feb. 2024.

Van Dooren, Thom. "Spectral Crows in Hawaii: Conservation and the Work of Inheritance." *Extinction Studies: Stories of Time, Death, and Generations*, edited by Deborah Bird Rose et al., Columbia University Press, 2017, pp. 187-216.

Wolff, Karl Felix. *I monti pallidi: storie e leggende delle Dolomiti.* Ugo Mursia Editore, 2016.

     Anna Perdibon

10 Green Magic: Regenerating the "Witches" of Colobraro and Their Plant Knowledge

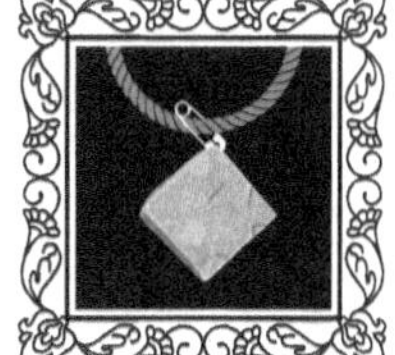

Juliann Vitullo and Arina Melkozernova

Colobraro, a small town in the southern Italian region of Basilicata (Lucania), has suffered for decades, if not centuries, from institutional neglect, depopulation, and stigmatisation as a "backward" area known for witchcraft and curses. Here, we consider the creative transformation of this town, its regeneration through the community's valorisation, preservation, and evolution of its ancestors' agroecology, rich biodiversity, and traditional stories, all of which embed everyday peasant practices and plants in a collective place-based history. By taking control of the narratives that had often been used to associate the town with a wild, irrational, and superstitious culture of "primitive" witchcraft, the community of Colobraro has been able to revive its traditional strategies for survival, connecting the historical traumas of the area to the loss of ancestral, reciprocal relationships with plants (Teti 28-32, 61). In so doing, the inhabitants of Colobraro ironically have challenged the assumptions about modernity that had earned Colobraro the nickname of "the town that cannot be named."

Due to the contemporary tourist industry, Italy is known today for its coastline, but it is a particularly mountainous country, and the region of Basilicata is the most mountainous area of southern Italy. Like many of the region's towns, Colobraro is located in the rugged terrain of the southern Apennines, about which the newly unified Italian government of the late nineteenth century developed long-lasting narratives. These narratives focused on Italy's need to civilise and discipline the mountainous south's untamed landscapes, wild animals, practices of witchcraft, and rebel brigands, who resisted the northern intruders. Marco Armiero has described this process eloquently: "nationalising mountains implied imposing meanings, appropriating resources, enforcing the authority of the State, redefining boundaries between wild and tame, wise and irrational, beautiful and ugly" (Armiero 4). The nineteenth-century narratives continued to shape concepts of the agricultural and pastoral cultures of southern Italy into the twentieth century, even beyond the post-World War II period of agrarian reform with its concentrated efforts to tame the land, the animals, and the cultures of the rugged terrain through hydroelectrical projects, including dams, that paid little attention to the historical relationships between plants, animals, and humans in the mountains. These campaigns of reclamation, which sought to create more health and prosperity in a region that was considered poor because of its topography, largely ignored the local peasant cultures that had evolved in the various environments, and that, due to their isolation, sustained a rich biodiversity based on interdependent relationships facilitating survival (Armiero 35-38).

The research of two influential post-World War II scholars, the Italian Ernesto de Martino and the American Edward C. Banfield, continue to define Basilicata (or Lucania), the ancient Roman region in which Colobraro enjoys a hilltop vista of the Sinni River Valley and the Ionian Sea, as a territory of peasant communities whose locations and practices have distanced them from modernity. While Banfield describes the nearby community of Chiaromonte as a society limited by its own ethos of "amoral familialism," which prevented it from developing (163-64),[1] de Martino seeks instead to understand and analyse the peasants' "magical world" of bindings, rituals, and spells in historical and psychological terms (De Martino, 2015a 118).

De Martino analyses the use of magical practices by Lucanian peasants as a strategy for dealing with what he terms the "immense power of the negative throughout an individual's lifetime, with its trail of traumas, checks, frustrations, and the corresponding restrictedness and fragility of the positive … of realistically-oriented action in a society" (De Martino, 2015a 85). He considers magical rituals to be not only responses to material needs, such as hunger or illness, but also techniques that "help the [individual] presence to reintegrate itself from these crises" (De Martino, 2015a 93). De Martino also notes that magical rituals were associated with moments of potentially significant physical risk, including pregnancy, childbirth, and the infant's early years, all of which were particularly dangerous especially in a society that offered little assistance for mothers and children. Yet de Martino continues to emphasise how these moments of crisis created psychological and existential challenges in addition to material ones (De Martino, 2015a 86).

One of the common magical rituals connected to the precarity of early infancy was the use of amulets, referred to as *abitini* in Lucania, or *u cingjokk* in the dialect of Colobraro.[2] The *abitini*, or "little shirts," were small cloth bags

                                    Juliann Vitullo and Arina Melkozernova

that imitated the shape of the amniotic membrane and so symbolically continued its protection. An amalgam of magical and Christian rituals, the *abitino* was
hung from the baby's neck during baptism. It could contain a range of items,
but it often included three grains of wheat to assure prosperity for the child
(De Martino, 2015a 35). Plants were also used as part of ritualised healing practices to prevent and cure illness. De Martino discusses how healers combined
the material and symbolic properties of the plants (De Martino, 2015b 298). For
instance, mint, which was consumed as an infusion or a tea, was thought to be
effective for curing digestive problems. Healers would also place the herb on
the patient's stomach in what de Martino describes as a symbolic or magical use
of the plant (De Martino, 2015b 298). Thus, the role of plants in magical rituals
combined tangible, healing properties with reassuring, symbolic meanings and
associations.

It was such links to witchcraft that contributed to Colobraro's reputation as
a town defined by sorcery and bad luck. In de Martino's research, women were
usually the magical healers, the *fattuchiere* (or witches); they used ritualised
actions, words, objects, and plants to protect and cure members of their community (De Martino, 2015a 4-5). The tight connection between women healers
and Colobraro was strengthened through the dissemination of an iconic photograph of a fattuchiera from Colobraro by the photographer Franco Pinna, who
worked with de Martino (De Martino, 2015b fig. 11). This photograph created
a chain of associations with women, magic, and Colobraro that diminished the
importance of other peasant strategies for survival, including traditional peasant ecological knowledge of plants (TPEK),[3] which had evolved with and helped
to sustain the region's rich biodiversity.

In recent years, some ethnobotanists have turned their attention to
Basilicata's quickly diminishing TPEK. This knowledge of relationships with
the landscape and the broader environment was acquired over generations of
foraging for and cultivating plants and provided everyday sustenance, as well
as remedies for mild illnesses, such as headaches or muscle pain. One study has
catalogued the descriptions and uses of local plants by one of the last traditional
healers of Basilicata, verifying his practices with other elderly people who
had similar backgrounds in the agricultural and pastoral work of the region
(Montesano et al. 3). With the respectful title of Zi' Matteo (Uncle Matteo), the
healer gained his knowledge and status by learning from another traditional
healer, yet he reported that, in most cases, knowledge of plants was passed down
through families by grandparents; women played an important role in this

transmission (Montesano et al. 8). Montesano's study describes more than fifty-two healing plants, both wild and cultivated, many of which serve as food, but are also known to offer a variety of medicinal properties. For example, wild asparagus shoots, when they are consumed as a food, either boiled or prepared with scrambled eggs and fresh cheese, can also be a diuretic. Garlic had multiple purposes; it was a spice in cooking, a vermifuge necklace for babies and children, and a relief from insect bites when ground, combined with parsley, and applied topically (Montesano et al. 4).

While recognising the importance of documenting Zi' Matteo's herbarium, our research instead focuses on the contemporary and collective efforts in rural, mountainous areas like Colobraro to regenerate the TPEK of past generations and to preserve the region's rich biodiversity for future generations. For the past two years, we have collaborated with two farmer ecologists from Colobraro, Concetta La Rocca and Teresa Bernardo,[4] who are active participants in local networks of custodians established to protect local plant varieties in danger of extinction. Rather than seeing themselves as continuing a tradition of sorcery, Concetta and Teresa consider their work a continuation of local peasant traditions, in which humans and plants co-evolved. The constant fear of hunger and the precarity of life among the *contadini* (or peasants) led to an awareness of their dependence on other forms of life and an attitude of respect and awe for the plants with which they have reciprocal relations. All three of Concetta's and Teresa's networks and communal projects focus on biodiversity, cultural diversity, and intergenerational equity. Connecting the historical traumas of the territory with the loss of their traditional plant knowledge, these projects emphasise the need to disseminate narratives and practices that encourage healthier and more sustainable futures. Our chapter focuses on how Concetta and Teresa have created spaces within their community that foster the reciprocity and resilience of the historical relationships between plants and people in Colobraro, and, at the same time, support the continuing co-evolution of those relationships.

Concetta La Rocca's family history echoes many of the points that Marco Armiero has made about the myths and material history of Italy's mountainous regions. While her parents were from Colobraro, they moved to Policoro on the Ionian Sea during the post-World War II period when thousands of Italians, many of them from more mountainous areas, immigrated to the coastal plains, after reclamation work had freed the area of malaria and made it easier to practise more industrialised forms of agriculture there. In the 1970s, the

   Juliann Vitullo and Arina Melkozernova

construction of the Monte Cotugno Dam on the Sinni River, close to Colobraro, altered the region's geography and flooded areas that had once been cultivated by peasants. Despite these geographical and social changes, Concetta grew up in the 1960s and 1970s with daily experience of the cultural and nutritional importance of plants in her family's and region's history. She learned about the vegetation around her family's farmhouse, including the names of the wild herbs in both standard Italian and dialect. It was still common for families to grow and conserve herbs to flavour traditional dishes, prepare herbal teas, and produce treatments for seasonal ailments; the plants that Concetta remembers being used most often in daily life are laurel, fennel, coriander seeds, pomegranates, peppermint, oregano, licorice, chamomile, poppy seeds, mallow flowers and leaves, garlic, onion, St. John's wort, and dried figs. Concetta also learned from her community about her ancestors' sacred respect for these plants through practices connected to both traditional healers and the Catholic Church.

In Policoro, where thousands of people had recently immigrated to the reclaimed coastal lands, there was only one nurse and one midwife for the growing urban population; consequently, many still depended on traditional knowledge. Concetta remembers that a neighbour with TPEK came to her home when her sister was suffering from pinworms, took her sister in his arms, recited a formula, and made a necklace of garlic that he put around her sister's neck so that it touched her skin. Her sister recovered. Concetta has another strong memory connected to the sacrality of the laurel plant, which had been recognised as a plant with magical properties by the ancient Greeks and Romans (Nava et al. 55-64). Every year on the Sunday after Easter, the residents of Policoro celebrated the Madonna del Ponte, a seventeenth-century wood statue of the Virgin Mary that had been found in a grotto close to the bridge over the Agri River; the statue was carried in a procession through the streets of the city. In the days before the procession, some men from Policoro went to the mouth of the Sinni River, where they collected laurel branches in order to create an arch for the place where the statue would be put at the end of the procession. Everyone would try to bring some of the blessed laurel home and use it during the following year as a talisman against bad luck. Concetta's knowledge of plants expanded in new directions when she studied botany at university, and she later decided to buy land for farming close to her family's hometown of Colobraro, rediscovering the tastes and smells of her childhood and of her ancestors on lands that had been abandoned.

While Concetta's relationship to local plants has been marked by the region's history of internal migration, Teresa's has been defined by *la restanza*, or the decision to stay rooted in the interior, mountainous areas of Italy that have been repeatedly devalued as backward. Her decision was not based on a sense of nostalgia for a bucolic past that never existed, but on an awareness that these places hold community memories and offer rich environmental histories and possibilities for the future. Vito Teti describes *la restanza*, a term he coined, as an affirmative choice to preserve marginalised histories and cultivate alternative models of development (Teti 47). Teresa grew up on a farm and later fell in love with a fellow farmer. Even though she spent much of her childhood reading books, she also learned from the landscape around her, particularly the plants. She remembers experiencing the inebriating aroma of a field of wild oregano for the first time when she was four or five years old and had been allowed to bring the animals out to pasture on her own. She collected a bouquet of the herb to bring back to her grandmother, who then suggested that she should wait until the plant was blooming to harvest it. This memory often comes to her mind now because wild oregano is no longer always able to bloom due to climate change.

Later in life, as an adult, Teresa remembers walking through a field of wild thyme and feeling so reassured by its aroma that she knew she did not need to cultivate allochthonous plants, like bananas, pineapple, or avocado, because her ancestors had left her everything necessary to sustain her environment and family. She also told us that the area around Colobraro has a distinctive, traditional polyculture landscape[5] that contrasts with the monoculture agriculture of the coastal regions; each home had an olive tree, a fig tree, an almond tree, and a garden with artichokes, peppers, melons, tomatoes, onion, garlic, and cultivated herbs, such as basil, parsley, and rosemary. All homes grew different varieties of artichokes, with their edible thistles and awe-inspiring purple flowers, and she still finds them magical because the plants can grow tranquilly in the rockiest of soils with very little water. Many farms also cultivated grains and legumes. Another characteristic that distinguishes the local landscape is the consistent use of fruit trees to create borders between fields and farms. With the help of a local project to preserve ancient trees, both Teresa and Concetta have recently learned that they have pear trees on their lands that are over three hundred years old. The importance of these trees to their ancestors is one of the reasons why Teresa and Concetta decided to protect local species in danger of extinction. It was this shared passion that inspired them to create spaces to

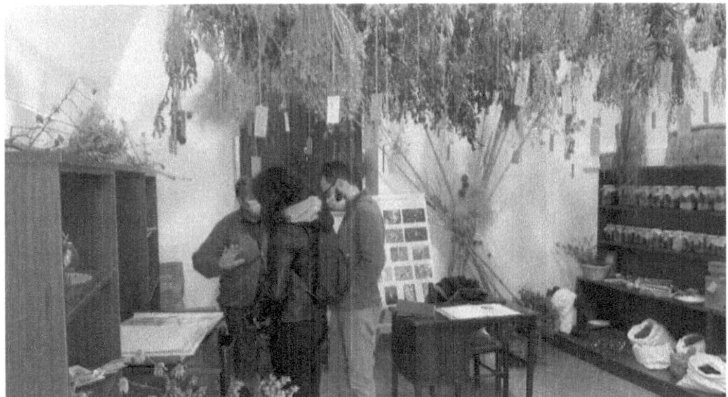

Figure 1. The Museo della Magia, the room of spontaneous herbs (Image courtesy of Juliann Vitullo).

support a future for the histories, knowledges, practices, seeds, and grafts sustaining their community's rich legacy of plant biodiversity.

One of the ways in which Teresa and Concetta have expressed their roles as custodians is through the creation of an herbarium within the town's recently designed Museo della magia (Museum of Magic), which celebrates the wild herbs in and around Colobraro, as well as the traditional, local knowledge of the town's ancestors who depended on the herbs in their daily lives for nourishing their families, healing physical ailments, and expressing their spirituality. The museum is connected to an annual theatrical performance that takes place in the streets of the town every August and is entitled *Sogno di una notte a quel paese* (*Dream of a Night in That Town*). Through this performance, Colobraro's residents reclaim their historical reputation for sorcery and address in a whimsical fashion the traditional belief that even saying the name of the town could bring bad luck. In 2019, the municipal officials of Colobraro received funds to transform an abandoned sixteenth-century Franciscan monastery into a local ethnographic museum that would examine the town's reputation as a centre of sorcery and the various origins of this reputation, the most famous being the research of the anthropologist Ernesto de Martino. The traditional connections between sorcery, women, and plants led to the decision to dedicate one room of the museum to the territory's rich diversity of wild herbs. Concetta and Teresa, together with the town assessor, Elena Napoli, and other volunteers, created "La Stanza delle Erbe" ("The Room of the Herbs") as a space to educate both future generations and tourists about the traditional relationship between peasants and plants and the important legacy of that relationship.

The first room of the museum allows visitors to understand the material, emotional, and spiritual importance of plants for the peasants of Colobraro and examines how the reputation of the town as a centre of sorcery and bad luck developed (Fig. 1). De Martino's research on Lucania has stressed how the rituals associated with magical forces met the historical and psychological needs of people who faced the "existential risk of being-acted-upon" and so developed traditions that provided a sense of control over the negative forces, such as illness, that put them at risk of traumatic events (De Martino, 2015a 113). However, de Martino does not consider the other survival strategies that the peasants adopted and that could be used to reinforce stereotypes of backward, southern Italian rural culture. The first room of the museum confronts these stereotypes by re-examining a photograph of a woman from Colobraro that became famous after it was published in de Martino's influential book, *Sud e magia* (1959); this photograph even appears on the cover of a later edition of the book. It is a portrait of an older woman humbly dressed in black, with noticeable wrinkles, pursed lips, and a rigid posture. The caption identifies her simply as a *fattuchiera*. Although other photos of the woman show her looking at the anthropologist in the foreground and with a child in the background, the image selected for the book removes these historical markers, creating a seemingly timeless, iconic image of a witch (Imbriani 204). The photograph was taken by Franco Pinna, a well-known photographer who travelled with Ernesto de Martino. He identified the woman in his own notes as Maddalena La Rocca, an elderly "witch" who had suffered misfortune, as all four of her children and her husband had died. He goes on to say that she had never seen a train or the sea and did not know when she had been born (Imbriani 203-04).

A local historian, though, has recently discovered that this story misrepresents the woman in the photograph; it is instead a portrait of Maria Francesca Fiorenza, who was a peasant and a weaver, like most of the town's women. Her four children had not died when de Martino met her, and there is no evidence that she was a witch. Rather, she was an extremely hardworking widow whose children survived because of her skills (Imbriani 204).

In addition to re-evaluating the stereotypical image of "witches" from Colobraro, the room in the museum also documents rituals that helped define the sacrality of the relationship between women and plants in peasant culture. One example is the *notte di San Giovanni*, which is the night of 23 June, the eve of the celebration of St. John the Baptist's birth and close in time to the summer solstice when so many plants are in bloom. Traditionally, women harvest local

     Juliann Vitullo and Arina Melkozernova

herbs and flowers, placing them in bowls of water, which they leave outside during the night so that the bowls collect the morning dew on the sacred feast day. In the morning, members of the family wash their hands and faces with this water as an act of purification connected to St. John's association with baptism. It is a ritual practice that promises good fortune, health, and prosperity, honouring the botanical fecundity of the season and the community's dependence on it. Although different mixes of local herbs and flowers are used, a common ingredient is *iperico* (St. John's wort), which carries St. John the Baptist's name in both Italian and English because it blooms close to the saint's birthday and is associated with healing.

This exploration of the sacred role of plants in the peasant traditions of Colobraro in the museum's first room connects it to the museum's second space, the herbarium, which celebrates Colobraro's wild herbs and their quotidian relationship to the town's peasant culture. In the spring of 2019, Concetta and Teresa organised a team of volunteers to collect dozens of wild herbs in and around Colobraro during the time that the herbs can be most easily identified because they are in bloom. Concetta, Teresa, and the volunteers then carefully dried bouquets of each specimen and hung them from the ceiling of the room with tags describing their common names, so that visitors who enter the room are immersed in both the herbs' visual diversity and their complex aromas. In addition, the walls of the room are decorated with apothecary jars full of the herbs' seeds, fruits, leaves, and flowers, reminding visitors of how peasants used all parts of the plants. Many of the herbs also have cards that provide botanical information, as well as explanations of how the plants have been deployed as food, medicine, basketry, textiles, and elements of rituals.

Teresa has also prepared a book of simple, local recipes for teas and dishes; each recipe features one of the room's wild plants. She included a photo, a "portrait," of each herb in order to help people in the community recognise the plants because the traditional knowledge of these plants is rarely transmitted through families now.[6] For instance, one dish, "a' mnestr di cicorie cà fef à purè" in dialect, focuses on the wild chicory plant, a bitter green that had traditionally been combined with fava beans, olive oil, and garlic to create a spring soup of fresh vegetables that was eaten with bread. Wild chicory is one of many greens, herbs, and roots that Massimo Montanari has described as the most important contributors to the distinctive bitter flavours of Italian food; these flavours originated in local peasant cultures centuries ago and are often associated with good health (Montanari 24-26). A 2007 ethnobotanical study compared wild food plant consumption in twenty-one local communities throughout Italy and determined that southern Italians used more wild and bitter greens. The authors attributed this practice to socio-economic differences that have caused greater "erosion" of the traditional knowledge of foraging for these plants in the more industrialised, wealthier north (Ghirardini et al. 12-13). Thus, a landscape's plant biodiversity and the place-based knowledge that helps sustain it also encourage a diverse, flavourful, and healthy palate.

While herbaria across Europe have traditionally been created for colonising countries to document and exploit the botanical resources of their colonies and so often contain more than twice the number of specimens than naturally grow in the region (Park), the herbarium of Colobraro turns that tradition on its head. It focuses on hyper-local specimens that grow in the town's own environment and celebrates the historical relationships between peasants and plants, which preserve botanical biodiversity.

Concetta and Teresa also participate in two agroecological networks of gardeners, small-scale farmers, and scientists in southern Basilicata. These networks creatively combine TPEK with scientific ecological knowledge (SEK) in order to create a seed bank and living, in-situ herbaria that sustain both the conservation and the continuing evolution of their landscape's agricultural biodiversity. As we have learned from Indigenous farmers, activists, and scholars, traditional ecological knowledge (TEK) is multigenerational, place-based knowledge that demonstrates humility toward practices inherited from ancestors and the "stories" of the surrounding non-human forms of life—animals, plants, soil, and water—which are treated as "persons, relatives, and community members" (Nelson and Vucetich 131). In order to understand the narratives of these non-human "relatives" and the connections between them, farm workers and communities that foster TEK protect knowledge "born through long tenure in a place" rather than "short-term observation," which often characterises SEK (Nelson & Vucetich 133). As Melissa Nelson summarises in her conclusion to *Traditional Ecological Knowledge: Learning from Indigenous Process for Environmental Sustainability*:

> if sustainability is to mean anything relevant for us, our more-than-human relatives, and future generations, then we must put our environmental ethics into action and get back in our tracks by re-rooting to specific landscapes. If we are able to embody kinship with our

Juliann Vitullo and Arina Melkozernova

natural world and practice reciprocity as if the future mattered, then we may once again become keepers of the green world (264-65).

These place-based, relational behaviours and storytelling practices sustain ancient species that are rapidly disappearing in a globalised food system, which, as Winona LaDuke emphasises, is becoming increasingly "concentrated in its monoculture and its ownership." She goes on to warn that just as we are starting to face the negative consequences of climate change, "we don't have all the seeds that we could have at the table" (11:27:00-11:34:00).

Both of the networks in which Concetta and Teresa work as custodians, the Agenzia Lucana di Sviluppo e di Innovazione in Agricoltura (ALSIA, Agency of Lucania for Development and Innovation in Agriculture), which is the centre for agricultural biodiversity at the National Park of Pollino, and the affiliated Associazione Vavilov, combine TPEK and SEK in innovative ways that highlight the importance of recuperating and protecting traditionally denigrated *contadini* cultures and their more-than-human botanical kin. The goals and strategies of these two interconnected organisations emphasise the contemporary importance of TPEK (or peasant science), offering creative collaborations that stretch into the future for practitioners of traditional agriculture who cultivate ancient varieties of edible plants. These collaborations are designed to assure that humans and plants continue to co-evolve as relatives in a shared landscape.

ALSIA developed as a community through a combination of regional and national agricultural policies that support the recuperation and protection of local biodiversity and the grassroots activities of gardeners and farmers who had already been active in reviving the local species that they had come to understand as a legacy of their peasant ancestors. The southern region of Basilicata, which is connected to the National Park of Pollino, was the first area in Italy to take advantage of the 2015 national legislation encouraging regions to create communities of food and biodiversity. The approach in southern Basilicata then became a template for other regions. Here, the community developed into an interwoven system of custodians, which first included agricultural custodians, gardeners and farmers who sustain mostly traditional plant varieties, but also animal breeds, at risk of extinction. The system now also contains interwoven networks of producer custodians, chef custodians, and most recently, school custodians, all of which are on a map of itineraries that highlight the community's TPEK and create new pathways through the landscape (Formica 15).

Together, these networks have managed to revive and protect over three hundred fruit species that were particularly important to the southern Basilicata landscape and peasant traditions.

Both Concetta and Teresa had been protecting ancient varieties of pear trees, including *la pera signora*, in their own *frutteti* (orchards) for decades before joining ALSIA. The *pera signora* is a variety of pear tree with small, sweet, and particularly aromatic fruit that ripens in July and lasts for a long time. As Teresa informed us, pear trees had once been common in southern Basilicata's polycultural landscapes, yet most of these trees, even the particularly old ones, had disappeared for several reasons, including emigration, the abandonment of many small farms, the construction of the Monte Cotugno dam, European Union incentives to clear the land, and attempts at more intensive forms of farming.

When Concetta and Teresa rediscovered these trees, whose fruit was among the flavours of their own childhood, they started to discuss their finds with other farmers. These conversations eventually led them to join ALSIA and become the *pera signora's* agricultural custodians. They help to regenerate the *pera signora* throughout their territory by sharing its fruits and the art of grafting. Their bond as friends and farmers developed through their care for the *pera signora*, a plant relative who had never left home but had been neglected. Concetta talked to us about how she purchased abandoned land close to her family's hometown three decades ago and had expected to garden there as a hobby, but the discovery of the fruit trees and flavours of her youth sparked a passion for recuperating the agricultural biodiversity that her ancestors had protected for their survival. Teresa also has a strong affective connection to the pear trees of Colobraro's landscape; in the only photograph she has of her parents together, they are in the shade of a *pera signora* tree.

Across a series of meetings during 2018, the founding members of the ALSIA community developed its design based on three shared concepts: biodiversity, protection of the rural landscape and its cultures, and the importance of a collaborative network of stakeholders (Formica 16-17). The community connected protection of the land's biodiversity to their traditional cultural identities, acknowledging the human role in the landscape and their affective ties to it. In addition, the founding members emphasised the need to recuperate the TPEK of the area's traditional "knowledges" and the "strategies for survival," making a direct connection between the historical traumas of their environment, its depopulation and economic challenges, and the alarming loss of their ancestral knowledge and biodiversity (Formica 17).

     Juliann Vitullo and Arina Melkozernova

In addition to developing their own inclusive network of land and food stewards, which celebrates their ancestors' efforts to survive and passes on traditional knowledge to future generations, the members of ALSIA focus on their relationships to the more-than-human stakeholders in their network. Because the region offers so many edible plants, there has been a particular emphasis on the role of agricultural custodians. Concetta took us to the ALSIA centre, where we learned about how plant geneticists and farmers collaborate to recuperate and protect local species through a conservation process of cataloguing plants and storing their germplasm in a seed bank. This system protects the rich diversity of traditionally native plants nurtured in ALSIA's own experimental fields. Most importantly, however, in response to external factors, such as climate change, that affect the biodiversity and food security of the community, the seeds are planted by members of the network to make sure that they continue to co-evolve in various gardens, farms, and schools of the community. In this way, the seeds of local species are saved, harvested, and shared among ALSIA members as the farmers of the region had traditionally done; the species do not belong to an individual or to a company, but rather to the community; they are a gift from the past for the future.

We also visited with members of the Associazione Vavilov, an affiliated non-profit network of gardeners, farmers, and scientists that provides yet another example of how the Colobraro community has consciously sought to interweave peasant and genetic sciences in their support of cultural and botanical biodiversity. Local farmers chose the Russian scientist Nikolay Vavilov as their inspiration because of his deep appreciation of the importance of TPEK in the co-evolution of human-plant relationships. An early twentieth-century plant biologist and geneticist, Vavilov travelled the world looking for areas particularly rich in agricultural biodiversity, before he was imprisoned, tortured, and killed by Stalin's regime. One of the areas he identified as a "centre of genetic diversity" was the Italian peninsula. Here, he found that the "genetic variation with the gene pools of domesticated crops and their wild relatives was high for both" (Nabhan 16). He also noted that many of the centres of genetic diversity were in mountainous regions that boasted a rich diversity of languages as well as of plants. This observation links directly to one of Vavilov's most important principles in plant geography, which he articulated in 1935:

> The distribution of plant species on earth is not uniform. There are
> a number of regions in the world, which possess exceptionally large

numbers of varieties. ... As far as the crops [concentrated in each of those exceptional regions] are concerned, it is possible to witness there the great role played by Man in the selection of the cultivated forms best suited to each area (qtd. in Nabhan 20).

Thus, Vavilov understood that biodiversity depended on an evolving relationship between plants and humanity, in which the place-based knowledge of those selecting the seeds and cultivars plays an important role. It is such knowledge that Indigenous scholars refer to as TEK (or Indigenous science) and that the gardeners and farmers of ALSIA recognise as the peasant science of their ancestors, as they connect their own work of recuperation and preservation of local species to Vavilov's legacy.

When Concetta introduced us to the current president of the Associazione Vavilov in October 2021, we shared a coffee in the town of Chiaromonte (Montegrano), and they then brought it to our attention that Chiaromonte was the town where the University of Chicago anthropologist Edward C. Banfield had conducted his ethnographic research for his 1958 book, *The Moral Basis of a Backward Society*. In that influential volume, Banfield blames the community's "amoral familialism" for what he describes as an ethical inability to work toward the common good. Developing this thesis, Banfield claims similarities between the peasants of Chiaromonte and the Indigenous peoples of the United States, saying that even though settlers in the western states were poor, they were capable of "self-government and mutual aid," while the peasants of Chiaromonte should be compared to the "American Indian rather than to the frontiersman" (37). Ironically, we found ourselves talking to a well-organised group of farmers whose ancestors Banfield might have interviewed and whose collective action was focused on preserving the knowledge and survival skills of the peasants Banfield had predicted might never be capable of organised efforts for the common good. ALSIA and the Associazione Vavilov have not only created networks to improve the common good, but have also extended the definition of that phrase to include non-human forms of life. During the pandemic, they concentrated on recuperating the *Dolce di Chiaromonte*, a small, yet sweet, local olive variety that peasants of the town often ate with bread. Possessing only three trees, they worked with a nursery to propagate the *Dolce di Chiaromonte* and were in the midst of an adoption campaign for the saplings when we were there.

Concetta and Teresa have found their work as custodians meaningful for themselves, as well as beneficial for the plants and landscapes they preserve.

Juliann Vitullo and Arina Melkozernova

They also see their work as educating others, including children in their community, about the reciprocal relationships with plants that are necessary to protect biodiversity. Concetta explains that traditional local species are often ignored because they are considered less productive, yet she urges the youth with whom she works in schools, and encouraged us too, to consider these species in terms of their co-evolution with peasants. Through repetitive selection over time, in some cases across millennia, growers were able to develop a broad range of pear trees that matured in different seasons; in addition, some varieties produced fruits that were easy to conserve during the winter. Consequently, it was not necessary to rely on the overproduction of one dominant variety. As Concetta herself explains to those she hopes will continue her work, it is the green magic of everyday, place-based relationships between plants and humans that sustained the children, communities, and landscapes of peasants like Maria Francesca Fiorenza, the misidentified yet famous witch of Colobraro.[7] It is this same green magic that regenerates the agricultural work of local farmers like Concetta and Teresa, whose ancestral and experiential knowledge with plants helps heal their community's historical traumas and contributes to a healthier and more sustainable future.

Notes

1   Please note that Banfield used the fictitious name of Montegrano in his volume to hide the identity of the town of Chiaromonte.

2   Concetta La Rocca shared the name of the amulets in dialect and told us that the u cingjokk often included three grains of wheat to ensure prosperity, three grains of salt for protection from evil spirits, and three leaves of both lavender and rosemary, whose perfumes encouraged beauty and counteracted envy.

3   We are indebted to Indigenous scholars, activists, and farmers, such as Winona LaDuke, Melissa K. Nelson, Robin Wall Kimmerer, and Vandana Shiva, from whom we have learned about different forms of traditional ecological knowledge (TEK). Despite important differences, we find affinities between TEK and traditional forms of peasant ecological knowledge (TPEK).

4   We conducted interviews with Teresa Bernardo and Concetta La Rocca from spring 2021 to summer 2023. These interviews occurred in person on their farms in Basilicata during October 2021, as well as via recorded Zoom meetings. Concetta and Teresa also replied to our questions with written responses and graciously shared photos with us. Unless other sources are given, they provided the information in this article about their role as agricultural custodians, their community projects, and their personal/familial/community relationships with plants. We

are grateful to them for sharing their knowledge and experience so generously and consider them co-collaborators in this project.

5   When we use the term "landscape," we have in mind the Italian scholarly tradition begun by Emilio Sereni. This tradition defines the agricultural landscape, or *paesaggio agrario*, not as a natural phenomenon that we simply observe, but rather as environments that have been "consciously and systematically" transformed by humanity (Sereni 17). In Rossano Pazzagli's research, the landscape is a mirror that reflects cultural values, including the resistance of polyculture to monocultural agriculture and the transformations of communal identities (Pazzagli 00:02:15). For the importance of fruit trees in the polyculture of the Mediterranean landscape, which has evolved over millennia, see Giuseppe Barbera's works (Barbera; Barbera and Cullotta).

6   Robin Wall Kimmerer explains that the "decline in plant knowledge is part of a generalized disconnection from the natural world in an industrialized society where the sources of our sustenance are hidden behind industrial processes" and that "we need to ensure that we are educating people with the capacity to learn from the land again, to retrieve the knowledge that is held for us by the plants" (Kimmerer 44).

7   Rosi Braidotti refers to this sense of interconnection between human and non-human others as "transversality," which she defines as "a transformative moment that turns the negative charge—for instance the experience of exclusion—into a collective force capable of activating a potential." She also notes that it is "a humble praxis of collectively driven change" (Braidotti 103).

Works Cited

Agenzia Lucana di Sviluppo e di Innovazione in Agricoltura. "Agrobiodiversità," http://www.alsia.it/opencms/opencms/Temi/dettaglio/Agrobiodiversita/. Accessed 31 Jul. 2023.

---. "Il progetto," http://www.alsia.it/opencms/opencms/biodiversitaLagPol/progetto.html. Accessed 31 Jul. 2023.

Armiero, Marco. *A Rugged Nation: Mountains and the Making of Modern Italy.* White Horse, 2011.

Banfield, Edward C. *The Moral Basis of A Backward Society.* University of Chicago Press, 1958.

Barbera, Giuseppe, and Sebastiano Cullotta. "The Traditional Mediterranean Polycultural Landscape as Cultural Heritage: Its Origin and Historical Importance, Its Agro-Silvo-Pastoral Complexity, and the Necessity for Its Identification and Inventory." *Biocultural Diversity in Europe*, vol. 5, 2016, pp. 21-48, doi: 10.1007/978-3-319-26315-1_2.

---. *Il giardino del Mediterraneo: storie e paesaggi da Omero all'antropocene.* Il Saggiatore, 2021.

Braidotti, Rosi. *Posthuman Feminism*. Polity Press, 2022.

Crescenzi, Aniello. "Su prodotti di qualità, biodiversità e officinali il sostegno al Pollino-Lagonegrese." *Agenzia Lucana di Sviluppo e di Innovazione in Agricoltura*, 6 Jun. 2023, http://www.alsia.it/opencms/opencms/agrifoglio/agrifoglio_online/dettaglio/articolo/Crescenzi-Su-prodotti-di-qualita-biodiversita-e-officinali-il-sostegno-al-Pollino-Lagonegrese/. Accessed 31 July 2023.

De Martino, Ernesto. *Magic: A Theory from the South,* translated and annotated by Dorothy Louise Zinn, HAU Books, 2015a.

---, et al., eds. *Sud e magia.* Donzelli Editore, 2015b [1st ed: 1959].

Formica, Annibale. "La comunità del cibo e della biodiversità di interesse agricolo e alimentare dell'area sud della Basilicata (Pollino-Lagonegrese)." *I Quaderni dell'ALSIA*, no. 16, Dec. 2020, pp. 15-21.

Ghirardini, Maria Pia, et al. "The Importance of a Taste: A Comparative Study on Wild Food Plant Consumption in Twenty-One Local Communities in Italy." *Journal of Ethnobiology and Ethnomedicine*, vol. 3, no. 1, 2007, pp. 3-22, doi: 10.1186/1746-4269-3-22.

Imbriani, Eugenio. "An Authentic Fake: The Sorceress from Colobraro." *Nuovo Meridionalismo Studi*, vol. 2, no. 3, Oct. 2016, pp. 201-207.

Kimmerer, Robin Wall. "Mishkos Kenomagwen, the Lessons of Grass: Restoring Reciprocity with the Good Green Earth." *Traditional Ecological Knowledge: Learning from Indigenous Practices for Environmental Sustainability*, edited by Melissa K. Nelson and Daniel Shilling, Cambridge University Press, 2018, pp. 27-56.

LaDuke, Winona. "TEDxTC – Winona LaDuke – Seeds of Our Ancestors, Seeds of Life." *YouTube*, TEDxTC, 4 Mar. 2012, https://youtu.be/pHNlel72eQc. Accessed 31 Jul. 2023.

Martellozzo, Nicola. "La 'patente' di Colobraro: la certificazione della sfortuna come strategia di patrimonializzazione." *Dialoghi mediterranei*, 1 Nov. 2019, http://www.istitutoeuroarabo.it/DM/la-patente-di-colobraro-la-certificazione-della-sfortuna-come-strategia-di-patrimonializzazione/. Accessed 31 Jul. 2023.

Montanari, Massimo. *Amaro: un gusto italiano.* Gius. Editori Laterza & Figli, 2023.

Montesano, Vincenzo, et. al. "Notes about the Uses of Plants by One of the Last Healers in the Basilicata Region (South Italy)." *Journal of Ethnobiology and Ethnomedicine*, 2012, pp. 1-10, doi: 10.1186/1746-4269-8-15.

Nabhan, Gary Paul. *Where Our Food Comes from: Retracing Nikolay Vavilov's Quest to End Famine.* Island Press/Shearwater Books, 2009.

Nava, Maria Luisa, et al. *Antica flora lucana: repertorio storico-archeologico.* Osanna Edizioni, 2008.

Nelson, Melissa K. "Conclusion: Back in Our Tracks: Embodying Kinship as If the Future Mattered." *Traditional Ecological Knowledge: Learning from Indigenous Practices for Environmental Sustainability*, edited by Nelson and Daniel Shilling, Cambridge University Press, 2018, pp. 250-66.

---, and Daniel Shilling, eds. *Traditional Ecological Knowledge: Learning from Indigenous Practices for Environmental Sustainability*. Cambridge University Press, 2018.

Nelson, Michael Paul, and John A. Vucetich. "Wolves and Ravens, Science and Ethics: Traditional Ecological Knowledge Meets Long-Term Ecological Research." *Traditional Ecological Knowledge: Learning from Indigenous Practices for Environmental Sustainability*, edited by Melissa K. Nelson and Daniel Shilling, Cambridge University Press, 2018, pp. 129-36.

Park, Daniel. "Colonialism Has Shaped Scientific Plant Collections around the World: Here's Why That Matters." *The Conversation*, 12 Jun. 2023, https://theconversation.com/colonialism-has-shaped-scientific-plant-collections-around-the-world-heres-why-that-matters-207375. Accessed 31 Jul. 2023.

Pazzagli, Rossano. *Un paese di paesi: luoghi e voci dell'Italia interna*. Edizioni ETS, 2021.

---. "Riconquistare il paesaggio della macchia mediterranea e delle dune costiere." *YouTube*, Università degli Studi del Molise, 14 Mar. 2022, https://www.youtube.com/watch?v=9lvCkVc3ick. Accessed 31 Jul. 2023.

Sereni, Emilio. *History of the Italian Agricultural Landscape*. Princeton University Press, 2014.

Shiva, Vandana. *Stolen Harvest: The Hijacking of the Global Food Supply*. The University Press of Kentucky, 2016.

Teti, Vito. *La Restanza*. Giulio Einaudi Editore, 2022.

Juliann Vitullo and Arina Melkozernova

11 Herbarium Ghosts: Spectral Serendipity in the More-Than-Human Archive

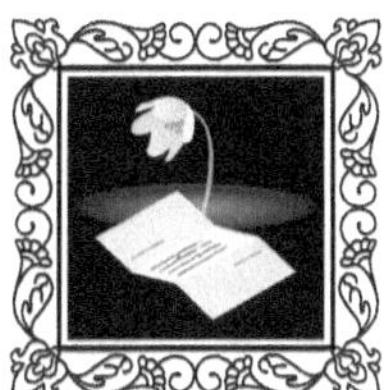

Nick Koenig and Anna M. Lawrence

Haunting collapses time, bringing the past into and thereby permanently altering the present.

—K. S. Coddington (752)

How might one see the ghost of a plant? Eerie driftings of fallen oak leaves and wilted chrysanthemums gliding transparently through the ether, or perhaps the desiccated remains of plant-matter leaving ghostly imprints on paper, rock, or skin? The ambiguity of plants as at once individual and collective, with bodies that lack clearly definable boundaries, might be echoed in their ghosts; spectral entanglements reaching across time and space, entwining around bodies and storying the land through their roots. Roots, as geographer Hannah Pitt contends, need not be that which we go "back to," but instead a manifestation of moving forward, a suggestion of potential becomings (473). Just as the spectral analytic of "haunting" collapses time, so too do plants. Following stories through roots complicates the flow of linear time, drawing past, present, and future persistently into relation with each other in the co-production and re-production of landscapes and political-ecological regimes.

This piece explores the haunting absent presence of plants—alive, imagined, and preserved—in the landscape and the archive by following the footsteps of human ghosts through fields, cemeteries, and gardens. Like our conversations on these topics, this chapter proceeds as a series of narrative anecdotes in which we share our perspectives on and experiences with botanical ghosts, both planty and human. We first came to think together about these topics several years ago as postgraduate students, sitting amongst the manicured hedges of a Cambridge college garden. Despite substantially different disciplinary backgrounds—Nick with training in biology and botanical science, Anna in historical and cultural geography—we discussed the different methods we use for sensing plants, how these might stretch across disciplinary boundaries, and the peculiar moments of serendipity in research when disparate threads suddenly coalesce and your identity as a researcher becomes inextricably bound up with the subjects of your research—human or not. For both of us at different times, these moments were marshalled by ghosts.

Through the stories presented here, we introduce the idea of "spectral serendipity": the invocation of ghosts in the research process which seem to guide the eyes and feet of the researcher by fortuitously present-ing the past. Rather than ignoring the ghosts that may appear to us in the archive or herbarium, we embrace the necessarily subjective nature of research—historical and scientific—and the intricacies woven around the figure of the researcher who is transformed, alongside their work, by the encounters they may have along the way (Mills). We reflect upon the human ghosts that have been conjured in our own research together with their various planty associates, considering the traces of the past that plant-ghosts might bring into the present, and the stories they might tell. In the following two narratives, we introduce two women and their plants: Dr Mary Wharton (a twentieth-century botanist from Kentucky) and her extensive collection of herbarium specimens and Mary Swainson (a nineteenth-century settler in Aotearoa, New Zealand) and her garden flowers.

Pursuing the (hi)stories of people and plants can be a difficult task. The fragile bodies and often abundant ghostly imprints of plants in herbaria often hide the contexts in which they were collected, and the people behind that collecting, especially if the collector was not a professional male botanist, so that both context and collector become obscured or even inaccessible to the researcher (Wintle). Conversely, looking for plants in archives built and catalogued around human interests and individuals presents the opposite challenge for the more-than-human historian: it is the people who are categorised, not the plants. Following Patricia Vieira's concept of "phytographia," we conceptualise herbaria as the vegetal remains that can be found within any archive—specimen-based or otherwise. Phytographia, as the "appellation of an encounter between writings on plants and the writing *of* plants," invites us to pay closer attention to inscriptions of plants themselves on human lives, words, and landscapes (Vieira 225). This concept provides a unifying interpretation of plant traces across different types of archive, offering a productive methodological tension between acknowledging the central role of the human in telling these stories, whilst attending to the agency of the plants in drawing them out.

                                   Nick Koenig and Anna M. Lawrence

A key and final dimension of our stories here is their relation to settler colonialism: both of our research subjects were upper-class, white women, living on stolen lands. The figure of the ghost has been much deployed in anti-colonial imaginaries that seek to uncover and interrogate the continued play of the colonial past in the colonial present (Cameron; Coddington). As Cameron observes, ghosts "unsettle the assumed stability and integrity of western temporalities and spatialities," forcing us to confront histories that are not "at rest" and those that remain politically invisible today (383). Here, we note the stories that are not present. The histories of Indigenous, Black, queer, or gender nonconforming botanists, collectors, and gardeners are at once ghostly and rooted in their perpetual becomings in and through contemporary landscapes. In sharing our own situated and personal encounters with ghosts—both human and plant—on settler lands, we hope to present herbaria as portals through which plant-human stories might flow, and through which alternative relations begin to flourish.

Nick in the Field

Sometimes you have to become a ghost to demand justice.

—R. Govindrajan (45)

Hiking through the foothills of the Appalachian Mountains in a region termed the "Outer Bluegrass and Knobs," I found myself moving through a wide-open field, looking and searching for vascular (or vein-bearing) species of plants. My ongoing project, called a floristics survey, had developed from a technical list of vascular plant species in a given area. This type of study is often considered by mainstream science as "unscientific" because a botanist will seemingly wander around a site roughly every two weeks, looking to make herbarium collections to document the plant composition of the area. However, these wanderings are extremely strategic and methodical. In the heat of August of 2020, I wanted to venture into a more remote part of the Miller-Welch Central Kentucky Wildlife Management Area to document species not previously deposited in a herbarium. My 2000 Jeep Cherokee, lovingly named Petunia, was a couple of miles away in a gravel parking lot. I had followed a horse trail used by visitors to the area as well as hunters to make a deep incursion into the 1800-acre, or 750-hectare, area. I had trekked through three open fields, crossed a stream, and passed through a couple of small forested regions. As sweat was beading—well, more like pouring—off of my forehead onto the grassy field, I gazed upon the next open field, contemplating whether to explore or not. I decided to go slightly further since the sun was still high in the sky on that humid Kentucky day, and I spotted brilliantly coloured fuschia flowers clustered on the middle of a stem no taller than my kneecap.

I was puzzled. During the summer of the COVID-19 pandemic, I had sought out these extremely people-depauperate fieldscapes to learn about the botanical diversity contained within the ancient foothills of the Appalachian mountains. However, the six creamy-pink petals with a subtle magenta line running halfway down them and the distinctly quasi-squared stem were completely unknown to my mental botanical image bank. I knelt down for a few moments, searching for clues of what family or genus the plant might belong to. I squatted patiently, waiting for the plant to signal *Hello! I am a ...*

As I looked at the plant and it looked at me, I felt a spectral presence in this ambiguity and mutual "unknowingness" I had with the plant. I was mystified because I can usually figure out what family a plant belongs to, but this plant had completely stumped me. While the plant might have not called out its Latin name, the sparse population in the middle of the wide-open, semi-wet field had signaled some ghostly, affective aura of botanical uniqueness. I snapped a picture on my phone, wrote down the GPS coordinates, the habitat description, and plant kin most likely connected to the plant of interest.

I then made the quick, but sweaty, walk back to Petunia, started her up, and blasted some music back to the herbarium preparation room, where I would gingerly place the plants collected for deposition in a wooden plant press for drying. However, I separated out the unknown collection first, furiously flipped open *Plant Life of Kentucky* (Jones), ran my fingers down the dichotomous trail of vegetal characteristics, and got the open, dreaded genus of *Lythrum*. My head was cocked sideways, but I followed the loosestrife key to the species *Lythrum alatum*, or winged loosestrife; the wings are a reference to the raised, lateral appendages along the plant stem. A relative of purple loosestrife, a noxious wetland plant that was introduced to regions of North America and that pushes out more sensitive and rare wetland plants, winged loosestrife calls much of the northern part of North America home, and sometimes even reaches into more southern regions like Kentucky, as the population in this wildlife management area had.

When I had learned about the common and scientific names ascribed to the plant, I had to know more about it: who else has met this more-than-human other in the region? Thankfully, for me, the era of botanical digitization of

Nick Koenig and Anna M. Lawrence

herbaria is well under way, so I proceeded to run a quick search for *Lythrum alatum* in Madison County, Kentucky. The search returned one result. My jaw dropped. The plant had been collected by the region's most renowned female botanist, Mary E. Wharton. I then studied carefully into the handwritten, cursive label created by young Mary Wharton in 1937. Eighty-four years prior to myself, almost to the day, the twenty-five-year-old Mary had been hiking just a couple miles north of where I was and had collected winged loosestrife (I was twenty-two at the time). Much of the history of Mary Wharton resides in the University of Kentucky archive in the form of letters and pictures. Her life began and ended in Kentucky, and she strongly advocated for protecting imperilled ecosystems by leading anti-dam protests and writing multiple plant field guides for the state. A species of dewberry (*Rubus whartoniae*) was named after her in 1942 ("Dr. Mary Wharton").

However, the digital picture of the ghostly remains housed at the University of Michigan herbarium and now laid motionless before me on the acid-free paper sheet sent goosebumps throughout my body at the synergies between myself and young Mary Wharton. While most assume that the biographies of humans will be stored within the pictures and stories we pass down, the "planty" collaborations of the "multinatural" (Latour) loosestrife-human collective had connected us through space and time via the vegetal body of the plant in an instance of what we call here "spectral serendipity." Often in herbarium collections, botanists will gather two specimens if the plant population is large enough: one for the home herbarium and a second to store as a backup. The hauntological spectre of Mary Wharton's 842nd of over eleven thousand plant specimens collected across her lifetime seemed all the more significant because it was a duplicate that I was viewing on my computer. The original had burnt in a herbarium fire at the University of Kentucky in 1948. The spectral remains of the winged loosestrife and the botanical histories encoded on the herbarium sheet were an alternative way for me to retrace the life of a woman botanist who has often been overlooked in Kentucky history. The sole remaining specimen at the University of Michigan herbarium bears witness to the spectral serendipity constituting one of the precursors to a form of spectral justice that I was—and am still—committed to: preserving and exploring the human and more-than-human histories beyond the dominant fields of the sciences and humanities (Govindrajan; Chao et al.).

The intense collapsing of the past, present, and human-vegetal futures through the dataset of digitised and real-life collections from Mary was an affective explosion I experienced throughout the day and carry with me today. The sites of herbaria continue to write complex stories of women overlooked in mainstream botanical histories. However, as discussed in our introduction and as we will reiterate in our conclusion, these stories of human-plant becoming, while focused on a historically marginalised group of women, usually revolve in scholarly narratives around white, privileged, (settler) women; multiple marginalised groups continue to be purposefully removed from historical botanical encounters. We consider later the ways in which we can reflect on these histories and work/play together in changing existing histories.

To close, I want to return to the opening quotation: "sometimes you have to become a ghost to demand justice" (Govindrajan 45). The site of a herbarium, along with the plant-botanist collective, is involved in the technical rendering of plants into species when they are viewed through a hauntological lens, sparking a thread of spectral justice that is obscured or made absent by a scientific viewing. Attending to emerging spectres, such as those of Mary Wharton and her winged loosestrife, we argue that those who engage with herbaria might gain a more vivid picture of the botanical histories that are often elided from narratives based on scientific categorisation.

Anna in the Graveyard

Sacred to the memory

of

Mary Frederica

...

The tender mother of three children

from whom

Her Lord and Saviour took her

in the prime of life

29th of September 1864

...

'She is not dead, but sleepeth.' Luke.viii.52

 Nick Koenig and Anna M. Lawrence

In January 2020, I undertook a research trip to the archives of Aotearoa in New Zealand, looking for traces of floral plant life—both literal and literary—in the letters and diaries of settler women from the early days of colonisation. My aim was to follow the flowers that flowed from England to the colony during the nineteenth century, exploring the role of flower gardens and plants more generally in negotiating life and landscape in the uneasy space between floral ephemerality and settler permanence. Searching for non-humans in traditional archives can pose a significant challenge, as records and their categories typically orbit around human individuals, collectives, and events. Unearthing the inscriptions of plants and "planty" concerns in such archives often requires considerable patience and luck. The story I offer here speaks to the transformative role of "spectral serendipity" and the affective relation of haunting in collapsing the webs of time and space strung between the archive and the more-than-human landscape in which they are rooted. In an embrace of ghost-story cliché, I start our story in a graveyard.

Every morning for a week, my walk to the Alexander Turnbull Library in Wellington took me through the Bolton Street Cemetery. Containing the city's original burial ground, which dates back to 1840, the cemetery extends out from the northeast corner of the Wellington Botanic Garden; it is a patchworked addition containing the garden's collection of heritage roses trained around metal hoops and staked among the graves. The ground upon which the botanic garden now lies was cultivated long before settlers arrived by local Māori from the nearby Pipitea pā. Today, the route through the garden to the library takes you across a long and noisy bridge that spans the Wellington Urban Motorway, a road controversially built through the middle of the cemetery in the 1960s, requiring the exhumation of 3,700 burials. On the east side of the bridge, near the path, stands a gravestone with a large, plain, concrete slab laid out in front of it, and a metal hoop for roses behind. The epitaph, as printed above, bears the name Mary Frederica Marshall.

Several days before I searched for this grave, I first encountered Mary Marshall (née Swainson) in a file of family records containing pages and pages of transcribed letters, neatly typed and numbered on translucent paper. Ghosts are quick to emerge when you read private letters, drawing you into the mundane dramas of someone else's life; as Sarah Mills observes, it is often hard to know when to let go of these archival encounters and their emotional entanglements with your own identity as a researcher (708). Mary had emigrated from England to Wellington with her family at the age of fifteen in 1841. The letters she wrote back to her grandparents in Birmingham captivated me. This was partly because they turned out to be useful sources, as Mary was a keen gardener, constantly asking her grandparents to send her flower seeds, bulbs, and roots from their garden to plant in her own.

> Do not forget to send me some seeds, and the bulbs of jonquils and daffodils—any that you can—narcissus I should like, and crocus and snow-drops (Swainson, 14 Aug. 1843).

> I have been very busy in my garden—it is about half the size of yours, which I remember you used to say was 'as large as a tea tray' (Swainson, 8 Oct. 1843).

But the letters also allowed me to watch Mary grow up before my eyes. I became involved in her personal life and felt compelled to read on, even once I had gathered all I needed for my own work. I watched her adapt to warm Christmases without mistletoe or holly, plant Birmingham anemones in her garden, observe clashes with local Māori who disputed her family's cultivation of their land, and win prizes for her rhubarb at Horticultural Society shows. I watched her get married at the age of twenty-three and send some of her wedding cake back to her family and friends in England. I watched her go through the loss of her first child at the age of twenty-four, born prematurely in March 1850. Before long, though, the letters came to an end.

I was far too involved in Mary's distant life to leave her story unfinished—in as much as a life can be *finished*, or perhaps rendered legible by its ending (Lorimer 6)—so I turned to genealogical websites to continue my research. There, I discovered that Mary was buried in the cemetery I had been walking through each day. The next morning, I found her grave. Mary had died at the age of thirty-eight, buried alongside her youngest son, who had died the year before. Later that same day, I returned to some of her letters in the archive. These, too, were neatly ordered, typed, and transcribed. Then, I turned a page and saw something odd—something that I had never seen in the many files of letters I had read: a quotation, typed, centred in the middle of the page, and with no date and seemingly no relation to what came before or after it. The quotation read as follows:

> For a thought written in warm, sunny life, and then suddenly rising up to us, when the hand that traced and the heart that cherished it are

Nick Koenig and Anna M. Lawrence

dust, is verily a ghost. It is a likeness struck off the fond human being, and surviving it. Far more truthful than bust or portrait, it bids us see the tears flow, and the pulse beat. What ghost can the church-yard yield to us like the writing of the dead? (Swainson 64).[1]

I do not really believe in ghosts, but, in that moment, it felt like I was being watched.

As suggested by Maddern and Adey, "the figure of the ghost is often used as a means of apprehending that which we cannot explain, do not expect, under-stand, or struggle to represent" (292). It is also, I would argue, used to centre ourselves in the stories of others—acutely self-referential (Cameron). Distant presences become more intimate, but only to those who sense them. I sensed a strange comfort, as if Mary was finally speaking directly to me. While mildly egocentric, this conviction compelled further reflection, inviting the spectres to move from the metaphorical to the material. Ghostly relations "tangle up the string of temporal linearity," staging conversations between past, present and future in considering who—or what—is allowed to speak (Maddern and Adey 292; Searle).

Reading Mary's letters alongside Patricia Vieira's concept of phytographia, I came to a question: what if the plants themselves were granted a haunting presence through her letters? It was not Mary's presence alone that I felt in the archives and the graveyard, but the presence too of her snowdrops and daffodils, anemones and rhubarb; plants that outlived their gardener by their persistent rooting on stolen land. The plants of Mary's gardens have their own stories to tell: of "civilising" the landscape, of escaping the manicured borders of the for-mal cottage plot, of memorialising and materialising distant relations, of mask-ing settler colonial violence with beauty (Lawrence). Plants have the ability to fabricate the spectral, collapsing space and draw the past into the present and promise of future through their bodies (Ginn); seeds sent from Birmingham to Wellington send out shoots of a flower that is, for all intents and purposes, materially the same as its sister plant on the other side of the world.

The heritage roses of Bolton Street Cemetery, some of which date back to the colonial era ("Bolton Street Cemetery"), similarly haunt the graves among which they grow, bidding us pay attention to *their* histories alongside those of the buried. For while the biography of a human spans the decades of their life alone, the biography of a plant extends in every direction and none, rhizom-atically reappearing and falling away with every flower that drops. Attending to the historical traces of plants—material and literary—suggests a different type of method and ethics that looks beyond the researcher's commitment to the individual human subject, and towards their emplacement within broader landscapes and communities: human and non, past and present.

Conclusion

Encountering human ghosts can thus prompt the consideration of their ghostly plant compatriots; spectres that are perhaps harder to conjure given the predominance of human, and increasingly nonhuman animal (McCorristine and Adams), imagery involved in imagining the un-earthly. Following the inscriptions of plants upon the earth—in real life, literature, or the spectral remains of the herbarium—draws our eyes to their co-constitution of our current material reality. Plant-ghosts are rendered material by their descendants, which corporeally collapse time and space in a present-ing of distant relations and conjuring of familiar companions: "I have some beautiful violets out, which quite smell of [our home in England], do you remember those under the drawing room windows there?" (Swainson, 23 Aug. 1846). The presence of plants "out of place"—"invasives," "weeds," unexpected ornamentals, or unseasonal food crops—raises the spectres of the plants which came before, alongside the histories of the plants that grow today and the emerging plant/more-than-plant assemblages to come.

Attuning ourselves to phytographic plant-ghosts invites reflection on the "response-abilities" (Haraway 71) involved in telling their stories. If, as we might hope, stories hold the potential to change minds and thus alter actions, how might we best tell the stories of plants? According to Austin, the biggest difficulty in representing plants as social actors is not reducing them to "anthropomorphic representations of what can be knowable to the human author/reader" (19). How does one hold the empathy-impelling concept of "plant-as-kin" alongside an acknowledgement of plant-otherness (Kimmerer)? We playfully put forward our concept of spectral serendipity to invite fellow researchers to reflect on the ghostly presences in their work as a means of holding the familiar and the uncanny side by side and up to the light. Ghosts already inhabit the space beyond the known; embracing their peculiar (mani)folding of space and time in leaf and petal pushes us to consider our shared potential in co-constituting speculative futures where we might do justice to the multitude of species and storied individuals who have called this earth their home.

     Nick Koenig and Anna M. Lawrence

It is important that we acknowledge here the dangers that come with the often romanticised telling of ghost stories. The stories we have narrated here have necessarily centred around ourselves as researchers; they were personal encounters mediated by our own identities, (overactive) imaginations, and irrepressible desire for enchantment. At the base of this desire sits an uncomfortable tension between a wishful naivety and a haunting fear that it is already too late for change—a precarious balancing between hope and dread. Enchantment, in relation to the ecological (and the political), is not straightforwardly aligned with an ethics of care (Krøijer and Rubow; Yusoff). While such a connection can occur, it is work that needs to be actively done, not an inevitability. As Cameron warns, "postcolonial" ghost stories risk constituting a "self-referential engagement with the colonial past ... perpetuating a kind of endless 'dancing around a wound'" and so failing to effectively mobilise change in the present (389). Haunting, in the minds of Eve Tuck and C. Ree, is the "relentless remembering" that will not be resolved by suggestions of settler innocence nor assurances of reconciliation (642). Bringing the past into the present requires both an attention to ghosts and a commitment to, or wariness of, "future ghosts" (Tuck and Ree 642). The seeds planted by written pieces, such as our chapter here, must be watered by actions taken beyond the page, both within and beyond the academy. We invite our readers to reflect upon the more-than-human ghosts that haunt their worlds, and how they might move forward with their roots towards a more just flourishing.

Notes

1   The quotation is from an 1853 novel, *My Novel*, by Edward Bulwer-Lytton.

Works Cited

Austin, Patrycja. "A Rustling in *The Overstory*: More-Than-Human Storytelling in Richard Powers's Novel." *Sensius Historiae*, vol. 38, no. 1, 2020, pp. 13-28.

"Bolton Street Cemetery." *Friends of Bolton Street Cemetery*, https://boltoncemetery.org.nz/. Accessed: 9 Jul. 2023.

Cameron, Emilie. "Indigenous Spectrality and the Politics of Postcolonial Ghost Stories." *Cultural Geographies*, vol. 15, no. 3, 2008, pp. 383-93.

Chao, Sophie, et al., eds. *The Promise of Multispecies Justice*. Duke University Press, 2022.

Coddington, Kate Shipley. "Spectral Geographies: Haunting and Everyday State Practices in Colonial and Present-Day Alaska." *Social & Cultural Geography*, vol. 12, no.1, 2011, pp. 743-56.

"Dr. Mary Wharton." *Floracliff Nature Sanctuary*, https://floracliff.org/dr-mary-wharton/. Accessed: 11 February 2024.

Ginn, Franklin. "Death, Absence and Afterlife in the Garden." *Cultural Geographies*, vol. 21, no. 2, 2014, pp. 229-45.

Govindrajan, Radhika. "Spectral Justice." *The Promise of Multispecies Justice*, edited by Sophie Chao et al., Duke University Press, 2022, pp. 33-51.

Haraway, Donna. *When Species Meet*. University of Minnesota Press, 2007.

Jones, Ronald. *Plant Life of Kentucky: An Illustrated Guide to the Vascular Flora*. University Press of Kentucky, 2005.

Kimmerer, Robin Wall. *Braiding Sweetgrass: Indigenous Wisdom, Scientific Knowledge and the Teachings of Plants*. Milkweed Editions, 2013.

Krøijer, Stine, and Cecilie Rubow. "Introduction: Enchanted Ecologies and Ethics of Care." *Environmental Humanities*, vol. 14, no. 2, 2022, pp. 375-84.

Latour, Bruno. *Politics of Nature: How to Bring the Sciences into Democracy*. Harvard University Press, 2004.

Lawrence, Anna M. "Pickled Moonbeams: Horticultural Dislocations of a Settler Colony." *King's Review*, vol. 6, 2020, pp. 24-29, https://www.kingsreview.co.uk/essays/pickled-moonbeams-the-horticultural-dislocations-of-a-settler-colony.

Lorimer, Hayden. "Dear Departed: Writing the Lifeworlds of Place." *Transactions of the Institute of British Geographers*, vol. 44, 2019, pp. 331-45.

Maddern, Jo Frances, and Peter Adey. "Editorial: Spectro-Geographies." *Cultural Geographies*, vol. 15, 2008, pp. 291-95.

McCorristine, Shane, and William M. Adams. "Ghost Species: Spectral Geographies of Biodiversity Conservation." *Cultural Geographies*, vol. 27, no. 1, 2019, pp. 101-15.

Mills, Sarah. "Cultural-Historical Geographies of the Archive: Fragments, Objects and Ghosts." *Geography Compass*, vol. 7, no. 10, 2013, pp. 701-13.

Pitt, Hannah. "Roots." *Environmental Humanities*, vol. 13, no. 2, 2021, pp. 470-74.

Searle, Adam. "Hunting Ghosts: On Spectacles of Spectrality and the Trophy Animal." *Cultural Geographies*, vol. 28, no. 3, 2021, pp. 513-30.

Swainson, Mary. *Letter to her grandparents in England*. 14 Aug. 1843. qMS-1337. Alexander Turnbull Library, Wellington, Australia.

 Nick Koenig and Anna M. Lawrence

---. Letter to her grandparents in England. 8 Oct. 1843. qMS-1337. Alexander Turnbull Library, Wellington, Australia.

---. Letter to her grandparents in England. 23 Aug. 1846. qMS-1339. Alexander Turnbull Library, Wellington, Australia.

---. Letters to her grandparents in England. 1826-54. qMS-1337. Alexander Turnbull Library, Wellington, Australia.

Tuck, Eve, and C. Ree. "A Glossary of Haunting." *Handbook of Autoethnography*, edited by Stacy Linn Holman Jones et al., Left Coast Press, Inc, 2013, pp. 639-58.

Vieira, Patrícia. "Phytographia: Literature as Plant Writing." *The Language of Plants: Science, Philosophy, Literature*, edited by M. Gagliano et al., University of Minnesota Press, 2017, pp. 205-20.

Wintle, Claire. "Decolonizing the Smithsonian: Museums as Microcosms of Political Encounter." *The American Historical Review*, vol. 121, no. 5, 2016, pp. 1492-1520.

Yusoff, Kathryn. "Aesthetics of Loss: Biodiversity, Banal Violence and Biotic Subjects." *Transactions of the Institute of British Geographers*, vol. 37, no. 4, 2012, pp. 578-92.

12 Nympha Voynichiana

Edward Colless

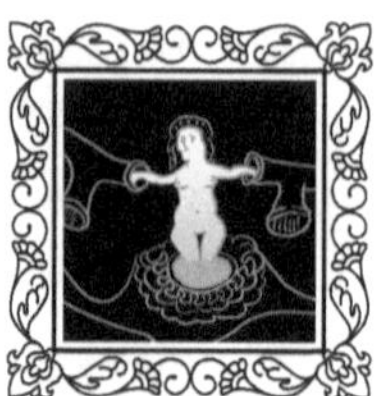

It has been called "the most mysterious book in the world," and not with-out good reason.[1] But in Yale University's Beinecke Rare Book and Manuscript Collection, it is modestly identified (like those efflorescent distant galaxies with drily deadpan, alphanumeric codes) by the formal title of Beinecke MS 408. "From the outside," as historian Deborah Harkness explains when she intro-duces Yale's 2016 facsimile edition, "there's little about Beinecke MS 408 to catch the eye" (Harkness vii).[2] "Not an especially glamorous object," notes another commentator, looking at the manuscript in its binding (Zhang). The volume is small, about the size and thickness of an airport paperback; and it is bound in soft, bare and, bland brown vellum limply stretched over thin board—a legacy, with its stitching, from the Renaissance and possibly some mid-nineteenth-cen-tury conservation. Its parchment content and inks have, however, recently been dated to the early fifteenth century, probably the 1420s; the manuscript was pos-sibly produced in the southern German-speaking states or in northern Italian speaking ones. However, these locales give no hint about the weirdly secret, unintelligible language this volume written in.

It has no title, no author, no attributed artist, no markings to indicate its ori-gin or its purpose. It has little scholarly or artistic context, and it has no prog-eny. Despite its unassuming guise, Beinecke MS 408 has been the object of cen-turies of intense curiosity and speculation, has inspired astonishment as well as incredulity, has generated conspiracy theories and academic feuds, has been associated with black magic and Cold War spycraft, has been smuggled, has been forgotten, and has motivated obsessive, and universally futile, endeavours at interpretation. MS 408: it is indeed an inscrutable galaxy, or at least an entire world—just maybe not this one.

A handwritten, illuminated codex of 234 pages (a number of these are fold-outs in various sizes), MS 408 has a stately, calligraphic text intricately and deftly interlaced with elaborate and vivacious illustrations of botanical speci-mens, with galleries of naked women bathing in oily liquid and frolicking in chorus lines like Maenads on a Greek kylix, with astronomical charts and horoscopic zodiacs designed for incomprehensible calculations, and with daunting diagrams of dizzyingly concentric, minutely cellular structures that have cogs and sawtooth gears and that could equally be microbial parasites, celestial spheres, or cross-section schemes for gargantuan civil engineering. Penned in an elegant, but also casually confident and consistent, hand without erasures or corrections, this remarkable script has defied translation, just as its language has defied detection.[3]

But while this script may be unintelligible, does that mean it is gibberish? Could it be a hoax? Studies of the script since the 1980s, using computer-aided analysis, have concluded that the text has twenty-five to thirty recurrent characters, suggesting it is an alphabetic or a consonantal (abjad) script, although there are no indications of word formation or grammar. Nonetheless, this could imply that MS 408 represents a "natural language," even with no convincing match to any known language. On this evidence, if the text were a hoax—nonsense or a parody of a secret, medieval scientific or occult treatise that was meant to defraud a potential collector and that is still capable of fooling twenty-first-century cryptography—it would need to have been generated by a cryptographic technique capable of mimicking the rules of a natural language. However, such an understanding of the fabric of "natural language" was not a competency of medieval linguistic science. Also, providing a motive for such forgery (via historical context or textual evidence) remains as difficult as translating or decoding the text itself. And, if the volume is written in code, then it is a code that the greatest codebreakers of the last hundred years have failed to identify (D'Imperio, 23-45).[4]

A language whose words do not follow any grammatical rules; nonsense that obeys unknown rules; a cipher that does not operate like any recognisable cipher. And it is not just the script that sends experts into vertiginous spins. The bizarre, botanical imagery and captions, appearing to be both instructive illustrations and meandering marginalia, seem tantalisingly close in style and content to medieval and antique sources, but, under scrutiny, they become indefinably remote, foreign, and uninterpretable. We see botanical specimens that do not appear to have any instrumental relation to their captions and that do not resemble real plants. Paleographers, philologists, linguists, botanists, mathematicians, cryptologists, kabbalists, iconologists—professional and amateur, as well as often expending decades of effort—have all repeatedly failed to crack MS 408. The scholarship concerning this volume has been as exacting and drily laborious as forensic archaeological registers of pot sherds in soil layers; but it has also been as provocative and inquisitorial as an espionage thriller or crime fiction novel. MS 408 persists today as an utterly mystifying and spectral book: so much about it stubbornly remains, after six hundred years, inaccessible.

Beinecke MS 408 is better, and more resonantly, known as the Voynich Manuscript (dubbed thus by afficionados and henceforth here referred to as "VMs"), from the name of the rare books dealer Wilfrid Voynich who, in 1912, found it among an assortment of manuscripts he had acquired from the Jesuit Collegio Romano in Rome. So idiosyncratic and recognisably unique is the untranslatable script in the manuscript that it has been labelled "Voynichese." Voynich himself poses almost as much of a riddle as the manuscript and the "language" adopting his name. Obituaries at his death in 1930 eulogise him; he was a generous polymath, fluent in perhaps twenty languages, and possessing extraordinary bibliographic erudition. He was the perfect, predestined recipient of this beguiling codex. More recent biographies depict him as a roguish character, occasionally a fantasist, steering his way through "a life of adventure, espionage, danger and dark secrets" while carrying an assortment of scars from knife and bullet wounds. But, then, these secrets and scars also seem like good credentials for someone discovering the world's most mysterious book.

Born of Polish parents in Lithuania (then part of the Russian Empire), Voynich graduated with degrees in law and chemistry from the University of Moscow in 1884; he was soon after arrested as a member of the Polish nationalist, revolutionary underground. A year and a half of imprisonment in Warsaw were followed by five years of exile in Siberia, from which he escaped on foot to Mongolia (where, by his own less than reliable account, he wandered for months in the desert), there joining a camel caravan to Beijing, and then eventually making his way via south Asia to Hamburg, at which penniless point he allegedly bartered his last physical possessions for passage on a merchant ship to England. Through a clique of fellow revolutionary Polish and Russian exiles in London and their supportive British intellectual circle, he became manager in the early 1890s of a translation, publishing and smuggling business for anti-Tsarist propaganda, which—despite his being monitored by the Russian secret police—gave him an entrée into the European book trade and, subsequently, to the antiquarian bibliophile market. Dissociating himself from Russian revolutionary subversion, he set up his own, quickly successful antiquarian dealership in Soho in 1898.

The manuscript discovered fourteen years later in the de-accession lot from the Jesuits has itself a biography as colourful as that of Voynich. The codex's provenance in the fifteenth and sixteenth centuries is a mystery, but it was certainly passing through some hands in Prague in the early 1600s, possibly those of Emperor Rudolf II. A book with arcane, eccentric botanical and astronomical illustrations would not have been inappropriate for Rudolf's attention. He was a renowned patron of both occult arts and alchemy, as well astronomy, and an enthusiast for innovations in the natural sciences, offering court patronage to Johannes Kepler, Tycho Brahe, and the celebrated botanist and horticulturalist Carolus Clusius. Rudolf II also famously collected for his *Wunderkammer*, his treasury of wonders and curiosities, in which a manuscript such as this would hardly have been out of place.

The signature of ownership by a pharmacist known as Sinapius (and associated with Rudolf's court as an alchemist and director of the emperor's botanical garden) was accidentally discovered through multispectral imaging of the first page of the manuscript; the signature dates probably to the 1610s. The codex was then owned by a Prague alchemist, Georgius Barschius, who, in 1637, copied parts of it and sent them to the famous Jesuit polymath Athanasius Kircher in Rome, known for his baffling, extravagant, allegorical attempts at deciphering Egyptian hieroglyphs. After two years, Kircher wrote back that he was stumped. Even he could get nowhere with this codex's incomprehensible cipher.[6] In a responding letter of the same year to Kircher, Barschius describes the text as "a riddle of the Sphinx" doubtless still trying to hook Kircher's Egyptological interest, but to no avail.[7] At his death, Barschius left his alchemical library, including the VMs, to his friend Johannes Marci, a Prague scientist. In 1665, Marci sent the entire manuscript to Kircher, plaintively revealing Barschius's sustained, dedicated but unsuccessful attempts at decipherment, with a request for the maestro to try again decoding it, for "indeed such sphinxes obey only their very own Kircher."[8] Kircher never replied, but passed the book on, at his death, to the Collegio Romano's library in Rome. There it remained, untouched in the dark and unknown, until 1873, when the government of the newly unified state of Italy, hostile to the Jesuits, ordered confiscation of all their libraries and archives in Rome.

Under the subterfuge of individuals keeping personal possessions, a collection of two thousand items was slipped out from the Collegio Romano, labelled "Private Library of P. Beckx" (a Jesuit Superior-General), and sent for safekeeping to the Villa Torlonia in Castel Gandolfo, on the coast south of Rome.[9] The villa was the family seat of Prince Torlonia, a personal friend of Petrus Beckx and a supporter of the Jesuits. Again, the document stayed in hiding until in 1903, when the Jesuits, strapped for cash after the Italian government's confiscations, put 380 documents from the library in Castel Gandolfo on the private—if not, in fact, clandestine—market with a catalogue containing two items from Kircher's library, one of which was described as "Miscellanea/codex membranacaeus saeculae XV." This was the VMs.

Voynich's purchase of it was not straightforward. The sale took nine years to complete, for reasons still unknown. And as if the manuscript did not already have enough obscurity, Voynich insinuated that he had unearthed it from a trunk long neglected among cobwebbed clutter in a castle in southern Austria, and that he was unable to give further details, as he had been sworn to silence by the castle's shadowy aristocratic occupants. His tale is a delightfully fantastic diversion, and—who knows?—perhaps inspired by the phantasmagorical, gothic novel *The Saragossa Manuscript* by Voynich's compatriot, the Polish count Jan Potocki (the novel was written in French from 1805 to 1815 and was published in Polish in 1847). This epic presents the story of a marvellous manuscript discovered in a sealed casket at an inn by a soldier during the Napoleonic war in Spain. The manuscript records the picaresque adventure of a man who, forty years earlier, became enmeshed in a series of nested stories involving kabbalists, secret societies, hauntings and seductions, dangerous escapades, magic, and hallucination. Almost a match for Voynich's biography, whether his tale was genuine or fabricated. But there was some truth to Voynich's story of his purchase.

The Jesuits made the sale of the VMs on the condition of Voynich's absolute secrecy, as the items were supposedly meant to be taken by the Vatican Library. This was a confidence that Voynich told his wife, Ethel Voynich (with a biography as compelling as Wilfred's), but that was kept in a sealed letter by her, to be opened—on her instructions written ominously on the envelope to her assistant and friend Anne Nill—only after her death. She died in 1960, thirty years after her husband, allowing a good half century of mystery and mystique about the manuscript to brew. Although he did well from selling other pieces from the Jesuit catalogue, Voynich himself was unable to sell the VMs. Anne Nill inherited it at Ethel Voynich's death and could only strike a deal on deferred profits from any future sale when she handed it to the rare book dealer Hans P. Kraus. After almost a decade of also failing to find a buyer, Kraus gifted it to Yale University in 1969.

Sounds like the VMs carries a curse? Recognising that there was something sinisterly out of place but promisingly out of the ordinary in it, Voynich dubbed this codex "the ugly duckling" of his catalogue (Hunt 17). He had found, secreted in its pages, Johannes Marci's 1665 letter presenting the codex to Athanasius Kircher and describing it as a secret work written in the thirteenth century by the Franciscan philosopher-scientist Roger Bacon and formerly belonging to Rudolf II. Oddly, it took several years before Voynich began sleuthing into the codex's Prague background. But then, taking Marci at his word, Voynich became convinced (and persuasively so to many others) that the manuscript had been at some point transcribed in code because it contained secret—that is to say, heretical—knowledge.[10] Trying to fill a gap in provenance between Bacon and Rudolf II, Voynich recklessly proposed (based on a highly dubious source) the sixteenth-century magus Dr John Dee as an intermediary and as the person who sold the manuscript to Rudolf.[11] Admittedly, Dee would not have been an unsuitable owner; he was a practitioner of hermetic and occult arts, was well versed in ciphers, and believed he had transcribed (by skrying through a black mirror with the help of his scurrilous medium, Edward Kelley) the language of angels, which he called Enochian. And he was in Prague in the mid-1580s where, with his reputation preceding him, had met with Rudolph. (Another version of this story had it that Kelley was the author the MS as a forged cipher and the culprit who sold this fraudulent manuscript to Rudolf II.) The connection to Dee also sounded pertinent because he had, with Enochian so to speak, invented a non-human language—even if its utterances were prattle. The Bacon-Dee connection became a canonical feature of Voynich research, even into the 1970s. Like most potential keys to the book's secrecy, however, this line of enquiry has now been thoroughly debunked. Lacking an origin story, the manuscript stays out of place. An "ugly duckling." A cuckoo, perhaps?

Or perhaps "alien" is a better word for it: a stranger. For the botany in its pages is a catalogue of stranger things. On each page throughout the first half of the volume, plant stems surge and dexterously twist or writhe upward from tentacular or tuberous or vascular root systems. In rusty browns, blood-streaked and soaked carmines, and in bilious piss yellows, these roots sprawl, spike, and spiral across the lower third of the page, thirstily soaking up obscure nutrients from the parchment itself. At times, these roots are extruded into filaments that flick and whip with the petulant agitation of animals' tails, stream outward to grasp with barbed tendrils at unseen prey, or even seem to contrive menacing, talismanic emblems, as if with the crooked, withered claws of a witch. On some pages, the roots appear intestinal, with engorged, bulbous knots clotting and shunting in peristaltic waves; elsewhere, they seem to be vines drooping ovaries and lymph glands, or swellings that hang above and drape across the literal bottom edge of the page, like pendulous, hairy testicles descending from etiolated, wormy ducts. Leaves of dusty jade, khaki, russet, and royal blue sprout into generously exuberant globules and clusters, fanning flamboyantly outward in starbursts, splayed like points of a coronet. Their serrate or dentate edges inflate and elongate into spikey insect feelers and mandibles. Petals unfurl from vaginal mouths ridged with glimmering cilia, puckering, gaping, lapping. They whirl and vibrate as a chorus of scurrying amoebae in Dionysian fever, haloes jittering around a regal orb. They flicker seductively as long lashes around the rims of solid cobalt eyes.

On later pages in the book, these plants assemble in loose ranks, their roots strutting like the legs of bloated animals on a blind march or convulsing and slithering with the undulations of jellyfish. Their foliage ceremonially mimics the plumage on a knight's helmet or, with ribbed and striped patterns, resembles medieval pennants billowing in the wind. And yet for all this vitality, there is no atmosphere, no soil or air, no sun in their world. Equally confounding and disconcerting are columnar sections of stems, telescoping and stacked in layers like storeyed wedding cakes or elaborately decorated pharmaceutical canisters. They are crammed into the pages' vertical margins, or appear as cross-section diagrammes of penile plumbing, secreting and spurting out the curlicues and filigrees of flowering viscera. All things here shimmer, shiver, quiver, pulse, arc, and stretch with a shrewd, at times lewd, animation. They bud, they sway, they climb in serpentine sproutings, they swell or sag in a sunless, unseasonal, moistureless, etheric medium.

At a distant first glance, these plants might seem to behave in the manner of a generic medieval or Renaissance taxonomy of medicinal herbs, a pharmacopeia or encyclopedia of plants detailing their remedial uses or dangers, their astrological and perhaps alchemical correspondences. But as compendia of traditional botanical and herbalist knowledge, herbal manuscripts relied on precision in copying visual and textual information from authorised earlier sources. Any variance from the canonical data might at most be supplemental annotations or scholia. In medieval Europe, there were three major traditions of these taxonomies. One was based on *De materia medica* by the first century CE Greek botanist Dioscurides, which had survived in the sumptuously illustrated version known as the *Vienna Dioscurides*, produced in Constantinople in 515 CE, copies of which were distributed in Greek, Latin, and Arabic to some European courts and monasteries. Print versions in Italian, German and Spanish began circulating widely in the late fifteenth century, well after the VMs was compiled. Although the botanical authority and discernability of its depicted specimens made *De materia medica* highly influential in elite circles, the lavish quality of its illustrations inhibited its circulation in pre-Gutenberg Europe. In comparison, the VMs illustrations appear rustic and untidy, certainly inaccurate. Another, far more popular, and thus accessible, second tradition was descended from a fourth-century herbal originating in Roman north Africa and attributed to Pseudo-Apuleius. Its illustrations were much less elaborate, and so much easier to copy; however, the style and layout bear little resemblance to the VMs. Moreover, its popularity was eclipsed in the twelfth century by a third tradition, that of the medical school of Salerno, notably Matthaeus Platearius's *Circa instans* (known also as the *Book of Simple Medicines*), an alphabetical listing of herbal drugs and their plants. Within their regular frames, the Salerno illustrations have a clean, in fact sanitary, formal propriety missing from the far more casually disposed VMs images. When compared to the Salerno style, the VMs pages feel contaminated, as well as playful and disorderly.

While there have been tentative identifications of plants in the VMs, based on empirical observation (habitually provisional, often contradictory, and usually disputed), it is almost universally accepted that the Voynich plants do not look like any of the illustrations from these traditional sources. This is not for lack of detail, as the VMs plants have intricately rendered leaf and flower morphology. In fact, it seems as if the specimens in the VMs assiduously elude clear connections to any transmitted knowledge of botany, via uncommon hybridisation or via untraceable deviation. In addition, the herbalist texts in common circulation were produced in workshops, by several scribes and illustrators at work on different sections or with different expertise, much like the work conducted in monastic scriptoria. But the script and illustrations in the VMs appear to have been, unusually, the work of two (or, at most, three) unhesitating, fluent hands. It could be that this was a grimoire composed by initiates of a very small sect with a fiendishly devised private language, a secret society perhaps of occultists about which we now know nothing.

And there is something fiendish about the febrile commotion of the plants, their roots, and their blossoms, even when they are squashed like bug stains on the page. It is not that uncommon for plants displayed in late antique or medieval herbalist guides and horticultural encyclopaedias to inhabit the shallow, synthetic space of lifeless, pressed flowers—almost the space of religious icons. But the graphic treatment of these Voynich plants is plotted like the ornate calligraphy of an illuminated letter fronting a liturgical text. Many of the botanical illustrations seem less instrumental or technical and more like the decorative, libertine improvisations found in an incipit of the *Lindisfarne Gospels*. Their posturing, mischievous tendrils, and gawping or leering rictuses even seem to satirise, if pre-dating, the diagrammatic abstraction of anatomical dissection, with its evenly lit, planar frontality of organs pinned out like emblemata; or, at least, these illustrations drolly resemble speculative medical schemas in the tradition of Vesalius and Galen. And, of course, almost all dissected plants divulge morphological as well as poetic analogies with human and animal reproductive systems—pistils, stamens, ovules, though, obviously they are hermaphroditic; these analogies can even seem to be anthropomorphic allegory. But in the illustrations of the VMs, the metamorphoses between species, between sizing, and between organic functions are amplified to hysterical magnitude, pathological as well as comical. This extroversion can be hallucinatory. With their baffling scale and meticulously drafted outlines of repetitive segments, some of these botanical specimens suggest the sort of beguiling, folk-tale features of the vegetation in Henri (*le Douanier*) Rousseau's paintings of fanciful, numinous jungles. Some even seem to have the whimsical, doodling improvisation of Dr Seuss's bizarrely elastic, laughing cat, who can balletically leap off a beach ball, juggling, like an acrobat, a teacup and birthday cake on his twisting, teetering stovepipe hat.[12]

Because of this aptitude for embellishment, the Voynich plants also display a propensity for the grotesque. Page after page, each of these strident miscreants adopts the morphological makeup of a *cadavre exquis*, exhilarating as proto-Surrealist fantasias but liable to the complaint that Hegel pronounced in his displeasure and disgust with plants' lack of anatomical decorum. In his *Encyclopaedia of the Philosophical Sciences*, Hegel observes that, despite apparent similarities with animals' sexual and vascular organs, plants do not possess the complex and discretionary internal configuration of insemination and gestation, nor of ingestion and metabolism (Hegel 183-99). It is not so much that plants can be called organs without bodies, but that, for him, they are nakedly, disgustingly extroverted organs; they are equivalent to the disparaging image of a groping octopus as a ravenous, unconcealed sex organ. What Hegel—in a bizarre tirade—found so repulsive in plants, and especially in their flowering, was their effusiveness: an obscenely complacent exteriorisation of sexual presentation, lacking the discreet configuration (*Gestaltung*) of form and function that induces an individuation (as *Gestalt*) and implementation of differentiated tools in animal, but more especially in human, bodies: hand, penis, eye, vagina, mouth, stomach, bowel, all of which provide for the sublimation of appetites (that is to say, the ability to digest food away from the feeding trough or carcass; and for *eros* to store up, enhance, and also govern libido).

The flowering plant for Hegel is a disarray of genitalia, and so it lacks a unitary essence of sexuality while it overproduces genitality in order to reproduce. Reproduction as flowering is an emission, a mode of excretion. The flower is the opening out, the inflammation, of a hole. Genitality is wasted, squandered in the flower. "Plants thus come to represent nature," remarks David Farrell Krell on what he calls Hegel's dialectic of genitality; they are "swooning nature" (127). Overcome by their own naturalness (*Natürlichkeit*), they contaminate the coming-to of Spirit. They hypnotise, they charm. Whenever Hegel employs the words *natürlich* and *Natürlichkeit*, adds Krell:

> he means that in nature or humanity which must be eradicated from
> a system of reason. Not cancelled and preserved, not aufgehoben, but
> eradicated. Whereas *Natur* is the Eve of Adam, *Natürlichkeit* is the
> Eve—or the Lilith—of Satan; if nature is the trash of the idea, the
> natural is the biohazardous waste in that trash, calling for special
> handling and careful evacuation (130).

The Voynich plants may be despoiling in that sense of Hegel's naturalness, debauched like Baudelaire's evil flower, or Blake's sick rose. To flip Hegel's complaint into a perverse affirmation of their unnaturalness, we could call the Voynich plants *ungestalt*—being without any identifying form. Entity without identity. There are hundreds of these mutating, roguish specimens illustrated in the VMs. And yet, even more remarkable than the profligacy of the manuscript's aberrant plant life, and despite myriad claims and counterclaims, not one of these specimens has ever been persuasively identified as any plant known to botanical science, not even as fantasias derived from ancient and medieval botanical sources, from magical herbalism, or from mythology. One could say that these plants are not of this world, but nor are they unambiguous contrivances. Each one is singular, yet also nondescript.

Krell's suspicion of Hegel's *Natürlichkeit* as satanic also incriminates the hordes of naked women who flourish and surge throughout the manuscript, mostly in hypnotically identical poses, with rhythmically interlocking limbs that suggest the same fever and inscrutable intent as the plants. "[L]ines of naked women," recollects Mircea Cartarescu in the all-too-brief but delirious, obsessional three pages given to the VMs in his monumental autofiction *Solenoid*,

> bathing in tubs and tubes, in green and turquoise blue liquids. Dozens of naked women with prominent stomachs, women holding, arms outstretched in a kind of horror, something that looks like a fish, sometimes an embryo, sometimes a flower. Rubicund, vegetative women, shoving their hands into sinuous, ramifying pipes, standing up in the same blue water in receptacles shaped like cornucopia that extend through pipes that look like veins or intestines (576).

Pond-scum, leaf-green, and petal-blue inky fluids incessantly and uninterruptedly, page upon page, drain into and flush out of interconnected communal baths, barrels, fountains, funnels, pots, and pools, lapping around the ankles and knees of these "vegetative women." This labyrinthine plumbing is as alimentary as it might be vascular or uterine, or it even might be a burlesque of horticultural irrigation with bilge or sewage. Yet none of these analogies seems adequate to account for the prolific strangeness in hydrodynamics of the various types of apparatus in which the nimble, curious, choric rituals of these figures are performed. Perhaps this ever-flowing fluid could be genuinely oneiric or a hysterical symptom: an index of the codex's ink transfigured into an obscene surplus of the text's and image's liquescent substances, discharging, spilling across and down the page as a secretion and trail, *ungestalt* but intermittently channelled and damned up, as the fecund solution in which—or out of which— these women sport like so many nymphs prancing in spermatic brine.

"Plant-like women," Cartarescu reminds us, repeating himself, as if trying to focus in front of a bestiary (577). Fauna or flora? These are not those all-too-familiar avatars of women caught in the act of bathing, such as the mythological Diana or the biblical Susanna. The Voynich nymphs perform without any of the perennial voyeurist dramatics of discovery and punishment that affect those women. There have been some efforts to identify these wading, plant-like women with emblematic ingredients of alchemical recipes, with components of distilling and condensing apparatuses, or with elements of more abstruse repertoires of alchemical symbolism (Rampling 46-51). But I would argue that the unashamed, even audacious, nudity with which these women assemble and parade more likely resembles, but then only to a limited degree, the medieval imagery of groups of women rapturously splashing about in a "fountain of youth," particularly in the popular usage of that theme within the chivalric romance poetry and courtly love supposedly contemporaneous with the VMs. In the European tradition, fountains of youth are usually rectangular or hexagonal masonry constructions, as indeed are some of the bathing pools in the VMs. But even with these iconographic similarities, the trail of tempting clues into the Voynich enigma inevitably evaporates. Alluding to baptismal salvation, fountains of youth are invariably situated in a paradise garden where, after a rejuvenating bath, amorous trysts can take place in the bowers. But there is no sign of a garden in the VMs, unless one counts the plants listed in the first half of the book. Instead of sublime garden features, the Voynich fountains evoke the vats used for tanning or brewing, or the cauldrons employed for cannibalistic stewing. And while the Voynich plants are otherworldly, they do not give the impression of being heavenly or Edenic. With the exception of one couple crossing arms in a handshake, there is little in the way of erotic rendezvous in this alien world.

Among Voynich scholars, these bathing scenes are called "balneological," borrowed jargon that denotes the effect of medicinal or therapeutic springs (distinct from any cosmetic benefits of mud baths), suggesting that the chorus lines of nymphs may be illuminating an enciphered manual on gynaecology or female hygiene (Brewer; Gibbs). But those murky spas of such a Voynich health resort do not exactly emanate the regenerative and tonic atmosphere of mineral baths, let alone the buoyancy of paradisical founts of life. Would cleansing, medicinal waters have the soupy, swampy opacity of the liquor flowing through the Voynich baths? This weirdly irrigated land is a Garden of Unearthly Delights, the botanical science of which is compiled as an anthology of unintelligible plants with their equally unintelligible texts. Even the word "botanical" itself begins to sound unintelligible in this milieu.

The Voynich botany does not belong to any herbal history, either in its mode of production or its image repertoire. What one might expect of a compendium, if it were situated in such an iconographic tradition, would be evidence of its own influence, as dutiful copies were derived from it or made after it. The VMs confounds this expectation. There are no signs of the historical transmission of motifs, either into the book or from it. It had no precedent, and it has no legacy. The book seems to have no past, just as it has no posterity. It is sterile. The idiom of these plants is alien to the herbarium tradition. Perhaps the herbal or horticultural discipline exercised by the makers of the VMs would more aptly be called "exobotany."

Not that this is to champion the VMs as an exceptional case of science fiction *avant la lettre*, as exoplanet world-building, or as the fantastic album of a dilettante botanist travelling to places as exotic as those visited by Jonathan Swift's intrepid Gulliver. Instead, think of the VMs as an artefact fabricated—pirating part of the subtitle of Henry Darger's fantastic novel—"in what is known as the realms of the unreal." Treat the VMs as an outsider romance. Indeed, if there is a book that demonstrates a similarly daunting unreadability to the VMs and similarly exotic dramatis personae, it would be Henry Darger's fifteen-thousand-page, compactly typed manuscript of his epic *The Story of the Vivian Girls*, in *What is Known as the Realms of the Unreal, of the Glandeco-Angelinian War Storm, Caused by the Child Slave Rebellion*.[13] This saga, probably the longest known work of fiction, was written over at least four decades—some scholars have even suggested six—and remained wholly unseen throughout Darger's lifetime. Though stylistically not stream of consciousness, it was written compulsively; its plotted, if sprawling, narrative of enslavement, rebellion, and apocalyptic battle is located on a massive planet over which the earth hovers, orbiting as its moon. On this planet, legions of countless little girls from the Catholic kingdom of Abbieannia, led by a clique of seven warrior princesses called the Vivian Sisters, engage in a grotesque, shockingly bloodthirsty civil war against adult slavers of the atheist Glendolinian clan, who wear military uniforms bizarrely topped with academic mortar-boards. Darger illustrated his monumental story with over three hundred intricate images in pencil, watercolour, and collage, some forming metres-long cinematic panoramas glued together from smaller, composed sheets.

As is well known, what makes Darger's illustrated manuscript exceptional in literature is that its author and artist was a reclusive, isolated, undereducated, asocial, and untrained amateur with a history of childhood and adolescent institutionalisation. In 1932, at the age of forty, Darger rented a tenement room in a northside Chicago suburb, near where he worked at menial jobs (as a dishwashing and a janitor) and close to the Catholic church at which he daily (often several times) attended services. This room was a home and studio, in which, apart from essential excursions, Darger lived, writing and painting hermit-like for the next forty years. After injuries from being hit by a car, which made him eventually unable to climb the stairs to his room, he admitted himself to a nursing home, where he died a few months later, in 1973, a day after turning eighty-one.[14]

Darger's astonishingly prolific, utterly secretive—and, to him, ultimately worthless—creative output was only discovered when, shortly before his death, his tenement room was cleared out by his landlord at the instruction of Darger (almost like Kafka's notorious command for his editor Max Brod to destroy his unpublished writing). Sorting through Darger's lair, the landlord found *The Vivian Girls* manuscript, hand-bound into fifteen mammoth volumes. It was among teetering stacks of newspapers, magazines, and comic books, a daily weather journal kept diligently for over ten years, numerous diaries, and innumerable balls of string, rubber bands, empty medicine bottles, and other debris accumulated across decades of scavenging and hoarding. The landlord also discovered two more gargantuan literary opuses: a ten-thousand-page, handwritten sequel to *The Vivian Girls* that was provisionally entitled *Crazy House: Further Adventures in Chicago*, and a five-thousand-page autobiography, only two hundred pages of which detail Darger's early life, the remainder being a fictional account of a tornado. It must have been a discovery as disorienting and awe-inspiring as Voynich's encounter with the "Miscellanea/codex membranacaeus saeculae XV."

Within this almost inhuman—and, in a way, anonymous—creative profusion, the illustrations of *The Vivian Girls* demonstrate an intuitive talent and idiosyncratic vision that would alone have been enough to define an artistic career. Alternately idyllic and brutal, they depict naked or partially clothed pre-pubescent girls romping serenely in wondrously superabundant Blakean or budding groves, sometimes sprouting ram horns and butterfly wings as if infused with animistic Ovidean vibrance. Or, in delicate watercolour and pastel washes, they suffer in pitiless but meticulously detailed Goyaesque carnage: as rebels, they are hunted by the slavers, strangled, mutilated, eviscerated, dismembered, beheaded, or crucified in blood-soaked killing fields. Both extremes of passion and fantasy were doubtlessly inspired by imagery of Catholic ecstasy and martyrdom. But there is a particularly hallucinatory quality to the Vivian sisters and their army of little girls that I would associate with the VMs. I do not mean their famously hermaphroditic physiology: when depicted frontally naked, they sport infantile penises. (This may be symptomatic less of sexual anxiety, misogyny, or paedophilia than of sexual ignorance and even innocence; it has been speculated that Darger may never have seen a woman naked. Even so, the physiology of these girls is a mark that becomes an expressive sign.) Rather—well, perhaps in addition to this—what the kingdom of Abbieannia shares with the VMs is the generally identical appearance of its female population.

Across hundreds of sheets bound into volumes resembling antiquarian manuscripts, Darger adeptly traced or collaged his Abbieannian intersexual figures from comics, children's books, and magazine advertising, but gave them matching facial features, expressions, and even poses.[15] Serial variation mimicking family resemblance across thousands of girls of the same age. In a fleeting aside on Henry Darger, Giorgio Agamben is so struck by the ingenuity of these creatures that he dubs them a novel species: *nympha dargeriana* (Agamben 18). These figures might run, leap, squat, fight, sniff flowers, or lie wounded and bleeding, but the impression of their innocuously self-absorbed, twinning, or mirrored similarities is undeniable. The balenological nymphs in the VMs pose in roundels and carousels or dance in a serpentine line, yet they also all appear to be multiples of the same figure, presented in three-quarter view, rotated, or flipped, with one hand hoisted onto their hip, as if printed from a template *ad infinitum*. Could we not bestow a scientific name on them, as Agamben does with Darger's nymphs? An exobotanical name for "plant-like women": *nympha voynichiana?* As with Darger's illustrations, the similarity of these women may have been a technical convenience; however, this technique also becomes a symptomatic mannerism that, in turn, becomes a signature device, a signature of the realm of the unreal.

Though resembling medieval herbals, the VMs is a singular—and thus incomparable—thing, as alien as Darger's unreadable world of the Vivian sisters. Cartarescu insists that the VMs was made by "some unknown person who had never made anything like it (because nothing like the Voynich manuscript exists anywhere in the world)" (577). It is the failure of the simile, manifested in the elusive grammatical function of the word "like" (as preposition, adverb, adjective, or noun suffix), which appears in so much commentary on the VMs, even with the sustained, symptomatic mannerism of the Voynich nymphs or Abbieannian girls. It is as if the Voynich codex can only be described through unproductive similes and likenesses that cumulatively reveal its derivation and evolution as unlikely. That is its signature: sameness and dissimilarity crushed into the infinite density of singularity and the incomparable. The unceasing invention in these pages far exceeds any indices of a familiar genre, any repertoire, or any attempt to assign sources for its imagery. But the volume also quashes interpretation. As one of the more prominent researchers has poignantly admitted online of his protracted work on the astrological charts in the manuscript, "The examples discussed in this post struck me as worthy of presenting, but I can't be sure that any of them are significant, and so far I have not

                                                    Edward Colless

found any consistent system throughout the whole zodiac section that would confirm these interpretations" (*Voynich Views*, 29 July 2018). Nick Pelling, a VMs researcher and computer programmer at the website *Cypher Mysteries*, called study of the manuscript "academic suicide" (Pelling). "How many," asks Mircea Cartarescu, of those compelled again and again toward the manuscript "had lost their minds, so they said?" (575). A lament that is ultimately uttered by any writer consumed with the damned, ungodly codex. Sound and fury signifying nothing. Cartarescu, again, puts this plight in hair-raising terms:

> I looked at them tens and hundreds of times, squinting, trying to go inside the hidden design, the deep wisdom. Always the same hopeless obscurity, the same glass wall separating me from the fascinating axolotl with an Aztec face, the same inability to find something in common with the Xipehéhuz, the elves, the strangers from another place and time who watch me at night from the edge of my bed (577).

In my own version of this "same hopeless obscurity," I squint at a dark hole inside the VMs: a demon that warps all commentary into a nullity, leaving only the anecdotal disappearance of the writer at the event horizon. At the risk of drawing another hapless similitude, could this dark be the demonic nullity that also appears in Jorge Luis Borges's story of a fatally phantasmic object, the eponymous Zahir (Borges, 1970)? A cruelly unforgettable thing, purposeless and senseless, yet also an ultimate thing. Ultimate, because it becomes the only and the last thing one can think of: a totalising, terminal, absurd singularity.

The antiquity of some of the examples Borges cites lend the Zahir an exoticism and patina of orientalism: it has been, he informs us, a bronze astrolabe, a tiger in a jungle, a blind man outside a temple, an illegible medieval codex, a vein in the marble column of a mosque, and even simply the bottom of a well. But what characterises this list is less its heterogeneity than its redundancy and inconsistency.[16] In Borges's story, the Zahir is a trivial, twenty-centavo Argentine coin, collected in 1929 by Borges himself; for his fictional alter ego, it becomes change late at night in a bar. Not that Borges's alter ego as writer realises what it is when he gets it, or even when he gets rid of it for another drink, attempting to obliterate it from his memory. But once seen, the Zahir cannot be unseen. Once you are aware of it, it persists and insists on your attention, drilling into your mind and brain and dreams with the obstinacy of an earworm, until it is all that you can be aware of. Its inconsequential obduracy eclipses the world. Unattached to justice, innocence or guilt; uncommitted to insight or understanding; indifferent to sensibility, vulnerability, prejudice, or prudence. It is simply the index of a pure and consuming, but unintelligible, cosmic spell.

Does that sound familiar?

Borges reports on his inexorable, monomaniacal fixation upon that coin by telling his story: a tale (autobiographical to a degree) of unrequited love, a case of melancholia and traumatised, desolate desire. In the throes of this morbid passion, he nonetheless displays a characteristically nonchalant if baroque erudition, recruiting esoteric, metaphysical conceits and fortuitously discovered arcane texts as diagnostic illuminations of his pathological condition and as evidence of a centuries-long conspiracy by the cosmos against the human race. Some of this conspiratorial material is fictitious or metafiction, and some of it is authentic; all of it is mischievously interwoven. What is slyly fermented is the unreliability of the narration as much as the alleged scholarship nested in it: Borges's sophisticated encyclopaedism, it turns out, is symptomatic of the narrator's encroaching psychosis.

In Islamic theology and jurisprudence, *al-zahir* refers to the manifest, visible—that is to say, exoteric—statement of the revealed word in the Qur'an and Sunnah: the prosaic commonality of doctrine.[17] The literalism of *al-zahir* insists that the revealed word is identical to its every utterance. It has one perfectly intelligible signification and one alone. Ironically, the Zahir in Borges's story is manifest as "hopeless obscurity" rather than limpid literalism; it represents a failure to get any "deep wisdom" of the object that possesses the writer. That failure is manifest in the esoteric density of Borges's erudite and elaborate, extraterritorial usage of the word that names his impulse to write (Lope-Baralt, 1999 29-69; Lope-Baralt, 2013 77). Borges's Zahir is identical to its every utterance, but that is what makes it unintelligible. True, the Zahir can be anything, but whatever it is, then it is unlike any other thing in the world. It is incomparable. At the story's conclusion, the Zahir closes its event horizon around the author as fatal echolalia:

> Dawn may surprise me on a bench in Garaway Park, thinking (trying to think) of the passage in the Asrar Nama where it says that the Zahir is the shadow of the Rose and the rending of the Veil. ... In order to lose themselves in God, the Sufis recite their own name, or the ninety-nine divine names, until they become meaningless. ... Perhaps I shall conclude by wearing away the Zahir simply through

thinking of it again and again. Perhaps behind the coin I shall find God (Borges 1970, 197).[18]

One cannot help but see this lofty gesture at *kenosis* to be—as I am sure Borges intended—sadly wishful thinking on the part of the story's eventually insane author, who hallucinates and interpolates consoling, but fictitious, testimonies into real historical texts and vice versa.[19] In one of these sources, Borges finds that while there is not one thing in the universe which cannot take on the monstrous aspect of the Zahir, ironically "the All-merciful does not allow two things to be it at the same time, since one alone is enough to fascinate multitudes" (Borges, 1970 195). The divine portion of the Zahir is its uniqueness, delimiting its disorder to one object in the world alone. But that "one alone" is the truly dark, ungodly thing at the core of its unintelligibility: perhaps a nymph traced and reproduced without proliferation, without multiplicity, without derivation or evolution; perhaps a plant like no other in the world. This is the monstrosity that also makes a passion for the VMs's enigma incurable, and the manifestation of that affliction indecipherable.

Perhaps behind the Voynich Manuscript, in the mad landscape of its dark exobotany, I shall find an ungodly world.

Notes

1 The phrase originated with the medievalist historian John Matthews Manly in an article published in *Harper's Monthly Magazine* in July 1921. Cited in Sherman, 43.

2 The digitised version of Beinecke MS 408 is available at https://collections.library. yale.edu/catalog/2002046.

3 There have been so many contentious claims about the language of the codex that an endnote can only gesture at the scope of speculation and philological research. One proposal suggests the codex was written in a transliterated, tonal version of Chinese, possibly using an alphabetic form of the language allegedly devised by the celebrated Jesuit missionary Matteo Ricci, which defying recent radiocarbon dating of the MS would place its origin in sixteenth-century China. ("Stolfi". See also Pelling. For a rebuttal see Schinner, 95-107.) Another theory, based on putative similarities between the codex and Mexican herbological codices produced in the mid-sixteenth century, in particular the 1552 *Codex Cruz-Badianus* (known as the *Aztec Herbal*) and attributed to Nahua scholar Martin de la Cruz, argues that Beinecke MS 408 was written in Mexico in a now extinct dialect of the Mesoamerican language Nahuatl. How and why MS 408 made its way into its European provenance is another story. (For summary and rebuttal, see Hansen.) Other claims are that Beinecke MS 408 is written in an extinct proto-Romance language, or in a lost dialect of Basque, in a poetic and phonetic mode of old Turkic,

or in polyglot or creole versions of Latin abbreviations, of Hebrew, Arabic, a modified Ukrainian, and even Sino-Tibetan, Manchu and ancient Khmer. (For a survey see Zandberger, "History of Research of the Voynich MS.") None of these claims has thus far gained anything near general assent among the vast academic and amateur community that has formed around this codex.

4   Titled *The Voynich Manuscript: An Elegant Enigma*, this was an in-house publication for the NSA by one of their cryptanalyst agents. Among others, cryptographers William Friedman and Elizebeth Friedman, who were considered to be world-leading experts, were introduced to the manuscript in 1925 and then spent some forty years working on the text. William, a founder of the NSA, led the World War II intelligence team that successfully broke the Japanese military code (called "Purple" in the U. S.), which was considered even more challenging than the German "Enigma" code broken at Bletchley Park in the UK. After the war, the Friedmans ran a study group at the NSA on the manuscript, but concluded in 1962 that it was either impossible to break or that, in the end, it was not a cipher. Elizebeth's title of a *Washington Post* article of that year poignantly declared: "The Voynich Manuscript: Still an Enigma." (Cited by Zimansky 437, n. 5.)

5   Gerry Kennedy and Rob Churchill, *The Voynich Manuscript*, Orion Books, 2004, cited in Hunt, 11.

6   Kircher was a professor of mathematics as well as a linguist (among many other accomplishments), and Barschius had sent the copied portions to Kircher via a Jesuit mathematician in Prague, Theodor Moretus. Kircher's admission of defeat with the translation was in a letter sent to Moretus in 1639, subsequently glued into Moretus's mathematics "diary." (Zandbergen, "Letter 39a.")

7   For a full translation of Barschius's letter see Neal, "Barschius ...." (Neal mistakenly titles the letter as "1637," although it is clearly dated in the signature as 1639.) Barschius's lure uses the "worldwide acclaim" for Kircher's 1636 *Prodomus Coptus sive Aegyptiacus (Coptic or Egyptian Forerunner)* and includes extolling Kircher as "the Oedipus of Egypt"—the epithet alluding to solving the sphinx's riddle, rather than the rest of the mythic story. "From the pictures of herbs," Barschius adds with a nod to Father Kircher's adjoined trade, "... it is my guess that the whole thing is medical, the most beneficial branch of learning for the human race apart from the salvation of souls." The relation between Kircher's heiroglyphs and the VMs is itself an alluring if thus far fruitless pursuit in Voynich scholarship. Most biographies indicate that Kircher's lifelong effort at deciphering Egyptian hieroglyphs began in 1628 when he came across a copy in a library in Speyer (where he had been ordained as a Jesuit priest) of the *Thesaurus Hieroglyphicorum*, a folio of twenty-nine engraved plates compiled by the Bavarian antiquarian Johann Georg Herwarth von Hohenburg (Godwin 59). By the time Kircher arrived in Rome in 1635 he had acquired a reputation as a linguist fluent in Hebrew, Syriac and Coptic, and also as owner of a mysterious Arabic document, allegedly written by a Babylonian rabbi Barachias Nephi, which contained supposed translations of hieroglyphs. On the recommendation of a renowned Coptic scholar Nicolaus-Claude Fabri de Pieresc, whom he had met in Avignon two years earlier, Kircher was appointed by Cardinal

        Edward Colless

Francesco Barberini to head a commission within the Jesuit Collegio Romano to find a key to the Egyptian hieroglyphic script. (Glassie 62-87.) As a book on the Coptic grammar that Kircher believed to be the source of a purely symbolic, indeed occult, Egyptian language, the *Prodomus* was the outcome of that commission and, as Peter N. Miller remarks in his study of the rocky relations between Peiresc and Kircher at the time, it was "surely the signal event of 1636 for any European Egyptologist." (See Miller, 135.) Little wonder that Barschius would at that time seek out Kircher's expertise.

8   For a translation of Marci's letter see Neal, "Marci ... 1665." Neal translates the Latin "sphinges" (sphinxes) as "riddles." (For a transcription of the Latin text and facsimile see https://collections.library.yale.edu/catalog/2041454.) Marci was likely prompted to renew the plea for Kircher's attention as a consequence of the much-anticipated multi-volume two thousand page *Oedipus Aegyptiacus* (*Egyptian Oedipus*) published from 1652-54. The baroque speculations on arcane ancient wisdom in this, Kircher's climactic work, with their flamboyant illustrations as well as multiple, elaborate and novel typefaces, would surely have tendered some optimism in Marci for the prospect of Kircher decrypting the enigmatic document he sent with this letter. (Malcom, 303-307; Findlen, 31-35. More generally Stolzenberg.)

9   The destination of the Villa Torlonia is at least one version of the story. Characteristic of the disputation rife in Voynich scholarship (in no small part due to confusion deliberate or otherwise by Voynich himself), some versions have this collection ending up in the Villa Mandragone in Frascati. (Zandbergen, "The Discovery of the Voynich MS by Wilfred Voynich.")

10   Voynich may not have been stretching credibility here. In 1640 Marci also wrote to Kircher about typesetting the "Coptic Arabic lexicon" (the *Prodomus*) with an intriguing allusion to secret knowledge, stating that "I have urged in my most recent letters that those founts of oriental letters should be engraved as soon as possible. If by chance any s*cr*ts needed to be published here we must not lack the requisite tools." (Neal, "Marci ... 1640.") Whether Voynich knew of this letter is uncertain. Again, characteristic of the quarrelling in the Voynich universe, even the 1665 Marci letter has been alleged to be a forgery created by Voynich. (SantaColoma, 11 Sept. 2015.) The same author has also argued that the alleged VMs provenance does not address the actual document Beinecke MS 408 (SantaColoma, 19 April 2020), which is itself a modern forgery (SantaColoma, 23 May 2016).

11   Voynich laid the groundwork for the theory of Dee's ownership in his lecture to the Philadelphia College of Physicians in 1921 (subsequently published as "A Preliminary Sketch of the History of the Roger Bacon Cipher Manuscript", *Transactions of the College of Physicians of Philadelphia*, 1921). In a series of vertiginous and devious steps, Voynich cites a 1909 biography of Dee by Charlotte Fell-Smith in which it is reported that Sir Thomas Browne wrote in 1675 to Elias Ashmole about an account of John Dee's time in Prague in the mid-1580s given to him by Dee's son, Arthur Dee. Browne wrote that Arthur referred to a "book containing nothing but hieroglyphicks, which book his father bestowed much time upon, but I could not hear that he could make it out." Voynich did not mention that Browne's

story cited in Fell-Smith's biography also mentions this book was found "in some old place" alongside a magical powder used for alchemical transmutation. (Quoted in SantaColoma, origins-of-the-dee-myth.) Dee's "book of hieroglyphicks" appears also in a 1904 publication, *The Follies of Science at the Court of Rudolph II* by Henry Bolton, in which the author describes the fantastic tale that Dee and Edward Kelley reputedly found the alchemical Philosophers' Stone (as magical red powder) in the ruins of Glastonbury Abbey with a book explaining its use composed by Saint Dunstan. (Bolton 6-7.) The invocation of Dunstan as an alchemist in this story was likely because he was the patron saint of goldmsiths.

12   One Voynich iconographic researcher even drew a passing comical comparison between certain nymph figures in the codex and "sneetches," after Dr Seuss's 1961 story featuring ostrich-necked, pot-bellied yellow birds. (*Voynich Views*, "No Stars Upon Thars.") The comparison is vivid.

13   The complete, scanned text and other writings by Darger are available at the Illinois Digital Archives (Illinois State Library and Office of the Illinois Secretary of State): https://www.idaillinois.org/digital/collection/intuit/search/page/1.

14   Darger's biography has been largely pieced together from limited sources in his own writing and guarded correspondence, but he still remains an enigmatic figure, both in an anecdotal register and as a clinical pathology. See Elledge.

15   A favourite source of his was the ubiquitous advertising motif for suntan lotion known as "the Coppertone Girl," which first appeared in 1944 and which depicts a toddler (much younger than his Abbieannians) on a beach whose bathing knickers are being pulled down by a frisky poodle to reveal an untanned bare bottom.

16   The capricious manifestations of the Zahir are comparable to the taxonomic farce of Borges's equally famous and fictitious "Chinese encyclopedia" (*Heavenly Emporium of Benevolent Knowledge*), referred to in Borges, 1999, 231.

17   The *zahir'm* is a counterpoint (and, in some schools of Sufi mysticism, a complement) to *al-batin*, which is a spiritual but hermeneutic discipline, an uncommon knowledge gained by fathoming the esoteric interior of doctrine. *Batin* was hidden—a poetic, when not unutterable, knowledge of an unseen god and thus reserved for an elite group. See Mahmoud, 66-68. It bears a nuanced correlation with Borges's Zahir.

18   The *Asrar Nama* (*Book of Things Unknown*) is a poem by the twelfth- to thirteenth-century Sufi mystic who wrote under the name "Farid ud-Din Attar" and who was better known for his epic poem *Mantiq ut-Tyar* (*The Conference of the Birds*). Teasingly contrary to Borges's citation, there is no mention of the Zahir in the *Asrar Nama*. On Borges's use of the Sufi symbolism of the Rose and the Veil, see Lope-Baralt, 1999.

19   This device for scrambling the authenticity of arcane sources is commonplace in Borges's fiction, as well as in some of his non-fiction. But in "The Zahir," it is a symptomatic index, and metastatement, of writing as pathology, comparable to two other great works pathologising authorial compulsion and monomania: the

indexing of Vladimir Nabokov's *Pale Fire* (1962) and the diaristic countdown to suicide in Guy de Maupassant's "The Horla" (1887).

Works Cited

Agamben, Giorgio. *Nymphs*, translated by Amanda Minervini, Seagull Books, 2013.

Bolton, Henry. *The Follies of Science at the Court of Rudolph II*. Pharmaceutical Review Publishing, 1904.

Borges, Jorge Luis. "The Zahir," translated by Dudley Fitts, *Labyrinths*, edited by Donald A. Yates and James E. Irby, Penguin, 1970, pp. 156-164.

---. "John Wilkins' Analytical Language," translated by Eliot Weinberger, *Jorge Luis Borges: Selected Non-Fictions*, edited by Eliot Weinberger, Penguin, 1999, pp. 229-232.

Brewer, Keagan. "'I Beg Your Grace That You Suppress This Chapter or Else Allow It To Be Written in Secret Letters': The Emotions of Encipherment in Late-Medieval Gynaecology." International Conference on the Voynich Manuscript, University of Malta, 30 Nov.-1 Dec. 2022, https://researchers.mq.edu.au/en/publications/i-beg-your-grace-that-you-suppress-this-chapter-or-else-allow-it- Accessed 2 Feb. 2024.

Cartarescu, Mircea. *Solenoid*, translated by Sean Cotter, Deep Vellum, 2022.

D'Imperio, Mary. *The Voynich Manuscript: An Elegant Enigma*. U. S. National Security Agency, 1978.

Elledge, Jim. *Henry Darger, Throwaway Boy*. Overlook Duckworth, 2013.

Findlen, Paula. "Introduction: The Last Man Who Knew Everything … or Did He?" *Athanasius Kircher: The Last Man Who Knew Everything*, edited by Paula Findlen, Routledge, 2004, pp. 1-48.

Gibbs, Nicholas. "Voynich Manuscript: The Solution." *Times Literary Supplement*, 8 Sept. 2017, https://www.the-tls.co.uk/articles/voynich-manuscript-solution/ Accessed 2 Feb. 2024.

Glassie, John. *A Man of Misconceptions: The Life of an Eccentric in an Age of Change*. Riverhead Books, 2012.

Godwin, Joscelyn. *Athanasius Kircher's Theatre of the World*. Thames and Hudson, 2009.

Hansen, Magnus Pharao. "Was the Voynich manuscript written in Nahuatl?" December 2018, https://nahuatlstudies.blogspot.com/2018/12/was-voynich-manuscript-written-in.html Accessed 2 Feb. 2024.

Harkness, Deborah. "Introduction." *The Voynich Manuscript*, edited by Raymond Clemens, Yale University Press, 2016, pp. vii-ix.

Hegel, Georg Wilhelm Friedrich. *Encyclopaedia of the Philosophical Sciences in Outline*, translated by Steven A. Taubeneck, edited by Ernst Behler, Continuum, 1990.

Hunt, Arnold. "Voynich the Buyer." *The Voynich Manuscript*, edited by Raymond Clemens, Yale University Press, 2016, pp. 11-21.

Krell, David Farrell. *Contagion: Sexuality, Disease and Death in German Idealism and Romanticism*. Indiana University Press, 1998.

Lope-Baralt, Lucy. "Borges, Or the Mystique of Silence: What Was on the Other Side of the Zahir." *Jorge Luis Borges: Thought and Knowledge in the Twentieth Century*, edited by Alfonso de Toro and Fernando do Toro, Vervuert, 1999, pp. 29-69.

---. "Islamic Themes." *The Cambridge Companion to Jorge Luis Borges*, edited by Edwin Williamson, Cambridge University Press, 2013, pp. 68-80.

Mahmoud, Mahgoub El-Tigani. "Comparative Research on the Zahir and Batin Thought." *European Scientific Journal*, vol. 12, no. 7, Jun. 2016, pp. 62-77.

Malcolm, Noel. "Private and Public Knowledge: Kircher, Esotericism, and the Republic of Letters." *Athanasius Kircher: The Last Man Who Knew Everything*, edited by Paula Findlen, Routledge, 2004, pp. 297-308.

Miller, Peter N. "Copts and Scholars." *Athanasius Kircher: The Last Man Who Knew Everything*, edited by Paula Findlen, Routledge, 2004, pp. 133-148.

Neal, Philip. "The letter of Georgius Barschius to Athanasius Kircher (1637)," http://philipneal.net/voynichsources/barschius_1637_english/ Accessed 2 Feb. 2024.

---. "The letter of Johannes Marcus Marci to Athanasius Kircher (1640)," http://philipneal.net/voynichsources/marci_1640_english/ Accessed 2 Feb. 2024.

---. "The letter of Johannes Marcus Marci to Athanasius Kircher (1665)," http://philipneal.net/voynichsources/marci_1665_english/ Accessed 2 Feb. 2024.

Pelling, Nick. "Chinese Voynich Theories." Cipher Mysteries, 14 May 2010, https://ciphermysteries.com/2010/05/14/chinese-voynich-theories Accessed 2 Feb. 2024.

Rampling, Jennifer. "Alchemical Traditions." *The Voynich Manuscript*, edited by Raymond Clemens, Yale University Press, 2016, pp. 45-51.

SantaColoma, Richard. "The 1665 Marci Letter: A Forgery?" 9 Sept. 2015, https://proto57.wordpress.com/2015/09/11/the-1665-marci-letter-a-forgery/ Accessed 2 Feb. 2024.

---. "The Modern Forgery Hypothesis." 23 Mar. 2016, https://proto57.wordpress.com/2016/03/23/the-modern-forgery-hypothesis/ Accessed 2 Feb. 2024.

---. "The Voynich has no Provenance." 19 April 2020, https://proto57.wordpress.com/2020/04/19/the-voynich-has-no-provenance/ Accessed 2 Feb. 2024.

                                                    Edward Colless

---. "The Origins of the Dee Myth." 22 July 2022, https://proto57.wordpress.com/2015/07/22/the-origins-of-the-dee-myth/ Accessed 2 Feb. 2024.

"Stolfi." "The Generalized Chinese Theory." 26 Sept. 1998, https://www.ic.unicamp.br/~stolfi/voynich/97-11-23-tonal/ Accessed 2 Feb. 2024.

Schinner, Andreas. "The Voynich Manuscript: Evidence of the Hoax Hypothesis." *Cryptologia*, vol. 31, no. 2, 2007, pp. 95-107.

Sherman, William. "Cryptographic Attempts." *The Voynich Manuscript*, edited by Raymond Clemens, Yale University Press, 2016, pp. 39-43.

Stolzenberg, Daniel. *Egyptian Oedipus: Athanasius Kircher and the Secrets of Antiquity.* University of Chicago Press, 2013.

Voynich Views. "Astronomical Coincidences in the Voynich Zodiac." 29 Jul. 2018, https://voynichviews.wordpress.com/2018/07/29/coincidences-in-the-voynich-zodiac/ Accessed 2 Feb. 2024.

---. "No Stars Upon Thars." 3 Dec. 2018, https://voynichviews.wordpress.com/2018/12/03/no-stars-upon-thars/ Accessed 2 Feb. 2024.

Zandbergen, René. "Earliest Owners." *The Voynich Manuscript*, edited by Raymond Clemens, Yale University Press, 2016, pp. 3-9.

---. "Letter 39a: Kircher to Moretus, 12 March 1639," https://www.voynich.nu/letters.html Accessed 2 Feb. 2024.

---. "The Discovery of the Voynich MS by Wilfred Voynich," https://www.voynich.nu/extra/mondragone.html Accessed 2 Feb. 2024.

---. "The History of the Voynich Manuscript," https://www.voynich.nu/history.html Accessed 2 Feb. 2024.

Zhang, Sarah. "Has a Mysterious Medieval Code Really Been Solved?" *The Atlantic*, 10 Sept. 2017, https://www.theatlantic.com/science/archive/2017/09/has-the-voynich-manuscript-really-been-solved/539310/. Accessed 2 Feb. 2024.

Zimansky, Curt A. "William F. Friedman and the Voynich Manuscript." *Philological Quarterly*, vol XLIX, no 4, October 1970, pp. 433-443.

13 *De-Flores Rhetorici*: D. H. Lawrence's Literary Herbarium

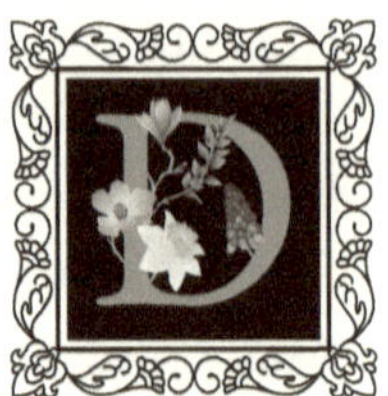

Sigi Jöttkandt

In his posthumously published essay fragment, "Flowery Tuscany," D. H. Lawrence takes us on a virtual tour of the flower-studded globe. We drift through England's daisies, buttercups, hawthorn, cowslips, and then America's goldenrod, stargrass, June daisies, Mayapple, and asters. India's hibiscus, daytura, and champa flowers come next. Crossing the ocean, Lawrence introduces us to Australia's wattle and "sharp-tongued strange heath flowers" (349) babbling in different languages. Doubling back, we find ourselves in Mexico, with its ravishing roses of the desert, and the creamy heartbells of the yucca, which dangles arm-length clusters like "dropping froth" (349). But then the arc of the sun heads counter-clockwise, back towards Europe and the Mediterranean, where Lawrence proffers banks of narcissus and anemone, asphodel and myrtle, crocus and parsley: "These are the flowers that speak and are understood in the sun round the Middle Sea" (349).

The tropological relation of words and flowers is as ancient as rhetoric itself. In the first century AD, the Roman scholar Quintilian heaped his scorn on "declaimers" whose "fermented" style seeks to persuade with a language "bedizened with flowers" (Quintilian 180). And yet his beloved Cicero had previously expressed the opposing view when he commended the Roman statesman Cato for adorning his speeches "with every flower, and with all the lustre of Eloquence." Similarly, in "On the Sublime," Dionysius Longinus traced Plato's "fair flowers of imagery" back to the example set by Homer's illustrious works. In the eleventh century, this association of rhetoric with flowers was consolidated by the Benedictine monk Alberic of Monte Cassino with his *Flores rhetorici*, which forms a figural bed. The twelfth-century Latin scholar, Matthew of Vendôme, felt that this bed was robust enough for philosophy itself to rest upon, as we hear in the latter's *Ars versificatoria*: "In the place of stated beauty, Philosophy and her hand-maidens, with beguiling zeal, so as to feed its labour on the myriad perfumes of the flowers is pleased to lie very often upon the flowers, very often to meander" (62). Yet flowers can also have a dessicating effect on speculative thought: "When the word flowers, the mind dries up," admonishes Eberhard the German in his *Laborintus* (qtd. in Murphy 180).

By the thirteenth century, we find flowers engarlanding language's fertile "plot of ground," their delicate petals blending form and content into intellectual perfume in Geoffrey of Vinsauf's *Poetria nova* (Dronke 31). And by the English Renaissance, the literary-flosculi connection was secure. The sixteenth-century George Puttenham describes figures and figurative language as "the flowers ... and coulours that a Poet setteth vpon his language by arte, as the embroderer doth his stone and perle". Henry Peacham, the educator and author of *The Garden of Eloquence* (1577), praised rhetoric as "the most excellent ornaments, exornations, lightes, flowers, and formes of speech".

When Lawrence summons this tradition in "Flowery Tuscany," it is to release the plant's sexuality from its crowning place in philosophical thought. Resistant to dialectics, the Lawrencian flower—radiant, ecstatic, generous, tenacious— takes on a different resonance, proceeding to blow up and blow out mimetic and teleological paradigms. *Flower, flowre, floer, florem*—the online etyomological dictionary gives us the root of "flower" in the Proto-Indo-European *bhel, meaning "to blow, swell, or to bloom, thrive" ("Flower" (n.)). "Flower" is thus connected to phallos, but also, and perhaps more unexpectedly, with bags, bowls, cushions, pimples, and eventually budgets, stomachs, and an ancient supernatural people of Ireland (the Firbolgs, arch-enemies of the Dannans). While the figure of reflection governs and regulates the rhetorical transfer of properties between mind and nature, forming the bridge between sensory and intellectual realms in the literary tradition that culminates with the Romantics, in Lawrence, a late-comer, we find philosophy's master-trope exposed to a different light, a de-anthropic one in which reflective paradigms waver. For Lawrence, the flower can never be tragic; it cannot double as a figure for human finitude, nor serve in an aesthetics of redemption. "For my part," Lawrence writes, "if the sun always shines, and always will shine, in spite of millions of clouds of words, then death, somehow, does not have many terrors. In the sunshine, even death is sunny. And there is no end to the sunshine" (361).

Whites, Pale-Golds

Lawrence's essay opens with spring on the horizon and the appearance of the first narcissus, little cups (*tazzette* in Italian) bearing the promise of the sun's warmth. And yet this is a false offering, it turns out. The cold *Narcissus poeticus* releases a frosty breath. It is a still-born spring, a shoot that revokes both the calendric and the tropological turn it was to herald. The narcissus pushes up sparsely, as Lawrence puts it, "among thorns" (351). It feeds off death. In Ovid, the narcissus sidles up to the grave of its namesake, "cold and shy and wintry" (351).

For Lawrence, "real" spring begins with the winter aconite:

> Some icy day, when the wind is down from the snow of the mountains, early in February, you will notice on a bit of fallow land, under the olive trees, tight, pale-gold little balls, clenched tight as nuts, and resting on round ruffs of green near the ground. It is the winter aconite suddenly come (351).

Stealthily, the linguistic, if not strictly botanical, cousin of toxic wolfbane and monkshood, winter aconite (or *Eranthis hyemalis*) overturns the "natural" unfolding of the seasons. The narcissus, mimetic reflection's most entrenched figure and emblem, is usurped here by an "ur" spring flaunting another myth of origin (*Ursprung*). Er-anthis sallies forth from another etymology, not the phallic blooming of the Latin "flower" but the Greek ἄνθος (*anthos*), thus emerging as the flower of a linguistic tradition that stretches back to Sanskrit's *andhas*, thought to be *Asclepias acida*, an intoxicating milkwood. Under the pretext of "winter," in a suspension of the mythos of spring, the aconite proliferates "in all odd places."

> The tramontana ceases, comes a day of wild February sunshine. The clenched little nuggets of the aconite puff out, they become light bubbles, like small balloons, on a green base (351).

As it explodes under the February sun, each "pale-gold little ball" miraculously becomes its own source of heat and warmth. "And by noon, all under the olives are wide-open little suns" (351). The aconite stands outside philosophy's specular, narcissistic complex. Allied with the loss of the *tramontana*, or the north wind, the aconite causes us to lose our bearings in the chrono-tropological system; in Italian, the phrase *perdere la tramontana* means to lose one's way, to be at a loss. Light as air, frail bubbles of "pale, pure gold" "crumbling to nothingness," the aconite throngs in any "land left fallow" as opportunistic, de-auratic others of identificatory paradigms (351). They open the way for another hiemal figure, the hellebore or Christmas rose.

Yellow-Greens

Hellebores appear as figures for what fails to represent, inhabiting a pallid region between the signifier and signified. These singular, self-enclosed hellebores resist becoming drawn into figuration, idealisation, models of meaning. They shrug off Lawrence's appropriative desire: though "short and lovely, and very wintry-beautiful," they exude "a will not to be touched, not to be noticed. One instinctively leaves them alone." Each flower, "wintry of winter," with "a quality of invisibility," seems to Lawrence to stand up as an anti-mimetic creature, rising "so lonely" from among the dry grasses, "like a little hand-mirror that reflects nothing" (352).

The "debris of winter," hellebores would rescind the theological gifts suggested by their common names, "Christmas rose" or "Lenten rose," allying themselves instead with what is left over, unwanted—unwanted, perhaps, because of the hellebore's reputation as a medicinal plant whose pharmakon might cure the "madness" of an aesthetic ideology that is intent on "assimilating the structure of language to the structure of a secure perception," in Paul de Man's phrasing (de Man, 1983 105). Indeed, this aesthetic programme, the metaphysical underpinning of the tradition of "Flores Rhetorici," whose system of figuration establishes the natural world as the basis for linguistic meaning, seems to halt in its tracks before the hellebore, which becomes more and more "assertive" as February goes on:

> Their pallid water-green becomes yellow, pale suphur-yellow-green, and they rise up, they are in tufts, in veritable bushes of greenish open flowers, assertive, bowing their faces with a hellebore assertiveness.
> … an uprearing hellebore assertiveness, like snakes in winter (352).

Another protocol of signification is put into play. Even as the hellebore arrests the metaphysical programme governing the oppositions of wild/tame, heaven/hell, winter/summer, and wanted/unwanted—leaving them hanging in mid-air as a frozen signifier, a wintry snake in the perpetual, but never completed, act of striking—the hellebores, with their concave bells, call to mind the idea of semaphores broadcasting wordless messages, radars, electric pulses, all of which operate via visual signals rather than linguistic signs. Wading through these silent trumpets, Lawrence brushes off the last red berry from the Tuscan Christmas holly.

Reds

Also called "butcher's broom," whose branches, rich in anti-bacterial properties, were once used for cleaning bloodied wooden blocks, *Ruscus aculeatus* relinquishes its "last red balls" (352), which roll off together with "winter" in Lawrence's sentence in a zeugma. The rhetorical figure of the zeugma yokes together two opposing semantic features under a single grammatical coordination, thereby producing an asymmetry between a grammatical coordination and its semantic opposition. The zeugma, in this way, operates as something that cannot be reduced to either grammar or syntax, but lies somewhere in between. As such, it draws explicit attention to what both metaphor and metonymy habitually prefer to overlook, namely, the contingent way a signified is "stuck on" to a signifier, like the holly, "a vivid red berry stuck on in the middle of its sharp hard leaf" (352). As he sweeps the fruit off the butcher's broom, Lawrence seems to shake off language's residual protocols. He faces resolutely south, shifting from the human temporal frame—"the brave day sunk in hideous night"[1]—to a pre-human Earth, and its material history in deep time:

> Then you sit down on that southern slope, out of the wind, and there it is warm, whether it be January or February, *tramontana* or not. There the earth has been baked by innumerable suns, baked and baked again; moistened by many rains but never wetted for long. Because it is rocky, and full to the south, and sheering steep in the slope (352).

Creams and Lavenders

Upon this "sunny baked desert," "on the sheer aridity of crumbled stone," the first hill-crocus appears: "you see a queer, alert little star, very sharp and quite small" (353). Like a herbarium specimen, Lawrence's hill-crocus is flat, more paper cut-out than three-dimensional flower, yet retaining its original colours—"creamy, with a smear of yellow yolk" (352). It seems to feed directly off itself, self-sufficient, ungrounded, "just lightly dropped on the crumbled, baked rock" (352). An extraterrestrial visitor whose visitation carries on the disintegrating of spatial and temporal markers initiated by the aconite, the unearthly crocus is allied with failed or interrupted messages, and with impenetrability and illegibility. In one Greek tradition, Crocus is the decapitated lover of the messenger god Hermes. In another, he appears as the lover of the "fairgarlanded" nymph Smilax (Nonnos 403-4), a dense thorny blindweed.

The hill-crocus is just one of a number of "spiky" wild crocuses, cream and mauve, but down in the valley, Lawrence discovers crocuses that have retracted their sharp edges to shape hollows, forming little lavender cups or bowls "sticking out of the deep grass" (353). The pointed star's epistemological projection, fingers radiating outward indexing other potential referential models gather into themselves in the evening to form "myriad folded tents" (353). In an "encampment" like that of "apaches," as hidden assassins, the crocuses burst forth the next day in "a perfect ecstacy of radiant, thronging movement," "surging in some invisible rhythm of concerted, delightful movement." "You cannot believe," Lawrence exclaims, "they do not move, and make some sort of crystalline sound of delight" (353), and as he sits still and watches, he begins to move with them in an anti-gravitational dance, "like moving with the stars," feeling "the sound of their radiance" (353) in a synaesthetic upending of the senses.

The star-shaped crocus is a member of the *Iridaceae* family, derived from "iris," a word of uncertain origin, perhaps emerging out of the Proto-Indo-European root *wei-, meaning "to bend, turn, twist." In Hesiod, the rainbow Iris, a messenger for the Olympian deities, is sent by Jove to avenge divinities who have betrayed their word. The iridescent "light" of the Platonic tradition is subverted or refracted. Was Homer's "saffron-vested Aurora" merely a front, a vector for Earth's irradiation by the crocus's "little star" (167) with its arciform rays?

Purples

By March, the unearthly crocuses have decamped, and in the newly deserted banks, the violets, which have been crouching in Lawrence's text "like tiny dark hounds" (354), finally emerge, flaunting and ruffling, "swarming brilliant purple" "till the air all sways subtly scented with violets" (354). Lawrence's violets have been playing a game of cat and mouse until now, appearing fleetingly in February. When the aconites burst, "in a cosy nook the violets are dark purple, and there is a new little perfume in the air" (352). Again, later in the month, when the holly and winter roll zeugmatically off together, the violets "are already emerging from the moisture" (352). They have projected proleptic faces upon the crocuses: "But before the violets make any show" (352).

Violets possess ionone, a chemical compound, which, according to Diane Ackerman, "short-circuits our sense of smell" (9). Violet's *ion* also evidently short-circuits our sense of place, violating the order of the proper. "Great, solemn-faced violets" serve as a sort of phyto-prosopopeia, one that de-faces the other flowers' "tufts and bunches" (354). These become "wan, more pallid" in the polyptononising violets' violet shadow. *Ion*, a word derived from the Greek, *ĭov*, means "to go." Desensitising the nose, the scent of violet satiates our olfactory receptors so that the odour seems to vanish, but what it really makes disappear is every other floral trace: "the air all sways subtly scented with violets" (354). In her study of scent in Victorian literature, Catherine Maxwell cites the British perfumer W. A. Poucher's assertion that the violet results in "intense olfactory fatigue." "After an hour's work on violets ... the professional nose forgot every smell it ever learnt—except, that is, for violets" (qtd. in Smith 79). Although Lawrence specifies these are indeed "sweet violets," *Viola odorata*, rather than their heath cousins, the *Viola canina* or dog-violet, they share the same hunting instinct, the same thrill of the chase. At stake, it seems, is control over the sensorium—the violet's generalised short-circuiting of the distinction of presence and absence, of here and there.

Blues

With the "blue, blue, blue" grape hyacinth, we arrive at what Lawrence regards as the most "fascinating" flower of all. It is the most fascinating, but also the most persistent, so that coming "for at least two months," "one tends later on to ignore it, even to despise it a little" (354). In reacting thus, Lawrence is simply taking the plant at its word; its Latin name, *Muscari neglectum* invites our disregard. This name literally calls for heedless treatment, indifference. Indeed, it carries a strong admonition *not to pick it up* (*neclegere*, from Old Latin nec "not" (from the Proto Indo-European root *ne- "not") + legere "pick up, select"). Why this nomenclatural prohibition? What risk might we run?

One discovers very quickly that this musky, botryoidal flower possesses Carrollian properties, shrinking its viewers down to microscopic size. "If we were tiny as fairies," says Lawrence, "how lovely these great trees of bells would be to us, towers of night and dawn-blue globes. They would rise above us thick and succulent, and the purple globes would push the blue ones up, with white sparks of ripples, and we should see a god in them" (355). Cobalt pyramids, referencing ancient mummies—Lawrence comments that the grape-hyacinth is the flower of the many-breasted Artemis, the Cybele of Ephesus—return us to another history of inscription: of hieroglyphics, sacred carvings, visual languages. With the grape hyacinth, we risk an epiphany, or seeing a "god," yet

   Sigi Jöttkandt

it is from a lineage of female divinities that rivals the Apollonian ones. In the Homeric tradition, Artemis is Apollo's twin.

Pinks

It is still March, but already the sloe and the peach are in bloom. "The sloe is white and misty in the hedge-tangle by the stream, and on the slope of land the peach tree stands pink and alone" (355). The sloe (or blackthorn), the peach, and also the almond and apricot, which swiftly follow, are in the *Prunus* genus. According to legend, the *Prunus persica* (or Persian apple) was brought to Egypt by the son of Darius, Kambyses II, who intended to use it for waging biological warfare. But, so the story continues, in the fertile soils of the Egyptian delta, the poisonous *persica*, whose kernel contains deadly prussic acid, became harmless. However, Pliny the Elder tells us this is "quite untrue." He maintains that the *persica*'s name derives from the fact it was planted at Memphis by Perseus.

Lawrence follows another route for the peach, considering it an "isolated individual" whose flesh is "not at all ethereal," "far from vulgar," "rare and private pink," and "beautifully sensual" (355). It is almost a person, or at least a *persona*, whose origin the *Oxford English Dictionary* suggests could be the Etruscan *φersu*, denoting a mask, a false face. The peach blossom "personifies" the obverse of personhood. It points to the way the prosopopeic figures of face, self, and identity have never been the incarnations of spirit they seemed to promise, but instead hideous dress-ups, "vulgar" encasings of "pink flannelette" (355). The word "pink" itself is a testament to this inversion, for we learn in the Online Etymology Dictionary that "pink" is a sixteenth-century innovation, arriving into English possibly from Dutch, and replacing the earlier Latin "incarnadine" (flesh-coloured). Lawrence, a modern Perseus, sets off a fusillade of pinks at prosopopeia's Gorgon: "And pink is so beautiful in a landscape, pink houses, pink almond, pink peach and purply apricot, pink asphodels" (355).

Blacks and Deep Purples

Daughters of the wind, dark violet anemones with black hearts come at Lawrence, "baying with all their throats, baying deep purple into the air" and "gulping the sun" (355). Anemones take their name from the Latin *anima*, meaning "breath." They are known as windflowers, and. in the Greek tradition, are said to arise from the blood of Adonis, the lover of both Aphrodite and Persephone who was gored while hunting boar. In ancient Greece, women celebrated the festival of Adonis by planting short-lived "Gardens of Adonis," seedlings of lettuce and fennel that would quickly perish under the midsummer sun, their passing keenly mourned. Lawrence's anemones implicitly cite this tradition but, rather than dying, they merely shield themselves from view, melting into the grey "at evening or early morning," their silky heads curving like umbrella handles. They possess "a peculiar outward colourlessness, that makes them quite invisible." "They may be under your feet, and you will not see them" (355-56).

Scarlets

But in the sun, they tell a different story. For under the sun's rays, the anemone, and above all, the "Adonis-blood anemone" presents "one of the loveliest scarlet apparitions in the world." Its colour is an unearthly one, emerging from the flower's sleek interior.

> The inner surface of the Adonis-blood anemone is as fine as velvet, and yet there is no suggestion of pile, not as much as on a velvet rose. And from this inner smoothness issues the red colour, perfectly pure and unknown of earth, no earthiness, and yet solid, not transparent (356).

Lawrence marvels at the miracle of a colour that seems to be "condensed light" (356), neither luminous nor transparent. It exhibits a "velvetiness without velvet, and a scarlet without glow" (356). Inhabiting the negative, the windflower consumes the categories employed to describe it and thus reactivates its shared heritage with the ghost: from Old English *gast*, Dutch *geest*, and German *Geist*, all of which mean "breath" or "spirit."

Revising the Adonis myth, Lawrence suggests that it is not human blood, but Venus's tears that are the material cause of the anemones, their immense number testimony to "how the poor lady must have wept" (356). Tears, welling from the goddess of love's woe, out of which we obtain the word, "wind," derived from Old English *wáwan* and Gothic *waian*, meaning "to blow, waft." All of the lachrymose gestures of literary grief and mourning are engulfed by the baying mouths of the anemone. A spectral flower, "unknown of earth," "yet solid" (356), the anemone is beyond mourning, beyond what Shakespeare, in his version of Venus and Adonis, called "the weeping morn" (Shakespeare, "Venus and Adonis").

Greens and Gold-Browns

We are now at the end of April, and the leaves are starting to emerge. Lawrence draws our attention to the fig trees and the "spurts of pure-green that have been burning like little cloven tongues of green vivid fire on the tips of the candelabrum" (357). These "tongues" morph into hands, spreading out and "feeling for the air of summer" (357). With the Lawrencian fig, talk is silenced as gesture; rhetoric's beguiling song turns caprine. Rather than ripening into the figures and tropes yielding rhetorical "fruit," these truncated "tiny green figs" are co-opted for zoomorphic speechifying. To Lawrence, they resemble "glands on the throat of a goat" (357), a discordant bleating beyond human language summoned by his Poe-esque rhyme.

What arises next is the vine-rosette's wine-scent of a "new year," but one that is no longer bound by any calendric institution, seemingly birthed instead by the whispers and tremors of the aspens, "all remarkable with the translucent membranes of blood-veined leaves" (357). These are "gold-brown," like the "thin wings of bats" suddenly become "birds." The aspens "wheel in clouds against the setting sun, and the sun glows through the stretched membrane of their wings, as through thin, brown-red stained glass" (357). It is red sap, the sap of summer, that runs through the aspens' veins; they have "the tender panting glow of living membrane just come awake" (357). Sheer life, life in its bare, trembling, scarce difference from the non-living, its mysteries hinted at by the "ladies tongues" the aspen's leaves evoke, "this is the beauty of the frailty of spring" (357), Lawrence comments, leading us into an entirely green world.

"So many greens, all in flakes and shelves and tilted tables and round shoulders and plumes and shaggles and uprisen bushes, of greens and greens, sometimes blindingly brilliant at evening, when the landscape looks on fire from inside, with greenness and gold" (358). Any idea one might have of nature as an outside is transformed into a Cubist interior. Our spatial models inverted, we enter "a time of green, pre-eminent green, in ruffles and flakes and slabs" (358). But in a space between spring and summer, a ghostly out-of-time and "out-of-date" quality intervenes (359).

Colourlessness

What happens next is something unspringlike, "out of the mood of spring" (358). The stone pines "keep their hold on winter" (358): "[h]ard, dull pines above, and hard, dull, tall heath below, all stiff and resistant" (358). The heath in flower is "stone-white." "It does not, casually, give the impression of blossom," but "[m]ore the impression of having its tips and crests all dipped in hoarfrost; or in a whitish dust" (358). While in the sun, the heath flower gives off "a sweet honeyed scent", which is accompanied by a "cloud of fine white stone-dust if you touch it" (359). What halts spring in its tracks, what heads summer off before its arrival is a "peculiar ghostly colourlessness amid the darkish colourlessness of the wood" (358). An "invisibility," a "dim whiteness" (359) eerily outlines the mythos of green that confers the ideas of "world," "phenomenality," and "life" onto the non-living system of linguistic signs.

"It is the ghost of the interval" (359), Lawrence intones, displaying here an unexpected affinity with disarticulating readings, with Derridean hauntology and teletechnics, with the logics of marking rather than of phenomenalising systems. All of this is seemingly at odds with the more customary image of Lawrence as a late Romantic, or "modern primitivist" whose work, in F. R. Leavis's summation, represents "an immense body of living creation in which a supreme vital intelligence is the creative spirit" (81).

Hesitating in this "out-of-date" interval, as if summoned by Lawrence's double negative—"Not that this week is flowerless" (358)—an ancient flower materialises. It is the orchid. Dating back at least as far as the Late Cretaceaous Period, that is, sixty-six million years ago, *orchidaceae* coexisted with dinosaurs, but, unlike them, they survived the great Cretaceous extinction. Perhaps this is why the orchids appear to Lawrence as "little lonely things" (359), wistfully recalling other, now long-gone variants of Earth's life. Yet here they are in the present, beneath a coniferous gymnosperm canopy, another survivor and relic of prehistory. And they are "still very much alive": the "ragged" bee-orchid; the "thick-flowering pink orchid" with huge bud-spikes, "hard-purple and splendid"; the "choice cream-coloured orchids with brown spots on the long and delicate lip" and with "exotic, tender spikes, very rare-seeming"; and the "pretty yellow one" (359).

Yet orchids alone "do not make a summer" (359), Lawrence reminds the ghost of Aesop's young man who, seeing a swallow, sold his coat in the belief that warm weather was at hand, only to freeze to death in the lingering winter. Orchids, like swallows, are too scanty. With their companions, the "little slate-blue scabious" (359), also known as the pincushion flower, they sit alongside "rosy cushions of wild thyme" and "fringes" (359) of irises in decorative, embroidery-like panels, "samples rather than the real thing" (359), mere ornament, without substance or backing—just as Quintilian warned.

                                                     Sigi Jöttkandt

Like fragments of cloth, remnants of fine needlework lost among the stones in the upper terraces, the orchids and irises end up in tatters, "torn and buffeted by too many winds" (359), together with what remains of the "Flores Rhetorici" tradition, its tropes and figures expelled from the linguistic "garden," metaphors "curl[ed]," metonymies "burnt," allegories pushed "rude[ly]" (359) from their secondary narratives, the sensory image dislodged from what was always a precarious ledge in the Idea.

Yet the winds finally cease, the sun "shake[s] off his harassments," and these tenacious tendrils, "half-wild, half-cultivated" illuminate Tuscany's stepped hills. The irises once again overpower the air with their orris scent. "There will be tufts of iris everywhere, rising up proud and tender," but this time bringing with them "a new crystalline lightness" (360). Once thought to be petrified ice, crystal's prismatic properties inject white light into the different spectral colours of the rainbow. The iris is a messenger of this crystalline light, deflecting and displacing heliocentric models. It disorders the sun's light, and divides it.

The Sun

A veritable Phaeton, Lawrence seizes the reins of the sun, first directing it northwards where night reveals itself as the unyielding principle of all things, a "grey or dark permanency" whose principle is potentiality. Lawrence remarks how, in the north, the sun offers only a momentary illumination before the darkness takes hold again:

> Man tends instinctively to imagine, to conceive that the sun is lighted like a candle, in an everlasting darkness, and that one day the candle will go out, the sun will be exhausted, and the everlasting dark will resume uninterrupted sway. Hence, to the northerner, the phenomenal world is essentially tragical, because it is temporal and must cease to exist (360).

For northern regions, reality is the "grey substratum," an underground of "cold, dark reality where bulbs live, and reality is bulbous."

Turning his face back toward the south, Lawrence discovers it is really darkness that is temporary. For the "southerner," he writes,

> if every phenomenal body disappeared out of the universe, nothing would remain but bright luminousness, sunniness. The absolute is

sunniness; and shadow or dark, is only merely relative: merely the result of something getting between one and the sun (360).

For Lawrence's flower, on the other hand, emerging from the Earth "without the assistance of imitation or analogy," as de Man puts it, the sun is not a metaphor. It does not signify anything other than itself. It is not a principle of fallen representation, nor a figure for the philosophical Absolute. It does not lend itself to Platonic allegories. The incarnation of words as flowers, literary language's most beloved and undying trope for naturalising our system of representation, yields to a de-naturing repetition, without origin or end, under Lawrence's pen. "Where are the little aconites of eight weeks ago? I neither know nor care. They were sunny and the sun shines, and sunniness means change, and petals passing and coming. The winter aconites sunnily came, and sunnily went. What more?" (361).

Commenting on Romantic poetry in his essay "Intentional Structure of the Image," de Man observes how the "fundamental intent of the poetic word is to originate in the same manner as what Hölderlin ... calls 'flowers.'" But he also notes how another model of imagination, buried in plain sight within this tradition, comes into play in certain instances when, in Wordsworth's phrase, "the light of sense goes out." De Man muses on how "we know very little about the kinds of images that such an imagination would produce," although he discovers their precursors in the de-totalizing vision of certain modern writers, whom literary historians tend to dismiss as "primitivist" (16).

Notes

1   From Shakespeare's sonnet 12, "When I do count the clock that tells the time."

Works Cited

Ackerman, Diane. *A Natural History of the Senses*. Knopf, 1991.

De Man, Paul. "Dialogue and Dialogism." *Poetics Today*, vol. 4, no. 1, 1983, pp. 99-107.

---. "Intentional Structure of the Romantic Image." *The Rhetoric of Romanticism*. Columbia University Press, pp. 1-17.

Dronke, Peter. *The Medieval Poet and His World*. Edizioni di Storia e Letteratura, 1984.

"Flower (n.)." *Online Etymology Dictionary*, https://www.etymonline.com/search?q=flower. Accessed 12 Feb. 2024.

Homer. *A Literal Translation of Six Books of Homer's Iliad*. J. Cumming, 1823.

Lawrence, D. H. "Flowery Tuscany." *The Norton Book of Nature Writing*, edited by Robert Finch and John Elder, W. W. Norton, 2002, pp. 349-361.

Leavis, F. R. *D. H. Lawrence*, Novelist. Penguin, 1964.

Longinus. *On the Sublime*, translated by H. L. Havell, MacMillan, 1890.

Matthew, of Vendôme. *Ars versificatoria (The Art of the Versemaker)*, translated by Roger P. Parr, Marquette University Press, 1981.

Murphy, James Jerome. *Rhetoric in the Middle Ages: A History of Rhetorical Theory from Saint Augustine to the Renaissance*. University of California Press, 1974.

Nonnnos of Panopolis. *Dionysiaca*, translated by W. H. D. Rouse, mythological introduction and notes by H. J. Rose, Harvard University Press, 1940.

Peacham, Henry. *The Garden of Eloquence: Conteyning the Figures of Grammar and Rhetorick, from Whence Maye Bee Gathered All Manner of Flowers, Coulors, Ornaments, Exornations, Formes and Fashions of Speech*. H. Iackson, 1577.

Puttenham, George. *The Arte of English Poesie*. N. p., 1589.

Quintilian. *Quintilian's Institutes of Eloquence*, vol. 1, translated and edited by W. Guthrie, Dutton and Richardson, 1805.

Shakespeare, William. "Venus and Adonis." *Poetry Foundation*, https://www.poetryfoundation.org/poems/56962/venus-and-adonis-56d239f8f109c. Accessed 12 Feb. 2024.

Shakespeare, William. "Sonnet 12: When I do count the clock that tells the time." *Poetry Foundation*, https://www.poetryfoundation.org/poems/90067/when-i-do-count-the-clock-that-tells-the-time-578cfa272532b. Accessed 12 Feb. 2024.

Shakespeare, William. "Venus and Adonis." *Poetry Foundation*, https://www.poetryfoundation.org/poems/56962/venus-and-adonis-56d239f8f109c. Accessed 12 Feb. 2024.

Smith, Roly. *A Camera in the Hills: The Life and Work of W. A. Poucher*. Frances Lincoln Publishers, 2008.

PART II

...hopeful green stuff woven...

—Walt Whitman, *Leaves of Grass*

14 Phytonic Oracle

Christina Stadlbauer

What will be described below is an artwork and poetic intervention that proposes a ritual in the form of an oracular consultation.[1] The Phytonic Oracle is a participatory installation based on the wisdom of plants. It was created by stepping into relationships with eleven selected flowers and allowing them to guide the process. The outcome is an attempt to give plants a voice, and an invitation to humans to witness the vegetal world.

To explain and describe this work within a framework of academic thought is a contradiction in itself. However, what can be meaningful is to situate the work in the fields of philosophy, biology, and art, and to describe the artistic research that is facilitated by the Phytonic Oracle.

Who Will Pollinate the Flower Clock?

It all started with a plant installation in 2021, which was part of the Mänttä Art Festival in Finland curated by Anna Ruth. I proposed an installation entitled "Who Will Pollinate the Flower Clock" as a re-enactment of Carl van Lynne's floral clock from the mid- eighteenth century.[2] The installation featured eleven plants that could grow in the climate of Finland, where the exhibit was taking place. The selected plants were pollinator friendly; that is, they would attract bugs, bees, and butterflies by offering nectar and pollen in exchange for the pollination services of the insects. In the Flower Clock, the plants open and close their petals following a circadian rhythm. Knowing when certain flowers open or close allows the observer to estimate what time of day it is.

My work with these plants entailed intensive engagement with their properties. I researched their needs, their preferences, their daily and annual rhythms, their preferred growing conditions, their pollinator interactions and any human use of them for their medicinal or toxic properties. It turned out that most of these eleven plants were generally labelled as "weeds," sometimes considered invasive, but primarily not species you would select to grow in your backyard. For the installation, these plants were inserted into a patch of land in

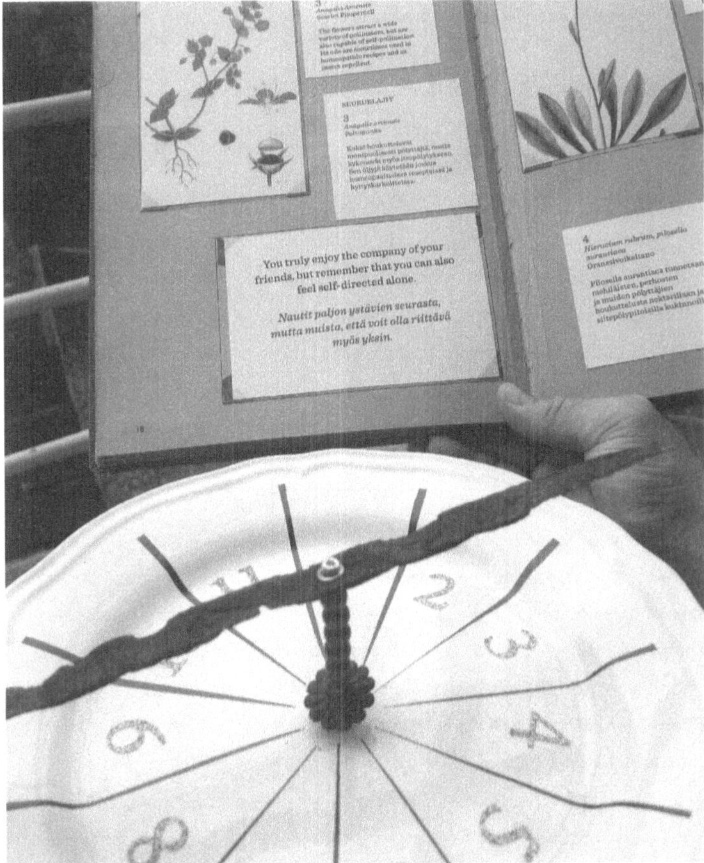

Figure 1. Phytonic Oracle book and tool. (Image courtesy of Christina Stadlbauer).

front of the museum and grew considerably well. The installation was set up for the art exhibition. However, it was also playing with the notion of audience, and expanding the usual group of museum visitors to include gardeners, local passers-by, and, of course, the insects that were attracted by the flowering field.

Made visible through my Flower Clock, the choreography of insect-flower pollination is a vital eco-system service, one that humans appreciate. Honeybees are a celebrated example of this and are known for their essential role in guaranteeing food supply. But pollination should first and foremost be seen from a plant's perspective: as a necessary intervention for propagation via fruit and seed and as a sexual act (Hustak and Myers). The insect pollina-tor cross-pollinates—that is, it transports pollen between different flowers—to ensure fertilization. The transport of pollen between the stamen (the male part of the flower) and the pistil (the female part of the flower) can facilitate the creation of seeds.

Pollination is an encounter between plants and insects, and it has effects that go beyond simple logistics. It clearly causes an immediate reaction within a plant that is communicated internally. As Calvo and Lawrence explain in *Planta Sapiens,* "when a hibiscus flower is visited by pollinating insects, the intimate act of pollination triggers signals which result in an increase of the respiration rate in the ovary sitting at the base of the flower" (Calvo and Lawrence 96).

The pollinator, in turn, is rewarded by picking up nutritious nectar and pollen, and is informed via various cues as to whether a flower has been already pollinated. These cues include visual evidence, smell traces from chemical substances, and a change in the electrical charge that can be sensed by an insect. This way, superfluous trips to already pollinated flowers—empty of nectar— can be avoided.

Such trans-species communication highlights the diverse ways in which different species interact, cooperate, and adapt to their environments through mechanisms that bridge the gaps between them. The signalling by plants about their pollination status is one such example. For instance, they can signal by opening or closing their petals—a common feature in the vegetal world (van Doorn)—to increase the chances of attracting certain pollinators that are active during specific periods of the day or night. The closing of their petals follows a circadian rhythm, but is also dependent on whether pollination has occurred or not (Fründ et al). Closing flower petals serves several purposes. Once pollination has occurred, the closed petals protect the developing seeds and reduce the chances of further pollination that might interfere with the successful development of seeds. Seen from the insects' perspective, closed petals are an unambiguous signal not to visit.

The Flower Clock installation had a human concern at its heart: the wish to know the time. But, as it turns out, the installation did not tell time very precisely. The opening and closing of the petals depended more on a plant's communication with its environment and with pollinators than on the time of day.

Thus "Who Will Pollinate the Flower Clock" performs a re-definition of time by proposing a "plant time" and points towards urgent concerns that are related to an ongoing loss of habitats and, ultimately, a decline in biodiversity.

The Phytonic Oracle

At the end of the exhibition, I felt a strong desire to continue working with the eleven flowering plants. Consequently, for the following year, I proposed a new installation that included the same plants but that took a different approach. This work would be more conceptual, shown in a gallery setting and designed for a merely human audience. What emerged was the "Phytonic Oracle," a prognostication tool that translates wisdom from plants into advice for life situations (Fig. 1).

I had harvested some specimens from the installation in the autumn, and these became the starting point for the Oracle. Additionally, with the information I gathered from botanical books, herbal medicine literature, online discussion forums, and also with inspiration from astrological readings and Tarot,[3] I began to develop a system for prognostication. The unique features of each plant became increasingly apparent to me through my prolonged, personal engagement with them.

For example, while many of the plants had yellow flowers—as seen in the field, in photographs, and in the dried version of the flowers—the yellows were very different from each other. The greens of their leaves, their shapes, their textures, their seeds, and their roots also all became relevant and enabled me to understand the plants at a level that transcends scientific descriptions and empirical knowledge. I developed a sensibility for these characteristics that allowed me to grasp their nature. I started to know the plants by engaging with them through my senses; touching them, smelling them, tasting them meant relating to them in diverse modes. This way of working influenced me. At one point, I was so immersed in the research that I was dreaming about these flowers. I became aware that, by radically opening myself to them, they had started to affect my thinking. Thus, the flower as object was not as important as my relationship with it. Such an approach to interacting with plants shifts one's "understanding" from a mere intellectual grasping to knowing via new forms of listening (Wilson 59). This shift can be considered embodied knowledge transcending the idea of one sole truth that can be measured and unambiguously characterised. In Shawn Wilson's *Research as Ceremony*, these multiple realities are acknowledged and described as the basis of "indigenous ontology" (73).

The Functioning of the Oracle

All the knowledge I had gathered, the understanding of the character of each plant, its unique capacity to inhabit this world and adapt to challenging situations, its taste, its looks, its feel, its colours, and its companion species became the basis of my Oracle book. I started a work of "translation" by transforming this information into meaning for everyday situations in human lives.

I created a compendium consisting of four categories: growth, pollination, value and habitat. Each of the categories is based on the particular characteristics of the plants and forms the basis for the advice offered by the Oracle. A plant's "growth" characteristic provides answers to questions about identity and personal development; "pollination" describes relationships, love, and emotions; "value" is assigned to work and purpose in life; and, finally, "habitat" is linked to well-being, housing, or travel. Though sourced from scientific information about the plants, my translation was performed intuitively and was grounded in the relationship I had crafted with the plants. Additionally, it was inspired by astrological readings, Tarot card interpretations, and other prognostication practices.

When we think about divination or prophecy as methods for predicting the future, the question of what lies behind the advice arises. Although there is nothing scientific or proven about any of these techniques, they have been used in times of confusion or crisis to reflect on possible futures. Whether they can foretell the future or whether they are just coincidentally correct guesses remains open to debate. In predictions, no claim of accuracy can be made, but seeking and receiving advice nonetheless creates a conversation with the subconscious or with a game with chance, and these methods do have a valid role in helping one to advance in life (Hon). The answers or advice from the Phytonic Oracle are not intended as stringent instructions, nor as the sole way forward that should be taken to heart. Rather, an answer expands the range of possibilities by showing one aspects of a situation that might not have been considered earlier. For instance, an unexpected way forward might be highlighted, a veiled notion might be reformulated, or a hunch might be substantiated. The Oracle's answers are vague and concrete at the same time, and can be related to a specific life situation that is at stake. The validity of prognostication lies therefore not so much in the "correctness," precision or stringency of a potential next step, but rather in the opportunity that it creates to contemplate possibilities and to reflect on blind spots or options that had not yet been considered.

  Christina Stadlbauer

Engaging the eleven plants as sources of wisdom might add an unexpected layer to previously established divination systems. Answers originating from the vegetal world follow different rules than those from the human world. The permanently sedentary existence of plants relies on resilience and adaptability that cannot be compared to human routes to success, which often involve mobility. Other dimensions of time or periodicity are observed when we consider plants, and these dimensions grant us glimpses into circadian or seasonal cycles of life and death. When seeking advice, such issues might help one to take a more distant standpoint in order to see the broader picture, or to refocus on what is simple or essential.

In the summer of 2022, the Phytonic Oracle was presented at Finlayson Art Venue as a participatory intervention. Visitors were able to seek out the Oracle during opening hours and made use of it. When visitors consulted the plants, a protocol had to be observed so that people could receive answers to very specific questions. This protocol added a ritualistic or ceremonial aspect to the visit and was as follows:

> The Oracle is in a dark, intimate room, and only one person at a time can enter. The visitor's question has to be formulated before entering the Oracle room. Once inside the Oracle space, the "Oracle tool" has to be operated; this is a metal pointer that must be spun, allowing the mystery to unfold. The pointer comes to a stop at a number between 1 and 11, indicating which plant is ready to respond. After determining in which of the four categories his or her question belongs, the visitor consults the Oracle book and retrieves its advice. The Oracle has then spoken.

From the guest book comments, I saw that some visitors made it a habit to come several times a week for advice and took the vegetal answers very seriously. What was a playful pata-botanic[4] proposition became an object of meaning and assistance to the visitors.

The situation created by the Phytonic Oracle proposes an alternative reality system. Asking advice from the plant kingdom takes us into the liminal, the magic, and the speculative. A person in a state of emotional confusion or mental disorientation seeking advice from an oracle is coming close to a ritual that needs to be carried out to overcome crisis. This act can be assigned to the realm of "magic" rather than to the domain of traditional problem-solving (Campagna 116). The visit to an oracle aims at restoring the conditions in which both the visitor and his or her world can regain their full presence, and can continue a mutually active and imaginative relationship. That is, this visit entails stepping out of the state of crisis, which can be described as a temporary inability to act, to imagine, and to overcome the temporary loss of our sense of reality (Campagna 116, 230).

As a magical intervention, the Phytonic Oracle therefore proposes to resolutely oppose the process of disintegration. Turning one's focus towards a world that is not informed by reason but instead playfully invites one into a state of sensing rather than of knowing may release the tension that prevents fluidity and connection with one's environment.

The ability to prognosticate is traditionally attributed to seers. It belongs to the realm of magic and non-scientific thinking. Recent research, however, has suggested that plants have a capacity to sense the future. As Paco Calvo and Natalie Lawrence point out, plants follow a different time-scale (Calvo and Lawrence 77). They are "slow" due to their immobility, which makes their movement only possible in terms of growth; that is, they grow towards a location. However, when they grow in a certain direction, the information that guides this growth and behaviour needs to be information about a future, one that will lead to success. If a plant invests a lot of energy growing in the wrong direction and then finds no nutrients, water, or light, it is in deep trouble. To predict and respond as early as possible to environmental change can be seen as anticipatory growth. Plants are thus forced to predict and, in this way, can be understood as being gifted with prognostication.

The Meaning Behind the Oracle: Changing Roles

The Phytonic Oracle is part of an artistic research strand that explores the possibility of communicating with non-human life forms. This research has been ongoing with different species and has led to speculative, absurd, and ritualistic works that question both our mainstream understanding of "intelligence" and the relations that we humans practise with the forms of life surrounding us. In the case of the Phytonic Oracle, the interspecies communication is between plants and humans—and vice versa. The Oracle becomes an amplifier for the "voice" of eleven plants that have a message for humans. When reading the Oracle, the visitor learns about the selected plants. She or he is introduced to vegetal life forms that constantly surround us everywhere and that often go unnoticed. The invitation is to acknowledge and witness the presence of these life forms. The Oracle seduces the visitor into conversation with the plant world, and a potential relationship is established. This cannot be assumed to be a conscious process, but rather the relationship might happen of its own accord. If the latter scenario occurs, the artwork can be considered successful.

Consultation of the Oracle encourages openness. The plant-human dialogue that is prompted suggests reversing the roles between "human and nature." Attributing wisdom to plants elevates them, makes them experts. The human visitor is looking for advice and comes to ask the plants. The answer she or he obtains is sourced from a "wisdom" based on the diversity that can be found in the plant world and that is conveyed via its forms, properties, resilience and capacity to adapt to changing circumstances. The usually dominant paradigm of human control is put aside: here, humans ask, and plants give a valid answer. Playfully and without judgement, the visitor's role becomes one of not knowing, and the plant world is granted the capacity to resolve complex issues, answer essential questions about life, and become our allies in facing unknown futures.

Working Methods and Conclusion

The working methods employed for creating the Phytonic Oracle and for my artistic research in general emphasise embodied understanding and learning grounded in watching and doing. During my preparation of both the Flower Clock and the Oracle, the plants became part of my daily routine; I was reading about them, growing them at home, seeing them as "weeds" on street corners, or drinking them as herbal teas. This was not a conscious search for them; instead, an openness, alertness, or awareness towards these flowers made me see them. Hence, I started relating to these plants in a different, more profound way, with every accidental encounter being as valid as intentionally looking up information about them. These plants affected my senses, offering me images, tastes, smells, textures. A conversation without words was unfolding, and this conversation became the basis for the messages in the Phytonic Oracle book.

To give a voice to other life forms carries the danger of anthropomorphising them, which misses the point entirely. However, using language, communication, and relationships as proposals to shift our viewpoints, playfully and open-endedly so that we do not insist on correct or exclusive approaches, might help to decolonise our stance towards other than humans (Despret and Bento). Speculation, science fiction, magic, and artistic interventions that refrain from logic or explanation might be able to generate a possible change of direction more effectively than a study based on scientific evidence.

Using a language distinct from scientific terminology can trigger a learning process by encouraging us to reflect on the importance of the beauty and the role of plants, on the need to preserve biodiversity, and on vegetal capabilities that have yet to be described. Art that interacts with botany and biology, and that dialogues with these life forms, assumes a responsibility grounded in high levels of trans-disciplinary skills (Scialabba) because the questions that this art asks span discourses from science to ethics and from ecology to economy. Which species are worth protecting? Where do we draw the line between weeds and useful plants? Should what is useful for humankind be valued more highly than what is useful in an ecosystem? How do we define "useful" at all without falling into a trap? Carefully defining strategies of inquiry and avoiding sticking rigidly to (pre)defined methods is key here (Wilson 39-40) and research based on artistic practice might be a helpful way forward. Relying on "Phytonic answers from the Oracle might give guidance and direction and unexpected support in life's most difficult and demanding situations."[5]

Notes

1   Participatory Installation, Plant Oracle, Christina Stadlbauer, 2022. This work was made possible by the assistance of Lynne Stuart, Gosie Vervloessem, and Petri Heino.

2   Horologium Florae. See also "Linnaeus's Flower Clock."

3   Tarot card deck by Rider-Waite.

4   "Pata" refers to a concept described as the "science of imaginary solutions." It was invented by the French writer Alfred Jarry ("pataphysics," or, in French, "pataphysique"), and it is understood as a "philosophy" of science. See also how FoAM has used "patabotany" (Kuzmanovic).

5   From "Instructions on How To Use The Phytonic Oracle," Finlayson Art Venue, Tampere, Finland, 2022.

Works Cited

Calvo Paco, and Natalie Lawrence. *Planta Sapiens: Unmasking Plant Intelligence.* Hachette UK, 2022.

Campagna, Federico. *Technic and Magic: The Reconstruction of Reality.* Bloomsbury Publishing, 2018.

Despret, Vinciane, Bento, Christine Aventin, and Juliette Salme. *Living in Mycelium.* In Vivo, Biennale di Architettura 2023.

Fründ, Jochen, et al. "Linné's Floral Clock is Slow Without Pollinators – Flower Closure and Plant-Pollinator Interaction Webs." *Ecology Letters*, vol. 13, 2011, pp. 896-904.

Hon, Tze-Ki. "Chinese Philosophy of Change (Yijing)." *The Stanford Encyclopedia of Philosophy (Summer 2019 Edition)*, edited by Edward N. Zalta, https://plato.stanford.edu/archives/sum2019/entries/chinese-change/. Accessed 22 June 2023.

Hustak, Carla, Natasha Myers. "Involutionary Momentum: Affective Ecologies and the Sciences of Plant/Insect Encounters." *differences*, vol 23, no. 3, 1 Dec. 2012, pp. 74-118.

Kuzmanovic, Maja. "Patabotany." *[foam]*, FoAM, 3 Jul. 2012, https://fo.am/blog/2012/07/03/patabotany/. Accessed 25 Aug. 2023.

"Linnaeus's Floral Clock—Horologium Florae." *The Linnaean Gardens of Uppsala*, Uppsala Universitet, 7 Dec. 2021, https://www.botan.uu.se/our-gardens/the-linnaeus-garden/our-plants/life-cycle-of-the-flowering-plants/. Accessed 3 Aug. 2023.

Scialabba, Anna. "The Decadence of Botany and the Crisis of Humanity." *Performative Habitat*, edited by Egle Oddo, Lori Adragna, Postmedia Books, 2022.

van Doorn, Wouter G., et. al. "Flower Opening and Closure: A Review." *Journal of Experimental Botany*, vol. 54, no. 389, 1 Aug. 2003, pp. 1801-12.

Wilson, Shawn. *Research is Ceremony*. Fernwood Publishing, 2008.

15 Vivid Frequencies: Using AR to Materialise New Affective Assemblages in More-Than-Human Ecologies

Anna Madeleine Raupach

Introduction

Vivid Frequencies is an augmented-reality (AR) artwork that accentuates co-presence with plants (Fig. 1). Experiencing this work through a web application on a mobile device, viewers moving around the Australian Botanic Gardens Mount Annan can watch or listen to the app digitally recomposing the camera view and sonic landscape of the surrounding physical world. The work responds to research by the Royal Botanic Gardens (RBG) Sydney that predicts environmental conditions in 2070 and models future growth maps for a selection of native Australia species. The audio-visual alterations in *Vivid Frequencies* are activated in response to the participant's proximity to these species on site, turning the scientific information of herbaria collections into living ecosystems. Translating data into a visual language and auditory soundscape, *Vivid Frequencies* dismantles and reforms the image of a plant in relation to the predicted growth, loss, or movement of the species over time. The audio composition indicates the average age of the species, with deeper, slower sounds signalling the viewer is close to an ancient being, and lighter, faster tempos suggesting shorter lifespans. Through this audio-visual code, the mobile device acts as a portal by which we can tune into divergent, non-human scales of time and space that are interwoven with ours.

In Part 1, I will begin by reflecting on herbarium collections as datasets. I explore how datasets become material ensembles through the construction and collection of physical specimen sheets, and how digitisation projects in contemporary collections codify and standardise metadata to expand opportunities for access and collaboration. However, there are significant omissions in these collections that cause tension around the extraction of plants from their natural environment, and I will discuss how *Vivid Frequencies* attempts to return

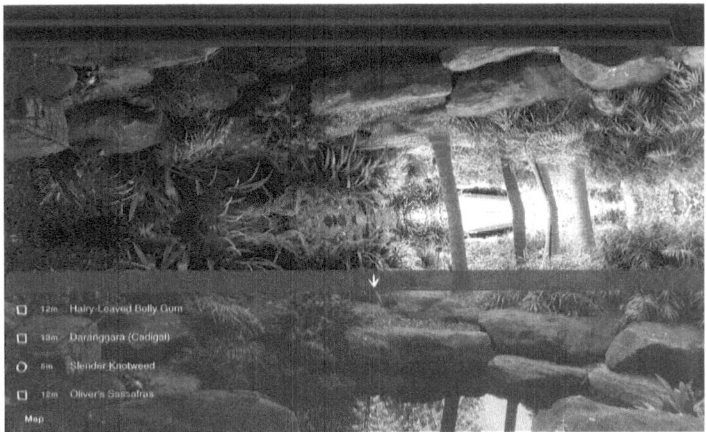

Figure 1. Anna Madeleine Raupach, *Vivid Frequencies*, 2022, site-specific augmented reality app. Developer: Dylan Shorten, Music: Kim Cunio, Video: Sammy Hawker. (Image courtesy of Anna Madeleine Raupach).

collected data to a living ecosystem in response to these problems. The Royal Botanic Gardens' Restore & Renew resource, which maps shifts in species distribution according to genetic analysis and climate modelling, will be referred to both as an example of beneficial use of herbaria data and as the basis for creative reinterpretation in my work. Part 2 will unpack how the audio-visual code and resulting aesthetics of *Vivid Frequencies* respond to herbaria data, in addition to participant and plant locations. Assigning visual post-processing effects and custom-made audio compositions to different species' GPS coordinates informs a dismantling and relayering of image and sound based on spatial and temporal qualities of the environment.

In Part 3, I will discuss examples of AR and audio artworks that respond to botanic gardens, herbarium collections, and site-specific environments, in order to distinguish how *Vivid Frequencies* integrates plants as active participants rather than passive subjects. This leads into a discussion of assemblage thinking and agency in Part 4, which explores how the expressive capacity of *Vivid Frequencies* emerges from a combinatory system of irreducible parts, and reflects on how this assemblage is symbolic of a complex ecology where agency is entangled and enacted between technological and vegetal systems. The chapter concludes in Part 5 by considering how AR can expand plant aesthetics back into lived experience via a diffracting of herbaria data into the vibrant matter of physical ecosystems. This creates an expressive apparatus for interdisciplinary research that accentuates how plants affect humans just as much, or even more, than humans affect plants.

Herbaria as Datasets

Beginning this project at the National Herbarium in 2021, I was immediately drawn to the material artefacts accumulated on the specimen sheets: the name of the collector and their handwritten notes, stamps and catalogue numbers signifying the various institutions that have been custodians of the file, and the barcodes and colour profilers used to capture this physical residue in machine-readable metadata. This coded language symbolises the plant's history in human hands—a history that is continuing to unfold through the major digitisation projects many herbarium collections are now undertaking. When I visited the National Herbarium, specimen sheets were being lined up on a conveyor belt to be photographed and converted into replicable formats of digital code, completing the metamorphosis of the organic, non-human into digital, human form. While extremely tempted to create work responding to these rich visual assemblages, my aim was to challenge the human dominance that informed their creation. My research instead explores how the herbarium can cultivate attunement to the presence of plants *in the world* by translating data into art experienced in the natural environment to which the specimen sheets refer. The process of creating this artwork will be discussed in Part 2; here, I will first consider the nature of the data itself.

Emma Lansdowne suggests that methodologies of herbaria enact a "scientific aesthetic regime" that promotes exclusion through their visual, political, and archival qualities (Lansdowne). By conforming to Linnaean taxonomy, herbarium classification systems flatten living and sensorial plants into a constructed, limited, and biased collection of material objects with a visual identity separate from the complex ecology to which the species are implicitly linked. This process of removal includes a "scientifically" justified exclusion of Indigenous knowledge and a decontextualisation of plants from their natural ecosystems. Acknowledging the ongoing complexities intrinsic to the work of decolonising collections, my artwork focuses its contribution on revaluing the herbarium by reconnecting its aesthetics with the living ecosystem, embedding their data into art that emerges out of co-presence with plants in the natural landscape.

Herbaria hold historical records for a baseline of individual species that make up the Earth's ecosystem and advance science that examines shifts in species redistribution. One way that herbarium data is evolving is through digitised and

                                    Anna Madeleine Raupach

networked catalogues. Referencing the digitisation of biodiversity data around the world, James et al. highlight the potential of online herbarium catalogues to synthesise knowledge. Improved access to biodiversity data specific to different ecological conditions increases knowledge of the associations, composition, and assemblages of species and plant communities across space and through time. This gives insight into the impact of invasive species, changes in environment, and human activity, and expands the ability to assess and predict environmental change. The RBG's Restore & Renew project is one such example of herbarium data being used to predict ecological shifts and subsequent restoration requirements due to climate change (James et al.).

The Restore & Renew web tool is the interface by which restoration practitioners can access genomic, evolutionary, and ecological data for over one hundred native species in New South Wales, and is also the dataset on which my *Vivid Frequencies* is based. Launched in 2019, this website is the result of research that combines collected samples with genetic studies to predict how current geographical areas will be impacted in future climatic conditions (Rossetto et al.). Species included in Restore & Renew were chosen to represent a range of functional, geographic, and ecological features. Using both new samples and historical records, metadata is mapped and leaf tissue is sent away for DNA extraction and analysis that informs climate matching for current and future conditions. The resulting web tool makes distribution, genomic, and climate data readily available to the public and is an example of how digitising and distributing herbarium data has transformative potential for climate change adaptation.

James et al. note that digitisation reveals inconsistencies in existing catalogues, meaning that: "Biodiversity data have been described as biased, fuzzy, haphazard, unstandardized, non-random, incomplete, and unique because of collecting bias and/or digitization gaps, and subsequently require quality assessment" (3).

To consolidate data across the varying practices and vocabularies of different research fields, James et al. suggest the need for global standardisation in streamlining the migration of herbarium specimen sheets into digital forms. For example, "Darwin Core" is an international standard used to facilitate the exchange of botanical data. Additionally, born-digital methods of data collection can improve systems by automatically linking GPS location and metadata to sample collection (James et al.). While global digitisation of herbarium collections has significant benefits for increasing the preservation and accessibility of biodiversity data, does conforming to standardised identifiers, labels, and definitions reinforce the scientific aesthetic regime that informed the original specimen sheets? Acknowledging this question, I suggest that the encoding of herbaria data opens new opportunities for it to be used creatively to reimagine and revalue our relationship with plants: scientifically, aesthetically, and experientially.

Vivid Frequencies: A Combinatory System

In a *Back to Earth* podcast sponsored by the Serpentine Galleries, the artist James Bridle refers to the concept of "using space for time" in reference to ecologist Suzanne Simmard's research on forest migration, according to which trees need to move an average of 400 metres per year to remain in their habitable environment, as the globe warms at its current rate (Sin and Pietroiusti). Investigating species redistribution, marine ecologist Gretta Pecl's research on "range shift" finds "terrestrial taxa, on average, moving polewards by 17 km per decade, and marine taxa by 72 km per decade" (Pecl et al., 2). Quantifying this distance makes tangible an imperceptible non-human behaviour, and evoking this phenomenon of plant mobility became the core challenge of *Vivid Frequencies*.

My research began by defining what the artwork should *not* do. I did not want to impose illustrative expression, such as the drawing techniques I have previously worked with, to depict qualities of plant time or mobility. Instead, I was asking if it was possible to highlight how plants already enact time and mobility by *allowing them to affect us* through the artwork, rather than the other way around. My work was to be situated at Australian Botanic Gardens Mount Annan, which is home to a collection of 34,462 plants and 3,313 different taxa across 416 hectares. Working at this scale, the first challenge was defining parameters that are appropriate for encompassing an ecology. The online flowering calendar and Garden Explorer map demonstrated filters that could be applied to delimit a vast living dataset. This digital interface for the gardens led me to the Restore & Renew web tool that aligned with my aim of expressing plant movement through time, and Restore & Renew's Target Species Directory became the dataset for *Vivid Frequencies*.

Through a process of "getting to know the data" (Ridler) for each species in the directory, I compiled images of the plant from plantNET, botanical illustrations, photographs of specimen sheets, and the current and future growth maps for the species created by Restore & Renew. From this information, three data points emerged as key for my work: where the species is growing in the

　　　　　　　　　　　　　　　　　　　　Anna Madeleine Raupach

gardens, how old it is likely to be, and how the species is moving over time. The first two data points enabled me to situate the species in time and place. The third was linked to the compelling measurements of the movement of plants over time. My question then became: how do I create a system that will allow these temporal and spatial behaviours of the plants to become expressive? Continuously reminding myself not to impose human-created imagery, I developed the approach of applying post-processing alterations to a live image as a way of bringing about a change in relations when a person, technology, and plant are in close proximity to each other. A post-processing effect is a full-screen filter that is applied to a live camera feed in the same way that a glitch affects a system, or a lens changes the appearance of the world it delineates. Using post-processing effects allowed me to set up a relationship between the participant and the plants that relied on proximity rather than direct interaction. Simply being in the presence of different plants would affect the aesthetics of the surrounding environment as they were translated through the camera of the mobile application.

Accessing the GPS locations for the species I was working with led to further insights into the inner workings of the herbarium. Requesting GPS coordinates required a meeting with the Herbarium and Botanic Gardens staff; I needed to explain that my data was not for commercial use and would not be shared with other parties. This gatekeeping revealed the security issues around herbarium data necessary for restricting access to psychoactive and threatened species that are at risk of poaching. After signing a contract for access to this information, I received a spreadsheet for the species to be part of the *Vivid Frequencies* app. The data fields I gained access to detailed the plants' taxonomy (Species, Genus, Family), Common Names, the year it became part of the collection, the GPS co-ordinations, and Garden Bed location. As well as the strict security measures surrounding access, another point that stood out to me when working with this data was that the CommonNameAllLang field opens space for different knowledge and naming systems to co-exist, and thus for decolonising work to be done. However, less than a fifth of the common names of plants in the data set I was given included names in Gadigal or D'harawal languages, signifying the enormity and complexity of this task.

To create my post-processing effects, I translated the current and future growth maps from Restore & Renew into a visual language. For example, predicted loss correlated to image desaturation, growth was expressed through multiplication of the image, species migration was indicated by pixel redistribution, and consistency of growth pattern was shown through mirroring. Within each of these categories, the effects were applied in a scale corresponding to how extreme the change on the growth map appeared. In addition to the visual qualities signifying spatial behaviour, the audio component was key in evoking the layered and multiple time scales of the different species comprising the ecology of the gardens. The age or lifespans of the species I was working with was one of the elements missing from the dataset I had acquired, so I relied on research from PlantNET to gain an understanding of the average lifespan of each species. As with the visual code, I sorted the species into nine age ranges, from perennial grasses to the ancient River Red Gum. Each temporal scale was then translated into 10-30-second compositions, in collaboration with the musician Kim Cunio, who responded to my request for pieces that could be layered over each other in any number of combinations. Cunio brought to the project a quality of sound that corresponded to the material nature of the plants and gardens, using a range of instruments that included timpani drums, Tibetan bowls, rain sticks, crotales (antique cymbals), and wooden blocks and beads. These various instruments created reverberating bass and shimmering tones that resonated with the plants in both cultural and functional ways.

The crucial element of constructing *Vivid Frequencies* was that I was designing only one part of a system that could be combined with any number of other components in its final form. Experienced in the gardens, the app activates the assigned visual and auditory responses for any number of plants that surround it. Consequently, the results are unpredictable, entangled, and always evolving. Areas that are home to certain communities, such as the Banksia Garden or Grevillea Walk, will evoke a prominent effect for those species in the data. However, at sites where many different species coexist, the specificity of effects become unclear, creating a sensory experience unique to that specific constellation of plants.

Plant Participants in Augmented Reality

AR has been used by many contemporary artists to engage with natural landscapes and ecology in alternative ways. A recent example is *Seeing the Invisible*, an app produced by Jerusalem Botanic Gardens in partnership with Outset Contemporary Art Fund. In this app, artworks by prominent contemporary artists, such as Ai Wei Wei and Refik Anadol, were transplanted into various botanic gardens around the world, including in Adelaide and Melbourne (Maor and Haring). These artworks are primarily based on 3D-generated models that

Anna Madeleine Raupach

float or are anchored to a specific location. The intention is to explore the relationship between the viewer and the digital art object, but there is little engagement with the surrounding plants.

In contrast, site-specific ecology is key to many of American artist Tamiko Thiel's AR works. Tamiko Thiel's and Will Pappenheimer's work *Biomer Skelters*, a collaboration with Liverpool John Moores University and the World Museum Liverpool, drew its premise and aesthetic from herbarium specimens and prints that were used to transform the city's botanical history into a participatory artwork that generates digital urban gardens (Thiel and Pappenheimer). The AR system detects users' heart rates and grows virtual plants in response to participants' biorhythms as they move around the city. Assigning native species to some participants and invasive species to others, *Biomer Skelters* stages a collective imagining of contrasting species' propagation and the connection between human bodies and urban ecosystems. Other examples of Thiel's works include *Gardens of the Anthropocene*, an outdoor, site-specific AR app that imagines a dystopian future where plants specific to the local area have mutated in response to rising temperatures (Thiel); and *Waldwandel / Forest Flux*, a collaboration with Bavarian State Forest Enterprise that brings AR into a gallery through a livestream to show the impact of climate change on Bavarian forests (Thiel). Thiel's work has pioneered and established AR as a platform for visualising environmental change. While these works primarily represent the non-human subjects as digital assets, in *Vivid Frequencies* and this chapter, I aim to position physical species as plant participants who share agency in the creation of an AR experience. Artists Rewa Wright's and Simon Howden's *Contact Projects* shares this approach by transforming plant surfaces into tangible interfaces that activate sound and digital augments through touch (Wright and Howden). *Vivid Frequencies* expands touch to co-presence and representation to affect, to broaden its scope to the entanglements of a living ecology.

Audio artworks also have a profound impact in augmenting the natural landscape. *Bushland* by Rebecca French & Andrew Mottershead is one part of a series of immersive digital experiences that invite participants to lie on the ground and listen to a 20-minute spoken narration of how our bodies decay and become part of the trees overhead after we die. Originally produced as *Woodlands* for a UK-based environment, this work was adapted for Australian climates, informed by Aboriginal knowledge, and placed in dialogue with local forensic experts and ecologists (French & Mottershead). *Ripples* by Yi Wu is another example of an auditory system that blends external and internal sounds to guide listeners through the Atlanta Botanic Garden (Wu and Freeman). This work, like *Vivid Frequencies*, employs GPS locations of plants as anchor points for subtle alterations that fade in and out depending on the participants' proximity.

Using Thiel's work as a primary example, Wright suggests that AR systems can be understood as software assemblages, and that this conceptualisation advances our idea of AR from an information overlay to an opportunity for the emergent properties of relationships between components to play out:

> approaching AR as an assemblage rather than an information overlay,
> and concomitantly, an interface as a network of relations rather than
> an object, produces a more nuanced understanding of the relations
> between devices, software, artists, artworks, and participants (371).

Investigating *Vivid Frequencies* as an assemblage helps to define how a data-driven and mixed reality artwork can contribute to revaluing the herbarium. Two key ideas inform how I have approached my research. First, the mobile device is considered as an extension of the human body (Hayles; McLuhan), and second, the ability of plants to communicate across networks is emphasised (Kimmerer; Gagliano). These two concepts scaffold the way I use AR—through the prosthesis of a mobile device—to extend the human relationship with the vegetal world. By creating a conduit between the two coexisting communication systems of plants and humans, which otherwise operate on different planes, I offer the possibility for humans to "tune in" to vegetal frequencies, and so to become receptive to the rhythms and essence of the more-than-human world in new ways.

Assemblages of Agencies

Wright's proposition of AR as a software assemblage stems from Gilles Deleuze's and Felix Guattari's theory of the machinic assemblage. I define an "assemblage" as an entity consisting of multiple and diverse parts, whose interactions and relations form a self-organising composite with expressive and functional capacities that are otherwise non-existent. Manuel DeLanda's reading of Deleuze and Guattari's assemblage theory highlights the fact that parts of an assemblage are irreducible and that relations between parts of an assemblage are crucial to producing its emergent properties: "if the interactions cease to take place the emergent properties cease to exist" (12); therefore, "the lines or links are often more important than the nodes themselves" (29). These "links" can change and expand over space or time, for example through technology

                                      Anna Madeleine Raupach

or communication systems, and require maintenance to continue existing. Furthermore, in addition to material components, such as hardware or infrastructure, expressive capacities, including sensory, symbolic, and energetic qualities, are implicated in an assemblage as both distinctly individual parts and emergent properties (DeLanda, 28).

Vivid Frequencies fits the definition of an assemblage through its emergent properties, the vitality of relationships between its parts, and its expressive capacities. Its components include: the herbarium data in its many forms (specimen sheets, Restore & Renew research, and my data request spreadsheet); the living plants; the botanic gardens and their design, architecture, and pathways; the combinatory system that informs the visual aesthetics; the audio compositions made by Kim Cunio's musical sensibility and skill; the programming software and developer Dylan Shorten's coding style, user interface, interaction design, and map; the device used by participants; and the participants themselves, especially their actions. Associated with each of these components are many other features.

While assemblage thinking helps explain the mechanics of *Vivid Frequencies*, the vital materialities of Jane Bennett's *Vibrant Matter* and Karen Barad's definition of agency from the perspective of "agential realism" supports the core essence of what this work, as an assemblage, strives to achieve. Bennett argues for the vitality of all matter by emphasising the role of non-human bodies as "actants" with the capacity to cultivate a change in the world through abilities such as generating a force or initiating a reaction (10). She goes on to emphasise that "humans and their intentions participate, but they are not the sole or always the most profound actant" (10). Supporting this proposition, Barad defines "agency" as an "enactment" produced by a reconfiguration of relations between beings that are each made up of their own entangled affordances. According to Barad:

> Agency is a matter of intra-acting; it is an enactment, not something that someone or something has. Agency cannot be designated as an attribute of subjects or objects (as they do not preexist as such). Agency is a matter of making iterative changes to particular practices through the dynamics of intra-activity (178).

This distinction between interaction and "intra-action" expands on how agency is mutual and emergent, and echoes the approach of using co-presence rather than direct interaction to inform the experience of *Vivid Frequencies*.

Barad explains: "In contrast to the usual 'interaction', which assumes that there are separate individual agencies that precede their interaction, the notion of intra-action recognises that distinct agencies do not precede, but rather emerge through, their intra-action" (128).

Considering agency as a shared enactment advances the argument for the agency of more-than-human participants in the assemblages of the herbarium, as well as in site-specific AR. In *Vivid Frequencies*, the plant and person sharing the same space generate together an expressive effect. This co-presence can be identified as the enactment producing a reconfiguration that creates an agency shared between the human and the plant. It materialises as a fleeting and expressive visual and auditory experience completely dependent on the "intra-action" between a human and more-than-human assemblages. However, this raises questions about intention and power dynamics. As Barad writes, "The acknowledgment of 'nonhuman agency' does not lessen human accountability; on the contrary, it means that accountability requires that much more attentiveness to existing power asymmetries" (219).

Archaeologist Yannis Hamilakis writes of similar power asymmetries in addressing the political implications of assemblages that preference certain voices and potential futures over others (Hamilakis). This is seen in how herbarium specimen sheets contributed to the erasure of First Nations names and knowledge, and the ongoing political effects of this erasure emerge via the lack of data in the assemblage of the herbarium. Hamilakis suggests political agency of assemblages occurs when they are intentionally composed rather than when there is a coincidental co-presence of parts: "That deliberate act of bringing together assumes the ability and power of a social agent to do so, it entails certain prerogatives, but it also brings about certain social and political consequences" (175).

This inherent bias reinforces the scientific aesthetic regime of original specimen collection, but it also opens space for artists as "social agents" to address gaps in herbarium collections. Creative interventions can integrate the assemblage of the herbarium into new assemblages that inject the sensorial and affective components currently missing from herbaria.

While Hamilakis describes human intentionality as a defining feature that enables assemblages to hold political power, Bennett questions how non-human actants share this purposeful behaviour (13). I suggest the behaviour of plants described by Gibson and Sandilands as "performative" demonstrates an intentional behaviour by growing, flowering, and dispersing in specific ways to

     Anna Madeleine Raupach

cultivate reactions in the ecology (2). While using the *Vivid Frequencies* app, I was fascinated by traits of plants, for instance Banksia flowers or a caterpillar's cocoon on a leaf, and those characteristics of the plant and its living relationships influenced the affective power of *Vivid Frequencies* because they drew me towards them and initiated an audio-visual effect. In this way, both human and more-than-human intention is influential in my work's existence and aesthetic, and this links to Barad's notion of performativity that "allows matter its due as an active participant in the world's becoming, in its ongoing intra-activity" (136).

Revaluing the herbarium in this way involves complex negotiations of temporal perspectives. Both Hamilakis and DeLanda write of temporality within assemblages as layered and multiple. Hamilakis describes "a multiplicity of temporal modalities: geological times, archaeological / historical times, human experiential times, nonhuman animal experiential times" (173). DeLanda distinguishes "a multiplicity of flows, each with its own variable rates of change, its own accelerations and decelerations" (14). *Vivid Frequencies* engages with different species' lifespans through its layered rhythms, and it thus evokes a recognition of potential change to the present landscape by translating shifts in species into visual qualities. However, it is over time that I hope the impact of *Vivid Frequencies* will do its work. My aim is for the affective experience that accentuates the plant-human connection to remain with participants as a potential re-enactment of the agency of more-than-human actors. *Vivid Frequencies* aims to synthesise past histories and future trajectories to highlight the significance of humans and more-than-human entities sharing the present moment, while both are moving at entirely different speeds.

Vivid Frequencies: An Affective Apparatus

In concluding this chapter, I discuss how *Vivid Frequencies* enacts qualities of Barad's definition of a "diffractive apparatus" through interdisciplinary research that explores climate-driven redistribution of species through the "vital materialities" of vibrant matter. First, I expand on the research concerning species redistribution. Pecl writes: "Critically, the pervasive impacts of changes in species distribution transcend single systems or dimensions, with feedbacks and linkages among multiple interacting spatial and temporal scales and through entire ecosystems, inclusive of humans" (Pecl et al., 2).

The impacts of species redistribution on agriculture and crop growth, food supply chains, and the traditional knowledge of local natural phenomena and associated cultural customs will have a significant effect on human well-being. The implications of non-human species shifts on human populations include conflict between regions and sectors over trade, economic threats and the geo-political limitations of human migration across borders (Pecl et al., 3). The breadth of research into species redistribution encompasses the friction between human and non-human ecologies as both change in different ways due to climate change. The inclusion of human well-being and cultural knowledge in Pecl's research is an example of cross-fertilisation of assemblage thinking between social and environmental science, but it also highlights the need for increased cross-disciplinary research. *Vivid Frequencies* contributes creative input towards this cross-disciplinary goal. By infusing scientific data into sensory experience within a natural ecology, my project aligns with Barad's "diffractive" methodology, which attends to the material entanglements of different disciplines in active and performative approaches, rather than representational habits, as a way of "understanding the world from within and as part of it" (88).

Aligning human participants with any other vital materiality in an assemblage has profound impact on how people conceptualise themselves within the environment. However, Bennett posits that the resulting challenge becomes how to facilitate communication—rather than perfect equality—between participants, asking:

> How can communication proceed when many members are nonlinguistic? Can we theorize more closely the various forms of such communicative energies? How can humans learn to hear or enhance our receptivity for "propositions" not expressed in words? How to translate between them? What kinds of institutions and rituals of democracy would be appropriate? (104).

Vivid Frequencies begins to answer some of these questions. However, it does so within the parameters of the site of the Royal Botanic Gardens, pre-programmed GPS location (rather than real-time sensing of surrounding plants), the limited data accessible from the National Herbarium, and the artistic sensibility of me and my (human) collaborators. The work's strength is in *simulating* a conduit between digital and vegetal communication networks that allows us to tune into more-than-human frequencies. By bringing perceptual materiality to imperceptible plant behaviours, *Vivid Frequencies* creates a contained experience that can be imagined expanding from the scale of the individual plant in front of us to that of global change. This imagined expansion is accomplished through an AR app symbolic of a "diffractive apparatus." As Barad suggests:

> Apparatuses are not merely about us. And they are not merely assemblages that include nonhumans as well as humans. Rather, apparatuses are specific material reconfigurings of the world that do not merely emerge in time but iteratively reconfigure space-time-matter as part of the ongoing dynamism of becoming (142).

As an apparatus, *Vivid Frequencies* links the human body to plants within an ecological network, creating an assemblage that distributes humans and more-than-humans as actants with shared agency that can generate affective power. The impacts and implications of reconsidering more-than-human bodies as vibrant matter—or plants as vivid frequencies—are profound and expansive. Through experience of this reconsideration within the Royal Botanic Gardens, I aim for *Vivid Frequencies* to both revalue the herbarium as a platform for re-engaging with plants in their natural ecosystem and accentuate more-than-human actants as affective bodies with whom we share agency in a way that remains with the participant beyond the mobile device, like a phantom limb.

Works Cited

Barad, Karen. *Meeting the Universe Halfway: Quantum Physics and the Entanglement of Matter and Meaning.* Duke University Press, 2007.

Bennett, Jane. *Vibrant Matter: A Political Ecology of Things.* Duke University Press, 2010.

Bridle, James, et al. *Back to Earth: Sowing the Seeds.* Serpentine Podcast, Episode 2, 2020, https://www.serpentinegalleries.org/art-and-ideas/back-to-earth-episode-2-sowing-the-seeds/. Accessed 10 Jun. 2023.

DeLanda, Manuel. *Assemblage Theory.* Edinburgh University Press, 2016, doi: 10.1515/9781474413640.

French & Mottershead. *Woodland.* Audio, 2018, http://frenchmottershead.com/works/woodland/. Accessed 30 May 2023.

Gagliano, Monica, et al. "Out of Sight but Not out of Mind: Alternative Means of Communication in Plants." *PloS One*, vol. 7, no. 5, 2012, doi: 10.1371/journal.pone.0037382.

Gibson, Prudence, and Catriona Sandilands. "Introduction: Plant Performance." *Performance Philosophy*, vol. 6, no. 2, 2021, pp. 1-23, doi: 10.21476/PP.2021.62372.

Hamilakis, Yannis. "Sensorial Assemblages: Affect, Memory and Temporality in Assemblage Thinking." *Cambridge Archaeological Journal*, vol. 71, no. 1, 2017, pp. 169-82, doi: 10.1017/S0959774316000676.

Hayles, N. Katherine. *How We Became Posthuman: Virtual Bodies in Cybernetics, Literature, and Informatics.* University of Chicago Press, 2000.

James, Shelley A., et al. "Herbarium Data: Global Biodiversity and Societal Botanical Needs for Novel Research." *Applications in Plant Sciences*, vol. 6, no. 2, 2018, p. e1024, doi: 10.1002/aps3.1024.

Kimmerer, Robin Wall. *Braiding Sweetgrass: Indigenous Wisdom, Scientific Knowledge and the Teachings of Plants.* Milkweed Editions, 2013.

Lansdowne, Emma. "Curatorial Subjectivity: The Universal Aesthetics of Herbaria." *Unlikely,* no. 4 (Art & Herbarium), 2018, https://unlikely.net.au/issue-04/curatorial-subjectivity.

McLuhan, Marshall. *Understanding Media: The Extensions of Man.* McGraw-Hill, 1964.

Pecl, Gretta T., et al. "Biodiversity Redistribution under Climate Change: Impacts on Ecosystems and Human Well-Being." *Science,* vol. 355, no. 6332, 2017, p. eaai9214, doi: 10.1126/science.aai9214.

Ridler, Anna. "Automated Dreaming: Using AI in a Creative Practice." *"Images of Machine Learning" Media Futures University of New South Wales Online Symposium,* 29 Jun. 2021, https://www.youtube.com/watch?v=LSasCBJak_k.

Rossetto, Maurizio, et al. "Restore and Renew: A Genomics-Era Framework for Species Provenance Delimitation." *Restoration Ecology,* vol. 27, no. 3, 2019, pp. 538-48, doi: 10.1111/rec.12898.

Thiel, Tamiko. *Gardens of the Anthropocene.* Augmented reality installation, 2016-17, https://tamikothiel.com/gota/index.html. Accessed 2 June 2023.

---. and Will Pappenheimer. *Biomer Skelters.* Augmented reality installation, 2013, https://manifestarblog.wordpress.com/biomer-skelters/. Accessed 2 June 2023.

Wright, Rewa, and Simon Howden. "A Technique and Method for Mixed Reality Performance with Digital Augments, Gestural Data, and Living Plants." *Advances in Creativity, Innovation, Entrepreneurship and Communication of Design,* vol. 1218, 2020, pp. 235-39, doi: 10.1007/978-3-030-51626-0_29.

Wu, Yi, and Jason Freeman. "Ripples: An Auditory Augmented Reality IOS Application for the Atlanta Botanical Garden." *NIME 2021,* 2021, doi: 10.21428/92fbeb44.b8e82252.

Anna Madeleine Raupach

16 *Walk Beside Me*: Growing an Awareness of Plants through Art and Cross-cultural Collaboration.

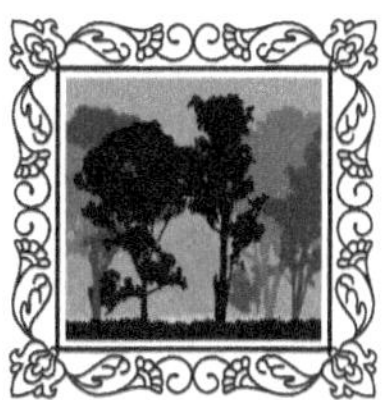

Erica Seccombe and Aunty Deidre Martin

We acknowledge, celebrate, and pay our respects to all First Nations Australians on whose traditional lands we meet and work, and whose cultures are among the oldest continuing cultures in human history.

Introduction

Walk beside Me is a work of art resulting from a cross-cultural collaboration between Aunty Deidre Martin, a Walbunja Elder of the Yuin nation, and Erica Seccombe, an Australian of European descent. Throughout this essay, Aunty Deidre is acknowledged with the title, "Aunty," the name given to highly respected women in Aboriginal and Torres Strait Islander communities who maintain custodianship of cultural knowledge and lore according to their kinships. This collaboration as a creative practice responds to the theme of plant blindness, a plant awareness disparity that describes the human phenomena of an impaired recognition of plants (Wandersee and Schussler). This work was commissioned by the 2022 *Tellus Art Project*, which is an alliance between University of New South Wales Art and Design, the Sydney Royal Botanic Gardens Herbarium, Bundanon, and Open Humanities Press. The research of the lead investigators, Prudence Gibson and Maria Sierra, initiates inter-disciplinary art projects framed by discourses in critical plant studies. In *The Plant Contract: Art's Return to Vegetal Life*, Gibson writes about the relationships between plant ontologies, politics, ethics, and art, emphasising that "the art world is a discipline that can provide an interpretation of the changed way we understand or conceive of plants" (13).

Through their collaboration, Aunty Deidre and Seccombe addressed cross-cultural plant awareness disparities in a ten-minute video entitled *Walk beside Me* and a colour-printed field guide of the same title that was to be a companion to the video. These works were first shown alongside the exhibition *Siteworks:*

from a Deep Valley at Bundanon Art Museum (26 November 2022-12 March 2023). *Walk beside Me* responds specifically to plants found in Bundanon, a biodiverse area holding warm temperate and dry temperate environments, as well as coastal rainforest and turpentine forests. This magnificent property is situated along the Shoalhaven River, 19 kilometres west of the township of Nowra and inland from the coast of southern New South Wales, or the South Coast, as it is called. Bundanon is on the unceded land of the Dharawal and Dhurga language-speaking groups, and recognises the Wodi Wodi, Wandandian and Yuin, the traditional custodians of the land in the Shoalhave,n where Bundanon, Riversdale and Eearie Park are located. Bundanon is named after the Dharawal word for "deep valley" (Bundanon).

A Biocultural Exchange

Increased education and enjoyment of plant life in society has been proven to combat plant awareness disparities and to generate new insights and familiarities, leading to stronger connections between humans and plants (Jose et al.). *Walk beside Me* strengthens an awareness of plants through a biocultural framework. Bioculture is an emerging term that describes the often intangible relationships between nature, culture, biodiversity, and heritage. In the face of growing globalisation, "understanding the intangible cultural heritage of different communities helps intercultural dialogue to grow mutual respect" (UNESCO). The notion of bioculture is founded in part on UNESCO's 2018 statement of protection and preservation of "intangible cultural heritage," which explains how heritage "is not the cultural manifestation itself but rather the wealth of knowledge and skills that is transmitted through it from one generation to the next". Importantly, cultural and community heritage is more complex than collecting artefacts or preserving sites, as

> [i]t also includes traditions or living expressions inherited from our
> ancestors and passed on to our descendants, such as oral traditions,
> performing arts, social practices, rituals, festive events, knowledge
> and practices concerning nature and the universe or the knowledge
> and skills to produce traditional crafts (UNESCO).

From a biocultural perspective, *Walk beside Me* celebrates the intangible cultural heritage of the plant knowledge of the Yuin peoples. The personal invitation from Aunty Deidre to walk beside her at Bundanon and to share her cultural knowledge of plants activates an awareness of these plants beyond a

   Erica Seccombe and Aunty Deidre Martin

Eurocentric viewpoint. With Aunty Deidre's spoken and written narrative alongside Seccombe's plant drawings and moving images, this body of work creates opportunities for viewers from the wider community to consider plants through a cultural lens. In the chapter "Totemic Life," from *Aboriginal Biocultural Knowledge in South-Eastern Australia: Perspectives of Early Colonists*, Philip A. Clark explains that the merging of the cultural and natural worlds in Aboriginal and Torres Strait Islander traditions is central to biocultural thinking because "the actions of spiritual ancestors during the Creation gave a deep social relevance to the country, imbuing it with their power and in doing so humanised it" (1). Unlike Eurocentric, which often considers Australian environments either empty lands or wilderness, the Aboriginal and Torres Strait Islander worldview has a profound respect for non-human entities, which they view as equally interconnected with human life. Grounded in these ideas, *Walk beside Me* contributes to the view that Indigenous knowledge systems are crucial to addressing and fostering more inclusive, holistic, resilient, sustainable, and culturally diverse responses to the significant ecological challenges of our time.

Entanglements

As this project involves one person of Yuin ancestry and one with English and Irish settler heritage from the Nowra region, the collaboration also addresses the entanglement of Aboriginal and non-Aboriginal societies since the British invasion of 1788. In the introduction to *Entangled Territorialities: Negotiating Indigenous Lands in Australia and Canada*, Françoise Dussart and Sylvie Poirier outline the importance of understanding entanglement between two cultural groups who are continuously and irreversibly connected by colonisation (Dussart and Poirier). Whether these groups are in direct or indirect proximity, the correlation and effect of interdependence and coexistence are not always equal or predictable, as "the phenomena of entanglement between social and cultural worlds, and thus between different meanings, praxes, and relationship with lands and places, may involve a higher level of complexity, or at least a different kind of complexity" (Dussart and Poirier 5).

The complexity of Aunty Deidre's and Seccombe's relationship with the region in and around Bundanon can therefore be understood as having begun long before the two first met in 2019. Since settler frontiers extended into the South Coast soon after 1788, it is probable that Aunty Deidre's and Seccombe's ancestors would have encountered each other through the dairy, shipping, milling, and logging industries. For example, Aunty Deidre's father, the land-rights activist Keith Stewart, was born in Nowra in 1929, and Edward Seccombe was the mayor of Nowra in the late 1880s. Although their respective families' experiences will have been vastly different across the 235 years of entangled social and political histories in the region, Aunty Deidre and Seccombe currently share a mutual passion for the South Coast environment. For Seccombe, *Walk beside Me* has been an opportunity to address her family heritage by learning more about Yuin culture, with the permission and guidance of Aunty Deidre. Through active acknowledgement of the necessity for a path to cultural reconciliation, Aunty Deidre's and Seccombe's collaborative art practice importantly embodies the spirit of resilience and empowerment, which is key to Yuin identity and to the continuous cultural and spiritual connection the land's traditional owners have with Bundanon.

For the Yuin, the land, rocks, ocean, rivers, plants, trees, animals, skies, and temporal seasons are all connected to traditional lore and are essential to their existence and well-being. The Yuin knowledge systems carry a deep sense of responsibility towards and stewardship for the environment, as sustainable practices continue to be integral to their cultural traditions and ecological knowledge. Across the various stages of colonisation, the South Coast, which Yuin peoples had cared for, landscaped, and lived in for over sixty thousand years, has been cleared and developed. The British colonisers were mostly blind to a First Nations worldview because they viewed nature through the lens of economic gain and domination. Endemic to this region, the great red cedars, *Toona ciliata*, were felled to the point where they were nearly extinct by the 1870s. These ancient and giant trees, which that can stand as tall as 35-40 metres, once created high canopies over Bundanon. The conflicting worldviews of the Yuin and British is noted by Clark: "while modern Western Europeans have seen themselves as having a separate existence from the 'natural' world, Aboriginal people consider that the social and physical aspects of their lives are closely intermeshed and therefore inseparable" (1).

Disparities

Plant blindness, which is a selective view of nature, leans on a philosophical definition of the word "blindness" as an unwillingness to learn, perceive, or understand, leading to close-mindedness, prejudice, or bias towards plants. Because "plant blindness" refers negatively to the physical disability of visual impairment, there are good reasons to change the term to "plant awareness disparity," which removes "blindness" but retains the original meaning (Parsley

                                        Erica Seccombe and Aunty Deidre Martin

601). This "disparity" in the perceptual Eurocentric bias towards plants, conscious or unconscious, is based on the anthropocentric view that humans are superior to nature and all other non-human entities. Even though plants contribute over 80% of the biomass on Earth, vegetation is considered non-sentient and therefore has been historically placed at the bottom of the teleological scale. The ideology that drives this thinking is of European origin and influences policies and laws governing industry, land management, environment, and climate change in Australia today.

Caused by humans, the catastrophic environmental challenges we presently face on a global scale make the debates surrounding blindness or awareness disparities towards plants crucially important. In "The Determinants of Planetary Health: An Indigenous Consensus Perspective," Redvers et al. give an overview of these debates from the perspective of an international group of First Nation scholars, respected Elders, and knowledge-holders who seek to define what they identify as being integral to the health and sustainability of the planet. In their view, First Nation perspectives are "in direct contrast to the human-centric worldview that continues to permeate climate discourse and action and from the so-called modern conceptualizations of health and wellbeing" (e156). The plant awareness disparity of the humancentric worldview, which separates nature from humans, "will only continue to perpetuate planetary harm" (e159). In the context of planetary health, Redvers's group agreed that there is a need for a new consensus on what constitutes a global ecocentric approach, and what the interconnected, defining features might be. While there has been increasing recognition of the importance of First Nation worldviews and knowledge in climate mitigation and adaptation strategies, "it [this recognition] has often been more symbolic than practically applied across the globe" (e156).

The archaeologist David Byrne's essay "Difference" is important for considering the concept of plant awareness disparity in the context of Eurocentric responses to plants and Yuin knowledge systems. The processes of colonisation and dispossession have also influenced the way in which the Indigenous Australians are viewed by the wider community. Writing about the South Coast, Byrne observes: "the memory of seeing Aboriginal people in the land has been lost to the invasion of white people, so that even the eucalypt forests were populated by the conflicting visions of loggers and conservationists whose natural habitat it had, in a sense, become" (290). As a consequence, this invisibility of seeming not to exist on the land extends to Aboriginal and Torres Strait Islander culture in contemporary mainstream Australia. Therefore, if members of the wider community cannot conceive of, or see, this culture in the present or the past, then they should never assume it does not exist.

It is often stated that Aboriginal and Torres Strait Islander people were included by state and federal governments under the Flora and Fauna Act until the 1967 Referendum, which constituted the formalised recognition of Indigenous Australians as citizens. Though factually incorrect, this assertion is quoted by Aboriginal and Torres Strait activists as an example of past and present injustices. The artist Vernon Ah Kee, a man with ties to the Kuku Yalandji, Waanji, Yidinji, and Gugu Yimithirr peoples in Queensland, explains, "Blackfellas jokingly say that we weren't considered people so we must be part of the flora and fauna act, but that's not even true. The fact is that we didn't exist at all" (Das). In this context, Aunty Deidre's own wording of the invitation to walk beside her, rather than using the common symbol of solidarity, was deliberate in actively revealing her position as being highly visible; she was neither behind nor in front. Walking beside someone also implies a sense of equality, suggesting a willingness to understand, listen, learn, and offer guidance, and to build a deep and meaningful connection. It signifies a desire for a relationship based on mutual trust, respect, shared experiences, personal growth, and, importantly, shared values.

The Contemporary Past

Byrne discusses working in the 1980s with a Yuin Elder, Uncle Ted Thomas (1909-2002), in mapping the archaeological evidence of his ancestors' habitation of the forested ridges below the Great Dividing Range along the South Coast (Byrne). He cautions that, from an archaeological perspective, mapping the Aboriginal stone artefacts in the terrain contributes to the academic heritage discourse on the origin of cultural objects—a discourse tha can also result in the disappearance of First Nation peoples from the 'colonial spaces they otherwise occupied"; as a precaution, "we must look to the dimension of *use* rather than *origin*" (296). While "origin" refers to the source and point of production of an artefact, "use" pertains to it intended purpose, function, or to the associated activities and knowledge. For Uncle Ted, while these objects are tangible evidence of his ancestors' occupancy of the land, which had existed long before colonisation (a fact he does not need to prove to himself), they also belong to him as part of the "contemporary past" (291). In archaeology, the term "past" implies a study of distant eras, while the "contemporary past" indicates the intangible cultural heritage of more recent times, which are still within the memory of living individuals and have direct relevance to the present.

As contextual and intangible heritage, culturally significant plants exist in the contemporary past as living entities and represent a continuous and active connection to Yuin culture. In the face of the Anthropocene, plants, ecosystems and their habitats are in danger and fragile, making it imperative to uphold Aboriginal and Torres Strait Islander cultures; the Australian natural environment must be protected. *Walk beside Me* is positioned within the contemporary past because Aunty Deidre's cultural knowledge systems and stories about plants have been passed down to her from generation to generation and continue to exist in the present. Her custodianship in sharing and promoting culturally significant plant stories and uses ensures that this knowledge is passed to the next generations. From her worldview, everything at Bundanon is intertwined, the edges of the past, present, and future are permeable, and all is connected to the spirits and the ancestors.

Aunty Deidre's narrative describing her cultural knowledge of plants at Bundanon has been recorded on the video and is printed in the field guide, which includes the Latin names of the plants she discusses. Seccombe and Aunty Deidre decided to include Latin genera to address a broader audience and so to make further cross-cultural connections to the plants. From Aunty Deidre's perspective, "it's a start for other people to begin their journey and do their research" (conversation with D. Martin). In her roles as a Discovery Ranger for New South Wales National Parks and Wildlife and as a cultural guide to the region, Aunty Deidre is often asked for the botanical plant names on the walks that she leads, to which she purposefully replies, "I'm just telling you what I know" (conversation with D. Martin). The Latin plant names do not appear in the video because Aunty Deidre does not need them. Using the European taxonomic system is complicated, as traditional knowledge systems should not be combined with Western knowledge to create "an assortment of information" (Redvers et al. e156). Therefore the Latin names could seem to defeat the purpose of seeing plants beyond the ideas of European classifications and hierarchies of things, plants, animals, and humans. However, from a cross-cultural perspective and in the interest of combatting plant awareness disparity, Seccombe and Martin inserted Latin names in the field guide to engage a wider audience in learning about and enjoying Bundanon.

Walk beside Me

Just as you will find on Aunty Deidre's walks, the *Walk beside Me* video, begins with a "Welcome to Country," in which Aunty Deidre acknowledges the ancestors and spirits of the land. She finds this welcome a useful tool for individuals to feel, hear, and smell nature and, therefore, to become more present within their surroundings. The information Aunty Deidre reveals to the audience about the plants is edited to ensure that sensitive cultural knowledge is retained and to discourage people from harvesting or preparing these plants for themselves. She closes her narrative by drawing the viewers' attention back to Country to encourage mutual respect of the ongoing connections between traditional owners and their lands. Aunty Deidre's full script from *Walk beside Me* is as follows (with the Latin plant names):

> *Welcome, my name is Aunty Deidre Martin. I am a Walbunja woman of the Yuin Nation. My connection to this country is through my father who was born in Nowra. I want to share some of my cultural knowledge of plants that you might find here at Bundanon. You can begin to learn about the bush in my way. So come, walk beside me...*
>
> *When you first walk into the bush at Bundanon, slow down and stop talking for little while. Pause, close your eyes and listen. Take a deep breath. Smell the air. Then you know you are welcome.*
>
> *I am sharing my knowledge of a selection of plants that have cultural significance, in ceremony, as food or medicine, and which are used in craft or tools. You'll never get hungry if you know what there is to eat and how to eat it.*
>
> *Many plants need to be prepared properly before eating. It is important to respect the natural ecosystems at Bundanon, so please don't disturb the plants!*
>
> *If you look closely, you might see some bright orange wombat berries growing on a vine in a tree. (Eustrephus latifolius)*
>
> *Shelf or bracket fungus is often used for ceremonies. I use it for Welcome to Country. (Polyporaceae)*
>
> *Bracken fern can be used to treat the sting of insect bites. (Pteridium esculentum)*

Erica Seccombe and Aunty Deidre Martin

Growing in sandy areas, the pennywort is known for its anti-inflamma-tory properties and can alleviate the pain of arthritis. (Centella asiatica)

Geebung fruit is ripe and ready to eat after it falls to the ground. We pick up the ripened fruit with caution as the death adder is known to wait underneath for small, foraging birds. The bark can be used for medicinal purposes to heal cuts and abrasions. (Persoonia pinifolia and Persoonia levis)

The young flowers of the banksia are sweet with nectar. As they dry they can be used as torches or lanterns. They make great hair brushes. (Banksia serrata)

The delicate and soft apple berry vine can be found growing in trees and scrub. We call them dharma, a sweet treat. (Billardiera scandens)

Lomandra, or spiny-head mat-rush, is used for basket weaving. It is also good for making splints for sprains and breaks. The seeds can be ground for flour. We've been eating gluten free for thousands of years! (Lomandra longifolia)

The crinum lily, or spider lily is toxic to humans and animals, but when it is prepared properly, it is known to soothe blue bottle stings. (Crinum asiaticum)

The sandpaper fig is an ancient tree which has very rough leaves that were used to smooth wooden implements. The figs are sweet and edible. (Ficus coronata)

Many of the plants here tell us the right season for hunting and harvest-ing. When the coastal wattle flowers, grows seed pods, turns its leaves upright, or the galls develop on the branches, it tells us the right time to see the whales making their journey, and when to dive for lobsters, fish for bream, and mullet. Ground seed pods can be added to bread. The leaves can be used as a soap. (Acacia longifolia)

If you look carefully you will see the native sarsaparilla vine growing amongst the rocks and undergrowth. It looks like the hardenbergia vine but you can tell the difference by the leaves and the taste. Sarsaparilla is known to have antioxidant properties and makes a great flavoured tea. (Smilax glyciphylla)

Discussing how to document the plants in the forest for the film, Aunty Deidre and Seccombe agreed that creating multiple camera viewpoints was important to create a sensation of deeper looking to create new cultural under-standings. To do this Seccombe used a macro attachment on a handheld digital camera, drawing the viewer's eye into closer proximity of the subject to focus on smaller details. The video is edited to create a visual narrative of walking beside Aunty Deidre on her country. As Seccombe notes, "from the outset, neither of us wanted create a documentary, so the outcome has evolved from us spending time together and talking, and with Aunty leading me to observe at the bush more closely" (conversation with E. Seccombe, 2022), Staying together at the Bundanon Artist Residency for short periods across the year provided Aunty Deidre and Seccombe with opportunities to capture plants in different seasons, but these stays were also fundamental for allowing them to establish a relation-ship of mutual trust. The edited, moving images result in close frames of Aunty Deidre's hands, and occasionally other people's hands, touching or reaching for certain plants in *situ*. It is only at the end of the video that Aunty Deidre's face appears in full focus, as she teaches Seccombe, who remains outside the frame, to make a call on a snake whistle. In the audio for the video, Seccombe has embedded the sound recordings of birdsong that she made with Aunty Deidre during their walks; these recordings help to capture and intensify the experi-ence of being at Bundanon.

Drawing Plants

The colour field guide printed as a companion to *Walk beside Me*, is a dou-ble-sided A1 sheet, which has folded into an A4 booklet but which can also be opened as a poster. Illustrating Aunty Deidre's text are Seccombe's stylised drawings of plants in a limited palette of green and ochre. Inside the first page of the booklet is a portrait of Aunty Deidre facing sideways; she is positioned alongside the words of her Welcome to Country. Seccombe's plant drawings are designed to be welcoming, attractive, and socially inclusive for a diverse audi-ence. While based on close observation, these drawings do not follow the strict

     Erica Seccombe and Aunty Deidre Martin

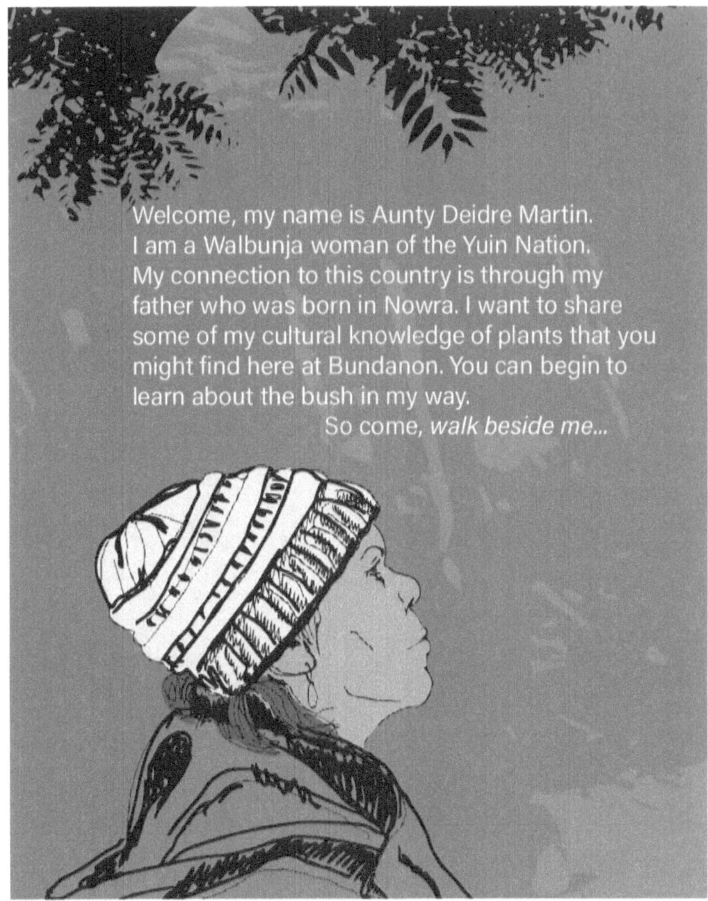

Figure 1. Detail of the field guide 'Walk Beside Me' 2022, A2 Booklet printed, folded.
Words by Aunty Deidre Martin, Illustrations by Erica Seccombe.
(Courtesy of the artists).

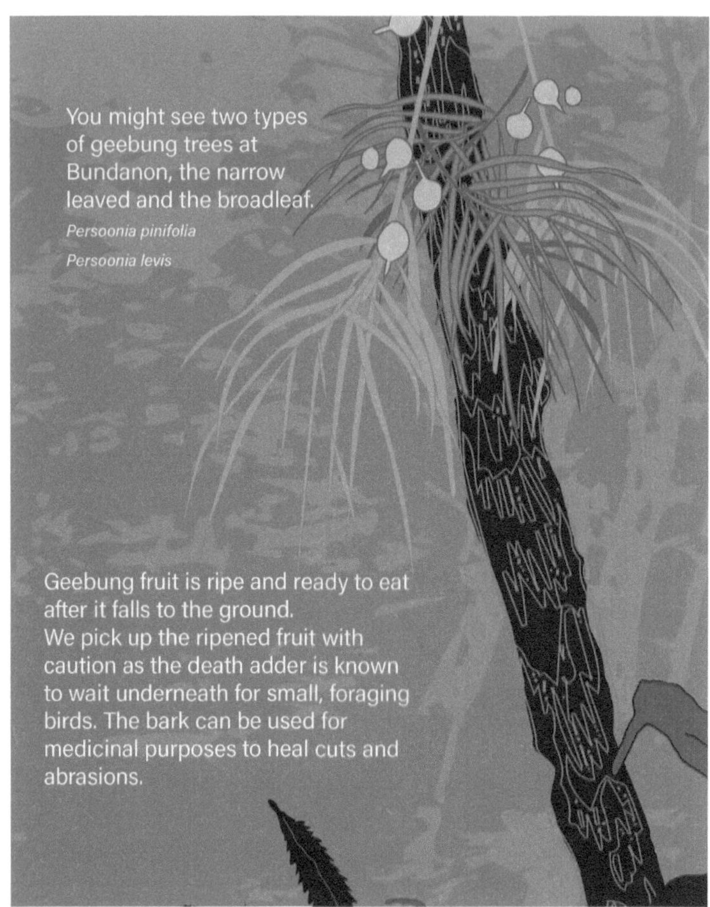

Figure 2. Detail of the field guide 'Walk Beside Me' 2022, A2 Booklet printed, folded. Words by Aunty Deidre Martin, Illustrations by Erica Seccombe. (Courtesy of the artists).

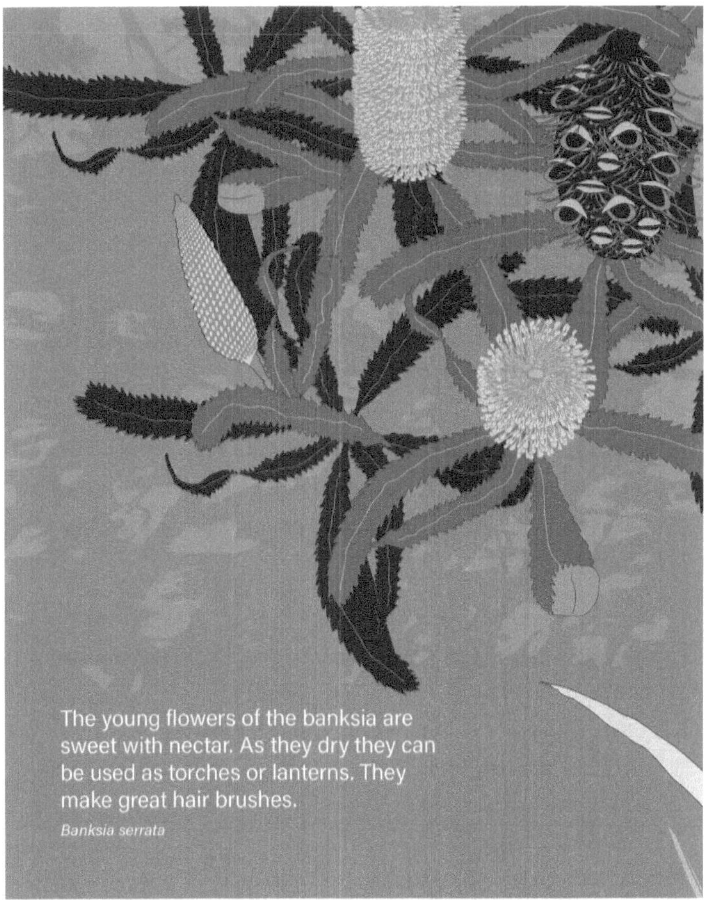

Figure 3. Detail of the field guide 'Walk Beside Me' 2022, A2 Booklet printed, folded. Words by Aunty Deidre Martin, Illustrations by Erica Seccombe. (Courtesy of the artists).

conventions of scientific illustrations; they are neither botanically accurate nor followstandard models of representation. The style is informed by Seccombe's previous large-scale commission: work for the Campbelltown Hospital Rebuild, New South Wales from 2019-2022. This project was antithesis of plant blindness, as it recognised that images of healing and culturally important plants in a large hospital create an environment where local people can feel at home and be restored by the nature that they both know and love. Steering the overall design of this project via illustrations of culturally significant plants in Dharawal Country, she consulted with Aunty Deidre and Elder Aunty Glenda Chalker, a Dharawal woman of the Cubbitch Barta Clan. Because of her European descent, Seccombe was concerned her illustrations of these plants would reinforce colonial tropes that shape society's knowledge of natural history and so perpetuate structures of power and domination (Das and Lowe). Asked if all three of them were comfortable with their collaboration, Seccombe wrote:

> Aunty Glenda put me at ease by advising me that the illustrations of the included plants should be easily identifiable to everyone, no matter what their heritage. Through this I have learned that the act of sharing knowledge cultivates inclusivity which supports empowerment, acceptance and cultural pride which contribute to a positive healing environment for First Nations People and for the wider community (Seccombe).

Seccombe's drawings of Australian plants belong to the present, yet her methods acknowledge the history of botanical women artists working in the early Australian colonies, for instance: Dorothy English Paty (1805-36), Fanny Anne Charsley (1828-1915), Fanny de Mole (1835-1866), Anna Frances Walker (1830-1913), and Marian Ellis Rowan (1848-1922). Apart from Paty, who is considered a talented amateur, these women all had professional careers in their lifetime, making both scientific illustrations and botanical art. Their botanical art was distinctive as subjective interpretation through reliance on aesthetics, and often told a story about a plant in its habitat and during its life cycle. Botanic art made by women is still viewed as a genteel, less serious, and feminine pursuit; however, more recently, the significant role of these artists is being better understood not only in art, but also in the fields of biodiversity research and conservation. The contemporary Australian artist Nazila Jahangir Anbardan discusses this revised history of female botanic art in *Women, Art, And Activism: A Feminist Analysis of The Life and Work of Botanical Female Artists From 17th to 20th*

Erica Seccombe and Aunty Deidre Martin

Century. Placing her research in a feminist framework, Anbardan explores how these artists have created a gendered perspective:

> a kind of worldview that itself is a temporary balance in the relation between women and the society or the world around them. A view that unites women from different races, classes, and so on and that allows for a multiplicity of their world views and the notion of the feminine (31).

She proposes that rather than viewing botanical art executed by women as subjugated, we should consider instead how it "resists the codes that are tacitly enforced by interpreters of the canon of art history" (31-2).

In his public lecture entitled, "Life and Death: The Newcastle Sketchbooks of Dorothy Paty," Nat Williams discussed his original research on Paty's watercolours of plants. These remarkable drawings were undertaken during her short life as a wife and mother in the new colony of Newcastle, which was on the traditional lands of the Awabakal and Worimi peoples. Of particular interest is Paty's drawing of a plant bearing a dark purple fruit, and colloquially known as "black apple," or *Planchonella Australis*. She dates this watercolour 13 November 1834 and titled it with the plant's former Latin name: *Achras Australis*. In a close study of this drawing, Williams discovered that Paty has lightly written the words, "Oombung," "M'Gill," and "Native apple" on the same page. (Williams). From these inscriptions, he deduces Paty had the opportunity to discuss this fruit with Birabahn (c. 1800-46, also known as Johnny McGill), an Awabakal man who was a guide and translator for the Reverend Lancelot Threlkeld (1788-1859), a missionary and linguist active in the 1830s. Williams suggests that Paty transcribed the sound of the name of the black apple in Awabakal or Worimi dialect. This discovery gives new depth to our understanding of her drawings and her short life. It also illustrates the lost or ignored opportunities in the past to better understand the connection of First Nation peoples to plants and their environments and so the need to try to interpret both from the First Nation point of view.

Conclusion

This nearly two-hundred-year-old exchange, which was almost lost to history, is a useful comparison to Aunty Deidre's and Seccombe's approaches and outcomes in their own cross-cultural collaboration. Rather than being sketched lightly in the margins, *Walk beside Me* gives a strong voice to cultural knowledge, and works to break down negative attitudes and biases towards human and plant relationships by generating an egalitarian model of exchange. For Aunty Deidre and Seccombe, the format, media, and aesthetics of this body of work, in both its digital and its printed versions, purposefully aim to disseminate information quickly and easily to a diverse and interested audience. For both parties, it was important that the video could be easily accessed online, and that the booklets were freely given away. In conclusion, the outcome of this creative collaboration, which addresses biocultural ideas in the context of plant awareness disparity, has demonstrated how cross-cultural dialogues can foster a deeper understanding and appreciation of the relationships between plants and humans. Bringing together different perspectives, knowledge systems, and artistic expressions, Aunty Deidre's and Seccombe's work contributes to the conservation of cultural heritage and the protection and recognition of biodiversity. *Walk beside Me* celebrates the richness of Yuin culture at Bundanon and further strengthens cultural resilience, inspiring deeper connections to nature in the face of the environmental challenges of our time. As Aunty Deidre concludes in *Walk beside Me*:

> *I welcome you to join me again to learn more about my Country and the rich culture of my people.*

Works Cited

Anbardan. N. J. *Women, Art, And Activism: A Feminist Analysis of the Life and Work of Botanical Female Artists from 17th to 20th Century*. 2023. MA Thesis, University of Western Australia.

Bridgewater, Peter, and Ian D. Rotherham. "A Critical Perspective on the Concept of Biocultural Diversity and Its Emerging Role in Nature and Heritage Conservation." *People and Nature*, vol. 1, 2019, pp. 291-304.

Byrne, David. "Difference." *Oxford Handbook of the Archaeology of the Contemporary Past*, edited by R. Harrison et al., Oxford University Press, 2013, pp. 289-305.

Clarke, P. A. "Totemic." Aboriginal Biocultural Knowledge in South-Eastern Australia: *Perspectives of Early Colonists*, edited by Fred Cahir et al., CSIRO Publishing, 2018, pp. 1-18.

Das, Sushi. "Fact Check: Were Indigenous Australians Classified under a Flora and Fauna Act until the 1967 Referendum?" *News*, Australian Broadcasting Corporation, 19 Mar. 2018, https://www.abc.net.au/news/2018-03-20/fact-check-flora-and-fauna-1967-referendum/9550650

   Erica Seccombe and Aunty Deidre Martin

---, and M. Lowe. "Nature Read in Black and White: Decolonial Approaches to Interpreting Natural History Collections." *Journal of Natural Science Collections*, vol. 6, 2018, pp. 4-14.

Dussart, Françoise, and Sylvie Poirier, eds. *Entangled Territorialities: Negotiating Indigenous Lands in Australia and Canada.* University of Toronto Press, 2017.

Gibson, Prudence. *The Plant Contract: Art's Return to Vegetal Life.* Brill Rodopi, 2018.

Jose, S. B., et al. "Overcoming Plant Blindness in Science, Education, and Society." *Plants, People, Planet*, vol. 1, no. 3, Jul. 2019, pp. 169-72.

Martin, Aunty Deidre & Erica Seccombe, *Walk beside me*, 2022, 10 min. Single channel movie, https://www.ericaseccombe.com/projects#/tellusproject/

Martin, Aunty Deidre & Erica Seccombe, *Walk beside me*, 2022, A2 Booklet printed, folded.

Parsley, K. M. "Plant Awareness Disparity: A Case for Renaming Plant Blindness." *Plants, People, Planet*, vol. 2, 2020, pp. 598-601.

Redvers, N., et al. "The Determinants of Planetary Health: An Indigenous Consensus Perspective." *Lancet Planet Health*, vol. 6, 2022, pp. 156-63.

Seccombe, Erica. "What Does a Hospital Feel Like?: Art, Health, Nature, Community and Culture at the New Campbelltown Hospital." *Arts Health Network*, 2010, https://www.artshealthnetwork.com.au/what-does-a-hospital-feel-like-art-health-nature-community-and-culture-at-the-new-campbelltown-hospital/ Accessed 20 June 2023.

---, and Deirde Martin. *Walk beside Me.* 2022, https://www.ericaseccombe.com/projects#/tellusproject/. Accessed 30 July, 2023.

UNESCO. "Oral Traditions and Expressions Including Language as a Vehicle of the Intangible Cultural Heritage." *UNESCO Intangible Cultural Heritage*, 2018, https://ich.unesco.org/en/oral-traditions-and-expressions-00053. Accessed 5 May 2023.

Williams, Nat. "Life & Death: the Newcastle Sketchbooks of Dorothy Paty." *National Library of Australia*, 28 Jun. 2017.

Wandersee, J. H., and E. E. Schussler. "Preventing Plant Blindness." *The American Biology Teacher*, vol. 61, 1999, pp. 82-86.

17 Sensing Plants—Hearing Country

Rebecca Mayo

In 2014, I spent several months in Austria on a residency. I visited the Natural History Museum's herbarium collection to view holotypes collected by Baron von Hügel when he briefly toured Australia in 1833-34. I sat with and handled handmade paper sheets on which different Australian plants were secured by tiny lengths of gum strip. Cuttings and seeds picked from their habitat nearly two hundred years ago were stored in red folders, marking that they were the first Linnaean-named specimen of that plant in the world. It was wonderful inside the museum, amongst the smell of camphor and wooden furniture. But I could not easily find an artistic response to these preserved, dried specimens. I felt time shifting back and forth—linearly—between me and the specimen, between the specimen and Hügel, alive and now dead. A dead end.

The Tellus Project offered me a second chance to engage with herbaria, while also attending to the contemporary rift between plants and people that is termed "plant blindness." This time, my residency was at Bundanon Trust, which is situated on the traditional lands of the Dharawal and Dhurga peoples. Bundanon, like the rest of the continent, has been transformed by the deep tread of colonisation, yet it remains a haven for more-than-human life. It is peaceful, full of sounds, smells, and feelings. It is a sensorium. Over the course of the year, I visited Bundanon several times, meeting and working with Aunty Deidre Martin (a Walbanja woman of the Yuin nations), the poet Lisa Gorton, and (later) Jacob Morris (a Gammēya-Darrawal Ngundah of the yuin marriŋ).

The Plant Sensibilia Machine provided an apparatus through which our collaboration could coalesce, on site and with an audience. It is an outdoor machine, designed to dye cloth with locally collected plants, and people can watch or participate in its process. A length of cloth, pre-printed with metal salts and sewn into a loop on the machine, circles through rollers, which are activated by a hand crank. As the cloth goes around, it passes through a heated bath full of plants and water. Gradually, over the course of the day, the plant molecules, released by heat and suspended in water, attach to the cloth. The

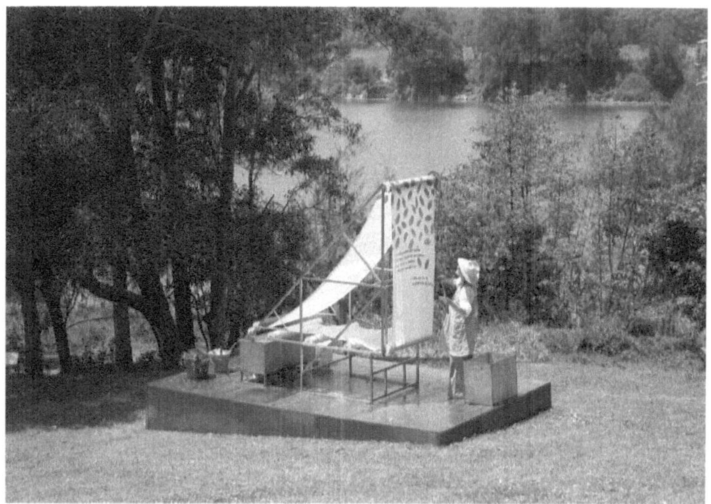

Figure 1. The Plant Sensibilia Machine: Acacia longifolia 2022 – 23. installation view, Siteworks 2022: From a deep valley. (Image courtesy of Zan Wimberley).

colour is strongest where the metal salts are printed. Poems written by Jacob Morris and by Aunty Deidre Martin with Lisa Gorton emerge through the steam, scents, and sounds of the Plant Sensibilia Machine, bringing plant and human collaborators together—in the present and on Country.

Aunty Deidre's poem tells us about her culture's relations with *Acacia longifolia*. An abundant plant, commonly known as Sydney golden wattle and as Wadananguli in the Dharawal language, its seasonal rhythms communicate and connect with the rhythms of traditional life and more-than-human life. Messages, signs, and ways of reading and understanding Country come forward, drawn to our attention with the soft colour of *Acacia longifolia* dye. The plant matter reveals why this plant matters. The fabric, a continuous loop through the machine, echoes the cycle of the seasons, as well as Dharawal understandings of time, which is spatial and without a beginning or end. Aunty Deidre's poem, activated by the Sensibilia Machine, speaks to the aliveness of her Country, to ongoing, more-than-human conversations. She teaches us to stop and listen.

Jacob Morris's poem extends plant-person interconnections: he reminds us of the vital roles of guardian and steward. He emphasises how plants are important life forces in their own right and warrant protection for this alone. His viewpoint stands in stark contrast to the instrumental ways in which colonial settler communities viewed the bush (and to a large extent still do). Majestic cararura (*Toona ciliata*, red cedar) once populated and watched over much of the east coast of Australia. A Gondwana plant, its native range includes southern parts of Asia, New Guinea, and Australia. It is one of two deciduous trees native to this continent. Since colonisation, ancient grandparent trees of this species have been harvested to build colonial furniture and buildings, and to be shipped and sold far and wide. Jacob's poem traces this story, and the story of Arawarra, his ancestor, who fought to protect these trees. The cyclical space-time continuum embedded in Jacob's poem is a call for reparative care, for Arawarra's remains to be returned to Country, and for the patterns and webs of life to be made whole once more.

The Plant Sensibilia Machine was designed to bring the studio process into the field, to put it in front of audiences, and to situate it in a specific place. Its mechanisms include the hand crank, simply geared with bike chains, so that the fabric can revolve around the machine, visible and readable to audiences as it slides in and out of the dye bath. During the four "Siteworks" weekends when the Plant Sensibilia Machine was activated at Bundanon, visitors gathered around the machine, asking questions, turning the handle, smelling the dye-bath, reading the poems, and listening to Aunty Deidre and Jacob. On hot days, the cloth dried on its way around the machine, floating in the air like a sail. At other times, children turned the handle so fast that the cloth remained damp, clinging to the rollers all the way around. Together, Aunty Deidre, Jacob, Lisa, and I have collaborated with plants and place to show another way of being and being-with plants—one that reflects life and relationships, as well as the intrinsic value of more-than-human life, its shared purpose, and its interdependence.

The value and importance of herbarium specimens is immeasurable. They are tangible records of which plants grew where, before grasslands became housing estates and forests were logged, and these collections assist ecologists in understanding how to protect life amid the threat of climate disaster. But to activate human-plant relationships, to reinvigorate our senses, to re-learn how to listen with plants and be on Country, we need to be working together with living plants. The herbarium specimen, however beautiful and important, is locked in linear time. The Plant Sensibilia Machine opens and reveals the possibility of collaborating with, and learning from, plants and places. It is an apparatus with the potential of activating and bringing together the voices that quietly ask us to listen.

Rebecca Mayo

18 ACACIA LONGIFOLIA

Aunty Deidre Martin with Lisa Gorton

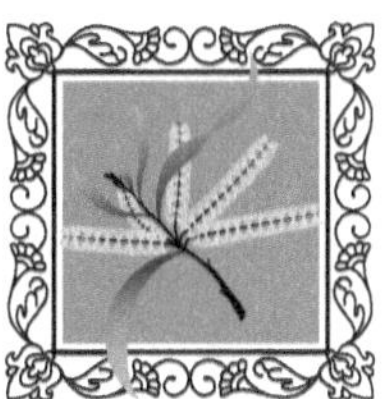

When its flowers first bud—

                    the whales are preparing to travel north—

When its seeds blacken in the split pods—

                    the lobsters are high up, feeding in the rocks—

          the seeds are collected, separated, roasted, and ground down—

When the galls swell on its branches—

                    the bream are swimming—

When its leaves change colour and point upward—

                    now like cloud shadow the mullet are dark in the sea—

                    it is time to make the nets—

Now the whales are starting south—

19 Arawarra and Cararura

Jacob Morris

I.

Strangers come
　and strangers steal.
the swing of their Mundabāŋ　　　　　　　axe
　left a wound yet to heal.

They came for Kundu,　　　　　　　　　tree
　the Cararura, cedar of Red,
but like the felled Kundu
　they too would fall dead.

For the Law has been broken.
　Justice Djawa as a knife,　　　　　quick
these Lawbreakers lost
　their Marramal and their life.　　hand
Spreading like Gāmbi　　　　　　　　　fire
　were whispers of horror.
cedar cutters and all
　came to fear the name Arawarra.

A Cannibal, A Savage,
　A Man O' pure Evil.
but to the Ŋandāmarra
　he's a Warrior, a Protector,

Hero to our People.

II.

Arawarra was different.
never punished by the crown.
   Ballaiyabi baŋgaŋ   he died an old man
and according to Customs
   buried in the ground.

The Jerra of Arawarra   story
   is not finished, Sad but True.
the following is an example
   of what a man can do,

For along came the Berrys,
   gadjak to their core.   rotten
they knew of Arawarra
   and wanted to settle the score.

Mabrra for Mabrra   eye
   or rather a head for a hand,
Alexander found Arawarra
   buried in the sand,

Now Alexander is respected
   for being so brave and bright
but he stole Arawarra's wallānuŋ,   skull
   desecrating his Grave out of Spite.

20 Finding Connections Amongst the Living

Maya Martin-Westheimer

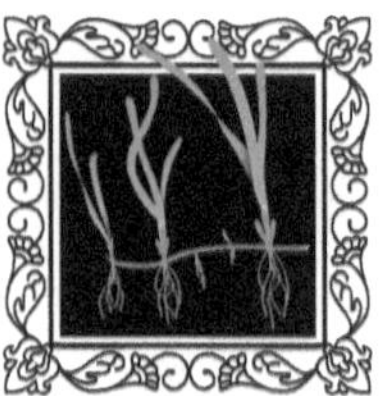

I wish to acknowledge and pay my respect to the Birrabirragal and Gadigal People, the Traditional Custodians of Woollahra and the Waters, Lands, and Country I live and work upon. I extend my respect to Elders past and present and the wider Sydney/Australian Aboriginal and Torres Strait Islander community.

I grew up on a farm in Myocum, New South Wales, ten minutes outside the town of Mullumbimby. This experience afforded me with the opportunity to observe nature's reciprocal relationships and the complexities and interconnectedness of living forms in the environment. I observed the growth of an entire forest and ecosystem, witnessed newborn cows taking their first steps, listened to the shrieking mating calls of koalas in the nearby eucalyptus trees, learned (through repeat visits) the favoured spots of the local possums, and saw first-hand the effects of floods and fires. I was immersed in the phenomena of the natural world. As an emerging curator, artist, and arts worker, I have found that these experiences have left a lasting impact on me, nurturing a deep appreciation for the intricate web of life that embraces us.

Since relocating to Sydney in 2020, I have discovered an equally deep connection with the Burroway/Moring/Vaucluse Point country in Nielsen Park, Vaucluse. The environment here has ignited a comparable sense of care and reverence within me. From June to September 2023, during an artist residency at the Woollahra Gallery in Redleaf and in collaboration with Floorplan Studio, I intensified my creative investigation of the complex intertidal ecologies of Nielsen Park, a heritage-listed site of ongoing significance to the Birrabirragal People. My goal is to come to an understanding of this place through a creative process and through collaboration with experts in diverse fields.

Deep ecology serves as the foundation for my personal philosophy, reflecting my experiences and approach to the land and environment. This concept emphasises the intrinsic value of all living beings and highlights the interconnectedness between humans and nature. Spiritual ecology, in its turn, is a term and concept developed and explored by various thinkers and scholars; no single individual is credited with its creation. It has emerged as a way of integrating spiritual and ecological perspectives, especially of recognising the deep interconnection between spirituality and the environment. Notable figures who have explored and written about the intersection of spirituality and ecology include Joanna Macy, Satish Kumar, Vandana Shiva, and David Abram, among others (Macy; Kumar; Shiva; Abram). Both deep ecology and spiritual ecology nurture ontologies of care, responsibility, and environmental stewardship.

When my family moved onto the farm in Myocum in 1997, the land had been severely damaged by logging, bush clearing, and cattle grazing, leaving it empty, degraded, and a relic of the nineteenth-century Big Scrub Clearing initiative that had cleared the subtropical lowland forest in eastern Australia. Less than 1% of the Big Scrub Forest remains today (Parkes et al. 212). Despite the challenges of the bare landscape, my family's efforts over the last twenty-five years have transformed the land into a sanctuary for life and biodiversity, emphasising the significance and impact of environmental stewardship.

Each time I revisit the Myocum farm, I bear witness to the forest's ongoing journey of growth and metamorphosis into maturity. Within these images, you'll find an ensemble of trees that tell the story of this ecological revival. The weeping lilly pilly (*Waterhousia floribunda*), foambark (*Jaguar pseudorrhus*), sandpaper fig (*Ficus coronata*), creek lilly pilly (*Syzygium australe*), red kamala (*Mallotus phillipinensis*), and the blue quandong (*Eleocarpis grandis*) stand as testaments to the resurgence of life and force of nature that can occur when there is the opportunity. Each of these trees plays a role in the collectively rejuvenated landscape.

Apprehending the stark contrast with the landscape from two decades ago is no easy feat today. As the new forest took root and thrived, the canopy of trees grew denser, delicately sifting and dispersing sunlight. This transformation has not only introduced shade, and therefore critical habitat and structural stability for the environment, but has also provided a perfect haven for native seedlings to prosper. The resurgence of the ecosystem demonstrates nature's remarkable adaptability and resilience, even in the face of significant human violence.

As a result of my father's use of native regeneration practices and weed management, the farm has undergone an awe-inspiring transformation. It now teems with life; it is home to wallabies, kookaburras, water dragons, lace monitors, goannas, snakes, possums, native mice, echidnas, yabbies, turtles, frogs, pheasants, honey-eaters, butterflies, and many more creatures. Once flat and degraded acreage, the homogeneous cow paddocks have been replaced with a complex and vibrant environment. Witnessing the land's hourly, daily, monthly, and yearly changes, I have come to appreciate the tremendous potential of care and the paramount importance of connection to the natural world, environmental stewardship, and fostering biodiversity.

In 2021, my experiences led to a collaboration with the interdisciplinary designer Sean Abrahams, and to our founding of Floorplan Studio. This contemporary, creative studio is dedicated to intersections of art, culture, and ecology. Floorplan Studio maintains an online forum and repository of projects and collaborations, and it initiates exhibitions and collaborative ventures. Our motivation in establishing Floorplan Studio was to cultivate increasingly expansive, experimental, environmentally aware, and culturally attuned creative endeavours.

Integrating contemporary design, ecology, storytelling, cultural insights, scientific understanding, and contemporary art, I seek to creatively facilitate projects that translate abstract ideas into tangible concepts and experiences. Through such projects, I appreciate the significant capacity of creativity to serve as a conduit for expressing complex connections.

Nielsen Park: Intertidal Utopia

Around eight thousand years ago, prior to major glacial thawing during the Holocene Period, the Sydney harbour would have had a different appearance, featuring coastal plains and deep gullies and valleys instead of water. The local Indigenous people witnessed the changes in this landscape. At one point in the harbour's evolution, the water rose a metre every year, and for hundreds of generations, coastal Sydney people could have watched from the Gap as the waters gradually consumed the coastal plains, creating the harbour we know today.

If you find yourself at Shark Beach, Nielsen Park, on a warm sunny day, you will be greeted by a turquoise, harbour-beach utopia. Beachgoers frolic, the sun glistens on the clear water, and the lush green foreshore adds to the picturesque

Maya Martin-Westheimer

scene. It is a place where you can dip in and out of the water, savour ice cream and snacks from the kiosk, and bask in the beauty of the harbour's calm waters.

When the beach closed for seawall re-engineering in March 2022, I found myself frequenting Bottle and Glass Point more regularly. As I studied this site, my curiosity and sense of wonder only grew deeper. I continue dedicating time to observing and documenting it through photography and video.

The gradual convergence of the sandstone coast and the harbour, coupled with the intricate rock formations sculpted by wind and water, imparts a unique character to the shoreline. Amidst this landscape, a diverse variety of flora and fauna flourishes, each carving out a niche in the ecosystem: oyster fields, crab caves, octopus grottos, sea hare paddocks, local cormorant sunbathing spots, and flat, rocky outcrops that serve as habitats for hermit crabs all interweave to compose the intricate tapestry of life within the park.

Nestled between Bottle and Glass Point and Circle Rock Island is a vibrant, subtidal passage adorned with golden kelp forests. The kelp acts as a natural barrier, guarding the entry to the shore. During low tide, hermit crabs gather in this passage for a captivating ritual of shell exchange, forming lines from smallest to largest. This practice is critical for their survival due to their lack of a protective exoskeleton. Since they do not grow their own shell, the hermit crabs must locate new ones as they become larger. These reciprocal relationships underwrite the park's rich biodiversity and ecological balance. A convergence of various factors has paved the way for these favourable conditions, cultivating a bio-diverse tapestry of life. The shallow waters of the passage, which are challenging to navigate, prevent boat traffic, creating a stable habitat for marine life.

The subtidal bay bordered by Glass and Bottle Point is a habitat for seagrass meadows, particularly the *Posidonia australis* species. Seagrasses, identifiable by their green, leathery shoots, play a vital role in stabilising sediments and preserving water quality within the Sydney harbour. These meadows serve the dual purpose of both nursery and feeding ground for an array of fish species, including bream, sea mullet, and leatherjacket. Additionally, seagrasses offer shelter and protection to vulnerable marine creatures like weedy sea dragons, as well as little penguins and migratory shorebirds (Woollahra Municipal Council).

The well-being of seagrass is influenced by various factors, for instance boating activities, pollution, and the changing weather patterns that are tied to increasing storm frequency because of global warming and climate change. Remnants of these invaluable seagrass ecosystems can still be observed near local harbour beaches. The importance of seagrass within the Sydney harbour is of such consequence that local institutions, among them the Sydney Institute of Marine Science (SIMS), have undertaken endeavours like Project Posidonia. This initiative is designed to actively involve local communities in the restoration of endangered Posidonia seagrass meadows (Sydney Institute of Marine Science).

Fringing Bottle and Glass Point is a coastal heathland with elements of Sydney Coastal Sandstone Headland Heath and the Eastern Suburbs Banksia Scrub, a critically endangered plant community. This community once occupied over 5,000 hectares of land in the eastern suburbs; however less than 150 hectares remain (NSW Government; Threatened Species Scientific Committee).

Nielsen Park stands as a vibrant living masterpiece, a remarkable showcase of nature's resilience and enduring interdependency within an urban setting. By means of creative initiatives and projects, such as *Rockpool Residency: Unseen Worlds*, I seek to celebrate this site and its unique ecology.

Rockpool Residency: Unseen Worlds Project: Going Deeper

My connection and relationship with Nielsen Park has unfolded through the investment of countless hours, days, weeks, and years—a process akin to nurturing any meaningful relationship. Nielsen Park, with its captivating intertidal ecology, beckoned me to immerse myself and explore its wonders at a deeper level. I realised that expecting to grasp the entirety of this place in one or two visits was overly simplistic and reflected a lingering Euro-colonial perspective of simplification of the environment and the non-human world. Being in the natural environment contextualises my own existence and place in the world.

The opportunity to participate in the artist residency at Woollahra Gallery provided an opportunity to launch *Rockpool Residency* in collaboration with Floorplan Studio. My passion for learning about and celebrating the essence of Nielsen Park and its inhabitants drives this project; it focuses on fostering environmental care and reverence, while also reflecting upon the ongoing Indigenous significance of Nielsen Park.

Rockpool Residency was conceived with the aim of gaining a clearer understanding of the intricate ecosystem at the site. We achieved this by bringing together diverse perspectives, ideas, and projects related to intertidal ecology and Nielsen Park's historical context. Our collaboration involves interdisciplinary experts, scientists, ecologists, artists, designers, and cultural leaders, all of whom contributed to an online platform that illuminates the Park's multifaceted nature.

Maya Martin-Westheimer

The project's development will be documented on the Floorplan Studio website via images, designs, artwork, interviews, and essays. Designer and co-founder Sean Abrahams is creating a dedicated online project space and identity in response to Nielsen Park, drawing from his own connection to it. Collaborators will also be encouraged to contribute their own images and text, thereby sharing their personal connections to the intertidal ecology and history of the location. This collaborative effort will enrich our comprehension of the site's significance.

Artists Marianna Ebersoll, Aurelia King, Lisa Myeong-Joo, and Anna Seymour are involved in crafting site-responsive creations. Each artist brings a distinct, multidisciplinary, and contemporary perspective to their work, and there is a broad range of project types, spanning ceramics, installation, social and participatory performance pieces, sculpture, video, photography, and beyond. These artistic responses provide alternative avenues for connection with and comprehension of a site via unique blends of medium and methodology.

To support a deeper engagement with the site, I have visited Nielsen Park and the rockpools with each artist, and we have taken time to observe and discuss the natural phenomena and happenings together on site.

Throughout the creation of *Rockpool Residency*, I have been reminded that scientific knowledge, or artwork on its own, only scratches the surface of the intricate relationships between species in Nielsen Park. Many of the relationships and processes taking place cannot be understood through numbers or text alone; they require different methods in order to be wholly understood, embodied, and comprehended. It is a world where hermit crabs and sea hares coexist, where iridescent algae glimmers like opals in the water, and where there is remarkable resilience in the currents.

Rockpool Residency: Unseen Worlds embraces the responsibility of creative exploration that incorporates sensitivity and mindfulness. To further share knowledge through this project, Floorplan Studio will create a field guide for the site; it will be available for free online, and park visitors, local residents, intertidal enthusiasts, and the general public will be able to download it. The field guide will include a creative map of the area and a local intertidal identification guide. Moreover, it will link to resources, including citizen-science databases, where one can upload one's findings.

I am collaborating with the Sydney Institute of Marine Science, marine biologists, Indigenous consultants, history organisations, and local ecologists and residents to gather more information on this environment and to engage with current debates. The Woollahra Gallery and Woollahra Council's Bio-Diversity team are also collaborating with us to share the information and resources produced throughout this project.

Rockpool Residency: Unseen Worlds will endure through online documentation, and there will be the potential for it to evolve into a larger exhibition context. Floorplan Studio and I are in the early phases of conceptualising a magazine dedicated to Australian art, culture, and ecology.

Works Cited

Abram, David. *The Spell of the Sensuous: Perception and Language in a More-Than-Human World*. Penguin, 1997.

Bauhardt, Christine, and Wendy Harcourt. *Feminist Political Ecology and the Economics of Care*. Routledge, 2018.

Bennett Jane. "Vibrant Matter: A Political Ecology of Things." *Perspectives on Politics*, vol. 9, no. 1, Mar. 2011, pp. 118-20, doi: 10.1017/s1537592710003464.

Carson, Rachel. *Silent Spring*. Penguin, 1962.

Irish, Paul. *Hidden in Plain View: The Aboriginal People of Coastal Sydney*. NewSouth Publishing, 2017.

Kumar, Satish. "Three Dimensions of Hindu Ecology: Soil, Soul and Society." *Religions: A Scholarly Journal*, vol. 2012, no. 1, Oct. 2012, doi: 10.5339/rels.2012.environment.16.

Macy, Joanna. *Spiritual Ecology: The Cry of the Earth*. The Golden Sufi Center, 2016.

Morton, Timothy. *All Art Is Ecological*. Penguin, 2021.

Nicolson, Adam. *Life Between the Tides*. Farrar, Straus and Giroux, 2021.

NSW Government. "Trees near Me NSW Vegetation." Treesnearme.app, treesnearme.app/explore. Accessed 8 Aug. 2023.

Operation Posidonia. "Sydney Harbour," https://www.operationposidonia.com/sydney-harbour. Accessed 8 Aug. 2023.

Parkes, Tony, et al. "Big Scrub: A Cleared Landscape in Transition back to Forest?" *Ecological Management & Restoration*, vol. 13, no. 3, Sept. 2012, pp. 212-23, doi: 10.1111/emr.12008.

Shiva, Vandana et al. *Ecofeminism*. Zed Books, 2014.

Sydney Institute of Marine Science. "Operation Posidonia," sims.org.au/projects/operation-posidonia. Accessed 8 Aug. 2023.

    Maya Martin-Westheimer

Threatened Species Scientific Committee. "Approved Conservation Advice for the Eastern Suburbs Banksia Scrub of the Sydney Region." 8 Dec. 2021, https://www.environment.gov.au/biodiversity/threatened/communities/pubs/2-conservation-advice.pdf.

Wohlleben, Peter. *The Hidden Life of Trees: The Illustrated Edition.* David Suzuki Institute, 2018.

Woollahra Municipal Council. "Bushland and Biodiversity: Threatened Species," https://www.woollahra.nsw.gov.au/environment/bushland_and_biodiversity/threatened-species-meet-the-locals. Accessed 8 Aug. 2023.

21 Augmented Herbarealities

Verena Kuni

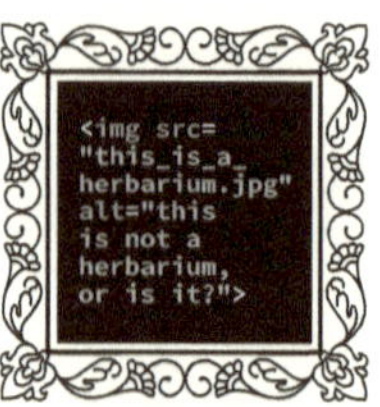

Herbaria are, by definition and by tradition, collections of preserved plant specimens that are regularly accompanied by related information. They comprise documents and collections, instruments and institutions, tools, and agents and agencies of botanical knowledge. Herbaria are a specific body of botanical knowledge deeply informed by colonial conditions, extractive endeavors, and other accoutrements of the ongoing Anthropo-Capitalo-Plantationocene (Haraway).[1] These accoutrements have led both to an ongoing loss of forms of knowledge that were not compatible with dominant institutional standards, orders, and regimes, and to an ongoing loss of plant species themselves. Hence, herbaria have lost their apparent innocence. Have the herbarium principle and herbarium practice finally come to an end? Or is it possible to overcome the herbarium's partly toxic heritage not only by raising consciousness—by fighting oblivion and suppression—but also by seeking new ways to keep the potential usefulness of herbaria, in order to create herbaria that encompass multiple perspectives on the past as well as for possible futures?

This chapter presents a response to the work of five contemporary artists in order to build on insights from interdisciplinary critical plant studies, cultural studies, the history of science, speculative design, and educational studies. With a focus on examples of critical and creative encounters with herbaria and the tales they may tell us, I still echo the traditional ways of learning from and with herbaria: actively keeping them and assembling them with one's findings. However, I do so by looking at our subject through the eyes of contemporary art(ists) in order to create multi-faceted "augmented herbarealities."[2]

The question is not so much why and how we should look at herbaria today. There are clearly many reasons, from learning about the treasures of past biodiversity, extinct and rare species and those that are still present, and the deep entanglements between colonial economies and the history of science. But we may rightly ask why and how we should create herbaria today. Botany has developed different practices of research and study, and while we can still learn a lot

   Verena Kuni

from just looking at plants over and over again, digitalised herbaria provide us with rich resources, so there is less necessity and need to embark on curious extractivism.

However, as the examples of artistic approaches discussed below demonstrate, a wider understanding of the herbarium that leads us to "augmented herbarealities" can make a difference.

Joan Fontcuberta (b. 1955, Spain): *Herbarium* (1983)

<img src="fontcuberta_herbarium_1983_exhibition.jpg" alt= "A wall, painted in a light, neutral color, and covered with rows of b/w photographs in portrait format, all of them mounted in passe-partouts and light wooden frames, each seemingly picturing a plant or a part of a plant, neatly extracted, in front of a light grey background">

This is not a herbarium. Or is it?

This collection is called "Herbarium," and we see vegetal specimens on display, each presented in isolation on a single sheet of paper, in portrait format, and seemingly identified with a Latin name according to the binominal nomenclature of traditional botanical taxonomy.[3] But there is no plant materially mounted on cardboard; we see only photographs[4]—not colour, but black and white. Certainly, the aesthetic gesture of abstraction can point us back to the history of scientific illustration. However, should a herbarium not come with a different setup and style of (re-)presentation? None of these photographs shows a plant in its entirety; instead, we see single parts, like flowers and blossoms, fruits and seeds, branches, leaves and twigs, sometimes even in close-up. There is no chance for us to understand how the plant to which the parts belong would have looked. At the same time, we are also desperately missing any hint about the habitat of each species, the place where it was found. Actually, none of the data usually collected with botanical specimen is revealed.

Thus we almost feel urged to come closer and to zoom in, so that we may hopefully be able to identify the plants ourselves. Indeed, some parts of plants that we can capture at a glance seem quite familiar: the dried seedpods of *Lunaria*, for example, or the majestic flower of a calla, a *Strelitzia regina*. There are once fleshy, now rather limp leaves that remind us of *Brassica oleacera*. There are stems of cacti. And there are twigs adorned with thick thorns.

However, the closer we come, the more we feel irritated. What seemed familiar now looks wrong, even uncanny. Is that not a dried *Buddleja davidii* blossom nesting in the calla flower? Do any thorns grow that regularly in rows? Is it due to our imagination that this flower looks like an animal's head, or is it actually one?

Of course, it is also the absence of colour that makes it difficult to answer such questions. This is the very stratagem of classic photography that helps to transform almost everything into timeless sculptures; "all art wants eternity."[5] The visual references to Karl Blossfeldt's famous *Urformen der Kunst* (1928) are more than obvious. Already at that time, photography proved to be a perfect tool for sculpting a second nature, a special way of world-building based on whatever it was that had been there (*"la chose a été lá,"* Barthes 1980, 120; "the thing has been there," Barthes 1981, 76). We know we shall not confuse a photograph with the subjects and objects it refers to. Nevertheless, we also know that however much a photograph may lie, there is still a factual truth contained within it.

This presence of factual truth, indeed, also applies to this collection of photographs. There have even been botanical excursions, though of a special kind, as the photographer went out to collect bits and pieces of debris and then put them together to create these special specimens: "small ephemeral assemblages constructed with industrial detritus, pieces of plastic, bones, plant and animal parts of a diverse sort, that I found wandering in the industrial outskirts of Barcelona" (Fontcuberta, qtd. in "Joan Fontcuberta").

Thus, on the one hand, Joan Fontcuberta's *Herbarium* is, in its own right, a collection of flora gathered on actual excursions. If we take the artist's comment into account, this collection can even be loosely located in time and space: before 1983, "the industrial outskirts of Barcelona". On the other hand, the reference to herbarium-related standards, especially those concerning the records of information, is considerably loose. All available—and relevant—data are contained in the photographs themselves.

This herbarium is not about plants. It is not about the strange flora growing in the peripheries of Barcelona, but about photography.[6]

As Vilém Flusser rightly points out in his introduction to Fontcuberta's *Herbarium*, "both biology and photography are basically concerned with information" (Flusser). Information is, however, only the basic ingredient of world-building. We need and use narrative tools in order to create science, or fiction, and often we have to take a closer look to decide what it is that is offered to us. That is what this herbarium tale can tell us.

                                                      Verena Kuni

Taryn Simon (b. 1975, US): *Paperwork and the Will of Capital* **(2015)**

<img src="simon_paperwork_2015_installation.jpg" alt="A room with white walls on which hang huge, massive wooden frames that contain color photographs, each featuring a festive flower arrangement in front of a blank background divided in two bold color fields; standing on the floor are several transparent vitrines, each of which contains two dark rectangular blocks made of concrete, on the top of which two staples of paper are displayed; one of the sheets on top of the staples shows a diminution of one of the framed photographs, accompanied by text, the other has pressed and dried flowers, each of which seems to have a related number and text line on the first sheet.">

This is not a herbarium. Or is it?

At first glance, monumental photographs mounted dominate the scene, and despite their vegetal subjects, it is not botany that we will think of first when looking at them. We see a precious flower arrangement, its aesthetic of artificiality additionally amplified by the two-toned blank background (Simon; Burisch). Only by coming closer do we become aware that there is also a tiny sheet of paper with text enclosed in each majestic, mahogany frame. This text is, indeed, an important key to understanding what we are looking at—not only because it comes with a list of the plants the bouquet consists of, complete with their Latin names and geographic origins. It also reveals the historic origins of the flower arrangement, and thereby points us to the concept of the project.

In the dry, tight style of archival records, the text tells us about an important political agreement, even including the date when it was signed. Alongside naming the official act and its participants, the text outlines the basics of the political background, motives, and results. Consequently, it significantly enriches terse titles like "Bratislava Declaration, Bratislava, Slovakia, August 3, 1968"; "Gdansk Agreement, Gdansk Shipyards, Gdansk Poland, August 31, 1980"; or "Memorandum of Understanding between the Royal Government of Cambodia and the Government of Australia Relating to the Settlement of Refugees in Cambodia, Ministry of Interior, Phnom Penh, Cambodia, September 26, 2014."[7] The flowers on the photographs are reconstructions of the original bouquets that were used as decorations in these historic events. The bouquets were displayed on the tables where statesmen sat together to sign treaties or other documents—paperwork that would regulate the dense entanglements of political and economic powers, national and global markets and geographies. The bi-coloured backgrounds have their source in the colors of the wallpaper and tablecloths of the rooms where the bouquets were displayed.[8] Thus, just as in botany, the focus is on the data, both of the bouquet and of its original habitat.

Of course, nothing of this is "natural"; every element is part of a series of highly controlled arrangements and acts.[9] This is obviously also true for the bouquets related to the seventeenth-century Dutch tradition of rich floral still lifes of impossible combinations of flowers that would normally neither grow nor blossom together in the same space and at the same time. Yet Taryn Simon has taken botanical work seriously.[10] With the help of professionals and the system of the Dutch Aalsmeer Flower Auction, she identified all the flowers of the bouquets in the original photographs of the political events and had them shipped to her New York studio. After she took her own photographs, a single exemplar of the flowers from each bouquet was mounted on herbarium paper, dried, and pressed to become part of a herbarium related to the photographs. In the end, there were thirty-six photographs in the wooden frames mentioned above and twelve concrete column sculptures. First used as Simon's flower presses, these columns now contain a folio with inkjet prints of the photographs and accompanying texts, as well a set of the original herbarium sheets with the dried specimens.[11]

This herbarium is about plants, about the intertwined histories of politics and aesthetics, and about forced coalitions both of plants and of humans.

It is important to note that one photograph falls outside Simon's meticulous system. Because there is no bouquet pictured, the centre of the photograph remains empty, and we are left with a bi-coloured screen. Indeed, on the original documents related to the event—the "Protocol Decision on the Principles of Resumption of a Full-Scale Freight Railway Communication through the Territory of Pridnestrovie. Tiraspol, Transnistria, March 30, 2012"—there is no big bouquet, only a small table with a vase with some flowers in the background (Ministry of Foreign Affairs of Pridnestrovian Moldavian Republic). However, the main reason for not recreating and photographing this bouquet was different: there were no real plants in the vase, only plastic flowers (Burisch).[12]

Anaïs Tondeur (b. 1985, France): *Chernobyl Herbarium* **(since 2011)**

<img src="tondeur_chernobyl_herbarium_2011_exhibition.jpg" alt="
Bright white walls on which, loosely spaced, but in regular distance
to each other, one or more frameless plates of photograms of plants
have been mounted; there is also a distance between wall and plate,
so each photogram casts a shadow.">

This is not a herbarium. Or is it?

We see a series of photograms, each of which shows the light, lucid, and, in some cases, even sparkling, silhouette of a plant. Some of the species are quite common, like *Linum usitatissimum* (common flax), a geranium or different *Phaseoleae* (beans). Others have been marked as "unknown" (Marder and Tondeur).

While such ghostly appearances may certainly remind us of traditional techniques of nature printing—if not the earliest examples from the sixteenth century,[13] then for sure the famous cyanotypes created by Anna Atkins—they can also evoke rather uncanny feelings (Atkins). This is, of course, due to the title of the series, unmistakably relating the folios to the eponymous nuclear catastrophe that took place on 26 April 1986, when one of the reactors of the Chernobyl Nuclear Power Plant exploded. The territory of the so-called "Chernobyl Exclusion Zone" remains significantly contaminated, as the herbaceous shrubs of the area reveal.

The plants contained in this herbarium are witnesses of the radiation that is still present in the zone, where they have been collected. Each of the herbarium sheets comes with a record indicating the radiation values—and, as is probably even more important, makes this otherwise invisible radiation visible to our human eyes: rayograms, literally.[14] Indeed, the project unites two practices and perspectives of camera-less photography: its key role in the history of science (the marks on photosensitive plates left by radiation led to the discovery of radioactivity) and its traces in avant-garde art (the artist and photographer Man Ray who originally coined the term for his photograms).

This herbarium is about (in)visibilities, about traces and witnesses, and about the bewildering aesthetics of forensic records.

Chernobyl Herbarium actually contains more than the floral *typographia naturalis* of the nuclear disaster. The project is a collaboration between the artist-photographer Anaïs Tondeur, the biologist and geneticist Martin Hajduk,[15] and the philosopher Michael Marder,[16] who returns to his own childhood memories in order to combine them with meditations on plants, contamination and deterioration, and relations between multiple dimensions of the invisible and the incomprehensible. Just as the plants have become white shadows, so too the original concept of a herbarium as a florilegium of recorded information that offers a collection of knowledge is reversed into its opposite. The herbarium becomes a loose collection of thoughts about losses, "fragments of an exploded consciousness" (Marder and Tondeur) of a vanishing world.

Driessens & Verstappen (b. 1963 and b. 1964, Netherlands): *Herbarium Vivum* (2013, 2018)

<img src="driessens_verstappen_herbariumvivum_wageningen_2013.jpg" alt="A park with trees, bush beds, and lawn; on the latter white rectangular boxes with a transparent front in each of which a single plant is growing; printed on the glass front, in black, are the words HERBARIUM VIVUM as well as the botanical name and specification of the plant contained; in the upper left there is also a red print with illegible words in an oval that looks like a logo.">

This is not a herbarium. Or is it?

On a short, mown lawn, between beds, bushes, and trees, we find pages erected on the ground. These pages are to be browsed by those strolling in the park; they are white, vertical, flat vitrines with transparent fronts and contain greens—as it soon turns out, living plants indeed. (Driessens & Verstappen).[17] A *herbarium vivum*, verbatim.[18]

Due to the relative flatness of the vitrines, the plants at first glance may even look pressed. Indeed, we may assume they would prefer to have more space so that they could expand in more directions. But at least they managed to grow, to flower, and, in some cases, even to yield fruit.

This is a herbarium in transition, each of its "pages" lasting for one life cycle of the plant contained in the "page." It asks us to return again and again to learn more about the plant's parts and phases—and thus obviously contradicts the traditional herbarium concept of a collection that provides botanical information about plants independently of the seasons.

What this herbarium shares with its predecessors, however, is that each plant is isolated from its original habitat and transposed to an artificial, standardised showcase. The plants in *Herbarium Vivum* are even, at least to a certain extent, immobilised in time and space; they are not drawn after life, but from life.

This work is both attractive and repulsive at the same time, and can trigger related emotions in the public. "Ah, so you are the plant torturers" is reportedly one reaction by spectators (Smale), while curiosity and fascination will probably still continue to draw numerous people to the installation. What could fit better into a "society of spectacle" (Debord) that loves live shows and concerts and that has a taste for reality TV and related media than a live herbarium?

Moreover, recently, the field of multispecies studies has emerged alongside a growing engagement with environmental issues, and a new plant craze may have led to alternative perspectives, but *Herbarium Vivum* nevertheless still fits perfectly into the tradition of human-plant relationship. Over centuries, plants have been prepared in similar ways—even via more radical procedures, as they are torn off the soil, cut, dried, and pressed—to become part of herbaria. There are numerous scientific experiments involving plants forced to exist and to grow under extreme conditions. Last but not least, the whole history of gardening and cultivation is clearly a panorama of cruelties towards plants.

All the plants chosen by the artists for the first version of *Herbarium Vivum*— cultivars of potatoes, tomatoes, cucumbers, hemp, mustard, borage, poppy, and tobacco—are examples of this history (e.g. Pollan).

This herbarium tells us what we do to plants, to living organisms just like us.

The second version of *Herbarium Vivum*, which Driessens and Verstappen created almost five years later, stresses our effect on living organisms (Driessens & Verstappen). Yet, it is different not only in terms of its design. This time, the vitrines mimicking a book were placed horizontally on the ground so that the plants could not grow upwards. Thus, except for the very first phase of development, during which we could take the boxes as propagation beds, the artificial arrangement appears even crueler than in the first version.[19]

In this version, the selected species can be identified as shrubs and perennials, common weeds that have been embraced by humans for their medicinal properties or originally wild plants that have long been appropriated by gardeners for their aesthetic qualities. Included are: field marigold (*Calendula arvensis*), narrow leaf plantain (*Plantago lanceolata*), orange hawkweed (*Pilosella aurantiaca*), common evening primrose (*Oenothera biennis*), scarlet pimpernel (*Anagallis arvensis*), as well as Italian grape hyacinth (*Muscari*), and fritillary (*Fritillaria*). Despite its eccentric appearance, fritillary is of wild origin, just as, despite its common name, the garden star-of-Bethlehem (*Ornithogalum umbellatum*) is.

Should we not admit at this point that, from a human perspective, all flora constitute a living herbarium, neatly divided into weeds and herbs and garden beauties, with useful companions and vegetal pests, with friend and fiend?

Alberto Baraya (b. 1968, Colombia): *Herbário de plantas artificiales* (since 2003)

```
<img src="baraya_herbario_installation_berlin_2014.jpg" alt="A
museum room with illuminated display cabinets each of which is
filled with different arrangements of botanical specimen, parts
of plants, whole flowers, fruit; some are shown on shelves, oth-
ers mounted on cardboard or in boxes; some sheets seem to come
with additional handwritten information, and in some cases even
photographs.">
```

This is a herbarium, is it not?

The folios on display show both the whole plant and some of its parts that are important for its classification, like a section of a blossom and/or a fruit, stems and/or twigs. Not only is there a written record of the place where the specimen has been found, but a photograph is also often added. In many cases, too, there are comments that embed the finding in a botanical excursion; these comments are enriched with, or sometimes actually consist of, further photographic records. Some of these records connect the human uses of the plant with its naturecultural environment and link the botanist-collector to people and plants, plants and people.[21]

Currently, we would expect a herbarium to be a record of botanical findings, and then to have alongside this botanical record perhaps an anthropological field book, a diary, and a conventional historian of science sorting through the documents to bring all of these details together and critically review them. Thus, what we see on these folios may look like a parody of the proud naturalists' and explorers' records from earlier eras of global colonialism and the dutiful pursuit of a science. But is it really a parody?

Looking closer, we may indeed muse about that for a while. Actually, all of the plants in this herbarium are artefacts; they are flora encased in plastic, fabric, paper and wire. Some are handmade, others obviously mass-produced; some bear an astonishing resemblance to botanical models, while others are products of floral fantasies. But all of them have a proper herbarium record.

Alberto Barraya's artistic endeavours consistently come with a wink, but they are deeply serious and very precise at the same time. They provide us with considerably rich insights into the many ways we use and need plants in our everyday culture, and they also scrutinise the strange roles artificial substitutes and surrogates of what is supposed to be "nature" can play.

This herbarium is primarily about human nature.

And this means, of course, that it is also about human culture, and about science being part of human culture. Page per page, frame by frame, vitrine by vitrine,[22] these specimen records demonstrate that scientific "objectivity" is an artful construct arising out of a related cultural craft—and that truth is not so much in a so-called "nature," but rather in open data and transparency.

Augmenting Herbarealities

Not only can encounters with artworks concerning herbaria tell us about the ways we create and use botanical data, as well as about the rules and standards for doing so.[23] They can also, more specifically, help us to understand the approaches to world-building that we have established on these very data. Artworks provide insights into the important role aesthetics play in the context of herbaria and plant studies, on all levels. And, last but not least, these "augmented herbarealities" can help us learn more about human-plant relationships, and the multiple ways these have been—and still are—formative for our contemporary natural-cultural environment, as well as for our past, present and future ways of being.

[This essay contains alt txt references that imitate html elements in websites. Similarities with existing images are not purely coincidental, but nevertheless it should be emphasised that all of the files mentioned above are fictions, inviting the reader to imagine what has to be looked for and looked at elsewhere.]

Notes

1   A slightly revised version became chapter 4 of Haraway 2016, a book that, as a whole, expands on how to overcome the deadly impact of this state of being.

2   If my neologism is obviously hinting at the term "augmented reality," this can be taken as an invitation to understand the herbarium as a powerful format and medium that is indeed able to augment reality—as the artistic herbarium tales in the following paragraphs will show.

3   For an overview of the project see Fontcuberta. Selected photographs are also displayed online; see, for instance, "Joan Fontcuberta."

4   The original photographs are silver gelatin bromide prints treated lightly with selenium, measure 22 x 26 cm, and are shown in exhibitions. That is, Fontcuberta's book from 1985 is not the only format chosen by the artist.

5   Alluding to the much-quoted phrase "Doch alle Lust will Ewigkeit" from the "The Drunken Song" ("Das trunkne Lied") in the last part of Friedrich Nietzsche's Zarathustra; see Nietzsche 1884, 111: "But all desire wants eternity" (transl. mine). While I am not the first and only one translating the poem's line that way (see e.g. McGrath 1973, 62), and while in German language the allusion "Alle Kunst will Ewigkeit" is widespread, the English translations of the verse vary, and different ones based on early translations are more common (e.g. "Eternity's sought by all delight", Nietzsche 1899, 483, or "But joys all want eternity", see Nietzsche 1817, 365).

6   The original book publication (Fontcuberta) already leaves no doubt about this fact; it comes with an introductory essay by Vilém Flusser that comments on the ambiguity of photographs as epistemic tools between document and deception. It was probably the first text Flusser wrote for Fontcuberta, and it was only the beginning of an intense exchange between the philosopher of media and the conceptual artist-photographer.

7   Simon's starting point had been the United Nations Monetary and Financial Conference (Bretton Woods, New Hampshire) in 1944, which led to the establishment of International Monetary Fund (IMF) and the World Bank, two institutions fostering economic globalisation. Tracking related activites of the participating countries, she selected thirty-six "signature events," signing ceremonies from the period between 1968 and 2014 in which the countries were involved.

8   It should be mentioned that although all backgrounds are two-toned, not all of them are literally bicoloured. When the original photograph is black and white, so is Simon's photograph of the recreated bouquet. The result is two shades of grey; see, for instance, "Classified 'Spare Parts' Deal. Oval Office, White House, Washington, D.C., United States, May 16, 1975" or the abovementioned "Bratislava Declaration [...]."

9   Of course, it is debatable whether there are human-plant practices that should be considered and/or called "natural"—and if so, what this means exactly. Botany as a science and as a cultural practice is concerned with concepts of nature, but concepts and related practices are never natural.

10   For an overview and more information about Simon's work in general, see the artist's website: https://tarynsimon.com/ (last accessed: 20 May 2023).

11   Each framed photograph measures 215.9 x 186.1 x 7 cm; the column sculptures are contained in vitrines measuring 111 x 56 x 78 cm. All prints are archival inkjet prints, text prints, and specimens mounted on archival herbarium paper.

12   For a different herbarial approach to plastic flowers, see the discussion of Alberto Barraya's project below.

13   Although the technique is mostly associated with its heyday in the late eighteenth and early to mid-nineteenth centuries, when it was used to create the so-called

                                                                                   Verena Kuni

herbaria viva, it can be traced back to herbals of the sixteenth century; see Thijsse 2022. For more insights into the technical features and construction of Driessens & Verstappen's *Herbarium Vivum* see the following paragraph; for an early example of a *herbarium vivum* see the related endnote.

14   The accompanying text reads i.e. "Linum usitatissimum, Zone d'Exclusion, Tchernobyl, Niveau de radiation : 1.7 µSv/h." Each rayogram measures 24 x 36 cm.

15   For a selection of Hajduk's contributions to the field, see his list of publications on ResearchGate, https://www.researchgate.net/scientific-contributions/Martin-Hajduch-2059616831 (last accessed: 20 May 2023).

16   For an overview of Michael Marder's writings, including several books on the philosophy of plants, see https://www.michaelmarder.org/ (last accessed: 20 May 2023).

17   The boxes are made of coated steel, coated wood, perforated steel, white spandex, and plexiglass; six measure 205 x 125 x 9 cm, and four are 127 x 75 x 9 cm. All of them are installed upright and open on the side abutting the ground, so that the plants are rooted in the soil.

18   The term "herbarium vivum" goes back to the seventeenth and eighteenth centuries, when it was widely used for herbaria that contained both dried specimens and highly accurate images of plants, the latter often based on nature printing; a famous example is Johann Hieronymus Kniphof's *Botanica in originali seu herbarium vivum* (1759). For selected pages, see https://commons.wikimedia.org/wiki/Category:Botanica_in_Originali (last accessed: 20 May 2023).

19   However, not only were the boxes too small to be mistaken for propagation beds, but they were also conceived to match the measurements of a book publication (16 x 23 x 2 cm). In addition, the boxes were placed inside, and the plants were grown under artificial light; see Bower and Tuinen (the book for which the project was created; photographs documenting the growth of the plants were shown in the accompanying exhibition), pp. 8-9 (photographs of the boxes are spread throughout the publication).

20   "Natureculture," of course, echoes Haraway 2008. This term, I would like to argue here, fits well both to this example and our subject in general.

21   For an overview of the different formats and presentations Alberto Barraya has developed since he started his *Herbarium of Artificial Plants* in 2003, see "Alberto Baraya." There are many different versions and instalments, each created on the basis of research expeditions undertaken by the artist.

22   These are merely the most prominent formats of installments the artist uses in exhibitions.

23   For arguments that would support a more detailed discussion of this perspective, see, for instance: Bowker and Star; Daston and Galison; Daston.

Works Cited

Atkins, Anna. *Photographs of British Algae: Cyanotype Impressions.* Steidl, 2020 [Sir John Herschel's copy; orig.: 1843].

Baraya, Alberto. "Alberto Baraya." Nara Roesler Gallery, https://nararoesler.art/en/artists/28-alberto-baraya/. Accessed: 20 May 2023.

Barthes, Roland. *La chambre claire: note sur la photographie.* Gallimard, 1980. English edition: *Camera Lucida: Reflections on Photography,* translated by Richard Howard, Hill and Wang, 1981.

Bowker, Geoffrey C., and Susan Leigh Star. *Sorting Things Out: Classification and Its Consequences.* MIT Press, 2000.

Brouwer, Joke, and Sjoerd van Tuinen, eds. *To Mind Is To Care.* V2 Publishing, 2019.

Burisch, Nicole. "Taryn Simon's 'Paperwork and the Will of Capital': Perspectives on Transience of Power." *National Gallery of Canada Magazine,* 18 Oct. 2019, https://www.gallery.ca/magazine/your-collection/at-the-ngc/taryn-simons-paperwork-and-the-will-of-capital-perspectives-on.

Daston, Lorraine. *Rules: A Short History of What We Live By.* Princeton University Press, 2022.

---, and Peter Galison. *Objectivity.* Zone Books, 2007.

Debord, Guy. *La Société du spectacle.* Paris: Buchet-Chastel, 1967. English edition: *The Society of the Spectacle,* translated by Donald Nicholson-Smith, Zone Books, 1994.

Driessens & Verstappen. "Herbarium Vivum 1 (2013)," https://notnot.home.xs4all.nl/herbariumvivum/Herbarium-Vivum-1/herbarium1.html. Accessed 20 May 2023.

---. "Herbarium Vivum 2 (2018)," https://notnot.home.xs4all.nl/herbariumvivum/Herbarium-Vivum-2/herbarium2.html. Accessed 20 May 2023.

Fontcuberta, Joan. "Herbarium, 1983." Àngels Barcelona Gallery, http://angelsbarcelona.com/en/artists/joan-fontcuberta/projects/herbarium/158. Accessed 20 May 2023.

Flusser, Vilem. "Introduction." *Joan Fontcuberta Herbarium.* European Photography, 1985.

Haraway, Donna J. *When Species Meet.* University of Minnesota Press, 2008.

---. "Anthropocene, Capitalocene, Plantationocene, Chthulucene: Making Kin." *Environmental Humanities,* vol. 6, no. 1, 2015, pp. 159-65.

---. *Staying with the Trouble: Making Kin in the Chthultucene.* Duke University Press, 2016.

McGrath, William J. "'Volksseelenpolitik' and Psychological Rebirth: Mahler and Hofmannsthal. *The Journal of Interdisciplinary History,* vol. 4, no. 1, 1973, pp. 53-72.

  Verena Kuni

Marder, Michael, and Anaïs Tondeur. *The Chernobyl Herbarium: Fragments of an Exploded Consciousness.* Open Humanities Press, 2016.

Ministry of Foreign Affairs of Pridnestrovian Moldavian Republic. "On Signing of the Protocol Decision on the Principles of Resumption of a Full-scale Freight Railway Communication through the Territory of Pridnestrovie." 30 Mar. 2012, https://mid.gospmr.org/en/tTL. Accessed 20 May 2023.

Nietzsche, Friedrich. *Also sprach Zarathustra: Ein Buch für Alle und Keinen,* vol. III, Ernst Schmeitzner, 1884.

Nietzsche, Friedrich. *Thus Spake Zarathustra: A Book for All and None,* translated by Alexander Tille, *The Works of Friedrich Nietzsche,* vol. II, T. Fisher Unwin, 1899.

Nietzsche, Friedrich. *Thus Spake Zarathustra: A Book for All and None,* translated by Thomas Common, The Modern Library/Random House, 1917.

"Photographs of British Algae: Cyanotype Impressions." *The New York Public Library Digital Collections,* https://digitalcollections.nypl.org/collections/photographs-of-british-algae-cyanotype-impressions#/?tab=navigation. Accessed 20 May 2023.

Pollan, Michael. *The Botany of Desire: A Plants-Eye View of the World.* Random House, 2001.

Simon, Taryn. *Paperwork, and the Will of Capital.* Hatje-Cantz, 2016.

Smale, Stephanie de. "A Personal Romance between Science and BioArt." *Waag Futurelab, De Waag,* 3 Mar. 2014, https://waag.org/en/article/personal-romance-between-science-and-bioart/. Accessed 20 May 2023.

Spencer, Daniel G. "The Chernobyl Herbarium, the Nuclear Sublime, and Progress after an End of the World." *Apocalyptica,* vol. 1, no. 2, 2022, pp. 39-61, doi: 10.17885/heiup.apoc.2022.2.

Thijsse, Gerard. "'Everlasting Gardens': Origin, Purpose, Spread and Use of the First herbaria." *In The Green Middle Ages: The Depiction and Use of Plants in the Western World 600–1600,* edited by Claudine A. Chavannes-Mazel, and Linda IJpelaar, 72-107, Amsterdam University Press, 2022.

Tondeur, Anaïs. "Chernobyl Herbarium," https://anaistondeur.com/chernobyl-herbarium. Accessed 20 May 2023.

22 The Scribbly Gum, or Confessions of a Reformed Plant Killer

Anna Westbrook

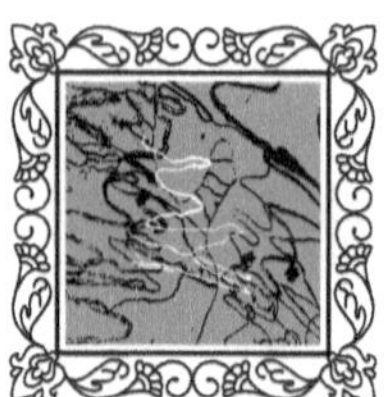

I am not a natural plant person. I do not garden. I am a languid, timid, unambitious hiker. My houseplants survive because my best friend messages me regularly to water them, rolls her eyes, and gives them kitchen sink deep soaks when she visits. Once upon a time, I wrote about the sublime, particularly the literary—what it is about poetics, (or erotics after Sontag), that can move a reader to tears, that may stir the *duende* (nodding to Lorca), and nudge one to the very lip of the well, to touch fingers across the void with one's ghosts? I'm not good with my hands, except for turning pages.

My mother, a self-described tree-hugger who grew up tanned-legged and feral in the bush, tried her best to imbue in me a Romantic sensibility, yet I was never attentive enough, subject to "plant blindness" and couldn't see further than the static of "green wallpaper." I preferred the ocean for its obvious turbulence and volatility, the smack of salt. Then, an undergraduate flirtation with Women's Officer ecofeminism turned me right off due to associations with chickpeas, potlucks, and patchouli. I love reading *about* nature, tracing the words of John Keats, Helen Macdonald, Olivia Laing, Rebecca Solnit, Mary Oliver, Ursula K. Le Guin, and Monica Gagliano, but I get restless being present *in* it… although perhaps presence in general agitates me. Give me a glass of wine and conversation, or the escapism of books, or the reliable chatter of podcasts enriching my pub trivia skills; it scares me to be still, silent, serene. It scares me that, eventually, we all return to the earth.

I tell my best friend, the plant-whisperer, E., that if only plants would *make a noise*, I'd remember to rehydrate them, like I daily tend to the cat, indignant at his half-empty bowl, because, to me, the animal world seems to possess more correspondence to the sacred or the desecrated. If I watched a pack of dogs and men on horseback chase a rabbit across a paddock to tear it apart, I would argue they were profane, outrageous, even though clearcut logging is immeasurably worse. If I am too tone-deaf to listen, could the plants please semaphore before they've crossed that subtle Rubicon of "fine" to "decidedly not." There's no existential squeal. The plants die quietly, suddenly, not with a bang nor a whisper.

"But they do tell you," E. tells me. "You're just not listening."

I feel deflated, rejected from some secret society, suspicious that I might be superficial, capitalist, and anthropocentric, blithely contributing to the climate disaster, and unable, excuse me, to see the forest for the trees. I am self-conscious in the same way as I have been as I waddled through French, or mathematics, or yoga, constantly looking over my shoulder, waiting to be sprung. Originally, I was going to write about mycelia, because I thought they were cool, almost extra-terrestrial, communicative, and fundamentally *intelligent*. I watched videos of Cordyceps, horror-struck as David Attenborough narrated the plight of zombified bullet ants with spores exploding through their heads. An individually unpleasant fate, but, ultimately, a natural correction of overpopulated species… this was before *The Last of Us*. The Cordyceps were a force, they did shit.

I flailed for an anchor of plant-animal interaction because I was inclined to thrust a humanistic logic onto the natural world, something that "made sense." How could I reconcile my own self-absorption with the fact that we are meaningless to plants, that plants do not care, that the genus *homo* may not, indeed, be the cumulative pinnacle of evolution? That I might not be exceptional… I live, work, and create on the Gadigal land of the Eora nation as a non-Indigenous person of Scottish, Irish, and French heritage. For too long, colonial narratives of "Australia" have centred around the myth of absence, inversion, and alienation—the pervasive and problematic Australian Gothic folklore of the desert dingoes, or the hanging rocks, or the big bad Banksia swallowing, disappearing, and stealing children. White children. Obviously.

During the Sydney lockdowns of COVID-19, I toyed with sourdough, binged Netflix, and embarked on a short but wild fling with another writer who kindled within me an appreciation of epic, dreamy walks. While I was hamstrung by apathy and writers' block, she diligently hammered out an entire novel, so nearly every day, I would leave my house in Surry Hills, not knowing what else to do. I wandered up desolate Oxford Street, entered Centennial Park via the Paddington gates, past the tiding of magpies on the reservoir, and proceeded slowly clockwise, getting out of the path of manic oncoming joggers and Range Rover double prams. I found a spot, tucked up a hill in the Woollahra corner, where I'd sit and read. I liked the ambience of being in the centre of town and yet so very far away. It seemed mildly dangerous and ragged as the light fell, wondering what everyone else were doing in their houses, with the sun setting perfectly west over the city's skyscraper gap—a forlorn Stonehenge.

I had come to the park all my life and was surprised that I'd found this unfamiliar nook. The trees here were different to the majestic ring of Moreton Bay figs, the stands of pine, a gate-crash of Californian palms, and soft, giving paperbark. Here, the grass retreated to a balding, sandstone outcrop, graced by a brood of scribbly gums. First Nations' people call the gums *Tarinny* and *Wongnary*. The Linnaean taxonomic *Eucalyptus haemastoma* was imposed in 1797 by botanist, James Edward Smith. *Haema* meaning blood, and *stoma* mouth, graphically, or "'red lips'" colloquially, and were meant to reflect the red discs of the tree's fruit, and yet completely overlooking the trees' most striking eccentric characteristic:—their scribbles,—a kind of non-human *logos*.

As a lifelong margin-doodling graffitist, these wily dropouts appeal to me, breaking from the formality of various eras of landscape planning and the relentless insistence upon standardised English garden design. At home, I dig out a half-remembered poem by Judith Wright: "The gum-tree stands by the spring. / I peeled its splitting bark / and found the written track / of a life I could not read." I would sit in the interminable present, not knowing when or if this pandemic crisis would subside. After the morning dose of Premier's reports and latest stats of infections and deaths, I dreaded teaching my university seminars of black squares I implored to contribute, to say something, anything. Give me, give me. These scribbly gums were a pleasant stripe of inscrutable, and often I would sit with my back against their trunks, lean in a gesture of supplication, nursing my iced coffee trying not to spill it in my lap, and cry.

***

Some as fine as filament, others fattening to Bunnings' sausages, they meander, spike, and trail off—the handwriting of a drunk. Science has an explanation for the mysterious articulation. Annually, the scribbly gum splits for the next distinctive layer to emerge. The cursive on the yellow-silver bark is a brown or ochre and is raised from the flesh of the tree. They are created by scribbly gum moth larvae: *Ogmograptis*, which devour irregular lines as they grow, subdermal, before pupating and erupting into their adult form, only to repeat. This is why the track-marks widen, the moths eat and eat and eat their fill. A feedback loop that doesn't necessarily hurt the tree, but the scribbly gain no benefit they simply provide a generous body.

Anna Westbrook

The moths have a sweet deal. Virginia Woolf thought a lot about moths, that they were curious, "hybrid creatures." She wrote about watching one expire on her window ledge: "Just as life had been strange a few minutes before, so death was now as strange. The moth having righted himself now lay almost decently and uncomplainingly composed. O yes, he seemed to say, death is stronger than I am." Compared to the matchstick of a moth's lifespan, these trees endure a millennium of *Lepidoptera* generations. I felt a torsion in thinking about the harm inflicted upon the trees. Could they feel it, or were they indifferent? And why was I drawn to the characteristic that had nothing to do with the gums but was something done unto them? Were they immovable hosts to the wanton appetites of a wilful, Dionysian, mobile creature? *Ogmograptis* was an opportunistic little bastard.

I wanted to quit teaching, but for what else was I qualified? I knew my "relationship"—although neither of us termed it that—was ephemeral, a lockdown comfort, but I didn't feel ready to let go. I beseeched the gums for answers, as though the moth trails were cards in the hands of a tarot reader. Despite their rosy lips but bloody mouths—like Lavinia in *Titus Andronicus*, robbed of hands and tongue so she cannot accuse her violators—we could not understand one another. "It's the end of the world every day, for someone. Time rises and rises," writes Margaret Atwood, unsparingly, "and when it reaches the level of your eyes you drown." Centennial Park is only 5 kilometres from the beach.

My friend T. told me about an experience with Ayahuasca she had on a beach in Mexico. She said that the guide told her that people who hold on too tightly always have bad trips. She saw people crying, vomiting, clawing burrows in the sand, while she felt like she was floating, undulating even, and that she could hear the trees breathe nearby. I don't think I would have the courage, or the stomach for it. My grip is too clenched.

Trees have persevered through four major extinction events; compared to how humans are faring, they will continue. Unbidden comes my training in philosophy, recounting the rhizomes of Deleuze and Guattari. Recent lab tests have proven that trees are capable of sharing information with each other, that they can alert one another to danger, that "mother" trees act as critical nodes in an intricate system of communication. My primary system of communication was a group chat on Signal, where we shared memes of vaguely amusing despair.

My friend C. and I had weekly, cocktail-hour phone check-ins where she laments how Naarm/Melbourne is so much worse than Sydney, that I can't even know—and I don't. She wasn't allowed to have a proper funeral for her father, and her marriage was a dropped porcelain plate during this stress test incapable of *kintsugi*. Perspective, I get it. If you slam the door, the entire set wobbles.

The Promethean wounding and regrowth. The most virulent parasite kills its host, a paradox of swift contagion that flames-out, known as the "Curse of the Pharoah." Yet parasitic relationships are constantly on a knife-edge, and some even turn co-operative. We, as humans, are swarming with freeloaders from gut to eyelashes. To the scribbly, this bludger is borne with good grace. The moth lays eggs on the bark in autumn, and, when they hatch, the caterpillars are ravenous. They plunge straight into the tree's flesh, gobbling. Once inside, they turn, like a tattooist's needle, right beneath where the next cork cambium layer will annually regrow. Then, when gorged, retrace the journey, munching the scar with which the tree has felted itself, a callus tissue, full of nutrients. After the banquet, the caterpillar bursts into the light to make new cocoons, to be reborn. If I was religious, I might find this comforting, the body of Christ, but, instead, I think about cyclical time—there's no momentum of "progress," just the rhyme of history.

Post-COVID, I return to the corner of Centennial, to the neutral, indifferent scribblies, and I close my eyes, knowing I am guilty of ocular-centrism, how sight dominates the hierarchy of the Western codification of "things"—a concept manifest in the enduring "look but don't touch" code of the traditional museum. How many people during these last few years have been deprived of that basic need? I'm grateful for the relative privacy of the grove, as I'm undertaking a thought experiment that looks like I'm feeling up a tree, and today I have a beer and not a coffee and am not in the mood to get fined. It rained last night, and the petrichor scent is strong. The gums are messy; they are shedding damp bark aprons. I remember what it felt like when I was wary to hug a friend, shake someone's hand, kiss a cheek. Things plod on like very hungry caterpillars in the dark.

***

There are two more species of scribbly gum which extend beyond the Sydney area into greater New South Wales. All are part of a family of more than 700 species of eucalyptus, each of which have come from Indigenous language. Professor Jakelin Troy, the Director of Aboriginal and Torres Strait Islander Research at the University of Sydney, argues the importance of proliferating the original First Nations peoples' names for trees to redress the disconnect settler-colonisers from the environment. My disconnect.

                                                      Anna Westbrook

Written amid the struggle to stop the Victorian government from cutting down ancient birthing trees, eucalyptus sacred to the Djab Wurrung (ultimately bulldozed for a controversial highway), Troy asserts that First Nations peoples have "always understood trees to be community members" and that after colonisation where we cut them down to clear grazing space, the Indigenous people "wept and cried with the trees." Is it a conceit to think that by planting more gums, more trees, we might offset some of the damage we have inflicted? "When we destroy trees," Troy writes, "we destroy ourselves. We cannot survive in a treeless world." When I touch a tree, I hope it touches me back, in some sense aware of my presence and lack of intention to harm. I think my mother would be proud of this, the incremental accomplishment of a slow learner.

After lockdown, I underwent a hysterectomy due to crippling endometriosis. During the lead-up, in chronic pain, I didn't think too much about the long-term. I wanted the agony, the daily bleeding, to just be over. It took many years and consultations to get this "outcome," as the doctors referred to it. Almost all GPs and specialists were reluctant to remove my womb, given my age, and what they called the "regret threat," that even my less than 1% chance of being able to carry a child to term, they fretted that I might resentfully sue. It is a hard thing to communicate, especially as a proud Auntie of five, that I don't have any strong attachment to the idea of having biological children. There's the pervasive intimation that the world is not only a human place, that we are illegitimate interlopers, that we are past global warming to an inheritance of global boiling. Frogs in a pot.

Much like the audacity of *Ogmograptis*, we leave indelible marks, carbon-dusted fingerprints, on the members of our community, on everything we touch. There's also that deep affiliation with having something inside you that you cannot control. Until you can, and you have it cut out. And you look at the scar's autumnal progression from crimson, to livid, to a distant shimmering horizon. Because what else is there?

E. comes round and says: "The plants are doing surprisingly well." This is a huge compliment for a recidivist murderer to receive. So, I'm off to water them.

23 Hyperlight

Tamryn Bennett & Ryan Gordan

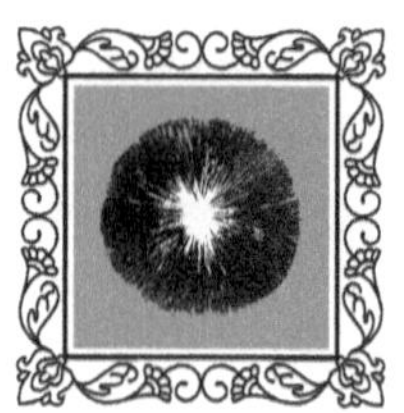

Our method is scientific,

but our opinions are not.

Cataclysm comes

as rebirth begins,

ghost pulse

between meteors.

Mediator from the stars

falls soft on earth

mushrooms speak

in the night of mind,

tongue of cosmos

nebulae fruiting with messages.

Older than thought

this unfolding,

spores scattered through galaxies

until here we hold a single breath.

Shape-shifting our bodies devoured

once humus, now acres of lace.

Webs fragile as spiders

trembling with existence,

we disappear.

Evolving near immortal

to become again and again

faint memories of forests.

Symbiosis of species and

civilisations in the orchard

mutual hyperlight

the blue hours ticking

to younger worlds

with suns more stable.

Tender allegory

of humble teachers

allochory release

to open the gates and see

the universe in all things

all things in the...

24 Remember

Tamryn Bennett

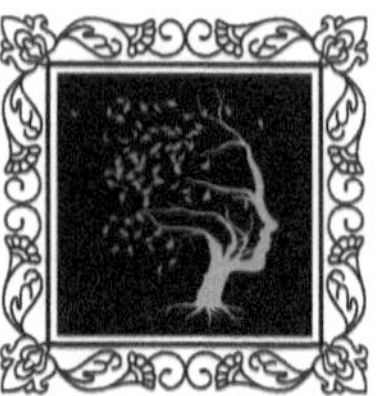

Written in wind

woven along river

tides before the first tree was felled

branches burned, turned to boat and book.

Holes in sky

ache in the soil

how many seeds were stolen

true names cut out like tongues

carried in coats to glasshouses.

Now we sit in the window

while you paint portals

we through the future

call it Sublime

canopy of palm

two hundred years above swamp.

All times echoing with knowings

beyond the sliver of science.

What has it silenced

in straight lines and shelves?

Linnaean structures and Latin

the need to still life somehow

separate ourselves from nature

as if inevitable decay

could be pressed from existence

Voices erased from pages

medicines burned…

And here we are

ears to the spine of eucalypt

picking bloody fungus

moss in your mouth

wild in your eyes

remembering when these mountains

would catch fire

writing new stories

all the seeds singing again

25 Adventures in the Undergrowth

Georgina Reid

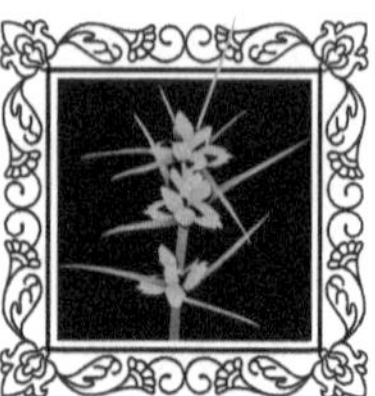

I'm prowling the garden like a psychopathic cowgirl. Secateurs in holster slung low on hips, ready for attack. Spade tucked under arm. I am a villain or a god, depending on who you are and where you take root. It is both violence and growth I'm after. The plants may or may not be quivering.

Today's victim is a blameless *Lomandra longifolia*, or mat rush: a strappy-leafed perennial plant endemic to much of the east coast of Australia, from Hobart to Cairns, coastal sand to country clay. There is nothing particularly striking about poor old *Lomandra*. Flowers, yes. But not gorgeous, iconic blooms like waratah, banksia, or wattle. Rather: tiny and hidden by not-so-tiny-and-very-sharp spikes puncturing shins of unsuspecting passers-by. Fragrance, yes, but not romantic and evocative like jasmine or frangipani. Rather: semi-toxic, like nail polish remover. They—yes, I am "they-ing" rather than "it-ing" because a plant is a being, not an object—grows in sun and shade, swamp and sand.

It is somewhat paradoxical highlighting the subjectivity of a being whilst also defining them by their scientific, binomial name. Genus: Lomandra. Species: longifolia. Classification, separation, objectification. Yet to name, surely, is to see and assign value. At a time in which all beings without eyes that can meet our own are perceived as an indistinguishable backdrop to the grand human odyssey, a name might act as a thread of recognition and connection. Love, even. I have many names for my partner, precisely because I love him. I wouldn't bother if I didn't.

I know *Lomandra*, too, has a spectrum of names grown of the soil, gifted by Country. I dig around in online, Indigenous-language dictionaries—Dharawal, Darug, Wiradjuri, Gamilaroi—but cannot find anything specific. I resort to asking ChatGPT. It (let us not forget AI is always an "it") gives me a list of entirely inaccurate words.

Language is a strange beast, created by stranger creatures. Is it the job of the writer to scribble around the edges, push and pull words and meanings, write into the gaps between what is said and what is meant, between what is named and what isn't?

***

Lomandra's skill (why not?) in adapting to a wide range of soil and climatic conditions means they're planted where others might fail. Petrol stations, road verges, roundabouts. A set-and-forget plant, if there were such a thing. In humans, qualities like adaptability, resilience, and vigour are celebrated and championed. We give medals to such people. But if you happen to be a person of the vegetal nation, yet still hold such qualities, you're in trouble. Either you're a weed (kill kill kill!), or you're unworthy of serious garden consideration (unless you're edible, because then you are a product, not a plant, which is an entirely different thing). *Lomandra longifolia* is disparaged by many gardeners. Not because they're weak, but precisely because they're strong.

Killing plants is rarely considered a problem. (Need to raze a forest for a new suburb? Sure, no worries, mate; I'll go and grab my chainsaw.) Many religions preach non-violence, and many people don't eat animals due to not wanting to perpetuate such violence, but what about plants? Who decided plant-people (over 82% of all the biomass on Earth) are excluded from being-ness and alive-ness, therefore fair game for our savage ways?

Gardening language does not typically evoke brutality. It is all "sanctu-ary," "respite," "beauty," "wholesomeness." It is pretty and placid. Except it isn't. Gardening is not about *making* a place. It's about finding a pathway *into* a place. Being *with* a place. It's about scratching around in the physical and metaphorical undergrowth.

Find a clearing to rest in this strange and slightly uncomfortable—yet famil-iar—landscape. Feel the branches scratching your shoulders, witness the many-legged critters rustling in the soil below. Sit with yourself and the world; with growth and death, terror and beauty. Sit, and contemplate this question posed by Amitav Ghosh in *The Nutmeg's Curse*: "What if the idea that the earth teems with other beings who act, communicate, tell stories and make meaning is taken seriously?"

What do you do, as a gardener, with this question? How do you dig yourself into a place, while at the same time acknowledging the being-ness of all those you are digging around and through and with? How do you hold both the inti-macy and brutality?

***

Here is a picture: a still autumn afternoon. Light bouncing off the glassy, molten surface of the river. No wind, no clouds. The garden, sandwiched between water and bushland, is glorious. You stroll (no one walks in a garden on day like today) down the path from the house towards the river. Tea tree leaves twinkle in the light, hakea limbs stretch towards yours, *Lomandra* leaves brush against your shins as you pass. You exalt in their caress.

Or not.

Not everyone, it turns out, appreciates forced intimacy with foliage. My partner, a very tolerant and accepting man, has had enough. He does not want to elbow his way through plants in order to access our house. I've held out for years, due to my conviction that vegetal fondling is a profound daily practice. To maintain the peace, I trim a few errant hakea branches, and decide to relocate an offending *Lomandra*.

I grab the spade I bought from a nice man on King Street years ago. English oak handle, polished with years of use. Narrow blade made of Sheffield steel— the good old stuff from the halcyon days of our carbon trip. A dangerous, efficient weapon.

Slam sharp steel into soil. Pierce what is alive and essential. Wiggle, loosening life from life. Repeat until plant is adrift. Lift.

Some questions I ask myself before, during, and after the act. Questions that should make me stop but don't... Does this act of destruction mean I don't believe in the intrinsic being-ness of *Lomandra*? Will my actions disrupt the stories the plant is telling with soil? Why should I make *Lomandra* move, instead of moving around *Lomandra*? Does it hurt, being hacked in half? Am I doing *Lomandra* a service, carving them into two, or is this a story I'm telling myself to assuage my guilt? Will Lomandra survive my violence?

I can't answer my own questions, but I don't stop. I place the newly mobile *Lomandra* horizontally on a flat rock and locate the blade somewhere in the middle of the clump. Left foot on spade. One two three. Thump. Try a few times, because they're dense and strong, unwilling to be broken. I use all my bodyweight to split the plant. I cut the long, fibrous leaves in half lengthwise, a propagation trick that my mother taught me years ago. (Remove half the foliage when transplanting/planting so the plant doesn't need to work as hard while roots are recovering.) Violence in service of life. Or so I tell myself.

Georgina Reid

Holes are dug, *Lomandra* is planted. One here, one there. A big bucket of water poured gently over traumatised foliage as a housewarming present.

I am an arsehole. I am a gardener.

26 Artist's Notes: Plants Out of Place

Betty Russ

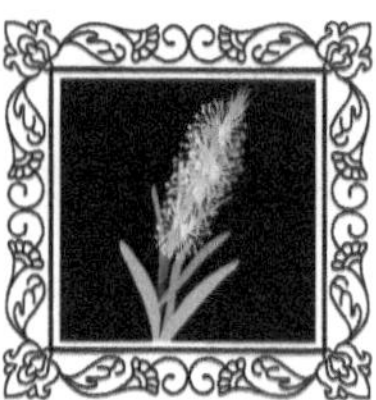

The idea of "plant intelligence," plucked from the realms of horror, science fiction, and, more recently, contemporary botanical studies, creates a critical context for contemplation and an opportunity to interrogate the real and imagined when it is restaged in the gallery setting. *A Leakage of Wholes*, presented in iterations across Meanjin/Queensland, Bundjalung/New South Wales, and Nipaluna/Tasmania, is a combination of embodied research and material investigation provoked by my inherent need to make sense of the uncertain future, and of my relationships to the botanical and more-than-human world.

What Western Linnaean taxonomic systems classify as "weeds," I suggest are really rebels, powerful tenacious nomads. In my art, I explore them as "plants out of place," possessing an immutable loquacity in the knowledge they hold of the capitalocene, and a clairvoyant insight into the schematic narratives of where we are headed.

The common water hyacinth, *Pontederia crassipes*, indigenous to the Amazonian basin, is one of the globe's most voracious "weeds," thriving on every continent except Antarctica. It chokes water systems all over the world, depriving the native ecosystem of oxygen, water volume, and sunlight. For humans, it can displace entire villages by destroying local fish populations. Unsurprisingly, it was spread by colonists for its ornamental qualities. Now, we face a mass crisis caused by industrialised agricultural practices pumping outflow into the water, full of nutrients that create optimal conditions for the water hyacinth. It is perversely beautiful to see when one does not realise what it is and what it does. It gathers in heavy flowering blankets with glossy, plump green foliage and delicate spears of mauve blooms. Devastatingly beautiful, and devastatingly deadly to native life.

To control the water hyacinth, the most common means is, unfortunately, poison. Some communities remove it manually and process it as compost. Others pound it, dry it, and weave it into practical objects. The system is obviously corrupted, but still the hyacinth persists. In my work, I speculate that, ironically, when our delicate ecologies collapse, it will be the weeds—the hyacinths, the tea tree, and other commonly displaced plants—that we look to for our critical dependence on the vegetal. I imagine weeds' capacity augmenting into voluminous sentience to resuscitate and repopulate after the inevitable decimation of their plant peers. I ask myself: how can I work with the speculatively sentient plants, acknowledging them as the potential operators and inventors of an apparatus of eco-revival?

Plant "consciousness", and imminent global catastrophe, have long created a tension around the vegetal, the more-than-human. Popular culture uses speculative fiction, science fiction, fantasy, and horror to simultaneously descant upon and ignore mounting eschatological terror. I am drawn to the unreal, the unimaginable, "the weird and the eerie" (to quote Mark Fisher's title), and provocative ideas that emerge from experimental investigations into other possible worlds. While mining the discourse of retro-speculative science fiction in my research, I frequently encounter histories of the future that are being realised in the present. This prompts me to look further and further back into ecological, human, and spiritual pasts that have become prophetic in their tales and truths. The vegetal world is ancient and continuing; it is past, present, and future. In my practice, I evoke the vegetal as a vocal signifier of what has been and what is to come.

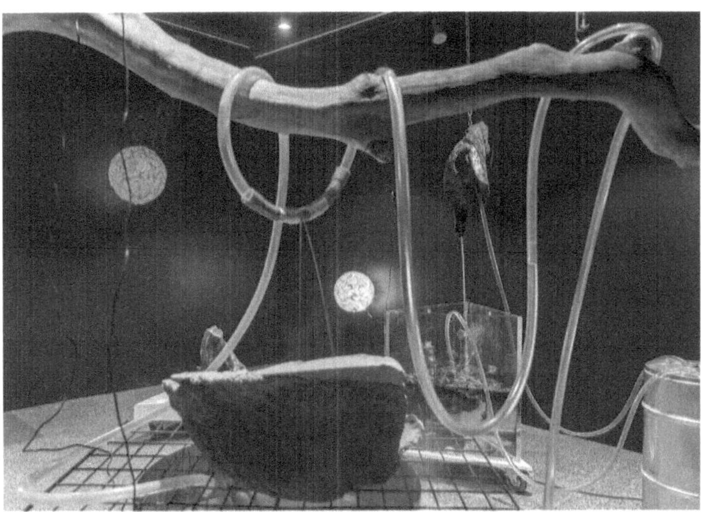

Figure 1. Betty Russ, *A Leakage of Wholes*, 2022. Installation view at Metro Arts. Photo credit: Louis Lim. (Image courtesy of the artist).

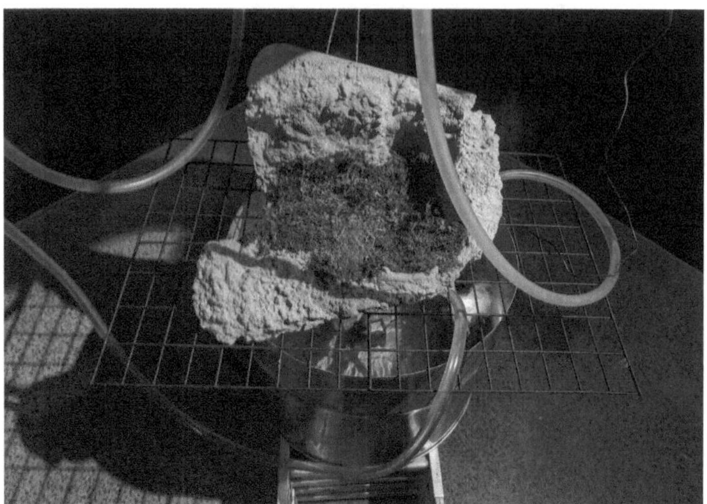

Figure 2. Betty Russ, *A Leakage of Wholes*, 2022. Installation view at Metro Arts. Photo credit: Louis Lim. (Image courtesy of the artist).

Living on Widjabul-Wyabul country of the Bundjalung nation, also known as Lismore, New South Wales, I am constantly grateful for the company of the *Melaleuca quinquenervia*—called the tea tree in English, and *kallara* in the Bundjalung language. The tea tree is an essential part of swamp and coastal ecologies and is used by the Indigenous cultures of the east coast of New South Wales and southeast Queensland; it is also native to parts of New Caledonia and Papua New Guinea. The tea tree is used for coolamons, food preparation, a source of sweetness, beverages, and as an antiseptic. It is also utilised for land stabilisation, windbreaks, and the essential oil is used broadly by the medical, cleaning, and cosmetic industries. The tea tree signifies seasonal shifts, and in this era of increasing risk of disaster acts as a vibrant, floral harbinger of climate change. The tree's trunk is akin to soft, papery human skin or sheets of delicate tissue, and I often find myself affectionately stroking it. Its sight, scent, and sound bring a sense of comfort and place to me.

While welcome in Australia, the tea tree is deemed a dangerous weed in Florida, where the Everglades is a perfect home for it—humid with brackish swamps. It was first introduced to the United States as a governmental effort to "dry up" the stolen homelands of the First Nations Calusa, Tequesta, Jega, and Ais. The tea tree is a counterpoint to the water hyacinth because it thrives in areas of low nutrients, high acidity, and moderate salinity, yet both can exist where they are tempestuously unwanted, brought by the most degradational, invasive menace of colonisation. They are both *plants out of place.*

Although weed control is essential for the maintenance of more delicate, threatened species and habitats, my work proposes that we reconceive our definition of weeds as something displaced rather than necessarily nefarious. I ask the viewer to consider the vegetal and more-than-human world with equity and a sense of partnership, giving time and respect to ancient and burgeoning ideas of plant agency, paying attention to their patterns and stories.

In my work, I tease out my tangential preoccupations with the brain candy of fantastic science fiction, and the mind-bending, world-time reality (following on from Ursula K. Le Guin) of the vegetal and more-than-human existence. I ask myself: if the idea of plant consciousness is absurd, then why do we anthropomorphically lay blame onto these plants out of place, as if they disobey us by persisting to flourish where they were involuntarily brought? Given that our environment is so catastrophically on the brink of inundation or fiery aridity, do we ignore, degrade, and disdain plants that may hold some key to our own survival? *A Leakage of Wholes* skewers assumptions and provokes reflection on the true meaning of "weeds."

27   The Life/Death of Plants: An Interview

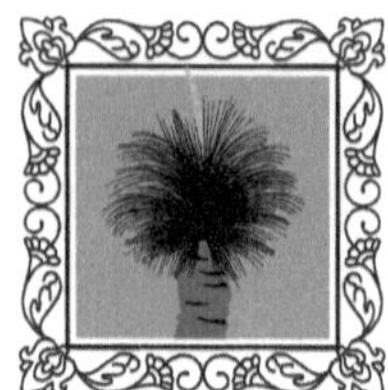

Marie Sierra and Prue Gibson

MS: If you were a plant, where in the world would you be?

PG: While I suspect I am kin to the banksia tree, I also know which plant I would like to be. After all, this tree is the banksia's cousin, and we all need each other to thrive. It's the Xanthorrhoea, a grass tree: the cadi tree of Cadigal land. They are warrior trees. Sturdy survivors. Sometimes it takes twenty years for the cadi tree's thick stem, the caudex, to emerge. Like a voice worth listening to, it takes time for the cadi to show herself. Rough, thickened, and coarse, the cadi's caudex is sturdy and immovable. Not a trunk, but a substantial, woody base. Not even a devastating bushfire could overwhelm the cadi trees. I know this for a fact.

In October 2020, a runaway bushfire at Sydney's North Head ravaged a site of endangered Eastern Suburbs Banksia Scrub, which was dense with banksias, cadi trees, coastal wattle and tea trees, leptospermum, prickly moses, and hardenbergia. The fire was the result of a disastrous hazard reduction, gone very wrong. 62 hectares were ravaged. When I visited shortly afterwards (I snuck in), the only plants that were green were the Xanthorrhoea trees. Some blackened banksias and tea trees showed signs of survival, but the scene was brutal, devastating.

The scrub has slowly started to recover since 2020, but the tea trees are growing too quickly and are crowding out the lower storeys. The view from the remnant scrub at North Head is an epic vista that inclines towards South Head, across the mouth of the harbour. It's impossible not to think of early days of invasive settlement when you have this panorama. It's impossible not to remember what Brenden Kerin from Redfern's Metro Land Council told me about the ESBS scrub—that prior to colonial times, there were regular cultural burns of the scrub to keep the low grasses down and the lower branches of the trees clear. Before settlement, the tea trees worked in synergy with the other trees and didn't grow too big. Non-Indigenous human impact has messed up the natural balance of the ecology.

That day I visited the scrub after the fires, my first instinct was to weep. As I walked across the soot, peppered with burnt phones and bottles (kids must have had quiet drinking sessions under cover of the bush) and hurdled the burnt logs, I felt the ash stick to my nostrils. There was still heat in the ground. I bent carefully to walk beneath blackened boughs and unstable burnt tree branches, and tiptoed across the dirty, aeolian, sandy soil. That was when I saw the dots of green in the mid-distance. Dozens of cadi trees that weren't black. The scene was either black or grey, save these trees.

The cadi trees, with their dark, thick stems and their waterfalls of sharp green foliage, welcome controlled fire and smoke. Their flowers are triggered by fire; this is called serotiny. Many of the Eastern Suburbs Banksia Scrub plants also welcome fire, such as the banksia whose cone follicles release seeds after fire. But... not that much fire. Not annihilating fire.

The Xanthorrhoea, the grass tree, is actually not a grass nor a tree. It's related to the lily species. As is often the case, our western English language is inaccurate and/or inadequate to match the complexity and sophistication of plants. Instead, this plant is the cadi. Proud, strong. Survivor. If I were a plant, I would like to have the strength of the cadi.

MS: What advice would you have for a fellow grass tree that has been languishing in a neighbour's front yard in a pot for some months while they are renovating? I think it may be asking to be rescued. Here is a photo of it. How did it come to this, and what does that say about our relationship to plants?

PG: There is a lot of shame associated with accidentally killing plants. It's easy to murder vegetal life. Too much water, too little; too much sun, too little. Not the right kind of soil, burned by too much manure. However, is there something about plant abandonment that is much worse? Humans abandon pets at alarming rates too. Is pet abandonment worse than plant-abandoning? Are cut flowers okay, but harvesting from the bush (crown land or national parks) is unethical?

The problem with the photo you have given me, Marie, is that it's hard to see the context. The ethics of this particular grass tree is difficult to evaluate, because I can't quite make out the details. The photo shows red- and yellow-topped garbage bins in the background and an autumnal, red-leaved tree in the foreground. In between are two plastic black pots. One looks like a neglected jade tree, and the other is the grass tree you mention. It has no green foliage, but only the wide caudex base—a caudex that could be a decade old, based on its breadth. Where the foliage should be splaying out at the top, there seem to be wounds. Did the foliage get knocked off? Was this grass tree the subject of a previous burn? The caudex looks very blackened, too.

I remember when I had my first real job, at the Art Gallery of New South Wales in Sydney—this would have been 1995—I walked through the Domain and across Martin Place to get lunch. I was walking with the curator I worked with at the time, Hendrik Kolenberg. As we crossed the square, we saw a father grab his son (aged about three years old) and give him about six really hard smacks, more like whacks, on the back of his bare legs. My stomach lurched and I remember, being pregnant, finding this violence upsetting. Hendrik put a hand on my arm and said: "you don't know what happened just prior to those smacks. You don't know what that child is like or what that father is like." In other words, don't judge someone else's life.

I often think about what I saw and Hendrik's reply. I once threw a pear at one of my sons when he was sixteen, in white-hot anger, and felt very ashamed of this. Shame is a powerful tool and an even more powerful benchmark for future behaviour. One of my plant humanities colleagues, Marcello Di Paola, has edited a book about plant ethics and creates a minefield of vegetal-value concepts. The book, *Plant Ethics* (Routledge 2018), focuses on relational versus value-in-nature plant ethics. Relational plant ethics interrogates the human practices that relate to plants, e.g. the normative criteria of plant cultivation (including flower-growing and cutting). Value-in-nature is less about the reasons to value plants. It's not about relations. Instead, it focuses on the values of the plants themselves, such as their integrity and their flourishing.

So, there is the notion of the value of plants, intrinsic to themselves. This suggests that plants have value, with or without human witness, or even with or without human consciousness. Then, there is the premise that plants have value because of what they do and how they thrive or flourish; this is the value-in-nature model. The only problem with this model is: what happens when the plants are no longer in nature and no longer thriving? Does their value deterio-rate over time, in time with their diminished flourishing?

Karen Houle writes about plant ethics in a way that extends her ecofeminist writings, by reminding humans of our entrenched dualities—left/right, either/or, good/bad approaches. These inherited approaches do not account for the

Marie Sierra and Prue Gibson

non-binary thinking of plants that might be more appropriate for the multi-plicities and distributions of plant life. Also in this book, Angela Kallhoff talks about "flourishing" as a kind of yardstick for value, against which plants are harmed or benefitted.

If we apply one of these ethical approaches to the abandoned grass tree, left in front of your neighbour's house, it could be Kallhoff's "flourishing" concept. Kallhoff describes "flourishing" as the development of a good life according to innate capacities. If plants, as we now know, can learn, remember, and decision-make (Gagliano), then these activities and organisational capabilities can be seen as "flourishing," or developing a good life. Plants undertake their activities in order to thrive, to develop well. A plant that "flourishes" is living a good life. It is vital and copes with stresses. Kalhoff says this provides a yardstick for assessing harm.

So, for Marie, her neighbour's grass tree is a good example. It had "flourished" before it was cast aside. We know this because the caudex (or thick trunk) is well established and wide. It has no foliage now, no green leaves anymore. Therefore, it is likely that it has been harmed or damaged. This grass tree has been thwarted in its "flourishing." Hence, this pre-moral position suggests that its treatment was unethical. Plants work hard at their own "flourishing." So, being stopped from that process of developing a good life is not ethical.

Marie's grass tree no longer lives a good life, no longer works to develop one: it no longer "flourishes." What follows is morality. Whose responsibility is it—the grass tree owner who abandoned the tree? Or Marie's responsibility because she has witnessed the non-"flourishing" and has a moral framework within which she may or may not act to restore that "flourishing." What, Marie, have you decided to do?

MS: I heard back from my neighbours about the grass tree. The workmen checked with the owners and said I could take it. They also thought it might be dead. If you are a grass tree, how do I know if you're dead?

PG: The cells of plants keep changing after death, like dead human cells do. Decomposition takes time. For plants, decomposition of leaves takes one to three years. A human body in a coffin can take ten years to decompose, or around ten days if left outdoors, with the help of such insects as maggots.

Usually we consider a qualitative end-of-human-life as being when the human has stopped breathing and their heart no longer pumps. What follows is a declaration of death. This declaration of death is less common with plants, and this is yet again connected to vegetal value. The timely pronouncement of human death is important for legal reasons, but plants do not enjoy legal personhood, although there are a couple of exceptions, such as the Whanganui river ecology in New Zealand. There, plants that are damaged or prevented from living can be represented in a court of law.

As a result, the timing and accounting for plant death is different from animal versions. Should a plant be considered dead as soon as it is harvested? When a plant is pulled up by the roots or cut away from the rest of a plant, it's possible to think this might be the moment of attributable death because it can no longer grow, draw up water, extend its roots for nourishment, or photosynthesise. However, a cutting could be replanted or grafted. The end, surely then, is not at the point of harvest.

Think of the cut flower industry, where there is economic value from the moment the plant was cut, through the floristry industry's various iterations and transports, to the moment it's placed in a vase in someone's home. Its longevity in the home is prized. But this may be considered a longevity of death, rather than of life. Humans are not harvested, as plants are, so the point of death has more clarity with the former.

Plants in the herbarium have a different story. In this case, plants are collected from the landscape, brought back to the gardens, and pressed between newspaper sheets. Then, once they are clamped between board, they are placed in the freezer for a week to kill off any insects. The idea is to dry out the cut plants, so they will later be mounted on a page of paper using tape and labelled.

However, are these plant specimens dead? They keep on changing once they are mounted. Their cells continue to work for some time. They lose colour and texture in their ongoing decomposition. I have smelled the scent of plants when I open herbarium specimen sheets. I have felt the life/death of plants taped to a page. I'm not sure I would use the language of death to these specimens because they maintain their value as archival artefacts. They continue to have value, as subjects for genetic testing and molecular research. Some are extinct in the wild and are the only record of previous life. For this reason, their liveliness lasts longer than their habitat versions.

It is a strange irony that plants' lives are not valued as highly as human lives when they are flourishing in their natural habitats, but, then, once they are dead, they are kept and revered in boxes in a human institution. You could argue plants are considered to be flourishing once they are dead because the herbarium valuing of plants is high, higher in many cases than in the landscape.

It begs the question: are dead plants in herbaria less threatening because they have lost their unknown and inaccessible liveliness? Humans do not still quite understand what plant life and independent agencies of plant lives mean. Humans still consider humans as having more agential life. As discussed above, plants are not considered lively even when they are thriving. Plant value as lively thriving or flourishing is considered less important than animals' and insects' liveliness or aliveness.

Human death can be attributed to abandonment and lack of care, and this could be considered the same with respect to plants. Plants can die naturally of old age or disease or drought, and this kind of plant death can be considered tangible and/or legitimate, only if we accept that we don't know whether or not plants choose to die.

To finally answer the question: how a grass tree knows it is dead? I suspect that a grass tree, kept in a plastic pot and located in a chilly Melbourne suburb, is already pretty confused—not just about death, but life too.

MS: I think it was indeed confused and had been for some time. In fact, its life was likely on a tragic trajectory from the time it was harvested for the commercial market—legally, one hopes—until its supposed end. I say "supposed" because after my exchange with the builders (who I determined were not gardeners, but a sort of backyard blitz crew), who left the plant in a certain part of this neighbour's front yard for me, it disappeared again when I went to collect it. The weather had been Melbourne winter at its dreariest—a fortnight of grey and incipient storms that made the days a linked-up chain of drizzly patches—so I wasn't walking past the plant every day. When I did walk down to the house again, where it had been sitting was replaced with a red Cordyline that had been "planted out." The grass tree was gone, undoubtedly in the skip that had been in the driveway for months, but had now also been taken away. They probably also thought it was dead, as apparently there is a high failure rate for them, particularly if not planted out, and from the way it sat in the pot, I think it never was. The owner of the house seems to be away for long stretches, and if it was potted for a long time, it probably dried out. So, it likely died of neglect.

I had noticed one thing about its caudex, which was that it looked like it had been ringbarked, but in a spiral. The groove it caused was consistently about 2 cm in width, presenting as an upward curving line around the caudex; it didn't look accidental. It was as if its dried frond stubs had been picked off in a "she loves me, she loves me not" game, which, of course, is an aggressive act on a plant. The hypothetical scenario, wherein it died because it was firstly transplanted from the bush, then never planted out, became dry, and was then physically damaged, when taken together, seemed like a very sad tale.

In reflecting on this, it reminded me that Klaus Eder has noted that our interactions with nature have such a "moral dimension" (Eder 26), but that our focus is often on the "use value" of the natural world. He notes that the "modern relationship to nature has reduced the symbolic significance of nature to a minimum. Nature has become a symbolic form without a significance of its own. Even garden plots, a refuge for the symbolic significance of nature, are being depreciated to the 'quick and easy'. Plants such as the thuja tree lose their earlier symbolic significance; they are nothing more than a hedge that requires no work, provides visual protection against others and creates the illusion of being evergreen. These remnants of symbolic signifiers of nature express a relationship to nature that strives to efface everything which cannot be measured by the yardstick of utility. Modern society has made great strides in the attempt to erase these broader symbolic meanings from its collective consciousness" (Eder viii).

You had noted what the symbolic meanings of a grass tree were for you at the outset of this interview. I thought it interesting you called it a cadi tree of Cadigal land, as I tend to associate them with south Australia, where they are sometimes called "yakka trees," a name derived from the hard work of harvesting the sap, which can be used as a glue. And they also occur not far from where I live in Victoria, at Wilson's Promontory, a three-hour drive south towards Bass Strait. In the end, it wasn't the Victorian weather that did the grass tree in, but a system that started with a lack of respect for its symbolic meaning, which set off a series of events wherein the use value supplanted any other meaning. When there was no longer use value, it was discarded.

MS: The next question. Is it possible to engage an allegiance with the grass tree and a discussion on plant blindness to entwine the use value in which contemporary society is so immersed with the symbolic significance of plants that Indigenous cultures worldwide value, create, and preserve? By identifying these differences, do we work our way towards solutions and shared approaches, or continue to endorse their separation?

                                                                     Marie Sierra and Prue Gibson

PG: I like your question about "use value versus symbolism." I think there is only a problem (or a division) when use tips over into instrumentalisation of plants—using plants with a greater human action in mind, without care or thought for the plant. Symbolism and meaning, whether Indigenous or non-Indigenous, are created, constructed, and shared, but they also constantly change and shift, as memory and association do too.

For example, last weekend, I decided to make some protection medicine for my three children. As content, I used three trees I'd previously chosen for each of my children: an angophora (the vessel), a casuarina (wise sage) and a frangipani (fertility, overcoming difficulty). These vegetal/cultural associations were derived from the complex web of my own lifethe stories whispered to me by family or blown from the pages of books, about trees. These cultural relations repeat, diverge, and refresh.

Prior to the vegetal cooking process, I set about gathering ingredients. There was a blanket of casuarina needles and seeds under the grove across the road from my house. I asked permission from the tree and gathered a few needles and seeds, along with a small amount of broken-off bark. The fallen and dried leaves of my back-garden, potted frangipani were perfect, and, again, I asked permission of the frangipani to shave off a little of its branch to dry in preparation. Finally, I had to travel to my childhood park to find some angophora leaves and twigs that had fallen in plentiful supply. I was confident I had not disrupted the natural seedbanks at each place, I had not over-harvested, I had not taken disrespectfully.

But isn't what I've just written typically white settler—to claim a stake of moral superiority? I think it might be a complex form of re-colonial imperialism to extract and extract. Have I not, in fact, just stolen vegetal stuff? I asked permission, but I didn't hear a human reply, nor a vegetal one that could be translated. I think I just hoped permission was granted.

I am not a tree, no matter how I wish I were. Even if I stand on one leg and throw my arms up in the air and wave them around (like we were taught to do when I was a pre-schooler), I am still not a tree. Morally, I like to think of trees as kin, to write about them as my community. But I've not heard back if this is acceptable. My only experiences are of sound and movement in trees and plants that I have come to know. While I feel deeply connected to them, I'll never know if the feeling is reciprocated. Perhaps this is the real source of solastalgia—that humans don't know the language, can't speak tree.

Nevertheless, I waited until this collected vegetal matter had dried, and then I burned it, using a sage bundle to keep the fire alight. I snipped a bit more of the sage into the fire too, as an extra cleansing uniformly followed across many cultures. Once the ash was cool, I tipped it into three glass jars and corked them. My children received their protection ash with their usual mix of kind reverence and mild confusion.

I'm not sure if the three trees involved will know what has happened. The frangipani bore witness, and the casuarina was close enough to notice the smoke. But I'll never know if they were complicit. I do know that I have been making concoctions and elixirs, charms and potions for over eleven years and that I draw on my own history of experience and reading, both real and imagined. It is unclear if my protection-ash-making is ethical or appropriate. It is unclear if it is appropriation or ventriloquy. It is unclear if it will work or fail. However, it is ongoing: these cultural acts emerge and then vanish. The urge rises up, and I can't resist. Like writing. Like my use of oxygen to breathe.

I have started to wonder whether plants care if we care or not. Plants don't need human consciousness or human witness or human permission to flourish, to thrive. So, why are those of us in the plant humanities spending so much time trying to impress them?

PG: My question to you, this time around, Marie:

When you realised you hadn't saved the neighbours' grass tree in time and that it probably had been chucked out in the skip, how did you feel? What will you do next?

MS: I was disappointed. I'm the kind of person who buys plants that are on the quick-sale table at a garden nursery to see if I can bring them back from the brink. Whatever success I have in that is really warming; about half of them come back.

But there was an upside. It turned my attention to the grass tree I already have in my front garden, which suffered quite a bit in the decade I was living interstate, much of which was during the drought. I planted it in about 1994, and, typically, it grew slowly, but quite well. It even flowered about three times over the next fifteen years—although flowering is a sign of stress, not of well-being. When I returned to it in 2020, it was barely alive. Much of the garden was unrecognisable, but it was the grass tree I was most concerned for as it really looked on the brink. I had planted it near to the house as it likes a little lime and the footings of the old brick house leech, just enough from the ageing mortar to keep it happy. I have a waratah that benefits from a similar position in another part of the garden.

I've cut away some the dried skirt to get some air circulating around it and removed all the years of dried leaves from the Corymbia, which dominates the space, that had gotten wedged into the base of its long, spiked leaves. Now that it's been in its position for nearly thirty years, I wonder if I planted it too close to the house, but I dare not relocate it. I've also been considering how to get it to flower again. I've read if you put a box filled with newspaper over it and set it alight, you can smoke it into flowering. How to do that and not set the house on fire is the conundrum that has held me back, but through responding to your question, I've done more research and read that another way to cause the stress that will encourage it to flower is to place a small stone on the growing tip, as "the stone causes enough stress that the flower will form, a little like a pearl forming inside an oyster" (Allgreen Nursery & Garden).

I thought I would see if I can put that lovely simile into action. I have a stone garden out the back, so literally thousands of stones from which to choose, particularly of the recommended 5-8-cm size. But first, I tried to have a look at its growing tip. It has lots of new leaf growth, so much so that I can't really see a tip at all. Peering into the centre from where the new green shoots emerge, it seems somehow wrong to be dropping something into the heart of this plant when I was just plucking litter out of it only three years ago. Its growth is finally progressing now—I know someone whose grass tree has grown much more in the same timeframe—and is due for fertilising in the autumn. It somehow doesn't seem quite right to stress it at all, but particularly when it's made good progress. Smoke-infused water could also work and would be a lot less invasive, so I'll set off to explore that method.

I hadn't previously considered that I could also propagate new grass trees from the seeds, and that is a possibility if it does flower and set seed. No special treatment is needed to germinate the seeds, but they do have a low success rate, so sowing many is recommended. It's not lost on me that had I done that in the other years it flowered, I'd have a garden of "young" grass trees now. They grow slowly, at around 2 cm per year, and can live to 350-450 years old. If it flowers in the next year, I could have new grass trees to enjoy if I grow into old age, by which time many more of the Xanthorrhoea could be classified as "vulnerable to extinction," as Xanthorrhoea arenaria and Xanthorrhoea bracteata now have.

Stepping back from that, a handful of grass trees in a suburban garden will make no difference to retaining a species, and I question whether that is a justification for the "use value" of controlling nature for my own purposes, those of being able to enjoy a grass tree that flowers—a further extension of the gratification I receive in "repairing" plants. What do you think, Prue; is this misguided and too singular to be of any consequence, or does every action of seeing plants matter?

PG: To be honest, I do believe in grassroots conservation. Your saving of one or more Xanthorrhoea trees is hugely important, because it keeps the tree's story alive. Even if some species are vulnerable or critically endangered, they're not gone yet. And even better than seeing plants is engaging with plants, as you do. If everyone made a point of engaging with even one tree, that is an improvement for ecological sustainability, but also for the quality of human experience.

PG: Do you think art/dance/narrative are good tools for spreading that plant-seeing message? How do you think art works to make the vegetal more real? And what plant are you?

MS: Our lack of ability to see plants is an issue of culture, so addressing plant blindness is best approached through cultural methods. I think all cultural practices are suited to increasing the visibility and awareness of plants, of "seeing" them. Visual art, music, dance, theatre can all be engaged in manifesting the vegetal, and not just in didactic ways, but in nuanced and enduring ways that become part of our social fabric. Awareness of the environment, of climate change, and of plants is derived from a posture that is culturally formed. However, culture is both enduring and agile, with a plasticity akin to the plasticity of the brain; it can continue to expand and develop. One of the key purposes of art is to "shape" a new approach to a preconception, an ideal, or a problem, which can deliver innovative perceptions by calling into question what we think we "know." In the case of plant blindness, art forms can cut through hundreds of years of anthropocentricism by giving plants a platform from which they can be both represented and recognised.

The grass tree I've had for years is doing well now after some recent rain, and getting a lot of new, green shoots. I might not give it smoke water for another year to let it recover further. The Corymbia and other plants in the garden barely flowered this past year, instead getting a lot more leaf from all the rain

                    The Life/Death of Plants: An Interview

last spring. It can wait—and let's be clear, that really means I can wait—a little longer, as a long period of neglect takes time to come back from.

Another treasured plant in the garden is the one I identify with the most, and that's the waratah. I planted it in a similar spot—close to the concrete footings of the brick house—even before the grass tree, to replace a banksia the previous owners had planted that had run its course. While I lived interstate, the waratah was not pruned annually and got tall and sparse, and I've been cutting it back after every spring flowering since returning three years ago. It is a bit hit and miss to prune, as sometimes it will shoot off older wood, but often not. It is very resilient in general, but also a bit fickle and challenging—with the reward being the incredible blooms in spring. It will re-sprout after fire, something it shares with the grass tree, so I might try the smoke water to see if it has any effect on its vitality.

It grows just above the fence, and there is someone in my neighbourhood that ripped off an entire a branch of it last year, reaching over from the footpath, which would have required partially climbing the fence, to get a prized flower. They are not common in the area where I live and very showy, so the temptation was too much. After that event, I pruned it to encourage growth in the opposite direction. Ironically, that flower thief is definitely a person that sees plants. They are notorious in our street come spring, as they're completely non-apologetic, even when caught in the act. I can't blame them for being able to see.

Works Cited

Allgreen Nursery & Garden. "Growing a Grass Tree in Your Garden," https://www.allgreen.com.au/garden-advice/growing-a-grass-tree-in-your-garden, 2022. Accessed 5 Feb. 2024.

Di Paola, Marcello, et al. *Plant Ethics: Concepts and Applications*. Routledge, 2018.

Eder, Klaus. *The Social Construction of Nature*. Sage, 1996.

Gagliano, Monica, et al. "Extended Cognition in Plants: Is It Possible?" *Plant Signalling and Behavior*, vol. 15, no. 2, 2020.

Houle, Karen. "Animal Vegetable, Mineral: Ethics as Extension or Becoming: The Case of Becoming Plant." *Journal for Critical Animal Studies*, vol. 9, nos. 1-2, 2011, pp. 429-32.

Kallhoff, Angela. "Plants in Ethics: Why Flourishing Deserves Moral Respect." *Environmental Values*, vol. 23, no. 6, 2014, pp. 685-700.

Kerin, Brenden. Barlow Street Forest Public Program Address, 1 May 2020. Sydney, Australia.

Notes on Contributors

Giovanni Aloi is an author, educator, and curator specializing in the representation of nature and the environment in art. He is the Editor in Chief of *Antennae: The Journal of Nature in Visual Culture.* Aloi is the author of *Art & Animals* (2011), *Speculative Taxidermy: Natural History, Animal Surfaces, and Art in the Anthropocene* (2018), *Why Look at Plants? The Vegetal Emergence in Contemporary Art* (2019), *Lucian Freud – Herbarium* (2019), *Posthumanism in Art and Science* (2020) and *Estado Vegetal* (2023). Aloi has contributed to BBC radio programs, worked at Whitechapel Art Gallery and Tate Galleries in London, and currently is USA correspondent for *Esse Magazine.* Aloi has curated exhibitions in the US and Europe and is co-editor of the University of Minnesota Press series Art after Nature.

Matthew Beach is an artist and researcher. Embedded within materialist discourses, his practice spans photography, printmaking, video, installation, and writing in order to explore the entanglements between place, the photographic, and care in more-than-human worlds. Two primary strands of inquiry include companion relations with (sub)tropical flora and gelatinous zooplankton. He is currently on sabbatical from his PhD in the School of Geography, Queen Mary University of London as a Sabbatical Officer within the Queen Mary Students' Union. Alongside sociologist and senior lecturer Giulia Carabelli, he co-curates Cabinet Cultures, an ongoing cross-industry research partnership exploring how humans attach value to and can collectively change attitudes towards houseplants. Previously he has been a visiting researcher and scholar in the Lamar Dodd School of Art, University of Georgia, artist-in-residence at The Sustainable Darkroom, and research and teaching fellow in printmaking at City and Guilds of London Art School. He holds a BFA from the College of the Arts, University of Florida and an MFA from the Slade School of Fine Art, University College London. More at http://matthewbeach.org/.

Tamryn Bennett is a poet and founder of Poem Forest. She grew up in a plant nursery on Dharawal land where she lives, writes and regenerates the escarpment.

Edward Colless is a freelance writer who has published in a variety of fields both academic and journalistic, working as an art critic, book reviewer and features writer, as editor and publisher, and has also ventured into travel writing and fiction. In addition to wide-ranging activities in tertiary education (art history, contemporary art, performance, aesthetics), he has also worked professionally in architecture, cinema, broadcasting, theatre direction, and in curating. Colless's current projects include the aesthetics of ruin, science fiction and fictional science, also hoaxed and outsider literature.

Prudence Gibson is an author and academic at the School of Art and Design, University of NSW, Sydney. She is Lead Investigator of an Australian Research Council grant in partnership with Sydney's Royal Botanic Gardens Herbarium. Her latest book is *The Plant Thieves* (NewSouth Books, 2023) which chases decolonial and psychedelic stories of plants and people of the Sydney herbarium. Other recent books are *The Plant Contract* (Brill Rodopi, 2018), *Janet Laurence: The Pharmacy of Plants* (NewSouth Books, 2015). She has contributed chapters to books for fellow plant studies scholars Michael Marder, Giovanni Aloi, Monica Gagliano and Catriona Sandilands.

Ryan Gordon. Fifty lifetimes as a skink, reincarnated once only as a humanoid, fascinated by what he sees which is mostly cactus-centric, has four heads with distinct personalities, grew up on a vortex. Fin.

Lisa Gorton is a poet and novelist. She holds a doctorate in English Literature from Oxford University. She has written poems for the catalogue of the Adelaide Biennial of Contemporary Art *Before and After Science* (2010), for *Melbourne Now* (National Gallery of Victoria), and for Izabela Pluta's artwork *Apparent Distance* in The National (2019) at the Art Gallery of New South Wales. Lisa has also contributed poetry to Izabela Pluta's artist's book *Figures of slippage and oscillation* (Perimeter Press, 2021), and for Buxton Contemporary's multi-disciplinary project *This is a Poem* (2021). Her awards include the Prime Minister's Award for Fiction, the NSW Premier's People's Choice Award for Fiction, the Victorian Premier's Prize for Poetry, the Wesley Michel Wright Poetry Prize, and the Philip Hodgins Memorial Medal. Her most recent novel is *The Life of Houses*; her fourth poetry collection *Mirabilia* was published by Giramondo in 2022.

Sigi Jöttkandt is an Associate Professor in English at UNSW. She received her PhD from SUNY Buffalo under the supervision of Joan Copjec, Henry Susan and Rodolphe Gasche. She is author of *Acting Beautifully: Henry James and the Ethical Aesthetic* (2005), *First Love: A Phenomenology of the One* (2010) and the *The Nabokov Effect* (2024), along with many articles on literature, psychoanalysis and philosophy. A co-founding Director of Open Humanities Press, she edits the SeedBooks series this volume appears in.

Nick Koenig (they/them) is a geography PhD student in the University of Idaho's Earth & Spatial Science Department exploring the intersections between tree ring science (dendrochronology), critical physical geography, and more-than-human narratives. Nick has researched and published on rare Clover species in the eastern United States—specifically Kentucky—analyzing the phylogenetic relationships in the genus *Trifolium* and served in various herbaria roles for the past five years.

Verena Kuni is a scholar in the field of art, culture and media studies, and a professor for Visual Culture Studies at Goethe University, Frankfurt am Main. Among her passions is the development of inter- and transdisciplinary projects and programs at the intersections of theory and practice, and she has a crush on experimental formats. Her research and teaching, projects and publications focus on transfers between material and media cultures; media of imagination; technologies of transformation; DIY and critical making; toys and/as tools; workshops, toolboxes, and kits for inventive methods and methodologies; creative entanglements between imagination and invention; (in)visibilities and (im)materials; visual epistemologies and (con)figurations of knowledge; biotopes, biotopias, and technonaturecultures; alternate realities; and (trans)formations of time. She has published widely, print and online, on contemporary arts, culture and media. More at kuniver.se

Anna M. Lawrence (she/her) completed her PhD in historical geography at the University of Cambridge in 2023, focusing on the sociopolitical lives of flowers in Victorian Britain and Aotearoa New Zealand. Her interests lie in how history might be used to rehabilitate alternative modes of plant-human relation within the context of ecological crisis. She has published work on the use of flowers in moral regulation, and on critical plant studies and vegetal geography.

Vanessa Lemm is Pro-Vice Chancellor and Executive Dean, Faculty of Liberal Arts and Science at the University of Greenwich, London. She is a globally recognised philosopher and editor of Nietzsche-Studien and associated De Gruyter book series, two premier publication venues shaping the field of Nietzsche studies world-wide. She researches the relevance of Nietzsche's philosophy for contemporary debates in biopolitics, posthumanism and animal studies. She recently published *Homo Natura: Nietzsche, Philosophical Anthropology and Biopolitics* (EUP, 2020). Her work has been translated into 6 languages.

Deidre Martin is a Walbanja woman of the Yuin Nation. A highly respected Aboriginal Discovery Ranger for the NSW National Parks And Wildlife Service, she is also the Founding Director of her cultural enterprise Bugiya

Naway Buradja (Yesterday, Today and Tomorrow). With over 20 years of experience in cultural and community work Aunty Deidre is committed to sharing her knowledge, her connection to Country and information about her culture. She connects to her heritage through weaving and collaborating with artists from Aboriginal and non-Aboriginal cultures. Collaborations include "Connections: Your Connection, My Connection, OUR CONNECTIONS," 2020 with artist Nicole Monks, commissioned by Shoalhaven Regional Gallery, "Walk beside Me" in collaboration with Erica Seccombe and "The Plant Sensibilia Machine" with Rebecca Mayo, Lisa Gorton and Jacob Morris, both projects were exhibited at Bundanon, NSW in 2022 and 2023.

Rebecca Mayo is a Senior Lecturer at the School of Art & Design, ANU. Her practice examines how an art practice built around process, repetition and labour can produce artworks that manifest through—and reveal—practices of care. She uses site- and species-specific plant-dye to make visible the interdependence between plants and people, and the resulting relations of reciprocal care. *Habitus* (Heide Museum of Modern Art) and *It's in the bag* (Caves, Melbourne) contributed to Climarte's Art+Climate=Change Festival in 2017 and 2019. Her work *A cure for plant blindness*, was exhibited at CLIMATE CARE: Reimagining Shared Planetary Futures, at the Museum of Applied Arts (MAK), during the Vienna Biennale for Change, 2021. Recently her Plant Sensibilia Machine has enabled textile and plant collaborations with Aunty Deidre Martin, Jacob Morris and the Utsav Malayalee Samaj Community in Melton, Victoria.

Jacob Morris is a gumea-Dharrawal Ngundah of the yuin marriŋ from the Southeast Coast of New South Wales, Australia. Jacob's great grandmother Lena Chapman was one of the last Dharrawal speakers from the South Coast. She kept language alive within her family. Warren Morris, Jacob's Uncle and mentor handed down the responsibility of language to him and his cousin Joel Deaves. As well as writing poetry, Jacob teaches language and dance at Nowra East Public School.

Anna Perdibon (she/her) is independent researcher, writer, storyteller and apprentice herbalist. She likes to call herself a "gatherer of stories and herbs." Her research focuses on new animism, ethnobotany and the Vegetal Turn. She explores human-plants relations in ancient, traditional European (Alpine) and Indigenous cultures, and their connections with storytelling, art and science to inspire steps towards eco-logical living. Her research, writing and teaching are dedicated to exploring, collecting and weaving together those stories, myths, practices and ways of life that cultivate respect, care, reciprocity and creativity with plants and the ecological community, in the past and the present. Anna organizes courses, talks and walks, and collaborates with projects that seek to enhance an ecological education with plants, stories, anthropology and art in Italy and abroad. She authored the book *Mountains and Trees, Rivers and Springs: Animistic Beliefs and Practices in Ancient Mesopotamian Religion* (2019), and academic and disseminating writings in English and Italian. As part of the educational project carried out by Border Crossings, she edited the booklet *BOTANY BAY. Heritage responds to Colonialism, Climate Change and Covid* (2022). Anna lives in the mountains of Trentino-Alto Adige, Italy.

Maya Martin-Westheimer is an independent curator, artist, and arts professional with a focus on the connections between environments, ecologies, and cultural histories. She employs collaborative methods and ecologically oriented philosophies to bring diverse perspectives together for meaningful creative projects. Maya's interests encompass deep ecology, decolonial practices, environmentalism, and cultural politics. Maya is the co-founder and director of Floorplan, a creative studio focused on the intersections of art, culture, and ecology, she holds a Master's in Curating and Cultural Leadership and a Bachelor in Art History and Curating. In 2023, she completed Seeds of Radical Renewal Leadership Course with Emergence Magazine and a three-month artist residency with Woollahra Gallery at Redleaf. Recent independent curatorial projects include Rockpool Residency: Unseen Worlds (2023-24), Cool Change (in the Middle of a Heatwave) (2023), Comfort in Chaos (2022), and Physical Absence (2019). As the curator and producer of Rockpool Residency: Unseen Worlds, Maya is currently developing a site-responsive art and event day at Nielsen Park. She is concurrently producing a Nielsen Park X Floorplan Creative Field Guide. With support from Woollahra Municipal Council and Create NSW, the Rockpool Residency project serves as a collaborative initiative, uniting scientists, The Woollahra Gallery, the Sydney Institute of Marine Science, artists, designers, and First Nations perspectives for an interdisciplinary project and event day. Maya's upbringing on a reforestation farm deeply influences her environmental appreciation, guiding her inclusive and collaborative approach to curating and the arts.

Arina Melkozernova is a PhD Candidate at the Comparative Culture and Language program, Arizona State University. Arina has a multidisciplinary background including art (Intermedia), science (Biology), Environmental Humanities, Digital Humanities, educational technology and instructional design. As a researcher, Arina collaborates with communities to restore their

   Notes on Contributors

"place-embodied" narrative. She contributes to building new research pathways within academia with criteria for inclusivity, data transparency and epistemological flexibility. As a teacher, Arina applies theories and methodologies from environmental humanities, biosemiotics, science, and indigenous ecology to discuss tensions and dialogues between Western and non-Western knowledge systems that exemplify the traditional cultural practices. Arina Melkozernova was named the recipient of the 2021 Future Steward Excellence Award from the National Digital Stewardship Alliance in recognition of her work in partnership with several Indigenous communities.

Elaine Miller is Professor of Philosophy at Miami University. She researches and teaches nineteenth-century German philosophy, particularly in aesthetics and the philosophy of nature, and and contemporary European feminist theory. Her books include *Head Cases: Julia Kristeva on Philosophy and Art in Depressed Times* (Columbia University Press, 2014), *The Vegetative Soul: From Philosophy of Nature to Subjectivity in the Feminine* (SUNY Press, 2002), and an edited collection, *Returning to Irigaray: Feminist Philosophy, Politics, and the Question of Unity* (SUNY, 2006). She has also published articles in the *Hegel Bulletin*, the *Palgrave Handbook of German Romantic Philosophy*, *Idealistic Studies*, *The Journal of Nietzsche Studies*, and *Oxford Literary Review*, among others.

Anna Madeleine Raupach is a multidisciplinary Australian artist and a 2024 Fulbright Scholar at the University of Southern California's School of Cinematic Arts. She is a Senior Lecturer at the Australian National University School of Art & Design with a PhD in Media Arts from the University of New South Wales (2014). She has developed cross-disciplinary projects through residencies with the Australian Network for Art and Technology, 2022; Powerhouse Museum, Sydney, 2019; Cité Internationale des Arts, Paris, 2018; and Common Room Network Foundation, Bandung, 2017, resulting in digital and physical artworks that are exhibited internationally in solo and group exhibitions.

Georgina Reid is a writer, PhD candidate and sessional academic at the University of Technology Sydney. She's the editor of *Wonderground* print and online journal and author of *The Planthunter: Truth, Beauty, Chaos and Plants* (Thames and Hudson, 2018). Her essays and poetry have been published in books and magazines internationally. Georgina lives and works amongst she-oak trees on the banks of Dyarubbin, the Hawkesbury River.

Heather Rogers is a digital environmental humanist and reproductive justice advocate. She is a graduate of the Digital Humanities program at McGill University where her research focused on women's contributions to botanical history, new materialism, critical plant studies, and the relationship between technology and nature.

Betty Russ is an artist and arts worker living on Widjabul Wia-bul country, Bundjalung Nation (Lismore). Working across sculpture, assemblage, installation, sound, and embodied research, her practice ferments between and around the philosophies and renderings of eschatological terror, speculative +/ science fiction, hauntology, spirituality, the-weird-and-the-eerie. Material manifestations protrude from hypnagogic fantasy, searching for psychological mitigation to the abject shock of the past, and sweaty white-knuckled fear of the future. Betty is also co-founder of Elevator ARI, an emerging artist-run gallery and studio space.

Erica Seccombe is a practicing artist with 30 years' experience working, teaching and contributing to the sector. She is a Senior Lecturer at the ANU School of Art & Design, living in semi-rural NSW on Ngambri, Ngunawal and Ngunnawal countries. Her interdisciplinary arts practice spans traditional lens-based imaging, print media and drawing, to experimental digital platforms using frontier scientific visualisation software. She is recognised as a pioneer of time-resolved (4D) micro-X-ray Computed Tomography through her investigations of immersive stereoscopic digital projection installations and 3D printing. A continuing theme arising in her work is the complex human relationships we have with nature and our natural environments, whether through social, cultural, or technological factors. Erica's practice articulates ways to position her own experiences and concerns as an artist of living at this time of uncertainty where human activity has had a dominant influence on the environment and climate.

Marie Sierra is the Director of CoVA alongside being the Dean of the Faculty of Fine Arts and Music at the University of Melbourne. She was formerly the Deputy Dean at UNSW Sydney, Faculty of Art and Design. Her practice as an artist and as an arts writer draws on her research on nature as a social construct. Examining issues around the consumption of both goods and natural resources, she has held numerous solo and group exhibitions within Australia and overseas. She has won awards for her artwork, and has had five Australia Council Grants, three Australian Research Council Grants, and an Australian Office of Learning and Teaching grant. She currently serves on the Melbourne Theatre Company Board and the Australian National Academy of Music Board.

Anna-Sophie Springer is a writer, curator, and director of the publishing atelier K. Verlag in Berlin. Through a versatile research-led and collaborative practice, she interrogates forms of cultural retention and creates interventions which aim to contribute to the strengthening of a more vibrant, feminist, and ecologically-responsible world. In addition to her work with K., together with Etienne Turpin she initiated and organized the exhibition-led research project *Reassembling the Natural* (2013–2023), as well as the *intercalations: paginated* exhibition series (2015–2023). She is the author of Inter Folia Aves (trans. Blanca Gago, greylock editorial, 2024) and co-editor of the two-part publication project Robert Zhao Renhui: Seeing Forest accompanying the 2024 Singapore Pavilion at La Biennale di Venezia. Anna-Sophie received her PhD from the Centre for Research Architecture, Goldsmiths, University of London and is currently Verwaltungsprofessorin in Transformation Design at the Institute for Design Research at HBK Braunschweig, Germany. The text included in this publication is based on her recent PhD thesis.

Christina Stadlbauer (AT, BE, FIN) is an artist, researcher and creative producer. She works at the interstices of arts and sciences, and develops research based artistic interventions including installations, performances, video works, rituals, lectures, publications. Her work has been shown in Europe and around the world - Kaai Theater (Brussels, 2011), Salo Museum of Contemporary Art (Finland, 2011); Pixelache Festival (2010–2016, Finland), Jardín Etnobotánico de Oaxaca (Mexico, 2012), Fundaciò Joan Mirò (Barcelona, 2018), Kanal Centre Pompidou, Brussels (2019) and others. Christina's work reflects her deep respect and engagement with non human entities and the relation between culture and nature. She obtained a PhD in Natural Sciences and her artistic practice is informed and influenced by her scientific understanding and background. Vegetal Speed-dating, Who Will Pollinate the Flower Clock and the Phytonic Oracle are examples of her work with vegetal life forms.

Bart H.M. Vandeput, aka Bartaku, practices the art of inquiry. He creates multispecies co-creation constellations interweaving light, energy, matter, plants and microbes. His eclectic intermedia processes play with tensions between process_result, living_non-living, human_more-than-human and self_ selves. He is a postdoc researcher at Antwerp University and a visiting researcher at natural science departments at Aalto, Ghent and Hasselt Universities. He is a member and co-founder of several art collectives. His works have been shared worldwide in various forms and media.

Juliann Vitullo is an Associate Professor of Italian Studies, a Senior Sustainability Scholar, and Co-director of the Humanities Lab at Arizona State University. She has written on various aspects of medieval, early modern, and contemporary Italian culture with emphasis on the relationship between textual traditions and the material world, including economics, gender, food studies, and environmental humanities. Her current book project, *Creative Co-evolution in Italian Food Communities: Rethinking what it Means to be a Farmer*, examines how cultural, scientific, and political strategies for protecting the biocultural heritage in Italy, especially in southern Italy, can contribute to an evolving and regenerative reconfiguration of the role of traditional farmers. It also focuses on the narratives that help sustain biocultural diversity, imagining a more resilient and healthier future. Together with Ian Moulton, she is continuing historical research with a volume focused on the relationship between food stories, objects, and practices from 1300-1650: *Encounters: Food in Renaissance Europe in 50 Objects*. Both her research and community-based teaching emphasize the importance of preserving the cultural and ecological knowledge of traditional and Indigenous foodways, including those of the Southwest US where she lives and teaches, for a more equitable and sustainable future. Together with her colleagues in Italian Studies, she has co-developed a curriculum with a focus on environmental awareness and questions of sustainability. She also serves on the board of the Clark Park Community Garden (Tempe, Arizona) and Slow Food, Phoenix.

Anna Westbrook is an interdisciplinary writer, scholar, gallerist, and educator across Literature, Arts & Culture, and Visual Art. She has a novel *Dark Fires Shall Burn* (Scribe, 2016), writes reviews and poetry, and was shortlisted for The Australian/Vogel award. Anna lives in Sydney with too many books and a cat.